# The CANADIAN Writer's Guide

## Thirteenth Edition

# The CANADIAN Writer's Guide

## Thirteenth Edition

Editor
Paul G. Cormack

Managing Editor
Murphy O. Shewchuk

Associate Editors
Jennifer Crump
Gill Foss
Bernice Lever
Sandra Phinney
Steven Beattie

Official Handbook of the
Canadian Authors Association

Fitzhenry & Whiteside

**The Canadian Writer's Guide**
**Thirteenth Edition**



Fitzhenry & Whiteside Limited
195 Allstate Parkway
Markham, Ontario L3R 4T8

In the United States:
121 Harvard Avenue, Suite 2
Allston, Massachusetts 02134

www.fitzhenry.ca godwit@fitzhenry.ca

Fitzhenry & Whiteside acknowledges with thanks the Canada Council for the arts, the Government of Canada through its Book Publishing Industry Development Program, and the Ontario Arts Council for their support of our publishing program.

**National Library of Canada Cataloguing in Publication**

The Canadian writer's guide: official handbook of the Canadian Authors Association / managing editor, Murphy O. Shewchuk; editor, Paul G. Cormack; associate editors, Jennifer Crump... [et al.]. — 13th ed.

ISBN 1-55041-740-1

1. Authorship. 2. Canadian periodicals (English)—Directories.
3. Publishers and publishing—Canada—Directories.
I. Shewchuk, Murphy II. Crump, Jennifer III. Cormack, Paul G.
IV. Canadian Authors Association

PN161.C33 2003 808'.02 C2003-903674-7

Cover design by Darrell McCalla
Cover image courtesy of Murphy O. Shewchuk
Printed and bound in Canada

# Contents

## 1. Inspiration



## 2. Action & Reaction

## 3. Look After Business



## 4. Develop Your Style



## 5. Nonfiction Techniques

## 6. Fiction Techniques



## 7. Children & Young Adults

## 8. Poetry & Lyrics



## 9. People & Places Past



## 10. Newspapers & Periodicals



## 11. Books

## 12. Theatre, Screen & Radio



## 13. Non-Traditional Markets



## 14. World Wide Web

## 15. Writer's Reference

# Foreword

## From the Editor

This edition of ***The Canadian Writer's Guide*** is, overwhelmingly, a new effort. There are new articles, new contributors, and a new editing process that linked Canadian authors digitally from coast to coast, and from country to country. But despite a newer, more modern approach the result is still a traditional "book" that, in time, will have the same wrinkled spine, turned pages and well-thumbed cover as previous editions. For many, like myself, it's a comforting result.

This is the thirteenth time we've come together to share a unique Canadian perspective on writing and publishing. In this edition we no longer recognize borders, and we've lost sight of cultural and other challenges that may have impeded our community. We've discovered friends across this country, and shared experiences from west to east.

Authors who have contributed before have contributed once again. They provide us with a solid foundation, and offer a voice of wisdom and experience for aspiring Canadian writers — whether they are new to the industry, the genre, or the medium. And they have invited other authors to share their perspectives on writing, on publishing, on editing, on learning. Together, Canadian authors have created thousands of books and tens of thousands of magazine articles, short stories and poems. Add to that output an unknown number of songs, radio, TV and theatre scripts and as many Internet pages. World wide, Canadian writing ranks with the best fiction and science fiction, the best research, the best biography, the best romance, the best poetry, the best travel notes, the best children's stories ...

In the months since Murphy Shewchuk sent out the call for articles, the nights have grown long to allow just a little more time to read through each author's contribution. And the contributions came — from all across Canada, from Scotland, from Australia, from the U.S.A., and from Cyprus. They've shared publishing tips and story ideas, and have allowed a rare glimpse into work-in-progress and work published. They've highlighted extracts from books and poems and plays and websites. And they've offered a number of ways to achieve literary success, or just to define it — one person, one genre, one really awkward editor.

The efforts of Canadian authors the world over have enabled this edition. Both published and nearly published authors have sent typed and digital contributions to British Columbia, and these were then e-mailed to a tiny hamlet in the north of Scotland for editing. Some have expressed surprise at this, but others have accepted that this was a natural progression for Canadian authors in new Old World markets. Our world has changed, and our industry has adapted rapidly to a digital market. But still there are books, and still there are authors, and still there are readers. And maybe this can be the one fine moment where all three join together — authors, new and old, reading their book: *The Canadian Writer's Guide*.

And as the early evening passes here near the Scottish Highlands, I know that the sun is rising for authors all across Canada — and perhaps that first light of day will glance across the pages of our next best seller!

*Paul G. Cormack*

Aberdeenshire, Scotland; November 2002.

## From the Managing Editor

This thirteenth edition of *The Canadian Writer's Guide* marks the second time I have taken on the challenging task of collecting input from a diverse group of writers with the intent of helping an equally diverse group of writers define and achieve their goals.

Although I have bestowed the title of "Managing Editor" on myself, I think that "managing" such a project is a lot like herding cats. I am a technician by training and a writer by osmosis. My technician side attempts to find order in things and, if there is no obvious order, to create some sense of order. My writer side tells me that writers thrive on chaos, seeking inspiration from within themselves and from the outside world and striving to put their own personal imprint on the chaos that surrounds them.

The result of this dichotomy is in your hands. I have attempted to take the sometimes conflicting opinions of the editorial committee and the often conflicting opinions of the 93 contributors and put them in an order that will help you take the next step forward in your chosen direction.

I have attempted to start the 139 contributions at the "inspirational" beginning and "herd" them through to the "award-winning" end in a sequential manner.

It is now up to you to decide if I have been successful.

*Murphy O. Shewchuk*

Merritt, British Columbia, Canada; November 2002.

# 1. Inspiration

# Becoming a Writer

*by Betty Dobson*

I became a writer when my thoughts became too personal for a diary. No surprise, since my parents did not believe in privacy for children. And they saw me as a child, even in high school. Instead of acting out like so many my age, I learned to craft fiction.

My early poetry read like encoded diary entries. I could write anything and, if questioned, claim I made it all up. Blooming crushes and broken hearts echoed inside me, growing to such a cacophony that I had no choice but to release them. Disjointed thoughts turned to rhyme, and the din to rhythm. The world made a bit more sense against a white backdrop.

Not that I really thought of myself as a writer. That distinction belonged to the professionals. I presumed that "writing for a living" took all the fun out of it.

So I plodded ahead, untrained and untried, churning out one insipid poem after another. My friends got hooked, coming back for regular doses of "Harlequinesque" poetry. But I knew I could do better. At least I hoped so.

Maybe that's when I truly became a writer — the moment when I thought to reach beyond this limited experience and into the unknown. It wasn't enough that I should learn to write. I had to learn about everything. A dollop of psychology. A smattering of sociology. And plenty of field work.

I discovered a fascinating world outside of my imagination, full of fabulous characters just waiting to be penned. The man on the bus who shook out his hat every three minutes. And the woman with pencils sticking out of her coifed hair. I dubbed her the street geisha. A few of my silent friends found their voices in poetry, like the swarthy man in black who loped past my appointed spot at the coffee shop. Others spoke out through fiction. "Sweet-apple" was my favourite, another patron of the Metro Transit system. He looked worn out by living. I wanted to know why, so I invented his biography.

A different sort of reality hampered my creativity in recent months. Faced with corporate downsizing, I chose to make the leap to a new employer and more challenging work. Coping with a new learning curve left little energy for writing. But the words inside my head wouldn't stay bottled up for long. I returned to my first love, poetry, then branched out to short essays, knowing that fiction would return in its own time.

When did I become a writer? I'm not sure. It's been an ongoing process, full of insights, perceptions and challenges. Writing is a lifelong education. If I ever think I've mastered the craft, then I'll know I'll have missed a step along the way.

—-

Betty Dobson is a freelance writer while she pursues her bachelor's degree in English and Creative Writing. An award-winning poet and essayist, she has also received academic recognition for the quality of her short fiction. Find her on the web at: www.writers.net/writers/inkspotter.

# If You Want to Be a Writer

*by Joan Eyolfson Cadham*

If you want to be a writer, know why you want to write. If you want to write for fun, that's wonderful. Do you want to leave a memoir for the grandkids, or enter writing contests? Your interest might be in letters to the editor or a weekly column in a local paper. Perhaps your writing aims will change. On days when words refuse to settle down on white paper, check to see whether or not your original intent is still valid.

If you want to be a writer, decide what genres of writing please you, and don't apologize for your choices. For years, I was convinced that *real writers* wrote for little literary magazines. I finally admitted that literary magazine writers often get paid in free copies, and, while I like to see my name in print, I most enjoy seeing it on a cheque. Besides, when I read, I generally reach for nonfiction. That's what I write.

**Writing is still cheaper than playing the VLTs...**

If you want to be a writer, admit that whether writing is a hobby or a career, it's going to cost money. Money for a cheap computer and a first class printer, for reference books, for notebooks and account books and idea books, for magazine subscriptions, for envelopes and stamps, for letterhead, for a comfortable desk and some shelves to hold all the books, and for the office curtains you buy on one of those restless days when absolutely nothing will write itself. Writing is still cheaper than playing the VLTs — though no less addictive.

If you want to be a writer — write. Every day if you can manage it. Regularly. If you have writer's block during your writing time, do something writerish. Rewrite or edit old copy, read your writers' markets, think up story ideas, read two or three articles or stories of the type you most want to write. Remember that the best way to learn to meet deadlines is to find some. Enter every writing contest you can find except for the horrible "suckers-only-need-apply" American Poetry Anthology scam.

If you want to be a writer, carry a little notebook and pen so that you can jot down vagrant threads of ideas. Be warned. If you don't write them down, they will immediately go off in search of a more worthy writer. You will never find them again and the missed opportunity may haunt you forever.

If you want to be a writer, remember that a writer can talk about the plot of a story or she can actually write it. It seems that describing an entire plot puts an end to any chance of writing a quality manuscript. Lots of people out there are talking about the best seller they will write when ... (fill in your own 25 excuses. It's a good exercise in creativity. Begin, of course, with "when I have time").

If you want to be a writer, read. Read books, editorials, magazine articles, and poetry that is so brilliantly written that the word pictures leave you shaken and sobbing. Read trash that is so poorly crafted it makes you laugh. Keep it to edit some day when you aren't feeling creative but want to do something writerish. Read the best sellers your non-writer friends are devouring, and try to analyze the appeal. Read and reread the classics because they are good for your soul.

If you want to be a writer, surround yourself with books on writing. Borrow books through the library. Ask for writers' books for your birthday. I keep my *Writers' Market* in the bathroom. I have never stopped looking for fresh markets.

**Hang around writers...**

If you want to be a writer, hang around writers. Go to readings and workshops. Try to find a writers' group — or at least one other writer. Meet regularly, face to face or via e-mail. Talk about writing stuff. Complain when the muse seems to have deserted you. Cheer when writing seems easy. No one but another writer will empathize, although a perceptive spouse will fairly quickly understand the effects of writer's block.

If you want to be a writer, never let anyone but another writer whose work you admire read an unsold manuscript. Other adults will either tell you that everything's wonderful or they will offer uninformed suggestions for revision and sulk when you don't take their advice. The only exception is reading manuscripts for children to children to whom you are not related. They are often surprisingly perceptive, honest and enthusiastic critics.

If you want to be a writer, on the days when words won't come, draw up lists of other jobs you might have that you would hate. I also think about being able to work in my favorite floor-length flannel nightie with the big ruffle and the flowing sleeves and I pour another cup of tea and bless the reluctant muse.

If you want to be a writer, be brutal with yourself about editing. When your work drives you mad and better words refuse to come, lock the manuscript in a dark closet for two weeks. It will behave much more politely when you let it out again.

If you want to be a published writer, dig “it” out of the drawer, put “it” in an envelope, add a return, stamped envelope (SASE) ... and mail “it.”

If you want to be a published writer, keep at least half a dozen manuscripts floating around all the time. Otherwise you discover you can’t write for wondering what is happening to the one manuscript that is out. When it comes back, the attack of “blues” keeps you from writing for another week. Manuscripts are rejected for a number of reasons, not all of which have anything to do with your writing.

**Find some way to handle rejection...**

If you want to be a writer, find some way to handle rejection. Kick doors, run through meadows scattering rose petals, go for a swim, rant for 10 minutes — then go look for new markets. Remember that Lucy Maud Montgomery had *Anne of Green Gables* rejected 13 times and, just to prove that editors haven’t gotten any smarter, several editors turned down the opportunity to publish Harry Potter because, they said, the books about the boy wizard didn’t have market appeal.

If you want to be a successful writer who makes money, keep accurate records regarding the location of your manuscripts, rejection slips with encouraging handwritten notes, and sales and expenses. When the paperwork is done, take time to celebrate successes.

—

Joan Eyolfson Cadham, who took her own advice, freelances full-time from Foam Lake, Saskatchewan, selling (and winning awards for) feature articles, editorials and columns for weekly newspapers, national magazines and CBC radio. She also has two nonfiction books published by Shoreline Press in Ste Anne de Bellevue.

# How to Write

*by Lisa Lange*

How to write. Get a pen. If you don't have one, borrow one from your bank, your workplace or your neighbour. Or get a pencil. Those cute little golf pencils are easy to find at golf courses or lottery booths. They don't have erasers, but they fit nicely in little hands.

Find some paper. Back of a phone bill or till receipt from the grocery store. Again, if you like little things, you can buy rolls of till tape from stationery stores. You would have to write tiny (the golf pencils would come into play here), but when re-rolled, they are easy to store.

And start writing!

It doesn't matter what it is. Your grocery list transformed into a poem. A complaint letter to the city turned into a romance novel. Or your journal entry turned into a personal essay. Just start writing!

When you have written all you can write, read your dictionary. Read your thesaurus. Read your Strunk and White. If you want to be a published writer, read writing magazines, borrow books on writing from the library, read the writing websites on the Internet. The website for the Canadian Authors Association (www.canauthors.org) is a perfect example. Then write again, rewrite, read again, and then rewrite all over.

When you have rewritten for the 20th time, take a break and talk. Talk to ordinary everyday people. These are the ones who feed your writing. Join a writing group and talk with other writers. A writing group is a perfect source of information for all writers, of all genres, skill, and publishing credits.

When your mouth is dry, your ears are sore, and your lips are chapped, drink some water, put cotton in your ears, close the door to your office or bedroom, put on lip balm, and start writing all over again.

That is how to write.

—

Lisa Lange is mother of two boys, Mitchell and Matthew, and wife of Richard. She is a full-time office worker, seamstress and writer, living in Victoria, BC. She is also a member of the Canadian Authors Association.

# New Writer Woes

*by Lisa Lange*

Remember when you were a teenager, looking for your first job? Being a rookie was always tough, and even though you might have wanted that bigger, better job, higher up the ladder, you knew that you would have to start small, from the ground, and work your way up. Well, sometimes for writing, it's the same way.

Your goal might be to be published in a big publication like *Reader's Digest*® or you may want to write that best selling novel. But sometimes you have to start small. Some editors want to see clips of your previously published work, for example, along with the query you are submitting. But just like getting a new job, they want to see that you have had experience. Well, as that age-old question goes, "How can I get experience, if I won't be given a chance to get some?"

I am a new writer myself, and ran into many of these same hurdles. But I soon figured it all out. As far as having clips to submit, try submitting your work to local magazines or newspapers in your area (in which you are most likely to get published, and where the editors are most likely to help new local writers). Editors, I have found, are more than willing to provide input and advice on what they are looking for, which in turn, can help when you are submitting to other editors.

### You *are* a published writer...

Try submitting to local papers who have writing contests. No, you might not always win money, but you get to have work printed, and therefore have a clip to submit to other editors. A prospective editor doesn't need to know that the clip you just submitted won you a cookbook in a local newspaper (like I did). It's a clip, and it means you *are* a published writer.

A recent avenue I discovered is volunteer writing. Yes, okay, every writer wants to get paid for their work, but this is a perfect opportunity to gain experience, exposure, and clips! Depending on the writing involved and the organization you are writing for, you are bound to learn a new genre of writing. It may not be your immediate interest in writing, but it can provide an opportunity to learn another style or skill. It might lead you down a career path you had never even thought of. But most of all, it keeps you writing! Remember that you are a writer, and whether or not you are being paid, writing will always help your writing in the future. Think of it as practice.

**Show 'em what you got...**

If you visit your local volunteer organization or approach local publications, someone is sure to be looking for writers. Most writing can be done at home with minimal out-of-home work (beneficial if you already work at a paying job, and/or if you are a parent). Your work can be submitted to the editor in hardcopy format, on disk, or via e-mail. This is your chance to show 'em what you got! This also looks great on your writing résumé and you can still say you are a writer.

So, not to diminish the concept of shooting for the top and reaching for the stars, keep that in mind. But remember that everyone, at some point in their lives, had to start small and work their way up. Never be discouraged, and never give up. You are a writer, so keep writing!

—

Lisa Lange is mother of two boys, Mitchell and Matthew, and wife of Richard. She is a full-time office worker, seamstress and writer, living in Victoria, BC. She is also a member of the Canadian Authors Association.

# A Writer's Friend

*by Joan Eyolfson Cadham*

I dialed the number. "Can you look at my editorial and tell me whether it hangs together?" I asked. I didn't ask whether she was too busy.

"Of course," she said. That's our automatic response.

In rural Saskatchewan, where we specialize in space and miles, most writers are a long distance from one another. My writing friend is 64 kilometres away. Fortunately, SaskTel has a program called "bundles," a flat rate for long distance calls.

My phone rang. "Got your copy in front of you?" she asked. "The idea works, I see where you're going, but why don't you reverse the position of your third and your fifth paragraphs? I think that would clarify your second point. And I love your references in paragraph six. Oh, and there are two typos. You've doubled the 'is' on line seven and I suspect you mean 'out' rather than 'our' at the beginning of paragraph four."

She was right — on all counts.

That's a real writer friend.

Every writer should have one.

Time spent with one honest writer friend is more convenient than a correspondence writing course, more fruitful than a once-a-week trip to see your analyst, more effective than solitary hours spent with writing guides — not that writers don't consider one or all of those other aids at some time or another.

But what is an honest writer friend?

She does not believe that your every word is a perfect pearl gently falling from your computer keyboard to your monitor then to your printer, ready to grace a waiting world.

She will not commiserate with your writer's block and understand that you are going to spend two weeks finding inspiration in the soaps, hot tea, and Belgian chocolate.

She won't agree that you can't afford to spend money on writers' guides, markets, conferences, and a good quality printer.

She shares some common ideals and principles with you. You don't need to write for the same markets. You don't have to belong to the same church. You don't need to vote for the same political parties. You must both want to be the best writers you can be, and recognize that "best" means "self-editing and rewrites."

She will listen patiently to your struggles to get to the computer — and offer three practical suggestions for getting started again. She will spot story ideas you missed and send them your way. She will insist you work to the absolute limit of your talent. She will expect that, like any good craftsperson, you will purchase the necessary tools for your trade.

When your subject or your writing skill warrants, she will encourage you to reach out to markets that intimidate you. She will spot markets and contests and writing jobs that should appeal to you.

She will celebrate victories. Her first thought will not be, "Why wasn't that me?"

She will call down the wrath of sixteen hungry cats on editors who reject your work with no comment — and immediately suggest another market.

She will help you save the flavour of an article while, together, over lunch, you cut it in half to suit a new and lucrative market.

And you, in turn, will do all these things for her, without question.

Where do you find such a friend?

Join a writers' group. If, after a reasonable length of time, you don't find a kindred soul, change groups — or start one.

Attend a writers' conference. Most of us are determined introverts and we find large groups intimidating. Take along an extroverted non-writing friend. Having someone at your side often helps when you want to meet people.

Check the byline on poems and stories you enjoy. My particular writing friend found me this way and phoned me. We both wrote for the same paper. One day she simply looked me up in the phone book and made a cold call. We've never looked back.

—

Joan Eyolfson Cadham moved from Montreal to Foam Lake, Saskatchewan in 1992 so she could write nonfiction and tell Icelandic legends full-time and still keep three cats fed. Her writing buddy also has hungry feline mouths to feed. All of the cats understand the value of a writing friend.

# A Writer's Fear

*by David G. Weagle*

You are a writer. At least you hope you are. No, you *know* you are. Writing is all that you have really wanted to do since you were a teenager. Perhaps, unconsciously, before then. You do know that when you were a child you would daydream for hours, creating wonderful stories in your mind. Your mother and teachers probably said you would be a writer someday. They were right.

Yes, you are a writer. You do not have an editor, agent, or publisher, but you may write articles and short stories, or you may be working on a novel. Your genre may be mystery, suspense, humour, children's stories, fiction or nonfiction. It may be that your passion is poetry. Yes, you write. But you have not sold anything, you have not been published.

**Someone unpublished is being presumptuous...**

Now, you are probably thinking that someone unpublished is being presumptuous in calling oneself a writer. You may not consider yourself to be a true writer until you sell something. Is that what you think? After all, what proof do you have that you can succeed? You may have a point, but you will be published, you will. What is holding you back? Do you know?

It is not a lack of support. Friends, relatives, and other writers who have read your work believe in you. They have laughed or cried when you wanted them to. They have been surprised, mystified, or shocked when you intended them to be. You have been told to send this story to that magazine, or that article to this newspaper, but you have not done so. Why? Well, family and friends, even other writers, are one thing; publishers are different. They are the experts. Will they like it? Will they buy it? Will they, horror of horrors, reject it? Maybe, but that is not really your greatest fear, is it?

Perhaps it is not rejection you fear. In my case, I was a banker for thirty-five years, so God knows I am familiar with it. I did not fear being rejected, or bad reviews, or public criticism. I write because I enjoy it and I have something to say. I think we all do. If you do not fear rejection, why have you not submitted anything? Could it be — and you may not like to admit this — that you fear yourself?

There it is. You are afraid to see your work in print. What if you do not like it? What if you pick up a newspaper or magazine, look at your article or story, and hate what you see?

### This is not literature...

What if you say to yourself, "Did I really write this drivel? This is not literature. This is not what I spent so many hours, days, or weeks, to create. This is junk!"

You feel yourself hoping against hope that nobody you know reads it, although you know that they will. That was my fear. Is it yours?

Think about it. What can be worse than self-criticism? Did you take all the right courses, attend seminars and workshops, and read "how to" books for nothing? Is my fear the same one that keeps you from sending your work to a publisher, or do you have another concern? If so, admit it. We are our own worse critics, you know. No one can beat up our fragile egos as badly as we ourselves can. Do something about it.

Take that first big step. Confess your fear on paper. After all, is not transferring our thoughts to the written word what we do best? Write it down and read it. Better yet, let someone you trust read it. Then take the next step. Send in that story, article, poem, query letter, or whatever else is in your word processor or pending file. Move ahead. You know in your heart you can do it.

I did. So can you.

—

David Weagle is a freelance writer and editor in Kentville, Nova Scotia. A recent graduate of Acadia University, his credits include short stories in *Winners Circle 5* and *Wordscape 4*, a monthly column in *The Authors*, short story evaluations, and in-house writing and editing for RBC Royal Bank.

# Traps for the Unwary Writer

*by Madelon A. Smid*

"I want to be a writer" is a dream suspended in the hearts of many. Two of the most common approaches often become traps for the uninitiated. Let the unwary be warned.

The *Creative Writing Class* seems like a natural first step. Yet it can quickly become a trap, keeping you from building a writing career. Everyone can profit from a creative writing class. The guidance of a good teacher and the support of your peers are pluses in developing your writing skills. But many first timers join a creative writing class persuaded that they are serious about writing only to be diagnosed many classes later with NPP (Non-Productive Procrastination).

Here is a checklist so you can decide if you have the symptoms of NPP:

- Are you taking your third writing class so you don't have to stay home and write?
- Are you bringing old pieces into new writing classes?
- Are you already checking out the next course before you finish this one?
- Are you constantly asking for critiques on one manuscript and rewriting it continually to please the last reader?

If you are the student returning for the umpteenth time with a tired piece of writing, you may need to acknowledge that you are using it as a form of procrastination. I came dangerously close to succumbing to #4 until I realized I would never find my writer's voice until I stopped listening to everyone else's. I'm lucky I pulled my "bleeding limb of creativity" free of this trap before it was torn off. A student of mine still hasn't recognized the danger. Eight years ago she began working on a category romance. She is still working on it today.

She has fallen into the "novel trap."

The *novel* hangs like an Olympic Gold medal just within reach. Ego tempts many beginning writers to focus on the idea of winning gold, to the detriment of their writing. Though many writers have successfully completed a novel, thousands more have fallen into the "novel trap" and may never be published.

You can say you're writing a novel, talk about your novel and fantasize about becoming a novelist without ever writing a word. You expect the novel to somehow just *happen* and while you are lying on the couch waiting for it to spring fully formed into your mind you can't possibly work on anything else. You can follow that dream for years, but eventually truth will out. The novel isn't happening, and with its collapse comes the destruction of your writing aspirations. You might have written a dozen stories or a hundred articles and then successfully tackled the novel. But by chasing the novel first, your dream ends ... along with a potential writing career.

If you are meant to write, there is a reward in any type of writing, whether it is scribbling away on your own, timed exercises in a support group, labouring over a poem or completing that novel. Every time you sell a shorter work, it will contribute to your confidence and initiate a more powerful urge to write again. Piece by piece they may help you find the discipline to tackle that novel. Each one of them teaches you something. All of them produce the "rush" that comes with creativity.

So if you have been plotting a novel for two years, don't despair. There is a cure, and the prescription is simple. Take one idea and write something before you go to bed.

—

Madelon A. Smid is the coauthor of the national best seller *Smart Women* (Macmillan Canada). Her articles are published internationally. She teaches creative writing classes in Saskatchewan, and continues to write both fiction and nonfiction.

# How Do You Get Your Ideas?

*by Sheldon Oberman*

Recently I finished a major project. So I caught up on sleep and my chores, hung out with some friends and began to relax. All the while I kept looking for my next idea.

Finally, it was time to get down to work. I went to my studio as early as I could. I made myself a strong cup of coffee and sat at my desk but I still couldn't think of anything. So I did some reading, cleared away old business, and wrote in my journal. I organized my planner and edited some earlier writing. I stuck it out each day till quitting time, 5:45 p.m. However, after a few days I was spending more and more time staring out the window, doing serious daydreaming. Then I had an idea. I'd write about how I get my ideas.

So there you have it. That's how I get an idea.

Of course, it's not the only way.

I get ideas while travelling or at the lake or playing with my young son or just as I am falling asleep or even in a dream.

They may be ideas about writing but they could also be about gardening or decorating the house, about teaching or performing or simply about what to say to somebody. For me, the real task is to enter a creative state of mind and use that creativity in whatever I am doing.

I asked ten of my teen writing students how they get their inspiration. I like the word "inspiration," because it means to breathe in. Take a deep breath. Relax. Something interesting may begin to stir.

This is what each one answered:

"Sometimes I get upset about something and I have to get 'under the influence' — like be all alone. Maybe I'll get drunk and surround myself with music. Or I'll drive to the railway tracks because trains scare me and I'll sit in my car and then I'll write."

"I have this place down in the rec room. It's sort of dark and there's a deep upholstered chair. No one ever comes down there. It's where I go when I want to have really deep thoughts or write really deep feelings."

"I have all these people who I know. And some of them I don't like or they're really bad in some way. So I turn them into characters in stories. In the stories they become good and kind and we have these terrific times."

"I'll go to a party or better yet to a concert. I'll be with lots of people and we'll all go crazy watching the band because the band is so into its music. Then I'll go home and get out my guitar and I'll play all night. I'll imagine that I'm on stage and everyone is watching me."

"I just keep remembering things. I want to write out what happened and what I learned. Lessons. Everything I've learned I want to write out like they're lessons."

"I don't write. I'm an inside kind of person. I don't get inspired. I don't like to think about things. I dream sometimes. I have some pretty wild dreams. But I don't think about them."

"I get inspired by comics like Adam Sandler. I'll watch one of his movies and I'll think about him for months. I'll try to act like him. I'll tell jokes or do things in a funny way — make everything funny."

"I have my room completely filled with posters, even the ceiling — all of them are musicians. In the middle is Jimi Hendrix — he's my dad's favourite. All I think about sometimes is what it would be like to be Jimi. Dad's always talking about him. He's even got his autograph."

"I'll be in my room — it's totally empty, nothing on the walls — and I'll read biographies. Then I'll start to pace in my room thinking about the guy's life and how it could be my life. I can pace that way for two hours with nothing in my room but my thoughts about that book."

"I get ideas when I take showers or when I go for long walks, or runs, like I'll get a runner's high and that gives me ideas for a story. It's got to be at night because there's no one around and no distractions. It's like I'm in this big force field, it's coming out of me and getting bigger and generating all sorts of ideas. It's how I like to feel."

There are so many ways that people enter a creative state of mind. The next question is, how do you get your ideas? Once you've answered that for yourself, the rest is up to you.

—

Sheldon Oberman is a storyteller, teacher and author of twelve books including *The Always Prayer Shawl*, *The White Stone in the Castle Wall* and *The Shaman's Nephew: A Life in the Far North*. He travels widely, storytelling as well as giving talks and creative workshops on personal, fictional and traditional stories. Visit his website at www.sheldonoberman.com.

# How the Morning Pages Inspire

*by Carol Kavanagh*

Creativity? We all have it. Inspiration? We have that too. It's just around the corner, but the problem is, we're half a block from the corner. How do we get from here to there?

The first step is a well-known tactic: get your butt in the chair seated at the table. Get the paper in front of you and your pen in hand or the keyboard at your fingertips. Did you ever procrastinate your way out of this? Me too, but if you *got* yourself there, then you could do some writing gymnastics: a character sketch, a piece of dialogue, a line of the poem that's bubbling in your head. This could get you started. The act of writing creates it's own inspiration.

But suppose you never got there, to the chair, I mean. Then you could try "morning pages." These are three, 8.5 inch by 11 inch sheets of lined paper which you fill with ink scrawl immediately upon rising, every day.

I hear you screaming already. This is much harder than getting your butt into the chair, but wait, just wait.

### We get free of the things that block us...

Sometimes we can't write because too many other things are blocking us. We can't get past them to get into the flow. These might be the report that's due at work, or the gas bill you can't pay, or Auntie's visit. Doing "morning pages" we get free of these things. And we recover our lost creativity.

One evening, as we sat around the dining table, I told my friends that I was taking this creative recovery program, which utilizes the morning pages. One buffoon, well, really a nice person, said, "Oh, so do you go there every week and say, 'My name is Carol Kavanagh and I'm a blocked creative!'?" Great laughter. Laugh, laugh if you must, but I shall enter the realm of the gods through creativity and you shall be cleaning out your garage.

So here I am, writing the "morning pages." Imagine this. The alarm goes off three-quarters of an hour early. I crawl from between soft sheets and a cosy duvet into a cold room as yet untouched by furnace heat, pull on sloppy woollen socks and a plush housecoat while trying to rub my eyes into the open position. Off to pee.

Then I sit down at a regular place where there is peace and quiet. It ought to be a special place not littered with the "to do" list, and all the things from which you're trying to get free. An alternative to this scene just described is to simply plump up the pillows in bed, pick up the blank pages attached to a clipboard which were lying in wait on the night table, and begin writing. This is what *I* do. I simply cannot bear to be cold!

**It is very white and very blank...**

So here I am, facing my first sheet of paper. It is very white and very blank. The idea with "morning pages" is not to think too hard. Simply write and keep the flow going. Don't stop. Don't worry about punctuation, spelling, capitalization or new paragraphs. It's a stream of consciousness. In the writing world this is known as "free fall." Whatever comes to mind ought to scrawl out onto the page. And no one except you will ever read these pages. Comforting thought? Hold on to it.

The pen goes to the paper. Things bubble up. There are feelings, complaints, questions. All the petty little irritations of life are recorded. Or perhaps a litany of yesterday's activities is being logged. Never mind. It's a start. It gets me going. For some important reason I need to start there. Grievances get aired and discussed. I whip through these like a race car at the Indy 500. And then, PLOP! I'm on a sailboat in the doldrums. It's as quiet as silence in the wilderness. At this point, I am allowed to write, "I cannot think of anything to write." A few lines of this and then next topic appears on the page. I'm back in the flow.

Now, here's the *important point*. During this process, something will zing through your head, a new scene of the novel, how a character wants to respond to something she's faced with, the perfect imagery for the next line in the poem. It's there, and you just run with it. You're at the corner and all the way around the block. You write the whole scene. You write the whole piece of dialogue. You get down that perfect line, and behold, there is another line.

This is how it happens. This is how you manage to be inspired and write every day. Is waking a time when the mind is freer and more readily available for inspiration? Yes. Are your problems far away? Yes. Does anyone bother you at this time of the morning? No.

The creative writing I described might not happen every day, but to give it a better chance of happening, tell yourself, before you begin the "morning pages," that you want to use this time to write, for example, the next piece of dialogue in your short story. Be specific if you can. Don't force it. Even if it doesn't happen, you're still doing very valuable work unlocking your creativity.

**Do *not* burn the gems and pearls...**

At week twelve you will have about 252 pages. Read them all! It will be horrible, all the worrying, complaining and snivelling. Do it anyway. You'll wonder at the life you lead, but never mind. That was then, this is now. Issues got out on the paper. They were real then and seem silly now. Good. Slowly, you achieved *distance* that lets you view the problems in a new way. Solutions came. New plans got developed. New insights were there. This unblocking has been a valuable activity, so to bring closure to it all, burn all the pages in a "letting go" ceremony.

However, do *not* burn the gems and pearls you've culled from among the 252 pages. These are precious! Rejoice! Your poem is written. Your story is almost there. The characters in your novel have taken over their own lives. Oh glorious chaos!

"Morning pages" help me to stay creative and inspired. They get me from the middle of the block to the corner and around it. I'm heading down the street full tilt, images, titles, and feisty characters clinging to me and they won't let go!

—

Carol Kavanagh is a registered psychologist who has published poetry and is currently working on short stories and a novel. A book by Julia Cameron, *The Artist's Way*, inspired her and she then took a course by that name, and began writing morning pages.

# Tap Your Innate Creativity

*by Barbara Florio Graham*

Often the difference between a *great* piece of writing and one that is merely *good* is that spark of creativity, that startling insight, that causes the reader to say, "Wow!" Whether you write fiction, nonfiction or poetry, you need to know how to tap into your own innate creativity, quickly and easily.

There is a myth that "creative" people are different from the rest of us. This has been perpetuated by comments such as, "Creativity is really the structuring of magic," from Anne Kent Rush.

That sounds exciting, but there's really no magic to it. An understanding of how the brain works will provide a means for anyone to access his or her creative potential.

The brain recalls a memory through visual images, organizing and locating the particular image and then associating or linking it with a name, word, or idea.

**Specialized in certain functions...**

Early experiments on the brain showed that the left side of the brain controls the right side of the body, and the right hemisphere controls the left side. These researchers also discovered that each side of the brain specialized in certain functions.

The left brain is responsible for most of our verbal ability as well as order, sequence, logic, and memory for words. Because 80% of the population is left-brain dominant, our educational system is based on developing left-brain skills: reading, writing, and arithmetic. We are urged, from childhood, to use our right hands to perform most routine tasks, including writing. Western civilizations read from left to right because our writing is based on words rather than symbols which form sounds or concepts, as in many Eastern languages.

The right brain processes and stores visual images, emotions, music, physical manipulation, and our perception of space and the world around us, our connection to nature, and higher mathematical concepts (such as geometry).

Notice the difference between arithmetic, a left brain activity which is simply different ways of counting, and higher math. The latter involves the visualization of complex mathematical structures. There is a close connection between an aptitude for math and musical talent.

Schools reinforce left-brain dominance by arranging desks in rows, positioning writing surfaces on the right side of chairs in universities, and a reliance on a specific order of classes and subject matter, reinforced by outlines, timetables, alphabetical listings, and charts.

Right-brain tendencies among children are discouraged, and the minorities who are right-brain dominant can have a difficult time learning in a "left-brain environment." No wonder so many exceptionally creative people — Einstein, Edison, da Vinci, Michelangelo, and Gates — had trouble in school!

### ***Craft* plus *art*...**

Writers are usually very verbal, so it's no surprise that most of us are left-brain dominant. The left side of our brain gives us order, control, and precision, the *craft* part of our writing. But we also need the right side, which provides freedom, risk, and chaos — the *artistic* additions. A well-crafted article might be boring, but a purely artistic creation can be confusing. *Craft* plus *art* is what we're all looking for.

Dull, boring writing comes from starting on the wrong side of the brain. Instead of taking control of the material in an attempt to be as precise as possible, we should begin our writing on the other side of the brain. This doesn't mean giving "full rein" to creative chaos, sacrificing solid research, organization, sentence structure and grammar. Instead we need to use both sides of the brain, but start with the right side when we're searching for a creative approach.

One easy way to do this is to allow ourselves to play as we did when we were children. Instead of staring at a blank piece of paper (or computer screen), start with crayons or finger paints, different colours of clay or fabric, "found" objects you can manipulate and rearrange. Let your mind wander as your right brain keeps its focus on colour, shape, and texture. Add other sensory input, from music or odours. Trying to get started on a mystery novel? Experiment with a variety of acrid scents. What ideas do pepper, salt, dill, vinegar, chlorine-based cleaning products, stain removers, medications bring to mind?

Feeling anxious about an article that's close to deadline, where you just can't seem to find an engaging lead? Find music that gets your toes tapping, create a collage of coloured papers and fabrics, repot a houseplant and feel the soil under your fingers.

Water seems to be extremely conducive to right-brain activity. You don't have to swim to experience this natural rush of endorphins. You may have noticed that many doctors and dentists have aquariums in their waiting rooms, and high-tech firms often have a fountain in a courtyard or foyer. Take a shower, or put a small fountain in your office.

An award-winning advertising firm in Ottawa has a Zen garden in its office. Recreate this effect yourself by taking a shallow, rimmed tray (or old baking dish) and filling it with sand (or bird gravel). Now you have a miniature sandbox in which you can trace patterns with a fork or invent a tiny landscape.

**Dance as you read aloud...**

In my online creativity course, each assignment explores not only a different sense but all of the visual and performing arts. If you're stymied by something you've written that just doesn't seem to flow, try moving around the room in a pseudo dance as you read it aloud. All the "bumps" will be obvious and solutions will arrive without much effort.

You can also use "mind mapping" or other techniques to organize material. Take a large sheet of plain paper and a marker, and write, at random, at all angles and anywhere on the paper, every thought, word, or phrase related to the subject you are working on. When you've exhausted all possibilities (or have filled every inch of the paper), pick up some coloured markers and group the words by circling in the same colour any that seem to belong together. You'll find yourself with four or five groupings, and then it's easy to decide how to order these into an outline.

So tap into your own innate creativity and add sparkle to your writing.

—

This article was adapted from Barbara Florio Graham's online course, *Tapping Your Innate Creativity*, which is described on her website, www.SimonTeakettle.com. Barbara is the author of three books and has won awards for nonfiction, fiction, poetry and humour. Her latest book is *Musings/Mewsings* (coauthored with her cat, Simon Teakettle).

# Writer's Block and How to Beat It

*by Keith Slater*

Writer's block must have been around since humans first put quill to parchment or chisel to stone. It might be the biggest problem (except death and taxes) that all writers have in common. It's that horrible feeling of being stuck for the next idea or word.

But writer's block doesn't have to be a problem. I've found ways to overcome it that have worked for over 40 years. They may not work for you, but it won't do any harm to try them. Perhaps they'll give you ideas of your own.

First, I tried to develop a greater understanding of the writing process. "How does my brain work?" I asked myself. ("On the rare occasion when it does," I added.)

The brain is like a computer. Thought waves are bits of electric current flowing round it and brain cells are memory banks. When we write, our brain gathers information from storage and builds a coherent thought in a "central processing unit," then our "printer cable," the muscles, moves a pen or a keyboard.

### The brain is a "shunting yard..."

I like to compare this with a shunting yard. The engine bustles about picking up railcars, collecting them into a single train, moving them around, then delivering them to a main line to be taken to their destination. With this analogy, it's easier to understand the problems of writers.

The first problem our brain "train" might experience is to run out of fuel. If we're tired, or hungry, the brain, like the engine, stops working. The solution is simple. Avoid working when energy is low. Find your best time, even if it's three a.m., and set it aside for writing. Plan your schedule around it, and defend it with your life! Take a walk, or have a snack to refresh the little grey cells. Give them a chance to stoke up the creative juices so they can flow again.

Problem two is too many railcars. Ideas run through your mind in hundreds, confusion reigns, the computer overloads, and the train grinds to a halt. Again the solution is clear. Plan your writing ahead. If unnecessary material floats around inside your head, jot it down to get it out of your "mainstream," and get back to the proper task. Once it's written, you can stop worrying.

The third problem involves too many tracks for the train. The plot is too complex, or characters take control, so you've no idea which direction to take. The solution is to decide on characters and plot before you sit down to write. Work on them in your head, and jot down notes before you begin writing. Build a story line. Integrate the piece by revising your notes, and take control of your writing.

Next, the track is a dead end, going nowhere. You've no ideas for the piece. What I do is set the piece aside until there is a way forward. If it never does, maybe it's one I shouldn't be writing. I try to identify why I can't make progress. Is it a subject I don't know well enough? Then I'd better do some research before I write about it! Or does the topic not interest me? Maybe I'd better cut my losses and get to one that does. Put it in the "pending" pile, and come back to it periodically to see if the "computer" has been working in secret. If so, get back to it.

**Nothing happens when you go around in circles...**

Problem five is the track-in-a-loop. There's nothing happening because you're going round in circles and returning to the same point. This one, I found, was from lack of planning. I trained myself to concentrate on one idea at a time and to know where it was going. Again, I try to identify the reasons for the loop, look for points to break out of it, and focus on those.

The sixth problem is a missing railcar. I'm stuck for a piece of information. I know where to find it, but it means going to the library. It's raining, so, "Maybe I can write my way around it if ..." No. I admit it. I can't manage without it. I have two choices. I can omit the entire section where that information is needed and get on with another part. Or I can work on a different piece, after noting what I'll need next time I'm in the library. Only as a last resort do I go for information, because that squanders precious writing time. I can find it later when I'm feeling less creative.

The next reason for writer's block is the one I find most serious. The driver doesn't want to start the engine, therefore nothing happens. If you have no wish to write, you're in trouble. Try to analyze the reasons. Is it this piece that doesn't motivate you, or is it writing in general? If it's that piece, you're back to one of the earlier problems and can deal with it. If it's writing in general, you have to find motivation and use it to drive yourself. Maybe it's the thought of all the fame and money that will be showered on you when your wonderful work finally bursts forth. Maybe it's the satisfaction of a job well done, or maybe you just want the thing finished to spite your Aunt Ermyntrude who always said you'd never make a writer. The reason doesn't matter. Find it, and use it for all its worth!

Next — what about the train with the wrong cargo? If you're not comfortable with the characters, the plot, or events as they unfold, this can stop your writing. The answer is planning. Only commit yourself to material you can handle with enthusiasm. Find the determination to succeed. Have the courage to throw a day's (or a month's) work into the garbage and start again if that's the only way to keep the creative urge going.

So, now that you know the causes of writer's block, how do you avoid it? There's a general approach to follow, one I developed as a student years ago and have used ever since.

**Know why you are writing...**

First, have a purpose. Be sure you really want to write in the genre you've selected. Know why you're writing; are these reasons enough? More importantly, will your reasons last a lifetime? If they're not strong enough, then maybe you're not a writer. Give it up, and put money on the horse; that's a surer way of making a million in no time at all.

If you *are* a writer, then you have to discipline yourself. No writer can sit back and let time drift. Plan your schedule with "writing" featured as prominently as possible. Are family, friends, or acquaintances distractions? Eliminate them (distractions, not people!). Disconnect the doorbell. Take the telephone off the hook. Threaten the family with dire vague consequences if they fail to respect your rights to privacy. Unplug the television!

Once you've arranged your space, then plan your writing. Know the direction it will take. Have the characters, the plot, and anything else you might need in mind before you write. Create your outline, divide it into segments if necessary. Have several projects in progress simultaneously, so you can switch to another piece if one gets blocked.

Then progress can begin. Build your work logically. The most valuable lesson I learned was to plan the writing for my next session as I was finishing the current one. That way, in a new session, I already had notes of what I wanted to accomplish. So make notes of where you'll go next time you write. Write something (anything!) to keep your mind flowing; writer's block finishes when writing begins! Maybe you'll scrap most of it next time, but at least it will be out of your system.

It's most important to avoid the temptation to reread and rewrite before the time is right. Finish the piece or section before going over it; then you'll have the direction established and won't be tempted to use revision as a means of getting off track. Make notes of major changes it might require as you go along, but resist the temptation to carry these out until the time is right.

Finally, cultivate the habit of focusing on the main purpose of your work, and keep it in mind continuously as you write. Be aware that writer's block can arise, and be prepared for it. Plan ways of overcoming it ahead, so it doesn't take you by surprise. Use my ideas as a guideline, and develop strategies that work for you. Don't be left standing when the train leaves the station on the way to a successful writing career!

—

Keith Slater is a recently retired Professor of Textile Engineering at the University of Guelph. He has published some 300 scientific articles, 20 books, 30 short stories, and 15 plays. He also taught a course aimed at developing written and oral scientific presentation skills in engineering graduate students, and has given workshops on various aspects of writing.

# Five Ways to Improve Your Chances of Getting Published

*by Julie H. Ferguson*

Professionalism, or the lack of it, can make or break aspiring authors. Sometimes it is hard to believe you are a professional when you have not had anything published but you must cultivate that quality. Undertaking tasks that demonstrate you are serious about your calling is part of the transformation. Editors and agents look for proof of these in query letters and bios.

**1. Membership in a writers' group.**

Writing in isolation is not only hard, it is foolhardy. Writers of all genres should present their written work for critique before submitting it to editors or agents. Writers' groups abound and provide the essential forum for your work where fellow writers can improve it. I know several successful authors who still belong to a critique group and maintain that they cannot write without it. If you cannot find a suitable group, the Internet has many where you can post your latest chapter or article for review by others working in your field or genre. Look for a group with varied membership — some beginners, but also some published authors, and many genres represented — for these are the individuals that will give you the most guidance and encouragement.

**2. Participation in writing/publishing courses.**

Nothing shows your commitment to writing better than regular attendance at workshops, courses, and writing classes. Although I teach at writers' conferences, I occasionally attend them as a participant and enroll in courses at my local university. I know one agent who not only insists that her clients attend courses but also checks with their instructors about their performance. An editor who sees no indication in a query letter or submission of your ongoing development is going to be anxious about your professionalism.

**3. Publishing credits/awards.**

Serving your apprenticeship includes getting something published that you can list in your bio so, as you work on your first book, also work on getting into print in magazines or online. Whether you get paid or not doesn't matter, nor does the subject material. Editors find it reassuring that a colleague has had enough faith in your writing to publish it.

Novelists and poets should also enter contests. Writers' magazines, websites, and writers' associations regularly list contests and their rules, so you can start small and build up to the prestigious ones.

**4. Attendance at writers' conferences.**

Surely one of the most motivating events in any writer's life, conferences are also essential to developing your professionalism. They provide current trends and changing requirements in your genre, especially in this electronic age, and allow you to mix with and present your work to published authors, editors, and agents. Your attendance at conferences demonstrates to publishers just how seriously you take your career and how hard you are working at improving your skills.

**5. Promotion skills.**

Publishers don't acquire books, they acquire authors. Authors who show potential for a series of books and for name recognition are ideal. Also, someone who is outgoing and personable, interviews well, and who can deliver workshops or keynote speeches with flair is going to make a publisher really happy. Writers, both fiction and nonfiction, need to develop speaking skills, connections, and promotional ideas for their books ahead of time, so that publishers get a two-for-one package.

—

Freelance writer and author of two nonfiction books, Vancouver-based Julie H. Ferguson leads workshops that provide aspiring authors with the knowledge, skills, and confidence to approach publishers. Her website is at www.beaconlit.com.

# The Evolution of the Editing Circle: The E-Circle

*by Sandra Stewart and Ian Walker*

An electronic editing circle (or e-circle) is an online editing group. Writers use the Internet as the exchange medium to critique each other's monthly submissions. Not a mutual admiration society, a way of venting one's frustration over rejection, or a marketing strategy, the e-circle is a great way for time-strapped or geographically challenged writers to learn from peer evaluation.

**Advantages of online editing...**

In a rural community, attending your nearest writer's group may require a two-hour drive — a downer in a thunderstorm. Your e-circle buddies are just a mouse click away in all weathers.

A further advantage is time management. In today's hectic workplace, the demands of your day job may preclude regular writing group attendance. Now you don't have to meet others in the flesh to receive feedback on your work in progress. E-circles are ideal if you can't devote a whole evening to critique, but can allocate a few short time slots each month. Expect to spend up to an hour reading each submission.

**Enlist today...**

Canvass fellow CAA members through e-mail, in meetings and at workshops, to enlist writers with similar interests into a close-knit group. You must be a working writer to participate. That means you have to submit your own work to qualify to review the work of others.

**Protocol...**

Before exchanging manuscripts, agree on a protocol that includes the turnaround time, the acceptable word or page count, the mechanics of sending files, as well as the etiquette of critique.

Points to consider:

- Do you want to appoint a host to lay out the rules and guidelines?
- Decide what will be the comfortable size of the group: keep it small, six members maximum, or you could find yourself with a bigger workload than you can handle.

- Choose whether to keep the comments confidential between editor and author, or whether you should copy all members.

**Trial...**

Once you've agreed on the process, run a trial. The trial will uncover e-mail software incompatibility, viruses, and more. You may have to experiment with various formats such as rich text (HTML), plain text, etc. until you find a method that works for each member. Rich text retains all word processor formatting, plain text does not. Attachments work well in some web browser/word processor combinations, but not in others. Member computer expertise is an issue you may need to explore to find practical solutions to technical difficulties. In setting up your workstation, be sure to install the latest virus protection software. Writers are prone to infection, so practice safe Internet intercourse.

Be prepared to comment on genres you don't normally read. This broadens your perspective as a writer, but can be hard work.

**Etiquette...**

A CAA e-circle ensures that its members are serious about writing and avoids the common Internet problem of rude and disruptive reviewers. Any crude or nasty criticism is completely ignored. Such a reviewer is not interested in improving your work. Under no circumstances should you retaliate and risk an outbreak of cyber rage.

The general rules of critiquing a manuscript should apply. Start with your overall impression, especially the strengths of the work. Make positive suggestions for improvement; forego negative complaints.

You must be brutally honest, but give a balanced opinion: good points as well as opportunities for improvement. Try to put a positive spin on your comments. For example, indicate a need for freshness rather than complain about clichés.

Reviewing the work of others helps you develop skills critical to see flaws in your own work and find ways to exorcize them. Insert detailed comment in the text immediately following the section to which it pertains. Use the standard copy-editing abbreviations.

**Results...**

E-circles motivate the writer to push ahead with "work in progress" to meet the monthly submission deadline. Our e-circle limit is fifteen pages of double-spaced text. A sample of up to eight thousand words reveals systemic deficiencies such as an unsympathetic heroine, lack of emotional impact, imbalance between dialogue and narration, etc.

Blind editors are objectively subjective so you get a fair appraisal of your work. The monthly critique the writer receives is a huge incentive to make revisions. However, you must view criticism with caution. Sift the comments and reject any that are off base. Remember that you don't know these people, and that literary style is a personal issue. Emotional reaction and gut feeling can be very informative. Questions the e-circle members ask about your writing often let you know how successful you are in developing character, showing motivation, engaging reader emotion, giving your story a place, etc.

**Side benefits...**

E-circle experience is good practice for pitching your work to the growing market of electronic publication.

A side benefit, but one that is by no means insignificant, is the forum an e-circle gives you to publicize and sell your work. You can broaden your circle of admirers and potential buyers for your next novel, as you reach outside your own community. You could be working with someone on the other side of the province, or the other side of the world. A circle of bright writers can be a huge asset.

**Show me...**

The success of its members demonstrates the effectiveness of any writing group. Our e-circle's originator published her first e-novel in October 2001. Her second novel went online in March 2002. Not only that, she won the publisher's award for excellence for both works. A second member was invited to lecture on the purchasing practices of wizards to an audience at Kent State University.

Give yourself an e-circle opportunity to get acquainted with Canadian Authors Association members, share ideas, and edge a little closer to a shared dream. If you can no longer endure that cruel editor in your local writer's group who trashes everything you submit, escape to cyberspace.

Writing group therapy should inspire you to write. If yours doesn't, surf into an e-circle.

—

Sandra Stewart won a prize for one of her many articles for local festival publications. She has presented academic papers on children's literature and is currently working on a fantasy novel for young adults. She is a newcomer to e-circles.

Ian Walker published an inspirational article in *Lifeglow.* His short fiction has appeared in magazines, newspapers, and anthologies. His first novel was published in 1995. He acknowledges the help and encouragement of writers' groups in cyberspace, and those close to home.

# Attend Writing Conferences

*by David G. Weagle*

Many writers ask, "Why should I attend writing conferences?" They make excuses for not going: costs of transportation, accommodation, meals, and conference fees, insufficient time, etc. Yes, it is sometimes difficult to justify the expense. Although it may be tax-deductible, one must have the funds in the first place. As writers, however, our attraction is the written word, and that is what writing conferences are all about. Reasons to attend include: networking, genre awareness, fellowship, exploration, business matters, ideas, and self-confidence.

**Networking...**

*Networking* only came into use as a noun in 1966, although "network" has been around since the sixteenth century. Exchanging information and services is as important to writers as it is to the "captains of industry." Without networking, we can write forever and not sell anything. Every time we hand out a business card, or talk about writing, we are networking. When we go to a workshop, monthly meeting, or a local reading group, we network. If this is so, why go to a conference? Well, simply, there you meet writers, publishers, and editors. A publisher once gave me her business card and invited me to call her direct. Wow! Where, but at a conference, would I get that opportunity?

**Genres...**

Do you enjoy writing children's stories, or murder mysteries? Is poetry your passion? Perhaps you prefer penning travel articles, book reviews, or political columns; maybe you write eroticism, romance, or crime? No matter, we all can learn more about our chosen genre.

When you join a local writers' group, how many members work in your genre — two, five, none? Would you like to compare notes with ten, twenty, or more? Of course you would. At writing conferences there are experienced, successful writers who will inspire, teach, and, yes, commiserate with you if necessary. Where else can you be certain to meet successful writers who are more than willing to pass on their secrets? Even best friends will often jealously guard their contacts. When there are a couple of hundred writers in one place, however, they give information more freely. Everyone loosens up a little.

Sure, you can attend a local workshop — but what happens? You spend all day listening to an accomplished writer, doing exercises, and talking to other participants. Then you go home, put your work aside, and deal with family matters. It may be days before you review your notes or talk with another writer — not so at a conference.

After a conference workshop, you are normally welcome to talk to the presenter; or you can return to your room and organize your notes, go for a drink or dinner with other writers, or join a group for informal discussions. Perhaps you have been struggling with your chosen genre, and will find some new motivation. Perhaps you need fresh fuel to make the embers of creativity burst into flames of inspiration.

**Fellowship...**

I went to my first conference expecting to be completely immersed in the art and practicalities of writing. How wrong I was! Authors do not only discuss literature. We are not always dreaming up the next poem, novel, or short story. Why — and I know you will find this hard to believe — at times we don't even discuss money. Sometimes we just enjoy shooting the breeze to get our minds off work for a while. Where better to do that than at a conference?

**Exploration...**

One of the great things about writing conferences is that they can be found in different parts of the country. The Canadian Authors Association, for example, held its last four in Alberta, British Columbia, Ontario, and Nova Scotia respectively. Accordingly, conferences provide an opportunity to explore our wonderful country. Rather than fly, I prefer driving because I can stop at interesting places along the way. Of course, that takes time and is expensive. If driving is not feasible, take a bus or train to see the country.

No mode of travel is cheap, but, if you normally take an annual vacation, it won't cost any more. Besides, travel to and from the conference is a business expense. Even side trips, if work related, can be tax-deductible. If you do fly, and have a few days to spare, rent a car and see some of the host province.

**Business matters...**

Make no mistake, writing is a business. It includes knowing what sells and where to sell it, what to charge, whether to use an agent or not, tax matters, copyright issues, contract terms, etc. Whether experienced or beginner, all writers occasionally struggle with such problems. At conferences, solutions come from other writers, panel discussions, seminars, etc. Taking part in the question periods following panels, for example, is important. Remember, you can never take too many notes.

Of course, it is one thing to know what sells, and where. It is quite another to learn how to sell it. That is why marketing seminars and publishing panels are so popular. Do not miss them. You'll find out when you need an agent and when you can sell yourself. No, that is not a typo; to sell your work you must sell yourself. Learn how to write an effective query letter. Ask if simultaneous submissions are acceptable (the jury is out on that one). What marketing books are recommended? Must you do readings and tours to sell your book? Can you self-publish successfully? Should you write for nothing in order to get published? What about payments of royalties and fees? Actually, the fee topic is probably best discussed at a seminar on freelance writing. Conferences usually have one. You will learn what, and how, others charge for their work.

**Ideas...**

A gathering of writers is also a great place to obtain new ideas and character descriptions for new projects. I confess that I sometimes lose track of what a speaker is saying. I love to watch people — their mannerisms, expressions, speech inflections, and appearance. My observations help make my fictional characters more realistic. If possible, I note any peculiarities in my notebook right away. If not, I do it at the first opportunity.

New ideas are abundant at conferences. Listen to other writers talking about their work and all sorts of topics will come to mind. As in brainstorming sessions, one idea begets another. An author describes her published crime novel, for example, and a listener decides to do a piece on the life of a judge. Writers help writers, even if inadvertently.

**Self-confidence...**

We all need self-confidence to succeed. One way to get it is to obtain feedback, both positive and negative. Your local writers might not feel comfortable about critiquing your work, but many writers at conferences will have no such compunction. By working up the courage to read or show your creations to other writers, you gain self-confidence. The more often you do it, the more confident you become. Furthermore, reading the works of others provides the opportunity to compare your work with theirs and, hopefully, increase your confidence in your writing ability.

Taking an active part in group discussions, workshops, and panel discussions is, for many of us, a frightening undertaking. At a conference, not taking part can make you a very lonely scribe in a sea of writers.

Sooner or later you will not be able to stop yourself from giving an opinion, and, wonder of wonders, the others actually listen. What a confidence booster!

**Are you ready?**

Now that you have decided to go, what do you need to take, apart from a passion for writing and an urge to learn?

First of all, and most important, is attitude. No matter what I have previously written, attending a conference is business — not a vacation. You are there to further your progress in your chosen profession.

Second, you will need material things. Take:

- More than one pen. If yours doesn't run dry, someone else's will.
- A small notepad for addresses, appointments, or cryptic notes during the day.
- Your notebook computer, exercise book, or binder paper, to record your notes.
- Comfortable clothes and shoes for all-day sitting and standing. Why be chic and uncomfortable? On the other hand, first impressions count.
- Cash. There may not be an ATM handy.
- Business cards. Computer generated ones are better than nothing.
- Cell phone. NO! Leave it home or turn it off.
- Camera and film.
- A journal. All writers should keep one.

Go to a conference. Grab the chance to hand your card to a publisher or agent, or to discuss your work with a friendly editor (not always an oxymoron). The benefits of associating with others in the writing business are invaluable. Some authors become lifelong friends. That is a bonus. As writers we need to broaden our experience to make our efforts more interesting to our readers. That is the essence of writing, and of attending conferences.

—

David Weagle is a freelance writer and editor in Kentville, Nova Scotia. A graduate of Acadia University, his credits include short stories in *Winners Circle 5* and *Wordscape 4*, columns in *The Authors*, short story evaluations, and in-house writing and editing for RBC Royal Bank. He has attended many symposiums.

# Mentoring: Learn From Your Peers

*by Barbara Florio Graham*

Comprehensive studies of the cultural sector were commissioned in 1995. When these were received by Human Resources Development Canada (HRDC), one overwhelming training need identified by writers was "mentoring."

I wasn't surprised that writers surveyed in all parts of Canada, those belonging to national or provincial organizations as well as unaffiliated writers in rural areas, considered individual mentoring to be the best way for writers to improve or upgrade their skills. For many years, writers' groups have provided informal mentoring to their members through workshops and networking, but one-on-one mentoring is difficult to sustain without funding. It is a time-intensive process for the mentor.

The alternative, informal mentoring, presents its own hazards. Some mentors get research support or other services from the writer in return for advice and direction — but they may have insufficient ability to pass on anything useful.

When the Cultural Human Resources Council (CHRC) obtained funding from HRDC for formal mentoring programs, the situation improved dramatically. It enabled the Writer's Union, the Periodical Writers Association of Canada (PWAC), and their counterparts in Quebec to set up mentoring arrangements which ensured careful selection of "mentor pairs" as well as a monitoring process. The first year that PWAC was involved, a group from the Ottawa Chapter put in an application to CHRC for a pilot project. Designed by the participants to boost their efforts at recycling previously published work, our program took the form of monthly workshops with individual sessions for each of the six participants as needed.

To fulfil CHRC's strict specifications, each of the participants had to meet alone with their mentor at least once or twice a month. Some met far more frequently than that; some just barely met the quota.

I was also surprised to see how divergent the group was, both in their needs and their contributions to workshop discussions. The group ranged in age from 28 to 57. One had only a high school education, but two others had post-graduate degrees. Their writing experience was also varied, from two young men who held full-time jobs and considered their writing almost as a hobby, to three experienced writing teachers (one male, two female) who were eager to find new markets and learn new techniques they could pass on to their students.

My oldest participant was an experienced writer and editor who had decided, as she was approaching retirement, to start her own publishing company! Although she began the workshop with the idea of recycling some of her articles into books or booklets, she soon became absorbed in producing her first children's book. Within a year, Sylvia Vincent had launched GWEV Publishing with *How Do Crocodiles Fly?*

Since then, GWEV has published six books, including two by outside authors, and has become a full-fledged small press. Sylvia's individual sessions with me called on my expertise in marketing and publicity more than in writing. And that's one of the first things I learned about mentoring. It's often not what you expect!

Many of my workshop participants needed help with time management skills, and I realized that this element should be a component of every mentoring program. You can't help someone develop their writing or related skills if they are always racing against the clock. I found myself developing systems and forms to track not only time but markets, queries, submissions, invoices and receipts.

Mentoring is not a magic wand that will instantly improve one's writing or marketing skills, especially if the individual receiving the mentoring is not willing to put in the time and effort required. The following guidelines should help.

**The mentor should:**

- Have some teaching experience, in order to present material at the correct pace, communicate effectively, and prepare handouts.
- Be generous with praise for positive efforts and offer only constructive criticism.
- Consider mentoring a real and important job, setting aside sufficient time to devote to the sessions, as well as making it a priority to respond quickly to questions and requests for help.
- Be willing to step back from his or her own work during the mentoring process, in order to spend considerable thought and effort on the protégé's project.
- Be firm, if necessary, insisting that the protégé fulfil his or her obligations.

- Be flexible, providing any necessary information and expertise as long as this serves the same result (helping to develop the protégé's writing career).

**The protégé should:**

- Be prepared to devote sufficient time and effort to the mentoring process.
- Have a clearly focused goal which he or she has the energy to pursue.
- Put mentoring sessions ahead of personal recreation and other pursuits.
- Respect any hours the mentor sets for receiving phone calls or faxes.
- Not expect the mentor to read work by the protégé unless it relates specifically to the project they are working on together.
- Consider the mentor's suggestions without becoming defensive or argumentative.

Some of the most successful PWAC mentorships combined individuals with special skills with others who were keen to learn (e.g. photography, desktop publishing, etc.). In Quebec, the program combined fiction writers with experienced editors who worked either on staff or freelance for various publishing houses. So mentoring can work on a variety of levels, including fiction, poetry, writing for theatre or film.

Mentoring can complement courses taken at a university, community college or online, especially if the course gives an overview of the material. Unfortunately, federal government funding for mentoring ended when responsibility for training was devolved to the provinces.

However, the Periodical Writers Association of Canada has since instituted its own informal mentoring program, where people pay mentors a fixed fee for one month of mentoring. A small percentage of this is donated back to PWAC. It's a win/win/win situation for everyone. The mentor receives payment for sharing his or her expertise; the protégé gains hand-on help and advice; the organization obtains donations as well as the satisfaction of assisting members to further their careers.

—

Barbara Florio Graham is a member of the Periodical Writers Association. She chairs PWAC's Mentoring Committee and Strategic Planning Committee. An author and online teacher, her books and courses are described at www.SimonTeakettle.com.

# 2. Action & Reaction

# The Write Way

*by Peggy Fletcher*

There is no magic formula to getting published. Creative writing is work. Those who tell you otherwise are misleading you. There are, however, ingredients which will help you find the right approach for your writing. The key ones among these are writing each day, or as often as you can, and reading as much as possible, especially those authors you would like to emulate.

Some people dream of writing a novel, a task which is difficult, and requires a great deal of self-discipline. Others love short stories and wish they could write like Alice Munro. Still others favor nonfiction and fancy themselves as photojournalists. Many choose poetry either in verse form or song. All hope they can become rich and famous when their work appears in print.

Are you the next Margaret Atwood? Maybe. But before you reach quite that high there are a lot of steps to be taken. A kind of apprenticeship you might call it. The difference between a serious student of writing and one who only dreams about it is the willingness to work hard at developing whatever talent he or she possesses.

A writing workshop is designed to help you decide what sort of writing you want to do. For some people that is as simple as keeping a journal or writing creative letters to loved ones. These writers have no real aspirations of getting published.

Those who do want to explore the field of creative writing that leads to the printed word can start in a small way by having letters to the editor published in their local papers.

Small weekly papers sometimes have space for writers who wish to share their thoughts or experiences with readers. Daily papers sometimes hire columnists for area content. These are some of the avenues writers can take when getting started.

A big mistake is to aim too high in the early stages. Although there have been times when first novelists or article writers have made the headlines, most writers will be disappointed with the number of rejection slips that arrive in their mailboxes because they didn't research their market. *Readers Digest®*, for example, does not even read a freelancer's work if it is sent in without an agent. The only "over-the-transom" articles *Readers Digest®* considers are pieces for the humour section and some nostalgic items. (Check the magazine for details.)

Church magazines and farm journals can be important places to try your first efforts. Small literary magazines can be found in the library and the editors may be receptive to poetry and literary fiction if the journals are studied. A lot of work goes into the marketing of creative writing. This sometimes puts people off. But most writers spend years building up a list of credits before they are published in book form. In the end, seeing your name in print is the goal.

**Tips on creative writing...**

- You do not need any special education to be a writer. All you require is a love of words and the willingness to learn to put them together in new and creative ways.
- If you have any particular problems with spelling or grammar, it is wise to have someone who is more adept in these fields edit your work before sending it out. Editors frown on sloppy English.
- There is a standard method of preparing a manuscript. It is useless to send your writing to a magazine without researching and preparing the script properly.
- Although you do not need an agent, many magazines are now refusing to accept unsolicited manuscripts. Look on the editorial pages for guidelines for contributors. If there are none, write to the magazine and ask what the requirements are for publication.
- Learning to use a computer is a plus these days. Many publishers require electronic files on floppy disks. Some will ask to have them filed through e-mail programs. This means you have to become familiar with the Internet. Most libraries have access to these computer areas. A basic computer course can help you.
- The pen is still a favorite tool of many writers. It is used for first drafts and for quick research notes. However the day when handwritten manuscripts could be submitted is long past. Only typed scripts are acceptable now.
- A notebook to jot down ideas and thoughts can be helpful in creative writing. Journals and diaries have long been favored for those who wish to write memoirs or travel articles. Keep it small so you can put it in your pocket.

- Reading your work out loud often lets you hear when there are awkward passages. Group workshops can be helpful in this respect. Although beginning writers are often shy about reading their work, it is important to try and overcome this. Constructive criticism is the best way to improve your writing.
- Most writers are avid readers. They read everything from the cereal box to the dictionary. While many of us have favorite authors and styles of writing, it is wise to expand your own reading habits to include different forms and genres. For instance, if you love mystery and horror stories, but seldom read romance or science fiction, try the latter.
- Poetry writing is never done for money. It is difficult to get published in book form, and poetry is a demanding genre. Light verse can be found in some magazines, but serious poetry is aimed at the many literary magazines that exist throughout the country. Self-publishing is not uncommon among poetry writers. Songwriters also have quite a challenge in finding a market for their lyrics. Sometimes they team up with musicians or singers to accomplish this.
- Beware vanity presses. These can be recognized by their bold advertising that asserts they want your writing. Respectable publishers never advertise for writers. Vanity presses want your money and their sales people will tell you anything to sell you a high priced book of little value.
- Unlike vanity publishing, co-op efforts or self-publishing may be an avenue you wish to explore. The co-op press is usually established by a group of writers who believe in themselves and who feel the bigger publishers neglect them. The authors often pay for poetry, short story collections and local histories, and small press runs prove to be satisfactory. The main disadvantage is the lack of distribution. However, if you are willing to work at it, the rewards are satisfying.

—

Peggy Fletcher was born in St John's, Newfoundland and now lives in Sarnia, Ontario. She taught Creative Writing and English at Lambton College, and is Family Editor at the *Sarnia Observer*. Peggy has published four books of poetry, one of short stories, and this has been supplemented by work in anthologies and magazines in Canada, England, Australia and the United States.

# The Value of a Freelance Journal

*by Christina Truman*

I had nearly reached the two-year mark as a freelance writer, and I was beginning to think I should just throw in the towel. After all, I had given the gig an honest go, but in return, it had not given me what I wanted, and what I needed: more assignments, and more money.

Although I had become a regular contributor to various local publications, and even landed a couple of national assignments, I was nowhere near the place I wanted to be. I wasn't what I'd consider a successful freelance writer. At least not like the writers I kept hearing about, those who made $1 a word. The ones who were so busy they had to turn down work. Who landed assignments with national magazines with ease. Or so it seemed.

What was wrong with me? Why wasn't I landing high paying assignments? Why weren't editors calling me with good news? And so the pity party began. I should have bought a few kazoos, balloons, and streamers for the occasion, because the party went on for a quite a few days.

"Woe is me," I declared each day when my virtual mailbox was empty.

**I took a good look at what I had done...**

And then I started to take a good look at what I had done for the past two years. How many queries had I sent out? How many follow-ups had I fired off?

The answers were embarrassing. But they were also encouraging.

Maybe the reason I wasn't getting assignments wasn't a statement about me as a writer, but rather a statement about my salesmanship. Maybe I'd get more yeses if I banged on a few more doors.

And so my idea to keep a journal documenting each query sent, and each acknowledgment received, was born.

I soon realized that keeping a freelance journal made my efforts tangible and, as a result, encouraged me to work hard. My journal was someone, or in this case, something, to answer to. Something that made me accountable for my daily work.

Here's what it looked like for the first month:

**October 4**

Sent "Life Through a Bus Window" essay to CBC's *First Person Singular.* The essay is about my honeymoon experience on the West Coast after the September 11 bombings and how it felt to spend 72 hours on a Greyhound bus. Felt good about essay, but wondered if CBC had been inundated with essays regarding September 11 topic.

**October 5**

Received surprisingly quick response from CBC saying my piece was not for them.

"There are some nice moments in it. But a FPS needs to be more than a memory or series of them. A personal essay needs to be anchored by an idea, driven by narrative," wrote the editor.

Editor included guidelines in rejection, and said I should feel free to try again.

Felt bummed, but not ready to give up. Will have to send an essay about a life-changing experience. Light bulb went off. Speaking Circles.

**October 10**

Sent *All-Canadian Mutual Fund Guide* an article entitled "Investing With a Conscience: Is it Possible?" after reading a post on PWAC-L (an electronic list accessible to members of the Periodical Writers Association of Canada) suggesting the magazine was looking for articles. The article originally appeared in *The Windsor Star* in February 2001. I'd like to recycle this piece. I received less than 10 cents a word the first time around.

**October 11**

Sent " Where the Wild Things Are" to *International Wildlife Magazine.* Article was published in a local magazine approximately a year ago. Hoping I can find another market for this piece, which focuses on the endangered species of Pt. Pelee National Park.

Sent "Living Out Loud" essay to CBC's *First Person Singular.* Essay is about my dread of public speaking and how a group called Speaking Circles has helped me to overcome my trepidation.

Poured soul into article. Took courage. Hoping that CBC accepts.

**October 16**

Sent article about bringing out the best student in your child to *Today's Parent* magazine. The article appeared in the August 2000 issue of *Windsor Parent* magazine. Originally received 10 cents a word for article. Looking for more.

Submitted article to *Homemaker's* magazine about an amazing pet rabbit that has helped to comfort and heal many emotionally wounded adults and children. The article appeared in the May/June 2001 issue of *PETS Magazine*.

**October 19**

Received response from *All-Canadian Mutual Fund Guide*. Editor responded that he was "swamped with requests to contribute to the magazine" and was unable to adequately follow up with many people who contacted the magazine. Said he wanted to acknowledge that he received my e-mail.

Next.

Submitted 2,400-word assigned article about customer service to *WOW Magazine* (a local trade publication for professional women). Will receive 20 cents per word. Hoping I can re-sell the article after it is published.

**October 22**

Submitted 2,000-word article entitled "Fitness for Families" to *Windsor Parent* magazine. Will be paid approximately 10 cents a word. Mad at self for taking on this low paying assignment.

**October 23**

Asked to do a rewrite on article for *WOW Magazine*. Editor does not want "first-person" lead in. Given source in Boston to contact for story.

**October 24**

Called source in Boston, and interviewed him for an hour. After transcription, and story is complete, will add another 4 hours to story. Will not be paid for extra time.

**October 26**

Applied for following position found on writersweekly.com:

Freelance Feature/Human Interest Story Writers: Experienced journalists required in various cities across North America to write 500-800 word biographies, tributes and dedications on a freelance basis.

**October 31**

Got assignment about wedding photography for *Biz X Magazine* (a local business magazine). Will be paid 15 cents per word.

Sent e-mail query on "Cloud Gazing" to *Cottage Life*.

Synopsis:

Queries sent: 1

Manuscripts sent: 6

Rejections: 2

Acceptances: 0

New assignments accepted: 1

Articles submitted: 2

Jobs applied for: 1

By the next month, my journal had shown five queries sent instead of one, and an acceptance from CBC Radio. By December's journal, I was elated to include in my journal entries that I had sold an article to the *Globe and Mail*'s "Facts and Arguments" page.

Now, keeping a journal has become part of my routine. If days go by without any journal entries, I know that I'm not working hard enough, and that my goal to land more national assignments will be that much farther away.

I've been told that to be a successful freelance writer, I need to send out one query every day. Although I'm not there yet, I'm convinced that if I keep up my freelance journal, I'll reach my goal, and by this time next year, my virtual mailbox will be full.

—

Christina Truman's work has been featured in numerous national venues including the *Globe and Mail*, *CBC Radio*, *Canadian Health and Fitness*, *Schizophrenia Digest*, and *PETS Magazine*. Her articles have also appeared in *The Windsor Star*, as well as numerous local publications. She resides in Amherstburg, Ontario with her husband.

# Diversify Your Writing

*by Denyse O'Leary*

Whether you are a full-time or part-time writer or hobbyist, you will eventually want to diversify. Perhaps you have done yourself proud in writing fiction and nonfiction for children on pet care issues. But now you want to write for adults as well.

As a professional writer, I have faced this situation several times. The question is, how to quickly establish a whole new network of contacts and publications? Here are some pointers that worked for me:

*Establish the reason(s) why you want to diversify.* As a public service? Because you need the extra income? It would look good on your résumé? Or do you need the information yourself?

This last motivation — personal need — is not as odd as it sounds. That has been the reason I got involved in a number of nonfiction areas that paid off quite nicely over the years. For example, in 1996, when relatives wanted me to help them find out if their basement apartment could be rented legally, I researched the issue for them. Afterwards, I sold an article based on my findings to the *Toronto Star.* Everybody won. My relatives were happy to learn that the apartment was legal, I was happy to get paid, and a number of *Star* readers have since told me that the article was quite useful.

**Suppose that you must improve your income...**

But the main reason for clarifying your reasons for wanting to diversify is to evaluate your opportunities accurately. Let's say, for example, that you have written for children about pet care issues. And now you wish to write for adults. If your goal is public service, you could place the information in Humane Society newsletters. But let us suppose that you must improve your income from writing in order to help pay family expenses. Then you will need to research *Writer's Digest*, *The Writer*, and similar publications for paying markets on pet care news — all the better if they pay in U.S. funds.

However, there is a third possibility: You may need to publish pet care information for adults primarily in order to qualify for a related position. Then you may have to aim at the top publications, such as *Dogs in Can-*

*ada* or *Cat Fancy*. Clarifying goals enables you to zero in on the right markets for you.

*Emphasize related qualifications in your query letter.* Writing for children does not prove that you can write for adults. But if you have any writing credits, you will get to the top of the editor's in-tray sooner in your new area than if you are obviously a novice.

*Look for holes in your target publication's coverage.* Six articles on puppies in two years and nothing on old dogs? If a puppy is well cared for, does it not become an old dog eventually? The editor may have noticed the problem too. Time to dust off your file folder on old dogs and pitch some stories to the adult pet care market.

*Lastly, join a writers' group, mailing list, or association in your new interest area.* Don't be shy; let other writers know what you aspire to do. It may be that someone else is trying to offload the area you want to get into. A third person may want to get into the area you are trying to expand out of. In other words, other writers might be happy to trade contacts with you. In my experience, groups and newsletters are the best sources of legitimate new leads and publishers.

Diversification is a lot easier if you see it as a staged process rather than a "must do now" item. Give yourself at least three years before you evaluate what you have done and what you have learned.

—

Denyse O'Leary is a Toronto-based freelance writer and the author of *Faith@Science* (Winnipeg: J. Gordon Shillingford, 2001). O'Leary writes regularly on science and faith issues. She also teaches workshops on business practice for writers and editors. She has two adult daughters, three gardens and a website (www.denyseoleary.com).

# Why Write a Query Letter?

*by Marilyn Fraser*

A query letter is a sales pitch to sell your product — your article — to a publication. A query letter is your introduction to the editor. You want to make a good impression and show that you are a professional writer. Editors are frequently swamped with inappropriate manuscripts and a query letter is, perhaps, the only way to break into a good market.

Query letters benefit both the editor and the writer. They enable an editor to determine quickly whether you, the writer, can write effectively using good grammar and correct spelling to express a coherent and well-thought-out idea. A query indicates your professionalism and allows you to present your credentials or your expertise.

**Slant your article in the appropriate direction...**

Querying saves you time and gives the editor an opportunity to provide feedback on the article you propose. You are then able to find out what the editor wants before you start writing and can slant your article in the appropriate direction. You find out beforehand whether the publication has already committed to an article to be published in the next issue on the same subject. In addition, the result of your query may be an unexpected assignment.

It is essential that you study the publication before writing a query. Read the magazine's guidelines and address your letter to the proper department. Be sure to spell all names correctly. Many publications now have a website on the Internet with their guidelines posted.

**The letter...**

A query letter should be no more than one page and should include five basic components:

- The hook, or the first paragraph, is designed to grab the editor's attention.
- The pitch, the next paragraph, explaining what you are offering. Title of the article, genre, and number of words.

- The body, presenting the details of your article, highlighting your preliminary research, your interviews, and perhaps tying your article to a recent discovery or development.
- Next should be your credentials, such as experience, training, and why you are the best person to write the article. Your credentials should include names and dates of magazines in which you have published in this particular market or on this topic, if possible. If you are a beginner and have no publishing credits, emphasize some of your other qualifications.
- The closing paragraph should thank the editor for reviewing your proposal, informing him or her of any simultaneous submissions, and suggesting a delivery date for the article. If you are not a "known" writer, offer to send the article on spec.

**Presentation...**

The query letter is your first impression to the editor. It should be well dressed, neat, tidy, and polite. Think of it as an interview. It should be printed on a good white or cream bond (no colours) and include a letterhead with your name, address, and contact information at the top followed by a formal salutation.

The body of the letter should be typed in a business style with block or modified block layout and a blank line-space between single-spaced paragraphs with no indents. The type should be 10-point in a classic serif style such as Times Roman, Palatino, or Courier. Be sure your laser printer has sufficient toner or that your typewriter has a good ribbon for clean type. Do not use a pinwheel printer. Use one inch (2.5 centimetres) margins all around.

After you have spell-checked your letter, proofread it carefully. Try reading it backwards, sentence by sentence, from the end to the beginning. This breaks the familiar flow of the words so the writer is better able to recognize spelling errors.

Include with your letter a business-size envelope, self-addressed and stamped with sufficient postage, or a printed postcard, self-addressed and stamped. The postcard makes a professional impression and is particularly helpful to editors by having lines for date, response time expected, recipient's name and title and the publisher's name. Did you know you could purchase United States stamps at Canadian postal outlets? If you are submitting to a country other than Canada or the United States be sure to include an appropriate IRC (international reply coupon).

Before mailing your query, do a final check to ensure you have included your name, address, telephone and/or cell phone number, and e-mail address. Make sure the letter is addressed to the proper editor and the names are spelled correctly. This is so routine that it is often overlooked!

**Some final tips:**

- Know the publication.
- Identify with the editor and the magazine's readers.
- Make sure your topic is appropriate for the audience.
- Address your query to the right department.
- Write your query as carefully as your manuscript.
- Slant your query to appropriate publications.
- Your hook should be written in the same tone as that of the magazine.
- If your query has sold so well that you get three responses, write three articles with a different slant for each.
- If the editor requests your manuscript, mark the envelope "requested material" so it won't go into the slush pile.
- Keep an original copy of your manuscript.

—

Marilyn Fraser has published *Cab & Crystal*, a Canadian magazine on earth sciences. She has been Toronto correspondent for an international corporate magazine. Other publishing credits include *Canadian Gemologist*, *CARP News*, *Mississauga News*, and *The Medium* (a university newspaper). Marilyn has published five chapbooks. She presently writes for canadianrockhound.com.

# Prepare Your Manuscript

*by Rosemary Bauchman*

It is said that first impressions are lasting impressions, so it is important that every writer has a clear grasp of proper manuscript presentation.

Whether you use a typewriter or a computer, your output should be on good quality white paper, size 8.5 x 11 inches, or the metric equivalent. Typing should be double-spaced on one side of the paper, with margins of 1 to 1.5 inches (2.5 to 4 cm) all around.

A title page is not usually required for short stories and articles, but is advisable for book-length manuscripts. Your title is centred in the middle of this page. In the upper left hand corner put your name and address. It is also wise to add your e-mail address and telephone number. In the upper right hand corner put the words "First Rights" or whatever rights you are offering. In the case of an article, short story or poem, you may wish to specify "First North American Print Serial Rights," retaining foreign, electronic and book rights for your future use. Below that print the exact number of words in your manuscript. Directly below that again, it is a good idea to type in "Usual Rates." This is a signal that you expect payment. If you are offering other than "First Rights," in the lower right corner state where the piece has appeared before and publication date.

**Use your "headers and footers" option...**

Page one should have your name and address in the upper left corner. In the upper right corner put the other information as to rights, word count and rates. Your title and byline are centred a quarter of the way down page one. The page number is placed in the centre of the bottom of page one. If you are using the "headers and footers" option on your word-processing program, you can set up the footer to read "Page __ of __ " where the program fills in the appropriate numbers on each subsequent page.

On the second and subsequent pages, you can use the "headers and footers" option to place an abbreviated version of your title in the upper left corner, then a slash and your surname (viz: Preparing/Bauchman).

Paragraph beginnings should be indented eight spaces, or one inch.

Try to keep the number of lines per page consistent. If possible, avoid breaking paragraphs at the end of the page.

Use paper clips to hold pages together, never staples. A longer work is clipped together by chapters in chronological order.

Shorter works such as magazine articles and poetry selections are best mailed flat in a 9 inch by 12 inch envelope. If you are including photographs or your manuscript on computer disk, be sure to sandwich your manuscript and enclosures between two layers of corrugated cardboard. In the case of enclosures, you may want to use larger, heavier padded envelopes to protect the contents.

**Enclose sufficient return postage...**

If you want your manuscript returned, be sure to enclose sufficient return postage. With smaller manuscripts include an appropriately sized self-addressed stamped envelope (SASE) for its return. Note that with the rising cost of postage, it may be more economical to include a standard No. 10 self-addressed, stamped business envelope and a "comment card" and ask the editor to destroy (shred or recycle) your manuscript if it is unsuitable. You can always print a new, clean copy for your next mail out.

Submit your book manuscript in the box the paper came in, or other suitable container. Carefully pack and wrap the package so that it will survive the postal system.

For book-length manuscripts, be sure to include a standard No. 10 self-addressed, stamped envelope for any preliminary comments the editor may wish to make. Also include a self-adhesive, self-addressed label that can be placed over your original label on the manuscript box.

If you are including illustrations, photographs or anything else that cannot be easily replaced, consider insurance and one of the tracing options available from the postal system. If your life's work is in the package, be doubly sure to have duplicates filed away in a safe place in case disaster strikes somewhere along the way.

With careful consideration to preparation, presentation and packaging, you ensure that your "first impressions" are favourable and that your manuscript is in the best possible condition when it reaches the editor.

—

Rosemary Bauchman is the author of six nonfiction books, numerous articles, short stories, poems and book reviews. She has conducted creative writing classes and edited material for other writers; has been a judge for fiction and nonfiction awards.

# Ten Self-Editing Tips and Tricks

*by Lois J. Peterson*

I wasn't around when publishers signed up authors, then helped them improve their grammar, punctuation, and anything else that needed fixing. But I do know that these days your submission's more likely to be accepted for publication if you learn to edit your work yourself before submitting it.

Self-editing takes time to learn, and discipline to exercise. But it can pay off.

Issues of subject, style, organization, and presentation affect how a piece of writing fares when it hits an editor's desk. This article's designed to help you look at text, and eliminate problems before you send it out.

Below are the ten most common problems encountered by the editors, book doctors and contest judges I recently polled.

**1. Adverbs.**

You seldom need them; eliminate them by using stronger verbs. Any one of a host of verbs can be used to replace the following adverbs: he walked *briskly*; she said *quietly*; the flags waved *lazily*; the children played *happily*.

Adverbs used alongside a strong verb are doubly redundant. In *she tugged sharply*, and he *hesitated briefly*, the adverb repeats the idea already implied by the verb. The word *hesitates* implies brevity; *tug* is itself a sharp action.

To discover how well you do in the adverb department, set the "find" function of your word processor to catch anything ending with *ly*, then replace the verb with a stronger one and eliminate the adverb. Count how many adverbs you find in your work, and aim to reduce their occurrence in subsequent writing.

**2. Clichés.**

These arise in ideas and scenarios, as well as in language. Couldn't the neighbour borrow something other than a cup of sugar? Are there only "spiteful" nuns at the convent school?

Using a mirror to reflect a character's appearance is passé, as are stories that end with a protagonist waking from a dream.

Although I used to think that clichés were acceptable, lately I've come to believe that writers should only use them if characters have no other way of expressing themselves. But the question arises — can a writer not convey lack of originality in an original way, rather than resorting to clichés?

**3. Contractions/possessives/plurals.**

One editor says she sees contractions, possessives, and plurals misused so often she ignores them, and fixes them later. A contest judge tells me that if there's more than one such error in the first page he's unlikely to bother with the rest of the piece. Your best bet is to write for the contest judge, and be relieved if a permissive editor catches you out.

If you're confused between its and it's, consider this: the possessives *his, hers, theirs, ours* and *yours* do not have an apostrophe. *Its* is just another possessive. It doesn't need one either.

But contractions do. *It is a hot day* becomes *it's a hot day*, in the same way that *she was not unhappy* contracts to *she wasn't unhappy*.

Plurals are easy. They never need apostrophes. *Seven dogs are in the yard, but my dog's asleep at home*, just about covers it.

**4. Repetition.**

Watch out for words repeated too closely on a page. Then, change them or move them. Only leave them where they are for a reason — for emphasis, irony, or to underline the meaning of the phrase or sentence.

In a recent story, I repeated the phrase *she took his arm* five times. Although the story was about an elderly man attended by female care-givers, I revised the piece so the reader would not be distracted by the repetitions, or worse still, would start looking for the phrase's next occurrence. Somehow Ed McBain gets away with *flying wedge haircuts* and *French heels* in almost every novel, often mentioning them more than once. But you might not want your readers to play "find the verbal tic" with *your* work.

The repetition of ideas often contributes to "too much tell, not enough show." *Junk Unlimited's CEO has a tidy office. Paper clips are ranged in military fashion around the magnetic holder. The few papers on his wide mahogany desk are placed edge to edge, and the phone sits right up against the desk's beveled corner.* The idea expressed in the first phrase is repeated through description. We know this guy's tidy by what we're shown, without the reader needing to tell us.

**5. Passive voice.**

An article was published recently claiming that the passive voice was not so bad. I forget where or by whom, and from the way I wrote that first sentence, you might agree.

The passive voice, in which an action is not directly attributed to a subject, is often used in business communications. *All cars parked in the forecourt will be towed away* might not be as confrontational as, *The manager will tow away John Bloom's car if he dares to leave it parked outside the front door again!* The second version might get prompter action. If you want to involve your readers, use the active voice so they can tell who's doing what to whom.

The only time you might need to use the passive voice is when your intention is to convey disassociation from an act or situation.

**6. Punctuation.**

I overuse commas. Lots of writers misuse semicolons. When does a period fall inside quotation marks, and when does it fall outside? The finer points of punctuation are discussed and explained in a number of library books on grammar and writing. Learn the right rules of punctuation and use them.

**7. Redundancies.**

My favorite is *the man put his hat on his head.* Where else would he put it? Now, if he put it on his elbow…

The *Writer's Digest* website once posted an impressive list of redundancies that included phrases such as *circle around, never before, young baby, raining outside, future plan* and *gather together.* See how many you slip into your writing without noticing. You'll produce tighter, more compelling work if you learn to edit out redundancies as you go, especially the ones you don't need.

**8. Speech tags.**

Beginning writers often make excessive use of dialogue tags such as *he explained; she retorted; he cried; she replied; they begged.* The good old *he said* and *she said* are discreet and non-intrusive. A writer's obligation is to convey mood, tone, and meaning through the dialogue itself, rather than depending on tags. But if these simpler tags begin to sound repetitive, try leaving speech unattributed when the speaker's identity is clear. Or use a combination of dialogue and action to convey who said what and why. *"Get down from there." Mary grabbed Jean's arm and dragged her down from the monkey bars,* works here without any attribution.

**9. Weak verbs.**

Oregon editor and critique-group leader Elizabeth Lyon's best advice is to avoid using weak verbs in power positions.

The weakest phrases are those that employ variations of the verb *to be*. These include: *there were; there are; it is; it was*. Power positions occur at the beginning and end of books, chapters, paragraphs and sentences — the doorways that meet, greet, and send readers on their way.

*There were four people sitting at the dining room table when George walked into the room. He'd never seen them before*, might be more powerfully written as *Four strangers looked up from the table when George walked into his dining room.*

*Minnie Howes dropped dead over her Sunday bowl of porridge* has more impact than *It was Sunday morning when Minnie Howes dropped dead over her bowl of porridge*. There are, however, times when weaker verbs are used with good reason. *It was Sunday Morning when Minnie Howes dropped dead over her bowl of porridge, and Thursday afternoon when her body was discovered by the gardener peering through the window,* tells a different story.

**10. Spelling and word use.**

It's all very well to spell-check a piece of writing, but don't expect it to catch everything. After recently wrestling with the spelling of *recognizance,* I was so pleased to get it right that it took a better editor than me to point out that the word I wanted was *reconnaissance*. Don't use the first word that comes to mind. Good diction makes for better writing.

If you don't know the difference between their and there, heirs and hairs, a spellchecker isn't much help. Try reading your work backwards, one word at a time. You'll be forced to consider every word out of context, helping you identify errors, or find more appropriate words.

These are not the only elements you should monitor as you develop your self-editing skills. But you can use them to start building your own checklist, adding weaknesses that reoccur in your writing, and things that others point out when they review your work. Check your writing often as you work to make it the best it can be.

The editor will thank you.

—

Editor Lois J. Peterson can spot errors in work submitted to her literary journal *WORDS*, but it often takes someone else to point them out in her work! Her edited fiction and nonfiction has appeared online and in print in five countries.

# The Joys of Writing and Rewriting

*by Lini Richarda Grol*

At one of our writers' meetings we had a special speaker who enlightened us about her writing, and more importantly, how to get published. She spoke enthusiastically about a newly published book. We listened in awe. After the speaker's lecture came question time. Hands went up, and she was bombarded with questions.

The first one asked, "Did you have to do a lot of rewriting before a publisher accepted it?" Our author shook her head and said emphatically, "I never rewrite, it kills the spontaneity of a story." We gasped and looked at our group leader who always urged us to rewrite our stories.

Another hand went up and someone asked boldly, "But don't you have to, if an editor asks you?" She then bent over as if sharing a secret with us. "Look, they like your story or they don't. No rewriting will make it better. If they don't like your story, so what?" She added with a shrug, "You take it back and send it somewhere else." Baffled, we looked at one another. She made it sound so simple. "Take it back and send it somewhere else." As if publishers and editors were sitting, waiting for our masterpieces.

**My heart sank...**

I remembered an earlier story I sent to every publisher in the writers' journals. Every time I saw that large manila envelope returned in the mail, my heart sank. I knew it contained a rejection slip.

Then one day my spirits rose when I saw a short letter on top of my story. The editor addressed it to me personally. I swallowed a few times, wiped my eyes and read, "Your story is a gem, but it needs a little polishing to make it sparkle." Reading further, I was on cloud nine. "rewrite your story and send it back to me; I think it will make a pretty good children's book." Wow. I swooned on that sentence and read it over and over again. I could see my book in the store windows with my name on the cover. I ran to my typewriter, eager to complete my soon-to-be-published book.

But when I looked more closely at my story, I dropped. The first page was awash in blue marks. In sheer disbelief, I turned the pages. Page after page was covered with blue pencil. How could this woman say that it was a good story when there was so much wrong with it? Was she poking fun? Did she sense that I was a novice? My thoughts raced. Was this for real?

How could I have been so naive to believe that she meant it when she wrote "a gem of a story"? I was furious at myself for believing her, believing that she was serious and that I had found a publisher for my masterpiece.

My "gem of a story" landed hard in the wastebasket. What was the use? I had to admit I was beaten. I grabbed my purse and went downtown to spend the afternoon buying an outfit. Ha, this was much more fun than spending time and money writing stories that no one wanted.

Grim but content, I went home and called my friends to show off my new outfit. But after they'd left that night I retrieved the letter, for her words "gem of a story" haunted me.

**It needs some polishing…**

I reread the letter with its praise and its possibilities. "Gem," she said, "it needs some polishing." Some? Some? Then I thought, "Stone gems need polishing, why not my story?" Humbled, I retrieved my manuscript from the wastebasket. Seeing all that blue, I realized that this editor must have spent a lot of time and scrutinized my writing line by line. Indeed, here and there it did sound stilted. I could do better. I'd show her.

That night, guided by her blue pencil marks and suggestions, I rewrote my story. It was in the early hours when, at last, I fell into my bed certain that the story now was a sparkling gem. The next morning, confident and happy, I put my story in an envelope, with a letter thanking the editor for her advice. I didn't have to wait long.

Within four days my story was back. This time the letter was signed "Sharon," and she seemed enthused. "You have done well," she said. "Your story shines in some places but still needs more work. Rewrite as marked and keep up the good work. I look forward to the finished story."

I was thrilled. But when I sat down to rewrite, I was seething. Blue pencil had again ravaged my so-called "gem of a story." I fumed. What does she mean it *shines*? Where? A cursed blue pencil obliterated whatever shine existed. My story landed in the wastebasket again and I stamped from the room. I swore that I had done with her and with writing … forever!

But as before, after a walk, I calmed down. I gathered up my battered story once more to give it a closer look. Then I saw what she meant and what she intended. Back to my typewriter I went. I typed painstakingly slowly to avoid mistakes and produced a perfect manuscript. I knew this was the last time and I made sure that my story sparkled and shone, as a true gem should. I read it through and smiled. Yes, this was it. This time Sharon would have to admit that my story was perfect. Enthused, I sent it off and anxiously waited for my contract.

But the story came back. Again with a glowing letter praising my efforts, with more of those dratted blue marks menacing every page. Something snapped, and I closed my eyes. How could this be?

But now I was obsessed with the story and a dream of seeing it as a published book. So, back and forth that story went. I doubted that I would ever see this story in print, let alone in a book. My hopes grew, though, when gradually my story came back with fewer and fewer blue marks on the pages. My heart sank when the story came back for the seventh time.

**One more rewrite...**

I groaned when I read Sharon's latest letter: "You are doing well. One more rewrite. Don't squeeze in what I have cut out. Just rewrite it as well as you can. Send it back in and we'll send you a contract and a well-earned advance."

Finally, there it was.

I read her letter over and over and went back to my story. Yes, there were still some detested blue notes on pages, but I knew now that my story was homebound. That last rewrite was sheer joy. I'll never forget the moment I signed the contract, or when I finally held that book in my hands. Sharon later wrote, "You should be proud of your book." I am, indeed. For thanks to her and everyone who worked on *The Bellfounder's Sons*, it was more beautiful than I had envisioned it.

Would I ever again rewrite a story if an editor asked me to? You bet I would.

—

Netherlands-born Lini Richarda Grol's novels, plays, poetry and "scissor-cut illustrations" have been published worldwide. She is a Life Member of the Canadian Authors Association, the Professional Women Writers of America and various poets' associations. One of her original stories, *Lelawala: The Maid of the Mist*, became a musical. It premiered in Toronto in June 2001.

# You Have to Please Yourself

*by Ruth Latta*

A friend phoned me the other day, his voice full of excitement. "I heard back from a publisher about the story I sent them. The editor thinks I should chop off the ending and tell the story from the woman's point of view, not the man's."

I sighed. How well I knew the thoughts running through my friend's mind. After receiving so many printed rejection slips saying, "Does not meet our needs at the present time," a personalized rejection letter with specific suggestions is a thrill. When our literary efforts are so often met with a thunderous silence, it is exciting to know that some human being actually read our work and reacted to it.

"Did she say she would publish it if you made the changes?" I asked.

"Well, no!"

"Did another editor make the same suggestions?"

"No, the story has only been out to this one magazine."

"If it were mine," I said, "I would seek a second opinion before subjecting it to major surgery. I would send it elsewhere and see what another editor thinks."

I felt like singing him a few lines from "Garden Party," a song made popular back in the 1960s by Rick Nelson. The refrain goes: "I've learned my lesson well. You can't please everyone. You have to please yourself."

Am I saying that I never revise? I revise. Any piece of writing can benefit from an edit. Everything I write goes from handwritten draft to computer printout. Then I reread it, a close friend reads it and makes suggestions, and back to the computer I go.

If an editor wants to publish something I've written, and suggests a few changes that do not distort the subject matter, then I am usually happy to comply. On a couple of occasions, I have taken exception to an editor's changes, explained my reasons for doing so, and had my own wording restored. I don't run back to the drawing board just because someone tells me to.

As my published credits mount, my self-confidence grows. At an earlier stage, I paid more attention to the views of friends, peer professionals and editors. One time I gave a friend a story of mine with some hard-to-diagnose problem. She told me there were three separate stories incorporated into one, and too many characters scampering around. "Ah ha!" I thought, with relief. "Right!"

At the computer, I used "Block" and "Delete" to separate the story into three parts. In my enthusiasm, I destroyed the original, but told myself it didn't matter much since it was so obviously flawed.

**The original had a plot...**

When I read the three segments, however, I found that not one added up to a story. The original, flawed though it might be, at least had a plot, which the fragments lacked. Suddenly I remembered that many of Alice Munro's stories are complex fictions with main plots and subplots. Some readers perceive her work as involving two or more separate stories bundled into one. Another memory came back — the advice of a writer-in-residence suggesting, as an exercise, that I merge and connect two different stories to create a more sophisticated dramatic tale.

Every attempt to reconstruct my original story left me sick at heart, and I never managed. A great loss to literature? Probably not. Yet I mourn its loss. Left intact, I might have found a way to better integrate the three strands of plot, or three parallel situations. Or it might have been published if I'd let it alone and sent it out. I butchered my story on the say-so, not of an editor, but a friend.

Since then, some of my stories have been deemed badly flawed by one editor, and greeted with enthusiasm by another. Now, only those in a position to publish my work can persuade me to make changes — sometimes.

—

Ruth Latta's latest work is a biography of Grace MacInnis, coauthored by Joy Trott, and published by Xlibris, 2001. Visit her website for further information about her published work at www.cyberus.ca/~rklatta/RuthLatta.html.

# Ten Assignments to Writing for Publication

*by Linda Jeays*

A few people are born writers. The rest of us learn to write one step at a time. With this in mind, I developed *Writing for Publication*, an evening course that I taught at a local university.

I worked from the premise that if my students already had a good grasp of the English language, they could expect to see their names in print by the end of the 10-week course.

How? By setting realistic goals. By climbing the ladder of success one rung at a time. Each week I gave the same basic assignment: Get your name in print. But each week the specific task was a little more difficult and the market harder to penetrate as a new freelance writer.

I made some assumptions based on my own experience. It was easier to get a book review published in the community newspaper than in *The Globe and Mail*; it was easier to get an article printed in a magazine for seniors than in *Maclean's*.

The strength of the step-by-step approach was that when an editor asked, "What have you written before?" students had clips of published work to show. Each published assignment, however modest, was a sure foundation on which to build success at the next level — and the next level was within reach.

For teaching purposes I set a harder task each week, but the students proceeded at their own pace. Some climbed that ladder long after the course had finished. I encouraged my students to complete each assignment several times, and some enjoyed the view from one of the rungs so much that they stayed there permanently.

These are the 10 assignments we used in the course. Start at the beginning. Take your time. Check off each assignment when you complete it, and then reward yourself as you climb each rung.

**Assignment 1:** Write a letter to the editor of your daily newspaper.

Read at least one week's back copies of the daily newspaper. Determine what the current topics are nationally, provincially and locally. Write a personal experience that sheds fresh light on one of the issues.

Or, contribute to the debate with strongly stated opinions, original insights, or researched facts and figures. Make sure your letter is a similar length to those usually printed and ensure that your vocabulary and style is suitable. Read your letter aloud: it should have a compelling tone of voice. A rebuttal to a previously published letter has a good chance of making print.

*Suggested topics:* smoking, health care, education, stay-at-home moms and dads, legalization of marijuana, capital punishment, minority issues.

**Assignment 2:** Write a report for your local weekly newspaper.

Local newspapers usually have limited budgets and few full-time staff. Freelance submissions that conform to the established style and content of the newspaper are often welcome. Don't plan on *improving* the paper, plan on making a contribution. The surest way into print is to write information pieces. For example, announce an upcoming church bazaar, provide details of lessons at the local tennis club, or profile the keynote speaker for a parent–teacher evening.

Go to community events with your notebook in hand. Offer your editor reports on minor league teams, scholarships won by high school students, and new business developments in your neighbourhood.

Book reviews and critiques of local music and drama productions (especially by schools and community groups) are usually accepted.

*Suggested topics:* school and sports events, local associations and businesses, local politicians, road construction, utilities, parks, recreational opportunities, books written by local authors, theatrical events.

**Assignment 3:** Contribute an article of 400 to 800 words to a small in-house publication.

Do you belong to an organization that publishes a regular newsletter or magazine for its members? This is an excellent target market for your first full-length article. You have insider status as a member of the group and "expert" knowledge of the concerns of the group. A small in-house publication can be a church magazine, a work circular, or union newspaper. Informal clubs such as a drama society, nature club, music group, badminton club, antique collectors' guild, or automobile association often present publishing opportunities. Editors may welcome nostalgic pieces, historical background to current club concerns, and profiles of experts in the specialty area.

*Suggested topics:* a personal anecdote, a report on issues raised at an out-of-town convention, your opinion of new products and developments. Tailor your work to the interests of the particular organization and then write something only you can write.

**Assignment 4:** Write a regular column for a local weekly newspaper.

Offer the editor of your weekly newspaper a regular column of local news, movie reviews, or gardening advice. Or, become a political reporter and write up council meetings and interviews with city hall staff and politicians. As you become more confident and can write readable, interesting copy to a weekly deadline, experiment with additional submissions in different styles: interviews, profiles, reports, reviews, opinion pieces, event-based descriptive pieces, and background articles. Also, venture into different fields — health, technology, fine arts — to discover your particular talents and to build a network of contacts for future in-depth work.

*Suggested topics:* city hall meetings, local business profiles, subdivision news, home safety, historical buildings, gardening, sports, cooking, youth organizations.

**Assignment 5:** Write a profile for a free magazine or newspaper found at your local supermarket or drugstore.

Many excellent newspapers and magazines supported by advertising revenue are free to readers, and pay their writers. They always need human-interest stories, and profiles written with a clear angle and sharp quotations from interview subjects. Study the different formats used in the publication and make sure your submission fits their style and content.

If you have a special talent for a particular kind of article — travel, fashion, housing, healthcare — ask the editor for writing opportunities in your chosen field.

*Suggested topics*: fascinating people, colourful events, and research of interest to the publication's target audience. Feed into already established departments, such as leisure, entertainment, and finance.

**Assignment 6:** Write an op-ed piece for the daily newspaper.

Op-ed columns specialize in strongly stated controversial opinions and "think" pieces. Be current and newsworthy. Tightly written humor and nostalgia are in short supply. Or, write about seasonal activities most readers will be contemplating in the near future. Develop material on statutory holidays, festivals and special celebrations, or write up a personal anecdote with a tie-in to a timely event. Follow the newspaper's regular format, usually 600 to 800 words, and brush up on Canadian Press spelling and style.

*Suggested topics:* Christmas, Hanukkah, Ramadan, Valentine's Day, Victoria Day, Thanksgiving, Remembrance Day, saints' days, anniversaries, birthdays. Unusual angles on any issue already being covered in the paper.

**Assignment 7:** Write a short article on a specialized topic for a limited-circulation magazine.

Look for limited-circulation, professional-quality magazines that cater to particular interests (such as camping or crafts) or to people in particular regions (teachers in Ontario, farmers in Alberta). Also, consider larger in-house magazines put out by institutions such as banks, museums, and hospitals, or special circulation publications such as those distributed through high schools. A profile piece or book review will often open the editor's door.

Become an expert on a topic that can be written up in different ways for different audiences. Query your editor. Follow the style and layout of the particular publication. Combine point of view, research material, and interviews from experts in the field. Be prepared to write on spec: the editor agrees to consider your piece, but not necessarily to buy it.

*Suggested topics:* disease prevention, alternative medicine, pensions, recycling, conservation, pet ownership, computer technology, science for the layperson.

**Assignment 8:** Write on assignment for a national magazine or newspaper.

At first, aim for lesser-known national magazines — such as those concerned with ecology, air travel, national safety standards — before trying better-known publications. Contact editors in their preferred manner. This can be by e-mail, fax, telephone, or written query letter with clippings of previously published work. Prove to the editor that you are a professional writer able to meet a deadline, obey a word count, and produce consistent work of a high quality. Your reward is a professional-level fee. Offer to write the first article on spec in order to develop a relationship with the editor that will lead to future assignments.

Network with fellow writers and attend workshops and conferences to meet editors. Be persistent. When your own article suggestions are rejected, ask what the editor does want written. Then write it.

*Suggested topics:* evergreen issues — child safety, disease prevention, women's issues, fine art, sports, parenting, tourist destinations—that are addressed in the magazine, or in the section of the newspaper that you are writing for.

**Assignment 9:** Write for a clearing-house organization.

Some newspapers and magazines have a central office that acts as a clearing house for different regional editions of its publications. The head office provides a regular core of articles to its satellites that then add their own local material. Some seniors' newspapers and religious periodicals work like this. The advantages are multiple or large fees, wide distribution, and your marketing is done for you.

Particularly in the U.S., some children's, women's, and gardening magazines have a similar central setup. You can submit five or six articles at a time and an editor will consider your work for several publications.

Newspaper syndicates can also be approached, but you must have a proven track record for professional and regular production of high quality material in a specialized field.

*Suggested topics:* finance, computers, defence and military matters, world politics, medicine or biotechnology.

**Assignment 10:** Write for annuals and anthologies published in book form.

Always follow up on opportunities to submit new articles or previously published work to annuals and anthologies. Your work is preserved in a more permanent form and adds value to your portfolio. Be aware of the difference between an authoritatively published compendium, and those that offer space in an anthology for a fee paid by you, not to you.

*Suggested topics:* thematic material suitable to "year-in-review" publications, anniversary issues, essay collections, trade compendiums, and special-interest anthologies.

Now, take a deep breath. You need not do all the assignments to become a *real* writer. Suit your endeavors to your talents, stress tolerance, and lifestyle. There is much satisfaction and enjoyment to be gained from writing for publications on the first few rungs of the ladder. Whatever you choose, once your name is in print you have found success.

—

Linda Jeays has done all 10 of her assignments. She still enjoys the challenge of softening the heart of a new editor and opening up a fresh market for her work.

# Strengthen Your Writing

*by Barbara Florio Graham*

In the writing workshops I give for federal government departments, non-government organizations, and corporate clients, participants often look for quick ways to improve their writing. Although each participant receives a copy of *Five Fast Steps to Better Writing* to remind them of the process summarized in the seminar, I add exercises to demonstrate various principles.

This exercise demonstrates Step Four: Strengthen.

After you *Prepare*, *Draft*, and *Revise*, and before you *Polish*, you need to strengthen verbs, sentence structure, and word choices to give your writing power and precision.

In the book and in my seminars I stress that the English language contains many weak verbs that provide a benefit to individuals learning to speak the language, but can be detrimental to fine writing.

These include all forms of the verb "to be" as well as: have, do, make, go, come, get, give, let, look, put, keep, bring, take, send, find, and see. Most of these weak verbs require a preposition or an adverb to denote a specific action.

For example, *come in* may mean enter, whereas *come over* could mean either visit or concede (as in "come over to my side of the argument"). You might say the boss *came up* with a raise, or the offer *came up* to your expectations, while other players *came down* to your level, *came down* with the flu, or *came out* to watch you. Someone may *come through* for you, or *come around* to your way of thinking.

In every case, you're using two words where one, more specific verb improves clarity. "Confiscate," for example, implies a legal seizure, whereas "take away" indicates just physical removal. When you write we must find out "what happened," is your intention to investigate, or merely to question?

Whenever you substitute a precise verb for a weak one, you provide the reader with a strong visual image. In addition, by eliminating parts of the verb "to be" and the helping verb "have," you force yourself to write active rather than passive sentences. This also follows an important rule for all written communication: *show* rather than *tell.*

Try the exercise that demonstrates this to participants in my workshops:

Write descriptions (about three paragraphs long) of anything you wish, using as many of the weak verbs listed in paragraph four as you can. Then take this draft and eliminate all the weak verbs. Be particularly careful of forms of the verb "to be," including am, are, is, was, were, will be, should be, etc.

Here is a sample paragraph:

> *It was quite an experience. I'd never seen the inside of a TV studio, the control room where everything takes place. There were five people sitting in front of TV screens and they had all kinds of dials and gauges and controls that they moved back and forth.*

Here is a revised version, strengthened by selecting more precise and descriptive nouns and adjectives.

> *The control room of a TV studio hums with activity. Three men and two women twirl dials and manipulate controls, keeping watch on their TV screens, each of which displays a different camera angle.*

Notice the dramatic difference in the two versions.

In some situations, of course, a passive construction offers benefits. For example, you may want to use the verb "to be" in a sentence describing the status quo, or to distance yourself from the information ("it was decided," instead of "we decided," when you don't agree with the decision). Occasionally the object is more important than the subject, and deserves to be placed at the beginning of the sentence (as in this sentence).

In general, you can improve your writing considerably by guarding against weak verbs and searching for more precise nouns and adjectives.

—

Barbara Florio Graham is the author of *Five Fast Steps to Better Writing* and has taught writing workshops to a variety of clients in Canada, the U.S., and abroad. Her online courses are described on her website: www.SimonTeakettle.com.

# Prune Your Prose

*by Margaret Springer*

"I prune so that a bird can fly easily through the branches," a farmer with rows of apple trees once told me. It's an equally essential skill for writers. Readers want to fly easily through the branches of your text.

How can we do it? Avoid the following, or use them sparingly:

1. Weak modifiers: just, so, such, very, really, at all, certainly, definitely, exactly, right, anyway, particular, some.

2. Hedging words: usually, probably, maybe, rather, perhaps, sort of, kind of, somewhat, quite, a little, look, seem, almost, slightly, -ish, -looking, -seeming.

3. Superfluous words:
(beginnings) There was, There are, Needless to say, The fact is that.
(in dialogue) well, oh, now, er, overuse of name of person addressed.

4. Time and sequence words: first, then, in a minute, finally, after that, suddenly.

5. Mid-air paralysis: began to, started to, proceeded to (use to show interrupted action only).

6. The "ing" disease: a string of "-ing" endings.

7. Adverbs and adjectives. Pretend they cost $2 each; use strong verbs and nouns instead.

8. Passive voice. Use active voice; check all usage of the verb "to be."

9. Overwriting: purple prose, Latin fog, gobbledygook and jargon.

10. Unnecessary emphasis: overuse of exclamation marks, italics, capitals.

11. Overuse of negatives: not honest (dishonest), not important (trifling), did not remember (forgot), did not pay attention to (ignored), not on time (late).

12. Authorial intrusion: editorial asides, author's comments, unexplained "I."

13. Clichés: too familiar, too wordy and/or redundant expressions (first and foremost, to all intents and purposes); also, tired adjective/noun combinations (vicious circle, run-down tenement, penetrating insight).

Prune out that tangle of prickly, unneeded words. Your writing will be stronger for it!

—

Margaret Springer has been pruning, chopping, chiseling and scraping words since her freelance writing career began almost 20 years ago. Since then her "words left in" have been published as fiction, nonfiction and poetry in a variety of magazine and book formats.

# Three Pigs — Building to Survive

*by Ingrid Ruthig*

It's a familiar tale. Rejection is The Big, Bad Wolf. However, The Wolf is an integral part of the story and if you remember that there are ways of combating it, you'll weather the huffing and puffing.

Begin by believing that editors are keen to accept work. Editors of literary journals, as well as those for publishing houses, usually admit to something similar. They receive and read huge numbers of manuscripts each year, and expect (no, hope) to be surprised, moved or challenged. Sadly, the required response to most submissions is rejection.

As co-editor of a literary journal, I too am often required to unleash The Wolf. But I'm also a writer and poet and sometimes The Wolf shows up at *my* door to remind me of how difficult it is to have work published in a market of limited possibilities and ever-increasing competition. Defeating The Wolf involves more than talent many days, and that's when the lesson of the Three Little Pigs can help.

**The house of straw...**

Remember Pig Number 1 and his house of straw? Talented? Who knows? He was too keen to cut House Building 101 for a pint at the pub, or perhaps he was just lazy. In the end, talent aside, his material wasn't ready, and The Wolf found an easy mark.

Don't cut class. Don't forego your homework. Read the journals you're considering submitting work to and save yourself (and editors) a lot of wasted time and effort, as well as disappointment. If you submit poetry to publishers of berries-to-beer recipes or do-it-yourself carpentry journals, they may enjoy the read. But they won't print it. Be willing to learn the market. Work hard and be persistent.

Take research a step further. Though it isn't always easy, take steps to ensure the publication normally prints the type of fiction or poetry you've written. It may be a house, but you're not likely to find a straw house in a land without straw.

## The house of sticks...

Next, the plight of Pig Number 2 and a house of sticks. Though presentation is important, don't just create a cute piece. Be certain it's solid. Become your own best critic. Read and reread what you've written; shelve it a while, let it simmer. In the early stages of any process of creation or design, you are likely to be too blinded by the colour and cut of your project to be able to see rough edges or poor joins. Come back when you've gained some emotional distance. Then select and cut, revise, rewrite. Remove the wobbles and anchor it firm. The Wolf won't use much puff on sloppy workmanship.

## The house of bricks...

Finally, take heart from Pig Number 3. Creator of the brick masterpiece, he knew how to pay attention to detail.

Build solid, stoke the fire, sit tight and challenge. Remember what it's like to discover the shiver of excitement at the end of a good piece of writing. Recall the echoes you heard long after you put the story or poem down. Be a reader first and keep in mind the sound foundations that make you nod and say, "Ah!" Then, ask if the same rings true of your own work. Be honest with yourself and your work won't be easy victim to someone's huffing and puffing.

You'll be closer to presenting editors (and hopefully, readers) with a glimpse of something they see or hear every day and yet do not "see" or "hear" at all. Plan to surprise and move someone. Show the ordinary through extraordinary eyes, but make sure you've built a house that The Wolf can't possibly blow aside.

—

Ingrid Ruthig is a poet, writer, architect, and poetry/visual arts editor for *lichen literary journal*. Her nonfiction has appeared in print and online both in Canada and the U.S., while her fiction and award-winning poetry have been published in various literary journals. She lives outside Toronto, Ontario.

# Proofreading: A Necessary Evil!

*by Deborah Wright*

So, you have just written an article and it's been published. You cannot wait to see this "baby" of yours in print. Well, guess what? You spell-checked it, you trusted your friends to cast a cursory glance at it for the content, and then you read the printed version that is in a popular magazine.

You are hoping that this particular article will lead to a great career in publishing because it is said, "There is a book hidden within everyone."

The problem is that when you read your article, you realize that the spell-checker (rightly so) read the word "you" and not "your" in the content. How can that have happened? It is because spell-checkers look for misspelled words, not their meaning.

I recently received a résumé from someone who wanted to be a proofreader. He wrote, "I have attached my résumé for **you** information." When that is spell checked with Microsoft® Word, it shows no errors.

What does it say to me about the person who thinks he would be a great proofreader?

**A second look is essential...**

Another example is how a professional proofreader needs another person to edit their writing. My partner and I created a website for our business of selling booklets on usage of the English language. We sent it out for criticism to some friends and relatives. We received kudos from most but the ones we valued most were those that specified where we had omitted information. Can you believe that we had not mentioned the price of these booklets in any of the pages?

There we were, trying to be light considering the subject was pretty dry and yet we omitted the most important part of the sales process.

Proofreading, sadly, is the first cut in company's advertising. An example of a client's belief in the process was shown by the fact that he sent me an outline of a mega-company's advertising. He said, "This has been sent to the client and their nine doctors have made their comments; our staff of five have also studied it — I am still uneasy, could you please take a look at it?" I found 35 errors — simply because my eye was a new one and I wasn't biased because I had written it.

Can you look at the following scenarios and imagine the impact on their businesses?

An accounting company who spells the word "financial" with "ai" instead of "ia"?

Someone applying for a job who hasn't figured out that résumé requires two acute accents?

A website that is promoted properly on all major search engines that has an obvious spelling mistake on the home page?

All these are examples of what is encountered on a daily basis by consumers trying to decide which company they should choose to assist their company in its operation. Which companies/personnel do you think they will consider hiring? An accounting company that cannot spell a word that is essential to their operation or one that pays to have a "second eye" to show them how their company would be far more professionally depicted?

Do you really think that a company would consider hiring someone who does not know how to spell the word "résumé" properly? (TIP: on e-mail type the word with an extra "e" and then choose the correct spelling.)

So, we come back to the basic question. Can a company/person NOT afford a competent proofreader? No, but be sure. Check out their references and ask for samples of their work. There is no designation as a "professional proofreader" and there should be — but that's another article!

—

Deborah Wright was born and educated in England. After founding a post-secondary institution in Victoria, BC, where she taught English, Deborah went on to become a professional proofreader. Her clients suggested she write informative booklets on English language usage. They are being used at Canadian universities and are available at www.punctuationtips.com.

# A Letter from an Editor

*by Jonathan Ball*

As a writer, I've seen the enemy. But as an editor, I've worn his face. Late in 2001, I accepted a position to create regular literary supplements for the University of Manitoba's student-run newspaper, the *Manitoban*. With a weekly circulation of 10,000 copies, not only on campus but across the city of Winnipeg, the *Manitoban* would give writers of fiction and poetry more exposure than most literary magazines could, while providing a great venue for new writers to break into print.

I was excited at the opportunity to get some good experience while helping out my fellow writers. I shook hands, signed papers, placed a call for submissions, and waited for the words to roll in.

I didn't have to wait long. Submission came upon the heels of submission, and my desk soon acquired what is known as a slush pile — manuscript atop manuscript in a virtual Babel of literature. I let it pile up for a little while, then dove into the sea of paper in search of publishable work.

I must say, I was surprised. Everybody, it seems, is trying to get published, and I was expecting a whole lot of bad writing. It was a pleasant shock to find that most of the submissions I got — most, not all — were creative, unique ideas, and well-written at that.

Most, not all. There were a few stinkers among the bunch, and these I declined interest in with a polite "thank you" note. Faced with a glut of good submissions, and only able to publish two a week, how did I decide what pieces to print?

Drawing on my own experience, and talking to many other editors, I discovered the following two primary considerations:

### Formatting...

Every editor is different, and there are no hard and fast rules concerning formatting, but the standard requirement is that submissions be PRINTED, double-spaced, on only one side of a sheet of 8.5 inch by 11 inch white paper. This goes for both literary (fiction) and non-literary submissions (articles, essays). Poetry is acceptable in single-spaced lines, but otherwise it's too hard to read and make notes unless the text is double-spaced.

Following standard rules of formatting, or specific rules when available, not only makes the editor's job easier, but it makes the writer of the submitted work seem like a professional, somebody who cares about their own writing. Except in very rare cases, whenever I received handwritten work I threw it out. The same went for work printed on one side of a piece of paper with scribbles or the text of a different piece of writing on the other side. If you don't seem to care if your work is published, why should any editor?

Close attention should also be paid to specific guidelines when applicable, especially word count. If an editor can only publish pieces that run under 1500 words, then they cannot publish your story that runs to 2000 words, no matter how good it is or how much they like it. At best, they can delete sections of the writing until it is down to the maximum word length. Except in rare cases (where I asked writers to rewrite their work to make it into the desired word length), I was forced to discard such submissions, which was a shame since many of them were fantastic. Most editors do not have the luxury of contacting a writer to ask them to rewrite a piece, and reject it out of hand.

**Style...**

Nothing is more attractive than good writing. While you need a good idea to serve as the basis for your work, the best idea in the world won't save you if you are a poor writer. Good writing is a matter of style — conveying your ideas in a clear, creative, and interesting fashion. Developing style is the hardest, most time-consuming, most intimidating task there is. There is no single thing that you can do to become a good writer, but a mix of several techniques can help develop your style.

The first thing any writer should do is gain an understanding of basic spelling and grammar. This is more important than anything else. Nothing will get a manuscript thrown out faster than spelling errors, and without good grammar there is little hope anyone will be able to understand you. Writers always try to explain poor writing by saying that they are breaking the rules in order to create new and interesting forms of writing. While breaking the rules can be advisable, unless you understand fundamentals your attempts will result in nothing but unreadable posturing.

After you understand how to write, all you need to do is write. Writing is an art, and is learned through practice. Reading the works of others should never be underestimated, as there is no better way to learn than from the Classics. Become familiar with the way that good writers write. Read and reread your favourite books, asking yourself why they are your favourite books.

Above all, edit and critique your own work. A surprising number of writers do not edit themselves, because editing means deleting, and it is painful to delete. It is also necessary. It is recommended that you delete at least ten percent of the words you write over the course of your editing, including as many adverbs as possible. Adverbs are the hallmark of weak writing, as they encourage flaccid description and move a writer away from the poetic language that makes writing both interesting and memorable.

**Editors want to publish the best writing possible...**

Writing this near the end of my contract, I need only turn my head a little to the right to see a stack of fine writing that will not make it into print. Some of the people are personal friends of mine, whose work it has pained me to judge under the harsh light of an editor's lamp. At the end of the day an editor, like a writer, just wants to do the best job he can, and publish the best writing possible.

Yesterday I picked up a piece of writing that I had read many times before from my slush pile, and in a moment of perfect clarity, understood it for the first time. In retrospect, this unpublished submission is better than most of the work I published in the past year. These things happen. Though editors seem like gods to the unpublished writer, they are mortal, and they make mistakes.

The next time you get a rejection letter, don't take it to heart. Good writing will get noticed. It may not get noticed the first time, or even the hundredth, but it will. Stephen King submitted short stories for seven years before a single one of them was accepted. The rest, as they say, is history.

—

Jonathan Ball is a journalist and a writer of fiction, nonfiction, screenplays, and poetry. *Son of the Storm*, an independent feature film based on a script he co-wrote with David Navratil, is being directed by Joseph Novak for release in 2003.

# Keep Your Editor Happy

*by Carol Matthews*

After wearing both an editor's cap and a writer's chapeau for a few years, one thing has become very clear to me. Talent is nice, but reliability is to be prized. Sound too simplistic? Imagine yourself as an editor, two hours after deadline, waiting to receive an article from your most talented writer. Finally it arrives at 4:45 p.m. on Friday afternoon. The words are like honey, the phrases make music, but ... it's 200 words too long, the theme has changed without any warning, and there's no contact list for fact-checking! The editor has to spend hours repairing the damage. Does he or she want to do this on a regular basis? What do you think?

When I asked other editors for their opinion on how writers could keep them happy, the answers were immediate and strikingly similar. These appeared in some fashion on every list:

**Stick to your word count...**

This means within 15 to 20 words of what has been assigned. Sometimes this requires a real hatchet job on your beloved creation, but better for you to do it before it is submitted, than for an editor after the deadline. Besides, all those unused words come in handy when you sell the idea to another market.

**Meet your deadline...**

Stay up all night if you have to, stay home from the party, hire a babysitter, skip your favourite TV show, do whatever it takes to get the job done when you agreed to do it. Whenever you can, file a story early — your editor, and you, will sleep better. If, for some legitimate reason you find you can't meet your deadline, give plenty of notice, apologize, and try to come up with a compromise that will satisfy both of you.

**Send a completed story...**

Don't try to add new facts once your story has been filed. Don't second guess your article and send in a totally new story two days after your editor has already edited what they thought was your finished product. If you're not sure you're on the right track, send a clearly identified first draft well before your deadline, and ask for feedback.

**Tell them early if you are having problems...**

Perhaps your primary source is out of town until after your deadline. Maybe your research is leading you to a different conclusion than originally planned. Maybe the facts cannot be substantiated. Let your editor know early so you can find a way to work around the required changes.

**Be open to criticism and changes...**

Editors are there to make your work and their magazine look good. Your writing will improve when you listen to your editors.

**Include a list of contacts...**

Expect your story to be fact-checked. Make sure you list all your sources and ways to reach the people you interviewed.

**Familiarize yourself with the publication before sending a query...**

Know their market. Study their style. Request sample copies and guidelines, borrow copies from the library, visit their website. Don't waste your time, and the editor's, by sending your query to the wrong magazine.

**Provide clean copy...**

No spelling mistakes, ever. Write in the proper format. Use Canadian English for Canadian periodicals, American English for U.S. periodicals. Use metric or imperial measures, whichever is appropriate, and never mix the two. Double-check your facts, dates, names, and titles.

**Build relationships...**

Once an editor has accepted your first piece of work, be sure to follow up with more quality queries, and follow through on deadlines and word counts. Editors prefer to work with writers they know and trust.

Keep your editors happy and you'll keep those assignments coming!

Special thanks to these editors: Carla Allen, Laura Bickle, Sandi Duncan, Carolyn Harriot, David Holt, Tamara Hughes, Diane LeBlanc, Philip Moscovitch, Aldona Satterthwaite, and Christina Selby.

—

Carol Matthews is a writer and editor living in Yarmouth, Nova Scotia. She edited *Commerce — Business Journal of Southwestern Nova Scotia*, for three years, as well as editing several newsletters. As a writer she specializes in gardening, nature and travel.

# 3. Look After Business

# What Is My Writing Worth?

*by K. Basarke*

We all write for the sheer love of it. Don't we? At one in the morning, when the protagonist is being a twit, the villain is becoming more likeable and you wonder if it wouldn't be easier to start over. Yeah, don't you just love it?

The joy of artistic endeavour is gone; the thrill of creation has faded. What keeps you going? Would you admit that somewhere in the deep recesses of your mind dwells a faint hope of locking in a "Stephen King" contract? And it is this pecuniary prod that keeps you at the keyboard.

But even if you do not aspire to these lofty heights, you must still decide what your writing is worth. Advice is free and plentiful. Mike Resnick, multiple Hugo winner, feels that if you accept less than three cents a word you are selling your work too cheaply. Others insist just as passionately that getting published is the key, regardless of whether you get paid or not. So what is a writer to do? The answer is: it depends!

A recent anthology wanted stories and offered payment of a single copy of the anthology. Did I want to sell them a story? You bet! The profits of the anthology were to go to support children with Down's syndrome. So I will give my work away — for the right reasons.

A pro market on the web wanted to buy one of my awkward-length stories. At seven thousand words, it had been turned down too often already. Did I take the offer? Nope! They wanted to buy all rights and I would want a lot more than they were offering for that kind of sale.

Of course I just sold a story for a penny a word because the editor supports newbies and it was all her small webzine could afford. Ah, logical to the end, that's me. So, how much is your writing worth?

It depends…

—

Ken Basarke has sold poetry and stories to *Pulp Eternity*, *Parsec*, *Blue Food*, *Jackhammer*, *Electric Wine*, *Storisende Verlag*, *Hugo's New Brew*, *Writer Online*, *Planet Relish*, *Visionair and Fantasy*, *Folklore & Fairytales* as well as *Dragons, Knights & Angels* magazine. His novels, *The Ursine Fix* and *The K'nith*, are at the publishers.

# Must We Be Starving Artists?

*by Linda Kay*

I had promised to talk to my journalism students about freelance writing during the last session of the semester. I told the class that they might turn to freelancing. Some might not find a staff position in journalism after graduation, but would still want to keep a hand in the profession. Others might not want a staff position, for family or other reasons, and opt instead to freelance.

I entitled my lecture: *How to Make a Living as a Freelancer.* I didn't get much past the title when a student in the first row raised her hand to question the notion that freelancing can generate a living wage. "Don't writers have to be starving artists?" she wondered.

Clearly, she wasn't the only student imbued with the idea that "one must starve to make art," a romantic perception worn like a badge in some circles. But status as a writer need not be proportionate to your level of poverty. Writers won't starve if they dispense with the romance and follow the first rule of freelancing:

**It's a business.**

If you treat it as a business, you will thrive. You'll earn a living from your writing if you're serious about not just the artistic production, which is serious stuff indeed, but also about the business end of it. As writers, we've been schooled to think the business end pales next to the artistic product. We somehow believe that crunching numbers will sully us or take our creativity away. It won't. It may not be as fulfilling as writing, but paying attention to the bottom line won't diminish our output or the quality of our writing. Precisely the opposite.

When I started freelancing in 1990, my husband noticed that I kept no records of my assignments. "Everything's in my head," I said, uttering a phrase that would become infamous in our household. That was my way of saying I didn't need to be concerned about the business end of my freelance writing, that it was tangential to my creative effort. After all, I'd never kept records at the *Chicago Tribune*, where I wrote a daily column. But I quickly learned there was a big difference being employed as a writer by a company and working for myself. There's the small matter of a steady paycheque. The paycheque came like clockwork from the *Chicago Tribune*. I realized soon enough that I needed to keep records of my freelance assignments if any money was to come my way.

As time passed, I learned there were four organizational tools for the freelancer that form the core of good business practice — and keep the artist from starving:

- Keep detailed production records.
- Write confirmation letters immediately upon receiving an assignment.
- Negotiate your fees and your expenses.
- Invoice promptly for your work.

Being self-employed requires that you:

**Keep detailed production records.**

When you work for yourself you cannot keep everything in your head. As assignments pour in, you will inevitably forget what you are writing for whom unless you keep a ledger. You'll also forget the word count and the due date, not to mention the agreed upon payment for the piece and for expenses. The taxman, of course, will also want to know exactly how much you are paid for your labour and how much you expend — and precisely when money is billed, received and dispensed. Save receipts for any work-related items.

Ledgers can be purchased at a business supply store. I enjoy the feeling of writing down each assignment in a ledger, but some folks might prefer to keep this information in a computer database. List the date the assignment was made; the employer; the subject of the piece (a slug line of sorts); the assigned length; the due date; the agreed upon fee; and the sum allotted for expenses. Save a column in the ledger for the date you ultimately receive the cheque.

This brings me to my second piece of advice:

**Write confirmation letters immediately upon receiving an assignment.**

Often assignments are okayed during the course of a telephone conversation. As a rule, most magazines are not so casual and will send a snail-mail letter confirming the assignment. But some won't — and newspapers never do. Same goes for newsletters and magazines published by private enterprise. To ensure that you have more than a verbal agreement, write a letter expressing your understanding of the conversation, noting key items like story angle, length, deadline and fees.

As an aside, before you accept an assignment, always ask if you'll be reimbursed for phone calls, taxis, parking, etc. I had a rude awakening once when assigned to write a profile on a tennis player who lived in Florida. I naturally assumed the employer would pay for lengthy phone calls to the player and her coach from Montreal to Florida. Luckily, I asked. "No," I was told, "we don't expense phone calls."

"Then I can't do the piece," I replied, calculating that the calls would eat up a good part of my fee.

That brings up the next point:

**Negotiate fees and expenses.**

I've already shown how failure to negotiate an expense fee can result in financial disaster, but the same goes for article fees. Make sure you know the accepted fee structure at a newspaper or magazine before you enter into a discussion about money. Learn the parameters in cases where there is no set fee structure. Call freelancers who have worked for the enterprise and ask them for help in determining a ballpark figure. I never ask someone outright what they were paid for a piece, but I do ask for an approximate figure they think I'll be offered given my experience and the type of piece I'm about to write. At one publication, I learned that the fee for an article accompanied with a photo could go as high as $500. When offered $350 by the editor, I began negotiating. I ended up with $500 — a lot more than I would have received had I not opened my mouth.

Lastly, while you may not feel like doing more work once you've pressed the send button and submitted your piece, don't forget the last piece of paperwork:

**Invoice the customer right away.**

First off, your work is still fresh in the employer's mind. Second, by the time the editor sends the invoice to payroll and payroll "cuts your cheque," weeks can elapse. Paying attention to the business side means the money will be in your pocket sooner, which means you can continue your creative work in peace and not worry about putting food on the table.

—

Linda Kay, graduate program director at Concordia University's School of Journalism, was a columnist for the *Chicago Tribune* before launching a freelance writing career in Canada in 1990. Her work has appeared in *Reader's Digest*, *Chatelaine*, *Newsweek*, *Inside Sports*, the (Montreal) *Gazette* and the *London Free Press*.

# Get Organized

*by Robert H. Jones*

A fellow writer recently asked how my workdays are structured. "Other than putting your butt on a chair in front of the computer and keeping it there as long as possible," he added, thereby stealing my thunder. "I'm interested in how you organize your day in order to maximize your output."

The truth is my days are not very well organized at all, but my office is. I state this despite the fact that people entering my basement workshop and office for the first time often ask if there were any survivors after the bomb blast. There is a difference between organized and neat.

**Not much structure to my workdays...**

Some folks produce best by following a set schedule. But after working for other people for 31 years, my first act when I tackled full-time freelancing was to forget we own an alarm clock. Thus, for the past 20 years I have slept as late as I wish, except when early morning flights or meetings are scheduled, or friends in Ontario forget about the three hour time difference and telephone at 8 a.m. their time. However, likely as not I am already up having my first coffee, or pounding computer keys. It is amazing how much work can be accomplished in three uninterrupted, early morning hours before the telephone and doorbell kick in. Conversely, I might also be in my office until midnight or later (which is the case as this is being written). Obviously, there is not much structure or organization to my workdays, so let's take a peek into the 11 x 11-foot disaster area where I work.

Four sets of shelves are filled with reference books, which equates to one shelf over 50 feet long. The books are in groups relating to subject material: saltwater fishing, freshwater fishing, fly-tying, writer's guides, mammals, birds, trees and shrubs, etc. One complete wall is lined with shelves containing 35mm slide pages which are separated and identified by category (steelhead, chinook, coho, bass, etc.), backed-up computer disks and CDs, stationery, a Canadian postal code directory, and 10 business card organizer books. Each holds up to 100 cards, and is identified by category: Writers, Government, Guides & Resorts, Tackle Reps, etc.

There is a small light table, two 5-drawer filing cabinets, two 4-drawer, one 3-drawer, plus four 10-drawer organizer cabinets. All are full, and everything is indexed by name or category. Stored in these filing cabinets are personal and business correspondence, over 2,000 35mm slide pages, 50 BC marine charts, and about 200 topographic maps (about 50/50 British Columbia and Ontario). Charts and maps are folded so their names and identification numbers are visible, albeit upside down in some cases, and each has a drawer index number in the upper left corner so it can be replaced in proper sequence.

One of the most important books in my reference library is a dog-eared British Columbia *Gazetteer.* When faced with an unknown place name, it reveals the proper spelling, which topographical map number to look for, and provides the location's latitude and longitude. As much of my output deals with saltwater fishing around Vancouver Island and the adjoining mainland coast, a 12 x 14-inch, hand-drawn map of this area is pinned to the wall by my computer. Blocked out with appropriate latitude and longitude lines, it shows me at a glance the general area for which I need a marine chart to pinpoint a specific location.

**Saves having to look up stumble-words...**

Also on the wall are pieces of paper with formulas for converting back and forth between metric and imperial, the province and state abbreviations for Canada and the U.S.A., a calendar showing assignment deadlines in red, and an extremely cluttered cork board. On it are pinned written reminders that "grey" is preferred over "gray" for Canadian publications; the differences between continual/continuous, farther/further, and e.g./i.e.; that the Norwegian lady who ties magnificently intricate flies is named Torill Kolbu; and the dejected little fellow in Li'l Abner who had the perennial black cloud over his head was Joe Btfsplk. While cryptic notes like these might read like gibberish to others, they save me from having to stop writing in order to look up the spelling for stumble-words I can never remember; the proper usage of grammar or punctuation; or spending far too much time hunting for some vague snippet of information that annoys hell out of me until I pursue it long enough to discover I didn't need it after all.

A clipboard holds several sheets of lined writing paper on which six vertical lines have been drawn. Three narrow rows are headed PUB (publisher's name), DUE (date), and SENT (date). A wide section in the centre is headed TOPIC (working title), followed by AMNT (amount), GST (#@+%!) and RECD (date). A red adhesive dot is placed beside each assignment when it is mailed. This is removed when payment is received, and a check mark indicates it has been published.

I often find that some of the best research material available is from articles I have previously written. For this reason, I maintain two types of computer files. The master is a chronological list indicating the publication name, date of publication, and title. Individual manuscript files are named for the publication. Each file is a complete manuscript identified by its title which, when opened, provides the date of publication.

Say I am writing an article about fishing for chinook salmon during the winter. My master index indicates which saltwater destinations I have written about, each of which probably makes reference to where and when winter fishing is best for chinooks, and which fishing tactics work best.

Reading through the index also provides ideas for new articles, and reminds me of which ones might be worth recycling to other publications.

All of this indexing and categorizing is not something I sat down and did overnight. It evolved over the years, from three-ring binders to computer files, and continues to do so as I discover new or better ways to keep track of things. Some of it takes time and effort to initiate and keep up to date, but the end result is worth it. With virtually everything in my office indexed, named, or sorted into groups, less time is spent searching for information, which results in more time for writing, editing, photographing, labelling slides, and that other thing I used to do… I think it was called fishing.

—

Robert H. (Bob) Jones has won numerous awards for his books and magazine articles. Editor of the Blue Ribbon Books series for Johnson Gorman Publishers in Calgary, Alberta, he resides in Courtenay, BC, with Vera, who is also a writer/editor.

# Make the Most of Down Time

*by Holly Quan*

Freelance writing can be a drown-and-drought occupation. Work often comes in waves, making you juggle several deadlines and burn your candle at both ends. But then you complete your assignments and — nothing. Suddenly you're in down time.

Virtually every writer experiences down time, for a variety of reasons.

Perhaps your muse has temporarily gone AWOL, your regular clients are on vacation, or assigning editors have stopped calling because you've neglected to send any query letters lately. Regardless of the reason, all is suddenly quiet on the writing front. Down time is tough on any writer but it can be especially frightening or discouraging for beginners. It's crucial to realize that down time happens and it's not the premature end of your career. Learn to recognize down time as an opportunity and use it effectively.

As a full-time freelance writer/editor, I've had my share of both the boom and bust sides of the self-employment cycle. I've learned to cope with down time and make it work for me. I've also learned that it's very easy to let emotions get the better of me and interfere with what can otherwise be a relaxing and productive period. Attitude is everything.

**To market, to market...**

If you know why you're in down time, you can take steps to prevent it, or at least reduce its impact. Slow periods occur for a variety of reasons, some of which are beyond your control. For example, a local or general economic downturn can affect your clients, who trim expenses and stop passing freelance work your way. Down time definitely has a seasonal side, too. Summers can be slow, and Christmas is usually quiet. More often, however, you experience a lull because you haven't been marketing.

One of the hardest things to do when you're busy is plan ahead. In the midst of plenty, you must still make time for marketing. Send query letters (one of my colleagues recommends sending one query every day; at the end of a month you've got 20 to 30 letters in circulation). Keep up your corporate contacts with quick phone calls or e-mail notes. Remind your clients that your current projects are about to end. "Hi, Carol, the newsletter will be finished on schedule next week, what's coming up after that?" is the kind of simple marketing technique that frequently leads to new work.

There are only so many hours in a day, though, and when you're busy with writing assignments your first priority is getting them done. If you simply don't have time to write queries or network with clients, make a list of ideas and contacts to follow up later.

Another smart tactic is to put money aside for the slow times. When you're working hard and the cheques are rolling in, set up a separate bank account as a rainy-day fund and be diligent about contributing to it. If you're worried about how to make your next mortgage payment you're not going to use down time effectively, you're going to panic.

**Keeping the lid on...**

Did I mention panic? Handling your emotions is probably the biggest challenge of down time. Depression is your enemy, negativity is a downward spiral. It won't help to berate yourself about queries you haven't sent or calls you didn't make. "It takes a lot of energy to worry and panic. Harness that energy," says Paul Lima, a Toronto-based technology and small business writer who's been freelancing full-time for 12 years.

Put that negative energy to work for you, not against you. Doing something physical is often a good stress reliever and it may be helpful to get away from your work environment for a couple of hours. Take a walk, go swimming, do some chores or gardening, shovel the walk. Such accomplishments are uplifting, a quick way to get your thinking back on track. And don't forget to breathe. I'm serious. "Deep breathing is a simple and effective technique to get your body calm and your head clear," recommends Lima.

**Make things happen...**

Don't hide under a blanket — make things happen. Because you've been keeping a list of query ideas and potential clients, now you can put that list to good use. You've got time to develop your ideas into dynamite queries. Search the Web for potential markets. Buy the local paper, make a list of businesses that may require your skills. Cold calling potential clients is much easier when you've got a portfolio package ready to send and down time is perfect for getting that portfolio together. Develop a marketing strategy, then follow it.

Now that you don't have looming deadlines, you've got time to network. Take an editor to lunch, have coffee with a current or potential client. Call up fellow writers. When you're in down time, often someone else is overloaded and may even pass a job to you (don't forget to return the favor next time you're swamped with deadlines). Networking involves family and friends, too; this is a great time to visit people you've been neglecting.

Down time is also a chance to take care of yourself. Relax, rejuvenate, enjoy. Heather Pengelley, a veteran freelancer in Montreal, advises, "When you're busy meeting deadlines, your creative side tends to get buried. Give your left brain a chance to express itself. Down time can be difficult, but without it, creativity dries up — so relax!" Treat yourself to a massage, even take a short holiday, but exercise restraint. Don't use self-care as an excuse to gorge on a bucket of ice cream.

You can also take care of business, both personal and professional. Visit the dentist, the doctor, get your car into the garage. Organize your files, get your bookkeeping up to date. Take a course. Read. Above all, maintain a businesslike attitude. Set daily goals and deadlines for yourself, keep regular hours. Don't procrastinate. No sleeping until noon.

**Keep the faith...**

Being a freelancer requires hope, faith and persistence. Especially during down time when it seems that the world has forgotten you. With the right attitude, down time can be relaxing and productive. Make sure that when the phone starts ringing again — and it will — you're mentally and physically ready to dive back into an ocean of work.

Meanwhile, take some advice from Sir Winston Churchill that seems tailor-made for freelancers experiencing down time: "When you're going through hell — keep going."

—

Holly Quan has been freelancing since 1988. She writes on travel, tourism, marketing, food and other topics for an assortment of trade and consumer publications throughout North America. She's also author of several guidebooks including *Adventures in Nature: British Columbia*. She lives in the foothills, southwest of Calgary.

# Your Own Clipping Service

*by Betty Dyck*

Have you ever seated yourself enthusiastically in front of your typewriter or computer to compose an article or begin a story and then remembered just the thing you needed for a "hook," or for rounding out an argument, in a recent paper? But which paper? What day?

Then the frantic search begins, sometimes involving more than merely minutes, ending in frustration. Even if you finally locate the material, the inspiration to write may be gone — or the time.

Several years ago I found the answer to this kind of problem, I began my own clipping service. Ideas for articles or stories are all around in newspapers, magazines, and periodicals. To make them more accessible for future use, I invented a filing system. Here are some of the ideas I found useful:

- As you are reading a publication, circle or tick off pertinent articles with a pencil for clipping later. Don't let yourself get behind in your clipping or it can become a chore.
- A sturdy cardboard carton big enough to hold file folders will do if no filing cabinet is available.
- Establish subject files and arrange them alphabetically.

Always date and document the article. You'll need the publication's name and the date, as well as the author's name, in order to give appropriate credit if you quote them later in your own writing. It also helps keep you aware of the age of your information — an important factor if you write topical articles.

—

Betty Dyck is the Winnipeg-based author of three nonfiction books, editor of two church histories, a published poet and freelance writer who conducts workshops on writing creative nonfiction and writing family histories.

# Keep It or Toss It?

*by Barbara Florio Graham*

I cringe whenever I hear a writer describe cleaning out old files. Which old files, I wonder? Are they destroying original notes they might be able to recycle into a new article — or outdated newspaper clippings that might be hard to find again?

But I can sympathize with the need to reduce the accumulation that threatens to topple whenever you reach for something. I, too, have file drawers that can't accept a single additional piece of paper, books that are double shelved, and bankers' boxes on top of bankers' boxes.

So what should you keep? And what can you (safely) toss? Here's the formula that works for me:

**What to keep forever...**

Back-up disks — Keep both software and your original work in a fireproof, waterproof security chest. Every six months or so, copy important new files to disk and store off the premises (you might find a colleague with whom you can share this service).

A mini portfolio — Assemble a portfolio with copies of your best articles, a list of everything you've had published (with dates), and your complete résumé. This should also be updated regularly and stored off-site. If you don't think this is necessary, just consider how you would recreate a list of published works after a fire or flood.

Original notes and tapes of important interviews — I'm appalled at writers who think they're saving money reusing audiotapes. There's always a danger that a tape that's been used many times might break, or produce a faulty recording because "ghosted" noise from a previous use leaked through. Audiotape is inexpensive. Use a new tape every time you do an interview (they're checked at the factory, so you don't have to worry about the tape not recording), and always put fresh batteries in your recorder (taking an extra set with you).

I transcribe my raw notes on the computer, then "archive" these on disks which I label with the date. That will usually allow me to find the correct disk by checking the date on the story file. If an interview tape is very valuable, store it in a labelled box, and put a reminder in your calendar file to fast forward and rewind these once a year (you should do the same with videotapes you want to keep permanently). Store all tapes in a cool, dry place. The basement of a house without air conditioning is the worst place to keep tapes!

If you have a metal blanket-box (they're often lined with wood), put the blankets somewhere else and use this box to store your most valuable items: portfolios, copies of anthologies in which your work has appeared, disks and tapes, important papers, etc. A metal box will withstand the kind of minor fire and flood damage that would normally ruin these things. They can often be locked, and can serve as a bench or coffee table anywhere in your house or apartment. I have a handsome brass one at the foot of my bed.

Keep financial files including business income and expenses, receipts, income tax returns, pay stubs, invoices, etc. for at least six years. When you finally dispose of these, keep in mind how much they reveal about you and your business. A small shredder costs under $50 and can sit over a carton or existing wastebasket. Get in the habit of shredding everything sensitive, particularly credit card receipts (except those used to claim tax deductions).

**What to toss...**

I set the following criteria for throwing things away.

Clippings — when I'm no longer sufficiently interested in the subject to want to write about it, as well as for people/situations/businesses which no longer exist.

Anything readily available elsewhere — perhaps in my own spin-off articles!

But there's another category. That pile of newspapers and magazines you want to read, but which you seldom have time to tackle. I call this my "File Unread" system. I keep folders (you may need boxes instead) which I have labelled:

TO READ: Fiction/poetry/essays

TO REVIEW: Writing/marketing material, including copies of writers' magazines I haven't had a chance to read; notes about new markets I've heard about but haven't yet investigated; magazines I picked up which may be potential markets.

TO READ/FILE: Nonfiction articles of general interest that I think I'd like to read, and may want to keep in my files for future reference.

TO FILE/CURRENT: This is the box or folder I'll tackle first whenever I have a few minutes to spare. These are items I clipped or saved because they pertain to current things I'm working on, queries I'm planning, or a subject of personal importance.

The idea of filing something before you've read it is anathema to some, but a necessity for a busy freelancer. There just isn't time to read everything, and even if you take the time to read it now, you'll have to read it over again whenever you retrieve it to locate facts or information.

There's an important rule I follow which helps me not to waste valuable reading time. If I'm going to read something, I mark it at the same time underlining or highlighting significant names or content. If I'm glancing through the daily paper, I either read an article that interests me and mark it to file later, or clip it for one of the "TO READ" folders. Looking through a newspaper or magazine without marking or clipping is a poor use of time.

Magazines get marked and clipped as I go through them. If I don't have time, then the entire issue goes into one of the "TO READ" boxes.

There are other "current" folders (in different colours), which I label "CURRENT/Fillers," "CURRENT/Fiction," "CURRENT/Articles," etc. You may label yours differently. I use these for clippings, ideas, and scribbled notes (some made in the car at stop lights) for articles I'd like to consider. Every so often, if I have some time (usually with my feet up in front of the TV at the end of the day), I review these and toss out things I feel are now out of date or which no longer interest me.

Another folder contains things I'm gathering for an idea I'm developing, but haven't yet found the time to query (or write). There is one for the new book, another to accumulate snippets that will eventually be considered for a short story collection I'm working on, another for bits of poetry that may be completely discarded when I look at them again, and another for filler ideas.

I don't know about you, but I never know when an idea will strike and I'm determined not to lose any tiny thread that might be useful. I keep a notebook and pencil in the sun visor of my car, in the bathroom (one just outside the shower where I often scribble a few words while I'm still wet!), beside the bed, etc.

I don't like to trust my memory. A fleeting thought, clever lead, great idea, elusive line of poetry is too easily forgotten in the business (or chaos?) of daily life. These folders are like a treasure chest that I can open any time I need inspiration, feel frustrated, or feel writer's block descending.

Colour is important to me, by the way, because I'm a visual person, and know — without checking — that the blue folder is the book one. A folder system also allows me to prioritize these from time to time, moving the yellow one forward and the red one back.

Once you get things into filing cabinets, another problem arises.

Eventually, those file drawers fill up, and the "what to keep, what to toss" problem arises again.

The secret is to create two folders for each listing, whether alphabetical or by topic. The front folder should either be a coloured folder or marked with a coloured tab. This is the "permanent, keep forever" folder, into which I place general information about this topic/individual/organization, contact names and numbers, an article or two that provides historical or other background information, anything that is unlikely to go out of date. This allows me to find these pertinent facts quickly, without paging through the entire file of clippings.

The second folder, which sits behind the first, is the "general" file. I place new clips in the front of this folder so that when I open it, I see the most recent article first. When the folder starts to bulge, I pull out handfuls from the back which I know (without having to check) is old, dated information. Because I never touch the permanent folder, I know I'm never inadvertently tossing vital material I may need later.

The colour-coded "permanent" folder is handy to keep by the phone when a story has gone to the editor and you expect the fact-checker to call. There are all the contacts, ready to hand. Colour comes in handy when you need to cross-reference between files. I put a note on coloured paper into the permanent folder with the location of cross-referenced material. No need to photocopy or worry about losing a small note in a huge, crammed folder.

I have often found new markets for old material, sometimes in ways I never dreamed of when I first did the research or interviews.

Reorganizing your files seems like a daunting task, but once you've started a system that works, it will give you one of the greatest gifts a writer could ask for — time to write.

—

This article was adapted from Barbara Florio Graham's online course, Time Management, which is described on her website, www.SimonTeakettle.com. Barbara is also the author of *Five Fast Steps to Better Writing*, *Five Fast Steps to Low-Cost Publicity*, and *Musings/Mewsings* (coauthored with her cat, Simon Teakettle).

# The Electronic Cottage # 1: Setting Up Your Own Virtual Company

*by Eric Fletcher*

What is it? An "electronic cottage" is a home-based business using telecommunications technology to procure, do, and deliver work.

A group of such businesses working together on an as-required basis can be organized as a "virtual company." There need not be an employer/employee relationship. Instead, skilled individuals can work together on different facets of a project, seldom (if ever) meeting face to face.

From our farmhouse located 50 minutes from Ottawa, Ontario, my wife Katharine and I telecommute with writers, editors, and translators throughout the world. Together, we have produced hundreds of documents, books, and articles in English, French, and Spanish. As people become increasingly interested in (or with downsizing, are pushed into) home-based businesses, starting an electronic cottage may make good business sense for you. We believe it's the wave of the future.

How, then, can you catch the wave?

Because it is a business, the steps to setting up an electronic cottage share many of the essential steps of establishing a new business venture.

**Develop a plan...**

- What are your skills? Make three columns: strong skills, skills you need to learn, skills you don't have to (or don't want to) learn. You may need to be flexible here!
- What is your business? This is often harder than you might think. Take your time, assess whether what you are currently doing is what you want to be doing in 2, 5, or 10 years.
- What are your short- and long-term goals? Be realistic: don't expect "the moon" when you start out.
- Who do you know who could help you define your business? Network! Read up on who is doing what and contact them for advice.

- Who do you know who might be potential clients? This can help define your target market.

Now tackle your formal business plan. If you need financing from a bank, a solid business plan is a prerequisite to borrowing money. Remember: just because you'll be running your own business and be your own boss does not mean you shouldn't have a plan!

Do you have a business partner? You must share a complimentary vision. Is your spouse your partner? The latter can pose additional challenges: you must clearly identify your roles and be able to communicate extremely well.

**Develop a realistic financial strategy...**

This is key. People are often eager to quit their jobs and be their own bosses. Do you possess the skills and financial wherewithal to manage a project, yourself, your spouse, your family both efficiently and professionally?

Here are some tips:

- Identify details of your current, continuing fixed and variable financial requirements. Shelter, taxes, and food are the basics. Transportation, insurance, and retirement planning are important. And don't overlook costs associated with your leisure time — without it, you'll burn out.
- How much money will it take to set up and operate? While many of the costs for materials (pencils to computers), knowledge (courses, resources), marketing, etc. may be tax-deductible, you will still need to earn the money before it is there to spend.

Accounting issues:

- Do you know an accountant familiar with home businesses? If not, network to find one.
- Pay an accountant to set up a system that works for you from the start.
- What can you claim as business expenses? What percent of your home can you write off?
- Should you operate as a proprietorship, a partnership, or should you incorporate?

Legal issues:

- Do you need copyright advice or protection?
- Will you require patent information?

- Will there be any potential personal liability issues from your business?

Insurance issues:

- Check your household policy. Computers beyond a specified value may require special coverage. If you have a laptop, ensure it is covered while in your car or at an off-site location.
- Does your car insurance coverage permit its use for business?
- What about personal coverage? Can you afford your own coverage in medical, dental, unemployment, or disability insurance?

Marketing and promotion:

Without this, you'll have no business! Many people mistakenly think that a home-based business means you can work your own hours, set your own schedule and wear what you want. Think again. Marketing is critical: plan to allocate 20 to 25 percent of your time for it.

- Project a professional image. Do you lead bird walks? Do you work at client's offices? Dress appropriately.
- Your hours are not your own. Clients expect you to work economically, efficiently, and produce work on time. Face it: most clients will probably work 9 to 5. Be scrupulous about being available by phone during normal business hours.
- Keep files of ongoing opportunities. Keep an electronic file of business opportunities that crop up. Keep a paper file of newspaper clippings, flyer samples that spark ideas.
- The Internet presents new marketing opportunities. Learn how you might create your own website and link to others to increase your exposure to untapped markets.

Pricing:

What is your competition charging? You may not be able to charge top rates at the outset — but don't undersell yourself either.

- Cover your overhead as well as direct costs.
- Hourly rate? Fixed price? Clients want a fixed price, you want an hourly rate.
- Ensure that you understand what your client really wants before you submit your bid.
- Do you have the terms of agreement in written form before you start work? Some clients do not want contracts. At minimum, write a letter of understanding, outlining what the job is and how you propose to achieve it.

**Be cautious about "being virtual" ...**

Don't just jump in to freelancing. There are peaks and valleys to freelance work.

- Can you budget? Can you save for a rainy day? Do you have a family or dependents to support? How will you survive the financial "valleys"?
- Have you considered part-time work or job sharing? Think it through before you leave a full-time job.
- Talk to your family or "significant others." Do you have their support? Do they need your financial support?
- Do you want to ski all day and work all night? Forget it! Even a cellular phone will not save you if this is your secret goal.
- Can you say no? Can you tell the persistent client who phones you to "talk shop" at midnight that you are unavailable until the following morning?

**Operating a virtual organization...**

- Who is your partner? Do you know how they actually conduct business vs. friendship? What are their ethics?
- If you need a partner, where will they work? Will you need to occasionally or routinely share space? How will you do this? Remember the liability issue.
- Virtual partners are not employees. Will you be able to mutually agree on priorities and work allocation?
- Virtual partners may truly never need to meet together. Writers, translators, and editors are good examples of this because work can be transferred electronically.
- Are you in a remote location? Can you get courier service? As a writer or editor, how will you deliver hard copy to clients if necessary?

Room of your own:

If you work at home, don't skimp. Purchase the best you can get for each functional requirement. Can you shut the door on your work? This is a psychological if not a physical necessity. Having a "virtual" office is not ideal if you cannot put it out of mind and sight. A door will ensure privacy for client conversations, sales calls, and interviews — and keep the kitten out!

- For your income taxes, you may be able to deduct a portion of your household utilities, property taxes, and other operating expenses proportional to the area of your office in your home.

- Details, details! Natural lighting is important, don't forget the reflection of light on computer screens. Having a ceiling fan is a good idea, as long as it doesn't blow your papers around.

Combating isolation:

Are you suited to operating without regular face-to-face contact? Will you miss the casual or focused chit-chat that happens in an office?

Professional organizations can be powerful networking sources for freelancers. There are a host of specialty organizations from romance to travel to medical writers' groups, technical editors' associations, etc. Members connect online, making memberships invaluable. What associations exist? Which interest you? The price of membership is part of your critical business expenses — and another potential tax write-off. And, if you become a conference speaker or part of the executive, your travel expenses (at minimum) are often paid.

Lifestyle:

Many factors influence people to become freelancers. Here are just a few:

- "Green lifestyle." Your decision to work at home is environmentally sound. Why? You may be able to substantially reduce your use of an automobile — and getting to your home-office will save commuting time and money!
- Control. You get more control over your lifestyle — if you manage it. What you do with your previous commuting time is up to you: sleep, read, spend time with the kids.
- Independence. You are the boss. You call the shots. You sink or swim. Can you deal with such independence?

If you can, you may be ready to set up your own electronic cottage.

—

Eric Fletcher telecommutes from his electronic cottage bordering Gatineau Park. He coauthored *Québec Off the Beaten Path* (2002) with his wife Katharine with whom he also writes travel columns, and is designing maps for three regional guidebooks. An expert on computer systems and publishing, he teaches and consults about electronic publishing. Contact: chesley@netcom.ca.

# The Electronic Cottage # 2: Essential Equipment and Services

*by Eric Fletcher*

What essential equipment and services do you need for your electronic cottage? First, make a budget. Separate the "must haves" from the "wants." Then do your research and buy the best quality "must have" products you can afford. Remember that office-related investments may be tax deductible. Get some guidance from your accountant.

### Things that don't need plugs...

*Furniture*. You'll probably need a desk, a comfortable chair, filing cabinet, etc. Consider ergonomic issues, such as the optimum height for a desk and chair combination.

*Personal space*. Where is your office? Does it have natural lighting? How can you make it personally inviting specifically as a work space? Should you invest in a fresh coat of paint on the walls?

*Mail and couriers*. What are your options? Identify your specific business requirements and then call Canada Post. If you live in the country, companies may not send some items to rural route numbers in the address. Research what "next-day" courier service *really* means if you live in the country. It may mean "whenever."

*Office supplies*. Can you get an account at an office-specialty shop? Does your membership in a professional organization qualify you for discounts?

*Custom items*. Can you design and print business cards or letterhead yourself? If you choose to have a printer or copy shop do it for you, keep the print run low in case you need to make changes.

*Storage space*. Don't get over-zealous in purchasing stuff! Where are you going to put it? Where will you put your inventory?

### Things you need to plug in...

*Surge protectors* help guard against power fluctuations or brown-outs which can be damaging to electronic circuits in your office equipment. If you experience frequent power outages, consider getting an uninterruptable power supply (UPS).

*Communications*. Telephone, fax, pager, cell phone, Internet and long-distance provider ... the options are many. What do you really need — and at what cost? Be wary of making long-term commitments for highly competitive services.

Combination telephone/fax/copier/answering machines can be a cost-effective solution, but be sure you can still function if one of the functions fails and the unit needs to be serviced.

Do you need a second telephone line? Balance your family and business needs. If you have kids, a second line may be strategically important — and an excellent "bargaining chip" when you are seeking "buy-in" from your family to set up your business.

Some kind of voice message service is essential for any home business operator. Do *not* use "cute" messages. Respond promptly to your calls.

Cable, satellite, and high-speed data lines may be needed for direct connect and data-intensive work, but they can be expensive. Do your homework.

*Computers*. What platform or operating system should you choose? Microsoft Windows or Macintosh? Who are your major clients? What do they use? What do your business colleagues use? Why? What do they like about the system? What don't they like? In general, get the fastest machine you can afford.

- Memory. The more, the better. Consider 128MB as a minimum.
- Monitors. A fast refresh rate to minimize flicker is more important than size. Be kind to your eyes. Thin screens are more expensive than conventional monitors but take up much less room.
- Hard disk. Words don't need as much space as software and images. A 20GB drive costs approximately what a 1.2GB drive cost a few years ago. Remember, as your needs progress you can add an extra drive.
- Keyboard and mouse. Ergonomic keyboards may look odd but can reduce the risk of repetitive strain injury (RSI). Get a mouse that fits your hand — you'll use it more than you think!
- Backup. Don't underestimate the value of your computer files. Recording them to a CD is easy and inexpensive — and CDs use widely accepted standards. Back up your files and keep a copy away from your house. Tip: develop a workable file-naming convention (where it is, how you store it) and stick to it!
- Modem. You'll need a modem to connect to the Internet. For a normal telephone line connection, a 56.6K modem is standard;

high-speed cable or telephone and satellite services require specialized devices usually supplied by the provider.

- Network. If you share your office with anyone, consider networking the computers to be able to share printers and other devices. Two machines can be networked with cards selling for under $20 each.

*Printers*. Excellent quality and dropping prices make laser printers extremely affordable and indispensable items for the electronic cottage. Ink jet printers have plummeted in price over the past few years but ink cartridge costs result in a higher cost per sheet than for laser printing. But even an inexpensive ink jet printer can deliver excellent colour at a fraction of the cost of a colour laser printer. Tip: choose a printer that can use archival inks so your pictures won't fade in light.

- Speed. Six to 12 pages per minute (ppm) is typical. But what do you really need? Your computer's operating system may allow you to print in background while you do other work.
- Special feed options. Do you need to print envelopes, heavy stock, different colours?
- Consumable supplies. The cost of toner and ink cartridges adds up quickly. Return empties for recycling and consider using rebuilt cartridges.

Computer pricing is volatile, but competitive. Check local newspapers for what is included in "typical" systems packages: the $1,500 to $2,500 price point for a complete "small business" system has been fairly constant for years.

The best deal may not be the lowest price. The attitude of the sales and support staff is absolutely critical: don't buy anything from anyone who cannot answer your questions in clear and simple terms. Insist on your rights as a consumer and business professional to get the service you need. And remember, you will also need to buy software!

*Other office plug-ins* (photocopier, scanner, bindery ...). Are there alternatives to these potentially costly add-ons? For example, your fax machine could double as a copier if you only occasionally need multiple copies. As well, many small businesses offer photocopying, scanning, printing, and binding services. It may be far more cost-effective to use a local service than to buy the equipment to do it yourself.

**Software and resources...**

*Word processors* make writing easier and more efficient. Everyone needs one! The brand is less important than being easily compatible with your clients and colleagues.

*Spreadsheets* make math accessible. Once you build a model (for tracking your inventory, distribution, and sales of self-published books, for example) it does the math and you can have fun with "what if ..." projections.

*Accounting software*. Get help from a professional to get you started. Once set up, an accounting package will keep you organized and give you a clear picture of your business status. Tip: technology is not everything. You need to have the discipline to do your numbers *regularly*.

*Industry-specific*. Computer-aided-design (CAD) systems are indispensable aids for some businesses. What is your business? Research what is on the market that can help you work more efficiently. Tip: there's a learning curve associated with all of these items. The cost (time being money) for you to learn how to use each software package must be factored in to your assessment of what you need — and when you need to buy it. Is it a basic need? Or a later goal?

*Internet*. An electronic cottage must have e-mail to function today. An e-mail address has become almost as essential as a telephone number. But through graphical web browsers, the Internet also permits wide, instant access to markets or research sources that are otherwise prohibitively costly — or that you would simply never hear about! E-mail and browser software is almost always included with computer systems. However, like anything else, Internet has its hidden costs. Plan for time you will undoubtedly spend browsing, searching, and getting sidetracked!

For access to e-mail and web browser services, you will need an Internet service provider (ISP). For the past several years, \$20 to \$30 a month for unlimited dial-up access has been typical. Cable or high-speed access is typically \$30 to \$60 per month. Since their name will be on the other side of the "@" symbol, your selection of ISP will usually determine your e-mail address unless you invest in your own domain name (e.g. @yourname.ca). If the company ceases operations, your e-mail address will no longer work so the lowest price may not be your best buy.

Many ISP plans include limits on storage space for a website with their plan. If you need a website, you can either have someone else do it for you or learn to create and manage it yourself. Either way, consider the ongoing maintenance costs: one specialist recommends allotting a minimum of 5 to 6 hours a week. Can you afford this? An out-of-date website is worse than none at all.

**"Nice to have" software...**

*Database*. This technology is powerful and easy to use but you will need to invest time to customize it to your specific requirements.

*Language spelling checkers*. Most word processors include a spelling checker for a single language. But what about French? Spanish? Depending on your business, you may need a foreign-language checker.

*Optical Character Recognition (OCR)*. Could you scan it instead of re-keying text? If so, perhaps you should investigate OCR packages.

*Games*. Okay, okay. Yes, this is an electronic cottage, but you gotta have fun, right?

—

Eric Fletcher telecommutes from his electronic cottage bordering Gatineau Park. He coauthored *Québec Off the Beaten Path* (2002) with his wife Katharine with whom he also writes travel columns, and is designing maps for three regional guidebooks. An expert on computer systems and publishing, he teaches and consults about electronic publishing. Contact Eric at: chesley@netcom.ca.

# Getting Permission for Quoted Material

*by Marian Dingman Hebb*

When you are preparing a manuscript for publication and are in doubt about whether you should be requesting permission for passages you have quoted, you should be able to ask your book or magazine publisher for guidance. But the publisher doesn't necessarily always have an answer — or the right answer. First as an editor and later as a lawyer, I have heard various "rules of thumb," usually citing the number of words that a particular publisher assumes may be quoted with impunity without permission from the author of those words. But there are *no* rules specifying a word count — under Canadian *or* U.S. law.

The amount you can quote is always a *judgment call*, which you can probably make as well as, and sometimes better than, your publisher. If the guess is wrong and you both are sued, the judge will make that judgment. Some guidance is provided by copyright legislation, and decisions in past cases that have reached the courts.

### "Insubstantial" copying...

The Canadian Copyright Act says that only a copyright owner can reproduce a work *or any substantial part thereof.* This means that other persons may reproduce *insubstantial* parts of copyright works without the permission of the copyright owner. But how much may be reproduced is not clear. How do you know whether what you are quoting is "insubstantial"?

First, you should ask yourself whether your quote forms a significant part of the work you are copying; for example, a line from a poem or song is likely to be considered substantial, and a few lines from a long prose work is likely to be viewed as insubstantial.

You also have to consider whether what you are quoting forms a significant part of the work you are producing; for example, it is probably not acceptable to use a quote from someone else as a title, chapter heading or introductory quote at the start of a chapter. For this, in my opinion, you should always obtain permission.

### Fair dealing...

In Canada, the Copyright Act provides a defence in respect of some copying of a copyright work by a person who is not the copyright owner. "Fair dealing" permits some copying without the permission of the copyright owner, *even if the copying is substantial*. Section 29.1 indicates:

Fair dealing for the purpose of criticism or review does not infringe copyright if the following are mentioned:

(a) the source, and

(b) if given in the source, the name of the (i) author, in the case of a work...

There is a similar rule for "the purpose of news reporting." Fair dealing is also permitted for research or private study, but this language does not in itself permit publication.

Under the rubric of "fair dealing," you may quote a substantial portion of a work, but only for the purposes of criticism, review or news reporting. "Criticism" may be interpreted broadly, particularly in case of textbooks and scholarly books, and may refer to ideas and general subject matter, not just the work from which the quote is taken. It is unlikely, for example, that a biographer could quote from another biographer without getting permission, if he or she is simply quoting as a substitute for his or her own description of some person or event. You can not use the words of another writer as a shortcut — without permission. This would not be "fair." However you may quote from another writer if your purpose is to critique either the work of that other writer or the subject he or she is dealing with. So it is necessary to qualify my previous example: it would be permissible to use an excerpt from an earlier biography in order to review the biography as a piece of writing or to disagree with the biographer's interpretation of the subject of the biography or events described. It would also of course be permissible to quote an "insubstantial" passage or snippet from the other biography. Remember that the "fair dealing" question only arises if the material to be quoted is *substantial*.

There is also a quantitative limit to what you can justify as "fair dealing." This too is implied by the word "fair" and again it is your judgement call. You need to take into consideration how much the text quoted forms the work from which it is taken and how much it forms your work, both quantitatively and qualitatively. It would probably not be fair dealing to quote the whole of a paragraph that is the pith and substance of short essay that has been published as a pamphlet. Nor is it likely to be fair dealing where you have quoted a large number of short quotes from the same source.

In considering whether your quotation is fair dealing, you also must consider whether what you are writing is competitive with the original work from which you have quoted, and what is the value of the quote to you and what is the value to the other writer.

### "Fair use" is the American term...

"Fair use" is the term used in American copyright legislation. It is somewhat similar to "fair dealing" in Canada (a term which we borrowed from British law, along with much of the rest of our copyright legislation), but "fair use" in the United States is considerably broader, covering "purposes such as criticism, comment, news reporting, teaching (including multiple copies for classroom use), scholarship or research." No specified number of words is permitted but the U.S. legislation gives the following guidance:

In determining whether the use made of a work in any particular case is a fair use the factors to be considered shall include —

(1) the purpose and character of the use, including whether such use is of a commercial nature or is for nonprofit educational purposes;

(2) the nature of the copyrighted work;

(3) the amount and substantiality of the portion used in relation to the copyright work as a whole; and,

(4) the effect of the use upon the potential market for or value of the copyrighted work.

You should remember that your use of quotes must comply with the law in both countries if your work is going to be published in Canada *and* the United States. Be careful if you are consulting an American writers' guide, as something which is "fair use" is not always "fair dealing."

### What is meant by "fairness"?

When determining whether a quote falls within the ambit of "fair use" in the United States or the narrower, Canadian "fair dealing," some of the the same questions need be asked to determine the "fairness" of reproducing material without the permission of the copyright owner.

- What is the effect on the original work?
- How much has been copied and how important is it?
- What is the value of the quoted material in relation to the whole of the work in which it is included?
- What is the benefit gained by the person who has copied?

- What is likely to be the result of the use of the quote or quotes on the original work quoted from? Do the two works compete with each other?
- How much effort has the quoting writer put into his work? Is he or she getting a free ride?

In considering "fairness," you must consider the totality of what is reproduced. Brief passages — in themselves insubstantial — may be *cumulatively* substantial, and if the reproduction is substantial, you must then consider whether it is "fair."

It has not been considered "fair" to quote from an unpublished work of another writer, probably because you are taking away from the original writer the right to decide whether or not to publish particular material for the first time. Nor has it been considered "fair" to quote the whole of another work, although an occasional judge has strayed from this rule, in one instance with respect to an epigraph on a tombstone and in another the cover of a magazine.

**You may quote "public domain" Material...**

You do not have to obtain permission to quote material in the public domain. In Canada, material originally protected by copyright usually enters the public domain and can be freely published by others fifty years after the end of the year in which the author died. However, there are a number of special rules in the Copyright Act for certain material, including writings not published during the author's lifetime (longer protection) and material in which copyright was published by government (shorter protection).

As books to be published in Canada will often also be published eventually outside Canada, you should bear in mind that you may have to get a permission that you may not require for Canadian publication. The period of protection in other countries may be longer than in Canada, for example, seventy years following the author's death in the countries of the European Union and extensions for various periods in a few countries because of World War II. The "life plus 70" rule is also the current rule in the United States, but again there are some special rules for unpublished works, works published by government and works published prior to 1978. Most countries belong to the Berne convention, which has established minimum levels of protection for authors, but every country has its own copyright legislation and sometimes this may affect the permissions you will need.

## Get permissions in writing...

When you are writing for permission, make it easy for the copyright owner to whom you are applying. The publisher of a book, particularly a book in print, is usually able to grant the permission and otherwise will forward your request to the author or other copyright owner. If you are quoting from a magazine, and if the author is a freelancer rather than an employed journalist, it is usually the author rather than the publisher from whom you will need to obtain permission.

It is not sufficient to put a disclaimer on a book to say that you have tried to contact copyright owners. Some copyright owners may accept that you have proceeded in good faith and will retroactively grant permission without a fee or with a fee which is within the budget of you or your publisher. However, it is possible that a person whom you did not contact will refuse permission (which could mean you will have to withdraw your book) or will insist on a fee which breaks the bank! If a lawsuit follows, it may be that the judge will assess the damages suffered by the person whose copyright you infringed at a much more modest level than he or she has endeavored to claim from you, but, even so, you could be stuck with considerable legal expenses including legal expenses incurred by the copyright owner whose rights you have infringed.

## Plan ahead!

Often writers and publishers leave getting permissions until the last minute. If you don't get the permission(s) required and time runs out on you, you may have to remove the quote and do some last-minute rewriting — or take an undesirable risk.

The time to start the permission process is when you are working on your manuscript. Then, if you discover there is likely to be a permission problem (a refusal, a fee which is too high, or an owner who cannot be found), it will be easier to deal with your material in a way which avoids the need for that particular permission or, in the case where you are unable to locate the copyright owner of a published work, you will have time to apply to the Copyright Board for a licence to use in Canada the material you wish to quote.

—

Marian Dingman Hebb spent ten years as a book and magazine editor before becoming a lawyer and specializing in arts, entertainment and copyright law. She has advised authors on contracts for more than two decades and has written self-help guides entitled *Help Yourself to a Better Contract*, *Ghost Writing*, *Writers' Guide to Electronic Publishing Rights* and, together with Maggie Siggins, *From Page to Screen — Negotiating Film and TV Contracts for Original Literary Works*, all published by the Writers' Union of Canada.

# Applying for Arts Council and Other Grants

*by Mark Morton*

As the Writing and Publishing Officer for a provincial arts council, I receive questions every day from writers wanting to know how to apply for a grant. I'll share my advice about that in a minute, but first there's some preliminary ground to cover.

First of all, before you can even apply for a grant, you have to be eligible. For most arts councils, that means that you have to have at least a modest record of publication. At the arts council where I work, a "modest record" means a few pieces of creative writing published in bona fide literary journals.

What's a bona fide literary periodical? It's a periodical that's "literary" in the sense that it primarily publishes poetry, fiction, or creative nonfiction; a periodical like *Prairie Fire* or *The New Quarterly* or *The Malahat Review* is a literary periodical, whereas a magazine such as *Chatelaine* or *Maclean's* or *The Canadian Mennonite* is not.

### A credible track record and editorial policy...

There are, of course, gray areas: is *This Magazine* a "literary" magazine? Probably. Is *Shift* a literary magazine? It contains fine articles about digital culture, but I wouldn't really deem it a literary periodical. A periodical also has to be bona fide in the sense that it has to have a credible track record and editorial policy. A periodical that's published only sporadically, that contains plenty of typos, and that tends to publish a lot of poems by the editors of the magazine may be "literary" but it's not bona fide.

Second, assuming that you as a writer are eligible to apply for a grant, your project also has to be eligible. For example, if you applied for an arts grant to write a cookbook or a how-to book, the application would be declared ineligible. Those genres are not considered "literary." The same thing usually applies to community history books, devotional works, tourism books, scholarly books, and many other genres that are merely commercial in nature, or that are intended for a specialized rather than general or "trade" audience. One more thing: most arts grants are intended to assist a writer in *completing* a project. If you've already finished your manuscript, your project will not be eligible. The rationale is that if your manuscript is done, then you're ready to send it out to a publisher who will then undertake all further costs associated with publication.

Now, assuming that both you and your project are eligible to apply for an arts grant, how do you proceed?

First, start by figuring out where you can apply. In Winnipeg, where I'm based, writers are fortunate in being able to apply to funding agencies at all three levels of government: the Winnipeg Arts Council, the Manitoba Arts Council, and the Canada Council. Not every city or province has an arts council, but yours might and, if so, you should consider applying. As to whether you can hold a grant from two or more funds simultaneously, that's a tricky question. If the two grants are for different projects, all should be well; if they are for two different stages of the same project, all might still be well; but if they are both for a single stage or component of the same project, the funds may not allow this.

**Call and request information...**

Now let's say that you decide to apply to your provincial arts council for a grant to assist you in completing a collection of short stories. Obviously, the first thing you should do as you prepare your application is call up your local arts officer and start schmoozing, right? Well, yes, you should call your arts officer and request more information, but the schmoozing part will get you nowhere, since the arts officers aren't the ones who decide who gets a grant and who doesn't. Instead, the arts officer simply puts together a jury of professional writers, who convene to review the applications and make their recommendations.

The jury makes recommendations based solely on the artistic merit of the applicant's writing sample and support material. Financial need is not taken into consideration: whether you are a millionaire novelist or a pauper poet, whether you are married to a doctor or a debtor, whether you live in Toronto's Rosedale or Winnipeg's North End — it doesn't matter so far as the jury is concerned. To them, the only thing that counts is the quality of the writing sample that you've included with your application.

Since the precise details of the application process vary from fund to fund, I won't get into specifics. I will, though, remind you that juries are made up of humans, and humans are turned on and turned off by a wide variety of things.

Bad writing is definitely a turn off, and will always result in no grant. Bad math, when you are calculating the budget of your project, will also not inspire confidence, and might jeopardize your application. Same thing with bad spelling, an arrogant tone, or missing support materials. It is, of course, theoretically possible to submit a careless, clumsy, or tactless application and still receive an arts grant, so long as your writing sample really wows the jury; but presentation *can* make all the difference when a jury has to make a decision between two closely ranked applications.

As you prepare your application you should also bear in mind your audience and your objective: your audience is a group of professional writers who have been asked to assess applications from thirty, forty, or in some cases a hundred and fifty applicants. Your objective is to demonstrate that your writing is excellent, that you have a proven track record, that your project will come to fruition.

After you submit your application, what are your chances of receiving a grant? I hate that question, because the word “chances” implies that jury deliberations are random, like spinning a roulette wheel. In fact, that’s not the case: a weak project will never be awarded a grant, no matter how many juries ponder it, and a truly excellent project will almost always be recognized as such and receive support. There is, I admit, a gray area: sometimes an applicant with a “good” project will be declined by one jury, will resubmit the same project to the next deadline, and will then be awarded a grant. In such borderline cases, failure or success depends to some extent on who is sitting on the jury, and on who else has submitted an application to the same grant deadline. That’s why most arts councils allow applicants to resubmit a declined application, to “even out” the slight vagaries of the process.

### Unlikely to provide written comments...

Remember, too, that a jury may not have sufficient funds at their disposal to award grants to all applicants that they want to support. In other words, if you aren’t awarded a grant, it may mean that the jury did not find your application deserving of support, or it may mean that they like it but simply didn’t have enough money to go around. Either way, it’s very unlikely that the jury will provide you with any written comments, since their primary role is to make recommendations to the arts council, not to give feedback to applicants.

Finally, I would stress that all arts councils take great pains to ensure that grants are awarded to the most deserving applicants, and that the whole process is transparent and legitimate. Everyone involved — from staff, to board members, to jurors — must avoid both real and perceived conflicts of interest. When I was hired to my position at the arts council, I had to step down from the various editorial boards on which I served. I even had to cancel my membership with a local bookstore, because it sometimes hosted readings funded by my arts council. Even for this article, I had to waive the small honorarium provided by the publisher because I wrote it in my "official" capacity as Writing and Publishing Officer. Such measures may seem extreme, but they're necessary to ensure that you — the writer — can have confidence in the granting process.

—

Mark Morton is the Writing and Publishing Officer at the Manitoba Arts Council. He also teaches English at the University of Winnipeg, and is the author of two nonfiction books.

# Grant Writing: Your Most Persuasive Writing Ever

*by Sher DiCiccio*

Identifying appropriate grants and completing an application are necessary steps, but the result may be unsuccessful if you do not state your case clearly and convincingly. A few basic steps, outlined below, apply to all grant applications but the comments on *writing style* apply to everything you write.

**First Steps...**

Identify potential grants by contacting local municipal, regional and federal offices, community foundations, and agencies related to your type of activity. These could include municipal cash grant programs and arts foundations or endowment programs, regional arts councils, the Canada Council and the arts council in your province. Once the appropriate organization has been identified, call to speak to the person in charge of your type of activity. For example, at the Canada Council, a federal organization that grants funds to artists, a grant officer manages each of the arts disciplines such as visual, literary or performing arts. Your first questions to the representative should be: "Do you have grants available for individual artists?" If yes, proceed. If not, you may wish to consult your local arts council to find an organization that may partner with you on a literary project such as a writing festival or series of workshops. Many organizations have websites with information and applications ready to be downloaded.

After you obtain your application package, read the terms of reference carefully. Make sure you understand the terms and conditions *before* you spend hours completing the application. The terms and conditions outline precisely what the funds may be used for and what reports are expected, and when. Inappropriate use of funds may result in the repaying of the grant even if the money was spent.

Create a budget and timeline for your work. Be realistic about the amount of time it will take to write. Will you travel to locations, interview people, take photographs? What consumable supplies such as paper, film, computer resources, etc. will you require and which items may be included? Additional funding should never be assumed. Similarly, do your homework to prepare your budget with accurate cost estimates the first time. Ask other writers who successfully obtained funds what information to include in your budget.

Then, determine if the amount of funding required matches that provided by the agencies you targeted. Asking a municipality for $30,000 from their total budget of $100,000 wastes everyone's time. The grant representative knows the funding budget and typical number of requests per year as well as the typical amount awarded to an individual. Use these numbers as a guideline to determine if a grant from that source meets your needs. Some municipalities do not grant funds to individuals. Instead the individual must identify a local arts organization with which to partner. Expecting a large sum of money from one source of revenue and not receiving it will also leave you scrambling to find funds later, often missing deadlines for other grants in the meantime.

**Partnering with an organization for a project...**

Choose someone from your organization who writes well. You must make your case using thoughtful, persuasive writing. Be concise, specific and accurate. Don't embellish. Don't ramble. Answer the question asked and if you don't know, call the funding agency representative for clarification.

To write persuasively about your project, you must understand the objectives; how the project will be evaluated; the mandate of the organization; and why it matters to the community outside your own group. Then write passionately about it. Convince them.

Back up your information with quantitative evidence about the organization and its successes. Such statistics may include the number of participants; volunteers involved and time commitment; membership numbers and demographics; and types of services the group provides. If an application does not provide tables or blanks to enter such data, create clear tables or graphs to make your point. Keep this information accurate and up-to-date. For example, your list of publications and résumé should be current, not recycled from previous applications.

For individuals making personal applications such as artists, let your activity speak for itself. Ask your grant representative if you may provide video, sound recordings, written manuscripts (or parts thereof) or slides of your work. Letters and awards received may also be appropriate.

Writing style matters. When completing longer applications that require profiles or descriptions of the project, make the application interesting. Use an active voice. For example, "the membership committee met" instead of "a meeting was held."

Use repetition to emphasize a point. Otherwise, use alternate phrases and words to keep it interesting to read. Watch the use of adjectives and adverbs — they only add clarity and interest when used sparingly.

Be specific. "In 2001, the number of participants increased by 25% to 3,212," not, "there was an increase in the number of people taking programs." Or, "I have written and published two previous collections of poetry and 12 individual poems," not, "I have written a few poems and collections."

**Answer *everything*...**

Finally, it may seem obvious but people often forget attachments or overlook sections of the applications. Answer *everything* even if the answer is simply, "not applicable."

Organize your information to correspond with an outline given for the grant or your own table of contents. Label everything. For example, give each sample of writing you wish to include a number or letter, and identify them on a list by title of work and the number you assigned.

In my 10 years as an arts administrator, I have participated in the grants process as someone writing the application, and as a member of a jury reviewing applications submitted to provincial and municipal funding agencies. Following these basic steps will help you identify the appropriate funding body and create a legible, organized and convincing case for a successful result.

—

Sher DiCiccio, Executive Director of the Waterloo Community Arts Centre, has worked in Waterloo since 1977. She is a member of the Association of Cultural Executives, the Canadian Authors Association (past president of the Waterloo-Wellington branch), and chairs the Arts and Culture Cash Grants Committee, City of Waterloo. She lives in Kitchener with husband Vic, and three teenage children.

# Get the Tax Breaks!

*by Arthur Bray*

Freelance writers are people who write independently, full-time or part-time, and whose services are not sold exclusively to any one buyer. If you are freelancing, regardless of any other employment, and meet certain criteria as specified in Interpretation Bulletin IT 504R2 Visual Artists and Writers, issued by Canada Customs and Revenue Agency (CCRA), you are self-employed for tax purposes. You should take advantage of all available tax breaks. Remember that you are in business and are obligated to act professionally by observing all tax laws and regulations, and not discredit the writing profession by acting unethically.

**The profit motive...**

A reasonable expectation of profit must exist before CCRA will allow tax-deductible losses arising from your writing. CCRA regards writers as "hobbyists" if there is no serious intent to be a profitable writer. Artistic expression in the form of writing receives no recognition for tax purposes unless the profit motive is present.

CCRA realizes that the nature of literature is such that a considerable period of time may elapse before a writer becomes established and profitable. It is possible that a writer may not realize a profit during his or her lifetime but still have a reasonable expectation of profit.

Factors that will be considered by CCRA in determining whether a writer has a reasonable expectation of profit are listed in IT 504R2. Get a copy from your nearest CCRA office or from their website at www.ccra-adrc.gc.ca and read it in detail. It is important.

**Income tax...**

As you are in business, you must report your profit or loss for income tax purposes, and there are two aspects to this reporting. First is the revenue and expense of your actual writing, and second is the cost of maintaining a work space in your home — your home office.

Claim your writing income and expenses on form T2124, Statement of Business Activities, and include it with your regular Tax Return. Writing expenses that are deductible from your business income are explained in detail in Chapter 3 of CCRA's Business and Professional Income guide (form T4002). Keep every piece of paper relating to your revenue and expenses to ensure ease of preparation of your return and to protect yourself in the event of a tax audit.

The next important point concerns the business aspects of your home office. The expenses you incur in writing are unrelated to expenses of maintaining an office in your home, because your writing expenses have no relationship to where you write. The work space must be either:

(1) your principal place of business (there need not be more than one place, and it need not be used exclusively for business), or

(2) used exclusively to earn business income and on a regular and continuous basis for meeting clients or other people in respect of the business.

You must use your work space for specified purposes and you may not claim related expenses exceeding your net income from the business for the taxation year. Such work space expenses could include, for example, the pro-rated portion of rent, property insurance, property taxes, mortgage interest, or operating costs such as heating or lighting, as well as building repairs. Do not claim depreciation on a portion of your home or you could end up paying taxes on any profit you make when you sell your house later. To determine the prorated amount of your household expenses, you must apportion your work space in a reasonable manner. This may be a percentage of the floor space of your home, or a fraction of the number of rooms, such as one sixth.

In the case of situation (1) above, you need not use the work space solely for your business, as it can also be put to personal use. However, you can claim a deduction only for the portion that you use for your business. For example, if you use your office for personal use 20% of the time, you may claim only 80% of your pro-rated work space expenses as a tax deduction. Refer to CCRA's Interpretation Bulletin IT 514, Work Space in Home Expenses. Writing expenses are claimed separately from home office expenses on form T2124. You then transfer the net amount of profit or loss to line 135 of your tax return.

**Goods and Services Tax and Harmonized Sales Tax (GST/HST)...**

Another important tax matter of concern to writers is the 7% Goods and Services Tax (GST), and the 15% Harmonized Sales Tax (HST) in Newfoundland and Labrador, Nova Scotia and New Brunswick where the GST is blended with their former provincial sales taxes. Many writers feel that because their revenue from business operations is less than

$30,000 annually, there is no need to register. Technically, they are correct. But if you have not registered, you cannot claim "input tax credits," which are credits claimed for the GST/HST you paid on taxable items used in your writing activities. If registered, and your credits are greater than the GST/HST you owe to the government, you may claim a refund for the difference.

It is also important to be registered so your GST/HST registration number can be shown on your invoices (if you use them) or your contracts or agreements. Your GST/HST-registered clients or publishers will then be able to claim their own tax credits. You could even have it imprinted on your business cards and cheques. Keep in mind that if you register so you can claim these credits, you must also charge GST/HST on all your written work. Your publishers or other clients must pay you the GST/HST and you then remit it to the government. For authors of books, remember that the GST/HST does not apply to payments from the Public Lending Right (PLR) for your books in libraries.

Writers do not usually send invoices, but, rather, the publishers send statements and cheques. You must collect 7% GST or 15% HST on royalties and payments if you register. In such a case, ensure that your contracts require the publisher to pay the GST/HST to you in addition to the royalty or other payment and to show the amount of the tax separately on the statement. Think about this: if you fail to arrange it with your publisher, you could find that in both old and new contracts, the GST/HST becomes absorbed in royalty payments. CCRA will hold you liable and you will have to pay the GST/HST from your own pocket.

**Remember, you're in business...**

My advice to those writers who have not already registered is to consider carefully the implications of the GST/HST. It is likely to be to your advantage to register. Why should you pay all that tax on your expenses and not get any of it back? Remember, you're in business! If you don't register, this then tells all your clients and publishers that you earn less than $30,000 annually from your writing. Do you want them to know that? This little fact can possibly affect the image they have of you. It is also nobody's business (with the exception of the taxman) whether your writing earnings are greater or less than this figure. If you are already registered, you must remain alert to changes as they occur. For example, there was the introduction of the Business Number (BN) which converted all business accounts you may have had with the former Revenue Canada to a single number. For many writers, that meant just your GST registration number, which then became the root of your new Business Number.

All businesses across Canada were automatically registered for HST purposes and are required to collect and remit the 15% tax on any taxable products shipped or mailed to recipients in participating provinces. Input tax credits can also be claimed for HST paid on purchases.

There is no lack of information available on income tax and the GST/HST to self-employed writers. All registered writers are on the mailing list for CCRA's quarterly newsletter, the GST/HST News, and you should read all issues carefully. Also, call CCRA and ask them to send you all relevant booklets and forms, in particular the ones referred to above. You will find the numbers in the blue pages of your telephone directory. Alternatively, if you have a computer and a modem, you can view these at the website referred to above, and print copies.

If you don't follow the rules, you may lose your tax status as a professional writer and there goes your profit.

—

Arthur Bray lives in Ottawa and is the author of four nonfiction books, two on Unidentified Flying Objects and two on financial planning. He is currently working on another nonfiction book on an unrelated topic.

# 4. Develop Your Style

# It Ain't What You Say, It's the Way You Say It!

*by Jennifer Stewart*

"It ain't what you say, it's the way you say it!"

What thoughts flashed through your mind when you read these words? What was your impression of the writer? (Now, now, don't be like that.)

Did you think to yourself, "This is going to be a very informative and erudite treatise on the use of tone in writing?"

No? Perhaps you thought, "What sort of dingbat uses 'ain't' these days?"

Closer to the mark? I thought so. You were responding to the *tone* of the writing. Tone is one of those difficult terms. We all know what it means, but it's really hard to explain it.

Tone can best be defined by using an example. When you're trading insults with your best friend, you might say, "I don't want you living next door to me, mate. You'll lower the tone of the whole neighbourhood!"

Tone is the pervading atmosphere of a place, or the general impression you receive about something. Tone is determined by the writer's feelings about the subject matter and the mood he/she was in when writing.

**Tone in speech...**

When we speak, we indicate our feelings in the way that we use our voices. We can change the pitch, pace and intensity of our voice to show whether we're being serious, sarcastic, sympathetic or sycophantic. How many times have you heard someone say, "Don't use that tone of voice with me!"

**Tone in writing...**

When we write, we convey the tone through:

- Our choice of words.
- The length and structure of sentences.
- The length and structure of paragraphs.
- The punctuation.

- The order of ideas presented.
- The format we choose to communicate our ideas.

Whatever you're writing, the first thing you *must* do, is decide on the tone you want to convey. What impression are you trying to give? Here are some of the many possibilities:

**Casual...**

- Use short sentences and paragraphs.
- Include plenty of colloquial expressions.
- Ask questions of your reader.
- Use contractions, e.g. you're, don't, I'll.
- Use personal pronouns, e.g. I, you, we, us.
- Choose shorter, rather than longer words, e.g. "He's a quiet chap," rather than, "He is a taciturn fellow."
- Use the active, rather than passive voice e.g. "You must remember to..." instead of, "It must be remembered that..."
- Vary your use of punctuation — dashes (—), ellipses (...), exclamation marks (!).

A casual style is friendly, relaxed and intimate. As a writer, you should feel that you are speaking directly to your readers.

**Formal...**

- Sentences and paragraphs are longer and more complex in structure.
- Vocabulary is also more complex and specialized (according to the subject matter).
- Punctuation is more formal (no place for dots and dashes here).
- Passive voice can be used (but don't overdo it — it can be too impersonal).
- Personal pronouns are usually avoided in favour of "it," "one" and "they."

A formal style is business-like, no-nonsense, no-time-to-waste writing. It is designed to inspire confidence in the ability of the writer to get on with the job.

**Persuasive...**

- Makes great use of emotive words. Consider your response to these pairs of words: home & hovel; confusion & shambles. By choosing the appropriate word, it's possible to sway your reader's feelings to your way of thinking.

- Sentences and paragraphs are usually short.
- Ideas are organized very simply, in chronological or reverse chronological order.
- Content is carefully selected to present one particular point of view.
- Personal pronouns are used, especially "us" and "them."

Persuasive writing can be used by advertisers trying to convince us to buy a particular brand of toilet paper or by governments trying to get us to rush out and enlist!

You can see from these short examples how important it is to work out what tone you want to convey in your writing. In material written for books, you have an audience that is prepared to spend a little bit of time. In articles written for magazines, your readers expect you to get the point. On the web, you only have a few seconds to persuade your readers to stay — if they receive a favourable impression, they'll keep reading, if not...

Take a look at your writing. What tone does it convey? Look at the word choice, sentence length, punctuation etc., and compare it with the short list above. Is this the tone you set out to convey? If not, you now have a few ideas on how to change it.

—

Jennifer Stewart is a freelance writer based in Queensland, Australia. She has had her own web-based writing business at www.write101.com since 1998 and has clients from every continent except Antarctica.

# Balancing Your Style

*by Devon L. Muhlert*

What writer *doesn't* want to appeal to a wider audience? Being able to relate to more readers results in wider appreciation for your work — and more sales. Personality typing can do this for you.

Of course the world is made up of individuals, not types. However, the Myers-Briggs Type Indicator® (MBTI) grew from efforts after WWII to help people understand each other better, and not to take offence at someone whose approach is simply different from your own. This article provides an overview of the MBTI®, and what it has accomplished for over half a century.

We all have blind spots about our work. Omissions do not jump out at us. If we saw them, they wouldn't be omissions. The MBTI® assesses your strengths and helps uncover alternate approaches to balance your writing. The MBTI® is also helpful in recognizing editors' working styles, and for editors to understand their writers' styles.

### Personality inventory based on four polarities...

Carl Jung made the original designations, which were later organized into patterns by Isabel Myers, consulting with Jung, and her daughter Katharine Briggs. The personality inventory is based on four polarities: how individuals relate to the world, how they gather information, make decisions, and organize. You favour one approach, at which you've become proficient through practice, similar to right- or left-handedness.

The first polarity addresses whether you gather energy from the outside world or from inside yourself. Do you draw on conversations or news stories when pondering new writing? You are probably an Extrovert (=E). If you prefer to think quietly on previous ideas or fantasies, you are likely an Introvert (=I). Extroverts spout ideas like confetti, talking through their process and not settling into a topic until unavoidable. Introverts, in contrast, have often nurtured a cherished idea to completion before committing it to paper. To them, Extroverts seem flighty and not serious about their craft. An "E" writer might easily get into trouble with an "I" editor.

### What about research?

Do you get the "facts, and nothing but the facts, ma'am?" Did you note the busker's hair colour, bushy beard, the look in his eye? Did the wind riffle through scribbled song sheets in his guitar-case, where a coin glinted in the sun? (Sensing=S) Or did you go home and think about homelessness and why society allows it? (iNtuitive=N)

The iNtuitive (N) thinks globally and in patterns, while the S personality gathers detail through the five senses. The N writer will do well to give the reader relief using concrete, vivid stories to illustrate abstract thoughts. Ns value original, unique approaches, but could benefit from the S need for sense experience.

The S personality, too, would benefit from the other polarity, because his or her writing might initially read like a shopping list of statistics. Ss can utilize more imagination to relieve those mundane details with story.

The third polarity involves resolving conflict and how decisions are made. Thinking (=T) and Feeling (=F) are official terms used, but they do not imply that thinkers don't feel or vice versa. Where Thinking is the preferred function, a T woman might write a treatise on justice, but never consider its effect on real lives. An F man, however, might literally feel for the person affected, to the exclusion of other criteria.

No types are gender-related — men and women come in all personality types. In our day, however, T men and F women are valued, so a T woman may appear hardened, and an F man, a push-over.

F writers need to care about their topic to get motivated. But Fs can seem over-emotional because they don't support their points with salient facts, which the T perspective brings.

Lastly, how do you engage? The choices are Judging (=J) and Perceiving (=P). J is not *judgmental*, it just means a J prefers working logically and sequentially. Given a deadline, do you sketch out how many words per day will be required and clear your schedule to adapt? That's a J style.

The P writer, on the other hand, begins extensive research with only a fuzzy idea of the end result. When the deadline stares him or her in the face, the P personality realizes he or she will never learn it all. With luck, last minute inspiration will strike to tie up all the loose ends, but even without that last piece of information for inspiration, it will get done.

Again, balance is the issue: Js would benefit from relaxing a bit and going with the flow, while Ps could learn to plan and schedule better to avoid last-minute panic.

As writers mature, ideally they allow their less-preferred polarity (their shadow side) more air time and attain balance naturally.

A crucial part of the MBTI®, though beyond the scope of this article, is the interplay of your four preferences. From a possible sixteen personality types, your specific dynamics can help explain your writing voice and genre.

For instance, an ISTJ would reel off the number of books that have been written on the career counselling, marriage counselling and other business applications of the MBTI®. He/she would announce the number of languages into which it was translated (over 300) and list countries in alphabetical order in which it is used. They could excel at writing formulaic mysteries or genres like Westerns.

An ENFP, however, likes possibilities, people and metaphors. Isabel Meyers was an ENFP, and read of a contest by a New York publisher for a New Year's deadline. By Christmas Day, she had four chapters to go, but both her children in tandem got the flu. Afterward, she wrote feverishly while a family friend typed through the night. Then she drove to New York on January 2 with her (naturally!) winning manuscript. ENFPs are good at personal narrative and poetry.

**All of us use both polarities...**

The two above cited are diametric opposites; the more letters in common individuals have, the better they will understand each other. All of us use both polarities at different times, much like a right-handed person uses the left hand and vice versa.

The MBTI® allows a dispassionate look at how we function in our writing, while allowing a glimpse of others' processes, which has the potential to round out our own approach. The MBTI® emphasizes the value of each type, and benefits accrued from collaborations of differing types (if they don't drive each other crazy before understanding each other's process).

So think balance: heartfelt pieces need hard data, and scholarly treatises are lightened with human stories. With the MBTI®, you can learn to use your shadow mode to compensate, helping yourself to balanced writing and to new readers.

—

Devon L. Muhlert uses the MBTI® in workshops. A photojournalist since 1991, she has two trade book manuscripts-in-progress, in classic P fashion, and fiction forthcoming in *Queen's Quarterly*. She is a songwriter, musician, and music director and taught creativity and photography for Continuing Education at Okanagan University College.

# Show ’em Your Style

*by Angie Riley*

“Ms Angie, you have a great sense of humour and personality; show it.”

This is the best advice that I received when I began writing and I still follow that advice when I set my goals for the year and put together my promotion packages. You have to let corporations, small businesses, magazines, advertising agencies or other organizations that hire writers, know that you’re out there and are available for work.

Well, how do you do that?

I’m glad you asked because you cannot be a successful freelance writer unless they know who you are and what you have to offer. Designing a self-promotion strategy that meets your needs and reflects your style and personality is very important.

The first thing you need to do when preparing promotional packages is determine who you want to target, how to approach them, when is the best time to do so and why is one target market better than another. Once your research is complete and you’ve decided how to proceed, you need to determine the best way to present yourself. You need to design a piece that shows your personality. I try to make them laugh, and show them something different.

**Let your originality and personality come through...**

I’ve done pieces with tasteful humour and pieces without and I have received a better response by far from those that made them laugh. The most important thing is to be yourself and to let your originality and personality come through in your promotional material.

I take the advice given to me from my good friend and use it in everything I do — writing and non-writing situations. To get a part-time job at a record store, I spray painted two vinyl records gold, transferred my résumé onto transparencies and then glued them on top of each of the records. I then glued the records to the foldout inside the album cover and tucked a paper copy of my résumé on the inside where the record would normally go. I got the job.

For a job as a pizza driver, I photocopied my résumé on hand drawn and coloured pizzas and put it in a box with a toy racing car on top. Then, I wrote, "They want it hot! They want it fast and I can deliver!" Again, I got the job.

**Stand out and be remembered...**

I've landed writing work and jobs inside and out of the writing world by being myself. My goal is to stand out and be remembered. My style and personality come through in everything I do and so far I have been successful.

Personality-driven self-promotion techniques have also benefitted my writing business. To approach new clients, I put together a promotion package that included a handmade accordion book with the letters of my name spelled out with key words and sayings underneath. For example, R is for reliable, reap and rewards and underneath "Rely on Riley and reap the rewards." Y is for "yes, yes and yes" and underneath "Yabba-dabba-do, this writer's for you." I also included a cover letter, résumé and the *Red Hot Book of Samples*. For a follow up piece to the target markets that kept my promotional material on file, I sent my résumé, a mini-hanger glued on foamcore board with my business card attached and the slogan, "I am still hanging around."

I've received a good response from all of my promotional endeavours. I do my research and approach targets that I believe will be receptive to my promotional approach. I work with clients that I am compatible with. I have developed my own style and do work that reflects it. I am happy working and my clients are happy with my work.

It could work for you.

—

Ms Angie Riley is a creative freelance writer based in Ottawa. She has written for websites, newspapers, small businesses and nonprofit organizations. She is currently seeking a publisher for her novels that are just as stylish as her freelance writing work.

# Work with Sound

*by Paul G. Cormack*

Writers, like other artists, create. Against a white backdrop, just a few sentences can yield a splash of colour or a series of images to reflect scenes real and imagined. But unlike some artists, musicians or sculptors for example, we sometimes forget to appeal to senses other than *vision*. What about *smell*, or *texture* or *sound*?

Tap your foot. Just lightly. Three or four times on the kitchen floor, or against the frame of your chair if you are standing on a rug or carpet. If you aren't standing, strum your fingers on the desktop or the edge of your keyboard.

Then stop.

What do you hear now? The whirring of a computer fan? The television … a computer game in a distant room? Children playing? The wind pressing against your window frame?

Think of your recent work; do "sound words" feature amongst the adjectives? What does your story *sound* like? *The Houghton Mifflin Canadian Dictionary of the English Language* contains a great many words that suggest sound. Take the word *buzz,* "a low droning or vibrating sound like that of a bee …"

Or *drip*, the "sound made by a dripping liquid …"

Or *zip*, "a brief, sharp, hissing sound, such as that made by a flying arrow."

Sometimes the words available to us — from our memories or dictionaries — aren't sufficient for the task at hand, and a new word may be more appropriate. English and French and Spanish are good at adapting to new words, or new usage. Think of *helicopter*, or *hélicoptère* or *helicóptero* as good examples of increasingly common language.

Writers have developed many words over the years to create a visual environment. But we've developed few for smell (other than *musty*, as in a worn, weathered book) and fewer still for texture or sound.

When I was working on a recent story, I needed to describe the sound made by the impact of a snowball. Fortunately it was winter, there was time available and enough snow on the ground to experiment. The best part of an afternoon was lost while I threw snowballs against the wall, the car, the garage window, my children. Then I heard it. Every time a snowball landed it went, "whoomf."

So I ran back to the computer and carried on with the story.

"Whoomf! Three, four, five snowballs slam against the door and the window. Lumps of snow stick to the green wooden exterior ..." (*Whoomf*, Cormack 2001).

It certainly seemed to work better than *hit* or *whack*. And it fit with the storyline better, particularly since the computer thesaurus suggested the alternative for my new word was *whoop*. That captured the atmosphere I was trying to create.

And isn't that what we set out to do?

—

Paul G. Cormack is a former radio news editor from Toronto. He now lives in the north of Scotland with his wife and three children, writes short fiction and works as a freelance editor. He is also an experienced technical author for the oil industry in the North Sea.

# 5. Nonfiction Techniques

# Writing Personal Essays

*by Lois J. Peterson*

All I wanted was a pair of boots for plodding around the muddy garden. At the local mall I found rubber boots for girls, boys, and men, and low-cut, high-gloss "fashion boots" for women. The outdoors shop had a good stock for kids, steel-toed boots for men, and hiking boots for women. At the secondhand store I found rubber boots for men and for children, and a pair of women's pink nylon boots that wouldn't get me through the first puddle. I finally found a yellow pair of rubber sailing boots at the ship chandler's, but I had no intention of wearing $89 boots in the potato patch.

So, instead of working outside in the yard, I wrote an essay about looking for "wellies." My vegetable garden didn't get dug that year, but I did make a few dollars for the essay (which paid for the boots I finally did track down).

**Everyone wants a glimpse into everyone else's life...**

There's a great market for personal essays in magazines, newspapers and on the radio. Everyone, it seems, wants a glimpse into everyone else's life and is eager for their opinions on just about anything. Consider the growth of "reality TV" — you no longer have to be a celebrity to find voyeurs peering over your windowsill or past your shower curtain.

Personal essays (sometimes called *opinion pieces* or *personal narratives*) allow you to have your say, get your gripes and raves off your chest, and have a shot at publication. Many new writers first get published with an essay on child rearing or job hunting, or how they helped a family member cope with a serious illness.

Perhaps you have strong feelings about the invasive use of cell phones, or want to share a compelling story about how one saved your daughter's life. You might feel strongly about environmental issues, or long to relate how your handicapped son learned to ride a bike. Perhaps you have a story to tell about a personal crisis, or a high point in your career.

Whatever you care about is fair game for an essay. And that's the first point. Be sure your essay is about something you care strongly enough about to be passionate about it. Readers wants to know what you know, feel what you feel, and understand where you're coming from.

Conversational topics that get you excited, or news stories that make your blood boil or get you laughing out loud, are likely to be provide good fodder for essays. Small gripes and observations also offer worthwhile material. However important or trivial the subject seems, make sure you set it in a frame that allows your reader to identify, empathize, and be involved.

Ever got stuck talking to bores at parties? They regale you with their life and opinions, but don't leave enough room to let you in to trade tales; they relate their story to nothing wider than their own experience.

Whether you're writing about your kid's first day at school or nursing an Alzheimic grandmother, make the frame wide enough to allow your reader to find parallels between your experience and theirs. Give them the opportunity to say, "Ah! Yes. I've never been there or done that, but I can relate to what the author's talking about."

**Share your memories...**

Perhaps you feel strongly about the use of fireworks. Set your opinions against the account of the day your box of fireworks exploded, or support them with statistics on fireworks sales, how many injuries are reported each Halloween, what it costs the local police department to patrol the streets on those nights, or share your memory of the first time you held a sparkler.

If you're writing about the "small" personal occurrence — a move, your first pet — put it in context that gives the reader insight to both the small moment and the wider perspective. Details draw the reader in, but generalizations keep them out. Be specific. Avoid using abstract expressions and phrases such as "the best day of my life', "my happiest moment as a parent", "I'd never known greater grief" to describe emotions of love, loss, anger, joy, satisfaction, etc. Make these emotions immediate by noting specific details to draw the reader into the experience. The old "seduction not instruction" rule — showing rather than telling — makes for a more compelling essay, as it does almost any piece of writing.

**Double check your facts...**

While personal essays allows for the use of many fictional craft elements — dialogue, setting, point of view, characterization — if you use facts to anchor your piece or as a springboard for your opinions, you need to double check them for accuracy. One factual error can prevent the reader from believing much else you have to say.

Here are some further guidelines to help you write essays that strike a chord with the reader:

- Personal essays by definition contain a personal perspective. You should be there. But watch your construction. If every sentence begins "I," you need to rephrase to provide a better rhythm and pace to your piece.
- No extra points for the number of facts you include. Academic essays contain more facts than opinion; personal essays contain more opinion than facts.
- Make connections. If you're writing about a global theme (poverty, unemployment, child abuse) bring the subject closer to home by relating it to specific, individual examples. If you're writing about left-hand turn signals, the search for the best french fries, or your daughter's graduation, again, set your views against a wider perspective so the reader can relate to it.
- The hook is the device you use to get your reader's attention. It's the doorway through which you welcome and orient them to the piece. Try using:

  **A question**. ("When was the last time you went without a meal?")

  **A quotation** from someone famous or something you've read/overhead. ("'Be careful' were the last words my father said to me each time I left the house.")

  **A strong statement** that your essay will either support or dispute. ("If you eat enough cabbage, you'll never get cancer.")

  **A metaphor**. ("The starlings in my back garden are the small boys in the playground, impressing each other with their new-found swear words. The crows all belong to the same biker gang. You need to know their secret sign to join their club.")

  **A description** of a person or setting. ("Michael once mowed the lawns around Municipal Hall wearing a frilly apron, high heels and nylons, with a pillow stuffed under his sweater so he looked pregnant. And it wasn't even Halloween.")
- Write as evocatively as possible. Employ all the senses. Using sight comes naturally to most writers; push harder to convey ideas and images through sound, taste, touch, and hearing.
- Think of your essay as a camera lens. You might start by describing a fine detail (your personal experience or perspective, a specific moment in the narrative), then open up the lens to take in the wide view (the general/global backdrop), then close the piece by

narrowing back to the fine detail. Or go the other way. Start with the wide view, focus in, then open up to the wide view again.

- Take your ideas from wherever you can. Note your reactions to everything, pursue passing preoccupations and distractions, consider what makes you glad, angry, passionate in what you read, see, and hear. Mine your own past for incidents, images, lessons and epiphanies.
- In a personal essay you have the freedom to think what you like on a subject, but your reader should go away with a good idea of why you feel that way.

A range of markets is hungry for submissions of personal essays. The American print magazine *Newsweek* carries one a week and pays $1,000; its Canadian equivalent, *Maclean's*, publishes "Over To You." The CBC AM radio program *This Morning* regularly airs "First Person Singular;" the *Globe and Mail* publishes personal essays on its "Facts and Arguments" page.

**Many magazines publish essays...**

Don't overlook smaller, less high-profile markets. Many consumer and commercial magazines publish essays, as do organization and business newsletters. Most local and regional newspapers carry essays, and more and more literary websites include them.

Before you submit essays, you should first check writers' guidelines for word length and the range of topics the market considers. You don't need to query; send the complete piece, and include an SASE and/or the required return information. You might consider submitting multiple essays to non-competing markets (publications whose distribution areas do not overlap), but do mention to the editors that you're doing this. Individual publication guidelines will often tell you if this is acceptable.

Many forms of writing require authors to keep themselves out of the story. Writing personal essays and opinion pieces allow you to have your say, and guarantees an audience who's willing to listen.

—

Lois J. Peterson's personal essays have been published in a range of print and online markets. She teaches others how to have their say in workshops in The Creative Writing Diploma Program in Surrey, British Columbia. The editor of *WORDS literary journal*, she publishes fiction, poetry, essays, and memoir.

# Make Every Word Count

*by Robert H. Jones*

Although I started writing for outdoor magazines in the mid-1970s, it was not until I began freelancing to the *Vancouver Sun* newspaper in 1981 that I learned the meaning of "making every word count." Outdoor section editor Phil Hanson specified a maximum of 1,000 words, with a preference between 600 and 800. As payment was by the word, I split the difference and submitted four 800-word articles. When my first piece was published, it did not appear to have been edited, but for some nagging reason seemed shorter and easier to read. After comparing the article to a carbon copy of its original, I realized several words had been cut. Upon marking them with a red pen, I discovered it had been reduced by nearly 100 words. I pondered those results for quite awhile, then took my red pen to the remaining three carbon copies, plus four more originals about to be mailed. All were cut dramatically, retyped, then mailed. When I met Hanson for the first time a few weeks later, he commented that I had "learned fast."

## Writing was easy; massaging was not...

In 1983, editor Burton Myers asked me to write a column for *Ontario Out of Doors* magazine. Although given free rein regarding topics, I had to stay within 600 words. I was dubious about being able to develop a plot; write a catchy lead; introduce various characters; describe surroundings and situations; then bring everything to a meaningful conclusion with so few words. It proved, however, simply a matter of writing a story, then massaging it — over and over — until the word counter on my ancient Kaypro II said it was 600 words. Precisely. Writing those "Leftovers" columns was fairly easy; massaging them was not. Entire paragraphs, which seemed so lyrical and important while being created, were replaced with one or two words — or deleted. Some columns took three days to write, while others (not many) were finished in three hours.

I discovered dialogue can replace descriptive narratives that ramble. By establishing a flow, the use of *said, replied,* and *answered* is required only often enough to avoid confusion. I also learned repetitive words or phrases can be rewritten to reduce their numbers. In most cases, common terminology can be shortened by removing or replacing a word or two: "in spite of" becomes "despite;" "do not forget to" becomes "don't forget to."

Some of the easiest words to remove are *that, the, and, I,* and *my.* To demonstrate this (assuming you are using a word processor), use the [Replace] command to replace "that" with "**". If your manuscript already has asterisks in it, choose symbols like ">", "++", "##", "[]". "That was the truck that hit that fire hydrant!" becomes "** was the truck ** hit ** fire hydrant!" Seeing an abundance of asterisks is a good indication you are overusing the word "that." Scan the entire manuscript, then see what can be rewritten to reduce the number of asterisks. When satisfied, go back to the [Replace] command, then convert the remaining asterisks back to "that" (capitalizing where necessary).

[Replace] can highlight other repetitive words, but avoid confusion by thinking it through before converting. For example: type a space before and after "I" and "the" to prevent words like *in, it, then* and *other* from appearing as "**n," "**t," "**n" and "o**r" (words starting a paragraph or followed by punctuation will not change).

**Learn to say more with less...**

Most editors are fairly flexible on word counts, and won't set their hair on fire and run around in circles if your article is 20 or 30 words over or under. However, when dealing with short columns, especially those with illustrations, you must be exact. When I started writing a humour column for *Real Outdoors* in the mid-1990s, editor Craig Ritchie asked for 600 words. As time passed, he decided to give the illustrator more room for his cartoon, so I pared back to 500 words. Although several columns had been written ahead of time, reducing them by 100 words was relatively painless. By getting used to writing tightly, you learn to say more with less.

I could go on, but I think you get the idea. Besides, editor Murphy Shewchuk said he wanted this to be 750 words. Precisely.

—

Robert H. (Bob) Jones has won numerous awards for his books and magazine articles. Editor of the Blue Ribbon Books series for Johnson Gorman Publishers in Calgary, Alberta, he resides in Courtenay, BC, with Vera, who is also a writer/editor.

# Conducting Interviews

*by Robert H. Jones*

When the editor of an art magazine asked me if a particular artist used the "dry brush" technique, I answered truthfully, "How should I know?"

"Because you write about art," she said.

"No," I replied, "I write about artists. They know about art; I know how to push buttons on my tape recorder."

This pretty well sums up an interview, which is simply a means of gathering information. For example: while researching destination articles for an outdoors magazine, a two-day trip to an area won't make me an expert on the myriad questions that readers want answered. However, there are usually local residents around who are experts, and when properly approached most will share their knowledge and expertise.

I find the most willing folk are involved with the tourism industry, wildlife and fishery biologists and technicians, artists, fishing guides and resort operators. Least willing have been politicians, senior and mid-level bureaucrats, and representatives from some of the industries involved in harvesting natural resources.

There are two types of interviews: personal and via telephone. Whichever method is used, it is important that the interviewer appears reasonably knowledgeable about the topic, and well prepared. This means preparing some basic questions beforehand, and having your equipment ready to set up quickly: tape recorder, microphone, extension cord, batteries (if required), and spare tapes to replace those which fill up. In the case of telephone interviews, having everything prepared ahead of time ensures the interviewee does not have to wait while you fumble around.

Let's examine the machinery. Some writers swear by tiny tape recorders that fit in their shirt pocket or purse. My Realistic Micro-26 has proved reliable and amazingly easy on batteries. However, I use it only when I can't use its big brother, a fairly hefty Realistic CTR68 with six piano-type keys. I like this large machine because it is sturdy and easy to use, and it doesn't move around on the desk while I am transcribing.

I prefer an external microphone because it can be positioned in front of the person being interviewed, while I sit across the table or to one side monitoring the tape and voice level. When playing back the tape, there is less extraneous noise, and the person's voice is loud and clear.

A jury-rigged mike stand has served me well for 20 years. It is fashioned from a Bilora Model 1600 swivel-head camera C-clamp, which has two L-shaped legs that slide out from the body to form a small bipod. A metal wall clamp used for hanging brooms and mops is secured to the adjustable head with a 1/4-inch nut. The mike fits tightly in the broom clamp, and the adjustable head allows it to be swivelled up or down so it directly faces the person being interviewed. In addition, the C-clamp can be clamped to the side or top of an easel, which allows an artist to sketch or paint as the interview progresses.

I conduct telephone interviews with a Telephone Recording Control device (about $30). This remains plugged in at all times, so hooking up or removing the tape recorder takes less than a minute. Warning: if you have a weak or noisy telephone connection, when it's time to transcribe the tape the sound quality will have you crawling the wall in frustration.

**Conduct interviews one-on-one...**

Whenever possible, insist on conducting interviews one-on-one. Having two or more persons involved gets confusing, especially when everyone starts talking at once or an argument ensues. If possible, select a room with no telephone, TV, radio or piped-in music, no window open to noisy traffic, and no external air conditioner.

Now, let's prepare to conduct a personal interview with mythical fishing guide Merton Mayers. First, prepare a list of logical questions relating to the topic of discussion. If possible, do some research on Merton beforehand. Has he guided somebody famous? Did he guide someone to a record-breaking fish? Is he involved with a conservation group? Sources of information might be relatives, friends, co-workers, or even Merton himself.

Before switching on the machine, explain how you intend to use the recorded material, then give a quick rundown of what you wish to cover. Ask if there are any topics or areas to avoid, which helps bypass questions that might cause tension or embarrassment. If there is something you are asked to keep off the record, honour the request. Don't confuse your interview with investigative reporting.

Artists like Robert Bateman, Ron Parker, and Fenwick Lansdowne were easy interviews. No strangers to newspaper reporters, magazine writers, and TV correspondents, they are living proof that practice makes perfect. It was just a case of switching on the machine, asking a leading question to get the interview started, then sitting back to listen. However, some folks are nervous when confronted with a microphone — others are downright taciturn. In either case, switch on your recorder, then hit the "pause" button while you chat them up. Eventually they will relax, especially if you get on a topic in which they have an intense interest or opinion. Once the flow of words begins, start the tape rolling.

Pay attention to what is being said. If Merton finishes expounding on a topic and asks for your opinion, be ready to respond with a reasonably intelligent answer or comment — but not at great length. This lets him know you are interested, and may jog his memory about something that might otherwise be overlooked. If something said alerts you to another question, jot it down and cover it later. Occasional interruptions on your part will help steer Merton onto or away from a specific topic, and give him a short breather.

**Ask for clarification...**

If you don't understand what is being said during the interview, you certainly won't while transcribing it later. Ask for clarification or descriptions to help relate to what he is saying. If he mentions fishing with Bjørnar Svenderhaaven on the Zymagotitz River, ask him to spell out the names while you write them down on a note pad. If you have a map of the area, ask him to point out the location. (A tributary of the Skeena River, it's near Terrace, BC.) Later, while transcribing the tape, check the spelling of place names against a gazetteer, atlas, or road map. Merton might be a great guide, but maybe he's a lousy speller.

Finally, you picked Merton's brain in order to write a travel destination piece on the Zymagotitz River. While writing your article, give him credit wherever it is due: "According to veteran fishing guide Merton Mayers..." or "few people know the Zymagotitz River as well as..."

One last point: Experience will teach you that the most important control on your tape recorder is the "pause" button. Other than short questions or comments pertaining to the topic, whenever you feel the urge to talk, hit the pause button. Otherwise, while transcribing a lengthy interview from tape to screen, disk, or paper, you will discover the sound you least want to hear is that of your own voice.

—

Robert H. (Bob) Jones has won numerous awards for his books and magazine articles. Editor of the Blue Ribbon Books series for Johnson Gorman Publishers in Calgary, Alberta, he resides in Courtenay, BC, with Vera, who is also a writer/editor.

# Get the Picture

*by Robert H. Jones*

Most editors of outdoor publications prefer package submissions — a manuscript plus an assortment of images. They will usually specify whether they want colour slides, colour photographs, black-and-white (B&W) photographs, or images submitted via e-mail. Rather than hire a photographer, many outdoor writers learn the basics of photography in order to make their product more marketable. A few advance to the point where they become as well known for their images as their prose. Conversely, some photographers take up writing and become very successful weavers of tales.

Photography can be exciting and challenging: muskies wildly leaping; cock pheasants rocketing skyward; bald eagles diving to pick up a fish from the water's surface. However, in the production of how-to-do-it articles, I am confronted with nothing more thrilling than a workbench cluttered with blobs of lead, fishhooks, pieces of wood, scraps of metal, feathers, and other assorted debris. Nevertheless, there are challenges to this type of photography: layouts, positioning, backgrounds, camera and lighting angles, depth of field, exposure times, plus a multitude of problems associated with colours and contrast.

**Avoid busy background clutter...**

My photo studio, workshop and fly-tying room are one; complete with dust, grime and cobwebs. Several projects might be under way at any given time, but when the workbench is required for photography, it must be cleaned off to avoid busy background clutter that detracts from whatever is being portrayed.

If several sequential pictures are required, how-to photographs may be shot in black-and-white; however, as most magazine editors now prefer colour, both techniques are covered below.

There are two basic types of how-to photography: vertical and horizontal. My verticals are shot from a standard tripod with the subject in front of the lens, while horizontals are shot straight down, with the subject beneath the lens.

Whether vertical or horizontal, some things remain the same. To increase clarity and contrast, a backdrop of some sort may be used. Whatever the material, it should be in contrast to the subject to make it stand out: dark subjects on light backgrounds and vice versa.

Some colours virtually disappear against certain backgrounds, particularly while shooting B&W. Avoid combinations like blue on green, red on brown, yellow on orange, or pale colours on light or neutral backgrounds.

Backdrops I have accumulated over the years include cloth, burlap, carpeting, woven bamboo, paper, cardboard, textured and painted wood panelling, and sheets of translucent plastic. If the subject is intricate, detailed or has a soft outline, a plain backdrop is chosen; if the subject is symmetrical or clean-lined, a textured background might be used.

For most vertical B&W work, a drop curtain of cloth is used. It consists of yard-wide lengths of pure white and dark green polyester rolled back-to-back on a length of round wooden dowel. The roll is suspended from a ceiling-mounted bracket located directly over and to the rear of the workbench. Changing the backdrop from light to dark is simply a matter of reversing the dowel, then unrolling the curtain.

For close-ups of lures or flies, 12 x 12-inch sheets of white, black, or coloured felt are used. The sheets are stored flat in a cardboard box measuring 2 x 13 x 13 inches. If a vertical background is required, the desired colour is fastened to the side of the box with a spring clip. The box is then stood on edge and positioned for best effect. This can be effective for shooting a fly clamped in a vise, or a single lure suspended by its nose.

**A perfectly stationary camera...**

The secret to sharp photographs is a perfectly stationary camera that is fired with a cable release. Also important is the depth of field areas on the subject itself, or in front of or behind it, which remain in sharp focus. The smaller the lens aperture, the more depth of field, and vice versa. If the subject has a fairly flat plane, it may be advantageous to throw the background out of focus, in which case the aperture is opened wider. In the long run it is best to determine beforehand which aperture setting produces optimum results. This is accomplished by shooting a test role of film with any lenses intended for this type of work.

When shooting black-and-white, I prefer a Mamiya C330 Twin Lens Reflex camera loaded with a 12-exposure roll of Kodak Verichrome Pan 125 film. This is usually sufficient for most projects, and the medium format 2 1/4 x 2 1/4-inch negatives are a pleasure to work with in the darkroom.

For close-ups, an 80mm lens is used. This is a near-macro lens that permits focusing within 10 inches of the subject. For a different perspective or increased depth of field, I switch to a 135mm lens. The tripod is positioned at least seven feet away from the subject, which is the minimum focussing distance for that lens. The basement floor has permanent marks on which to set the tripod's feet, and the bench top is marked to indicate extremes the subject can be moved to the right or left.

Up to three adjustable reflector lamps with 200-watt, incandescent bulbs are used for B&W lighting. Light readings are taken with a hand-held, Gossen Lunasix 3 meter, and in most cases I work with only an incidental reading. Positioning of the lights depends on the subject, and whether or not shadow sculpting is desirable. If a light-coloured background is used, one or two lamps may be aimed on the backdrop, and only one on the subject.

**Virtually grain-free prints...**

For B&W macro shots, a 35mm OM-1 Single Lens Reflex is used with 50 ASA film. This slow film provides virtually grain-free prints. The through-the-lens light meter is used in conjunction with the Lunasix 3. Lenses used include a 50mm macro, and macro-zooms of 28–105mm and 70–210mm. For extreme close-ups, a 2x doubler may be used, or the camera and one of the lenses may be attached to a bellows unit.

For colour, a 35mm OM-4ti SLR is used with either 50 or 100 ASA daylight film. The internal spot metering system is used to determine the best exposure time (up to eight readings can be computed and averaged out), but this is cross-checked with the Lunasix 3.

For colour close-ups or macro shots where backlighting is not required, a dedicated ring flash and reflector provides even light with no shadows. If light control is desired, blue photo-floods are used in the reflector lamps. In many cases the project is simply carried outside and shot in natural light; in direct sunlight for highlighting or shadow sculpting, or in a shaded area for subdued lighting with no shadows.

The secret to producing good slides and photographs is the same as for good writing: set high standards, then settle for nothing less. This means learning to use all of your photographic equipment properly and, equally as important, throwing away every slide or negative strip that fails to meet your self-imposed standard.

—

Robert H. (Bob) Jones has won numerous awards for his books and magazine articles. Editor of the Blue Ribbon Books series for Johnson Gorman Publishers in Calgary, Alberta, he resides in Courtenay, BC, with Vera, who is also a writer/editor.

# Don't Play Film Roulette with Airport Security

*by Robert H. Jones*

My trips that involve flying are usually work oriented, which means up to six cameras may be included in my luggage: three 35mm single-lens-reflex (SLR) and three range-finder (RF). The SLRs, a selection of "must have" lenses, power winders and a dedicated flash go into my carry-on bag, as does all of the film (usually 40 to 50 rolls of 100 ASA, plus a dozen rolls of high-speed 400 in case of wet, overcast conditions). The range-finder cameras and other photographic equipment, including specialty lenses, ring flash and spare batteries, goes into my unaccompanied luggage. This fragile equipment is first stored in a sturdy, high-impact polyethylene tackle box from which the innards have been removed to make space. Pieces of foam rubber placed between the equipment provides shock protection and prevents the contents from moving around.

Despite airline notices to the contrary, repeated X-rays at security check points will fog film. I do a fine job of destroying my own film through improper ASA and/or aperture settings, which have nothing whatsoever to do with existing light conditions, therefore I do everything within my power to thwart the airport security people from adding to my problems.

Film should never, ever be stored in unaccompanied luggage as it is subjected to X-ray scanning, and I'm told on good authority that the scanner settings are much higher than for carry-on. This situation has worsened since the World Trade Center attacks on 11 September 2001, with the increased use of even more powerful CTX-5000 and CTX-5500 Invision scanners.

Forget about lead-lined film protection bags. When a scanner operator sees an unidentifiable object in unaccompanied luggage, the scanner X-ray intensity is simply cranked up until the contents can be identified.

All film — unexposed and exposed — is carried in clear plastic Fuji film containers, which in turn are placed in clear plastic bags. Loosely, so the security guards can simply roll the bags around and check the containers as they tumble about inside the bag.

Prior to entering a security checkpoint, I remove the plastic bags from my carry-on luggage, then request that they be visually inspected as the remainder of my carry-ons go through the X-ray scanner. Ask nicely. Security staff endure a lot of jerks during the course of a shift, so I try to not be one. Even when I encounter the odd jerk who just happens to be an airport security guard.

Prior to continuing a trip that requires more flying, or preparing to return home, if my cameras contain partly-shot rolls of film they are rewound and the number of frames exposed — plus two frames — is written on the film cannister with a felt-tip pen. Prior to rewinding the partial roll, check the number in the film counter window. Whatever it reads, add two. In other words, if the counter reads 10, write 12 on the container label. Better to waste a frame or two that you can be sure of, than to lose two or more possibly good shots because they overlapped.

**Use blank paper labels...**

As ink and wax crayon can be easily rubbed off the smooth plastic surface of a film container, prior to departure I affix blank adhesive paper labels to at least a half dozen containers. I don't worry about which have blank labels until such time as I am making a move that requires going through airport security. It then takes only a few minutes to sort through the containers and switch fresh film into unlabelled ones, thus making the labelled ones available for partially used rolls.

If manually rewinding a film, hold the camera against your ear. Stop winding when you hear the film leader snap free of the take-up spool. To double check, activate the film advance lever a couple of times to ensure the film wind-up knob doesn't move.

When two of my RF cameras are finished rewinding film (a Nikon and a Canon), a half-inch or so of the leader is left exposed. Fine and well if the roll is only partly exposed; in fact I usually tug the leader out another half-inch or so just to make sure I don't lose it. However, if the film has been fully exposed, I wind the leader inside the container. I forgot to do this once, then later re-shot an entire roll of previously exposed film. As I said, I don't need any help from airport security staff to ruin my film, I do quite well on my own.

—

Robert H. (Bob) Jones has won numerous awards for his books and magazine articles. Editor of the Blue Ribbon Books series for Johnson Gorman Publishers in Calgary, Alberta, he resides in Courtenay, BC, with Vera, who is also a writer/editor.

# Writing as a Balancing Act

*by Sandra Phinney*

Editors expect freelancers to turn in "balanced articles." But what does this mean and how can you achieve it? Writing a balanced article means that you produce a piece that has both depth and scope. You achieve this if you cover several topics about a subject, include voices from different parts of your region (or across the country, especially if you are writing for a national publication), and provide opposing points of view.

**Taking the broad view...**

If you are to write about a variety of topics within a certain subject area, you need to give as broad a view as possible.

For example, an article about planting raspberries could cover the best way to prepare the soil before the canes are planted; how to test soil for pH; what to use for fertilizers (including organic solutions); planting procedures; spring and fall maintenance of a raspberry bed; and recommended varieties. You could also include time-tested recipes; folklore; comments or anecdotes from growers; yields and recommended plantings; storage tips; how to identify and prevent insect damage or diseases — ad infinitum.

The amount that you write will be determined by word count, but *what* you write about will depend on the depth or scope you want to achieve. You may choose to write about two topics in depth, or you may decide to skim the surface and broaden the scope by writing about seven topics related to the subject. Now, balance doesn't mean that you have to give equal space to each topic within your subject area, but at least you should be conscious of your choices, and how you can best balance the article. Of course, it is also important to factor in what your editor expects, along with what will satisfy the needs and interests of your reader.

The point is, when you sit down to write an article, think of as many angles as possible related to the subject at hand. Map out a plan before you start to research or interview. Think "balance" before you put pen to paper. It rarely happens by chance.

## Representing geographic regions...

Taking the concept of balance a step further, consider the geographic location that the publication covers. Are various regions represented?

Say you are assigned an article of 1800 words for a regional business magazine that is distributed in Atlantic Canada. The subject is quality control in the tourism industry. After you have mapped out the angles, the next step is to ensure that you achieve balance by interviewing people from each province. It will be important to talk with individuals who have different backgrounds, who represent various sectors and interests. So, before you line up potential interview candidates, visualize how each province can be represented. Who are the various stakeholders? Where will you find different "voices" to represent various viewpoints?

Your interview plan could include contacting the Minister of Tourism and the owner of a motel in Prince Edward Island; the chairman of the provincial tourism association and a travel agent in Newfoundland; the manager of a convention centre and the owner of a craft shop in New Brunswick; the captain of a ferry and the president of the Chamber of Commerce in Nova Scotia. So far so good! Now think about location and gender. Are there any "rural" voices in your article or is everyone from an urban centre? Do you have women's voices or are they all men? Again ... think of balance.

A word of caution: don't confuse balance with the word equal. If you interview eight people for this article, the interview split does not have to be even. You may end up with three people from New Brunswick, one from Prince Edward Island, two from Newfoundland, one from Nova Scotia, and at the last minute you decide to have a national voice and interview a director from the National Quality Institute in Ontario. Out of these eight, it works out that six voices are from urban centres, two from rural communities; five are women and three are men; and there is a good split between private, public, and not-for-profit sectors. That's fine. Overall, you still have a healthy mix and have achieved a good balance.

If you are writing an article for a national audience, the same principles apply. Simply select people to interview from different regions of the country.

## Representing opposing views...

A further note on balance has to do with opposing viewpoints. With many subjects, there are pros and cons. It is important for the reader to hear various opinions, including ones with conflicting ideas or who are opposed to the thrust of your article.

Imagine that you are writing a feature on the subject of naturopathy for a national health magazine that promotes alternative lifestyle choices. Your focus is about medical training; standards; trends; and consumer choices. Your interview list includes the president of the Canadian College of Naturopathic Medicine and the chair of Materia Medica at the same institution (2 males, city, ON). You also interview the first trained naturopath to practice in Nova Scotia and co-chair of the Canadian Naturopathic Association (female, rural, NS), and a doctor of naturopathy, chiropractic, and traditional Chinese medicine who heads a clinic in Vancouver (male, city, BC). Finally you find a patient who has selected a naturopath over a mainstream MD (female, rural, ON). A little heavy on the Ontario side, but not badly balanced otherwise.

Now, keep in mind that controversial issues can surround many of the articles you write. The subject of naturopathy is no exception, and this field of practice has its share of opponents. In order to complete a balanced article, you need to find a reliable source who can raise legitimate concerns and address them in an intelligent fashion. So a conventional doctor who teaches medicine at Cornell University in the U.S. (male, city, NY), who studied a number of alternative treatment modes and wrote a book on the pros and cons of various alternative treatments, would likely be excellent.

Once you have researched the issues, it is important to place the main concern(s) on the page so the reader can get a sense of what's at stake and, subsequently, form her own opinions. You can also provide balance in your sidebars by providing reading lists, websites, and contact information for organizations that represent a wide range of reliable sources for the reader.

If your article is balanced for depth and/or scope; has regional or cross-country representation including urban/rural, male/female voices, and presents opposing viewpoints, then you have covered the basics. Your articles will be balanced, your editor will be thankful, and your readers will be enlightened.

—

Sandra Phinney is a freelance writer in Yarmouth, Nova Scotia. She writes features for regional, national, and international magazines, and mini-documentaries for CBC radio. Sandra gives workshops on freelance writing and creative writing. In her spare time she writes poetry and fiction. Visit her at www3.ns.sympatico.ca/s.phinney/.

# 6. Fiction Techniques

# Where Do You Get Your Ideas?

*by Matt Hughes*

Every fiction author gets asked the question, as if story ideas were rare earths revealed only to a select few. But stories are all around us, all the time. You just need to know what to look for.

Some people say there are only seven basic plots in fiction. I think it's even simpler — there is only one story, but with endless variations.

It goes like this. First, we have a character — a man or a woman, a boy or a girl, an animal, an alien, a machine — who lives in a place and time that may be real or fanciful.

Then something happens that pulls the character out of everyday circumstances. Maybe a robot shows him an image of a princess who needs help, or a tornado lifts her house over a rainbow, or he meets a sultry blonde who wants him to find her missing sister.

From that point on, the hero(ine) struggles against mounting opposition toward a moment of decision: trust the Force, accept that there's no place like home, avenge your partner by turning in that sultry blonde who shot him.

The hero chooses, and finds himself transformed by the choice and by the struggle that led to it. Then maybe they all live happily ever after, or maybe the hero returns to his former life sadder but wiser. Not every story needs a happy ending.

So you want a story idea? Think about something that might happen — you witness a crime, you find a payphone that lets you call 1935, you discover your neighbour is not what she seems — then think about where that unusual event might lead. Then decide which way to go.

The rest is just writing.

—

Matt Hughes writes speeches for politicians and corporate executives. He has published three novels — *Fools Errant* and *Fool Me Twice*, Warner Aspect 2001; and *Downshift*, Doubleday Canada 1997 — and *Breaking Trail*, the memoirs of Senator Len Marchand, Caitlin Press 2000. His suspense fiction has appeared in *Blue Murder*, *Alfred Hitchcock* and *Storyteller*.

# Start Your Story Where the Story Starts

*by Matt Hughes*

Every novel has a point where the hero(ine) embarks upon the main conflict at the heart of the story. It's when Dumbo wakes up in a tree; it's when a Louis L'Amour cowboy dives for cover as a shot rings out.

That's the place to begin your manuscript. Why not first establish the character and setting? Because you may have only a few lines to hook that most crucial of readers — an agent.

Major New York agent Don Maass tells this story: One Friday afternoon each month, he and his associates gather around a table that holds a stack of sample chapters they have asked to see after winnowing through several hundred query letters. Now they decide which chapters to read over the weekend.

Each manuscript is passed around. Agents read the first page. If the manuscript grabs someone's attention, it goes in a briefcase. If it doesn't grab anybody, it's gone.

If that was the opening of a novel you spent years writing, that Friday peek was your only shot. Your story catches fire on page three? Too bad; page one didn't hook anybody.

So put your main plot point in the first paragraph of page one. Get your story started, and then layer in the back-story as you keep going. Your chances of landing an agent will take a quantum leap and that is the first step into the big leagues.

Besides, once you've sold the book, you and your editor can always rewrite the opening.

—

Matt Hughes writes speeches for politicians and corporate executives. He has published three novels — *Fools Errant* and *Fool Me Twice*, Warner Aspect 2001; and *Downshift*, Doubleday Canada 1997 — and *Breaking Trail*, the memoirs of Senator Len Marchand, Caitlin Press 2000. His suspense fiction has appeared in *Blue Murder*, *Alfred Hitchcock* and *Storyteller*.

# Stories: Lost and Found

*by Deb Loughead*

Beginning writers are often stumped for starting points in stories. Though the phrases and words might start flowing once the idea has been established, for fledglings, just reaching this stage can be the most confounding part of the entire process. Sometimes inspiration is extremely elusive.

In creative writing classes we're inundated with suggestions for revving up our creative engines. "Write what you know," they tell us. Or, try to experiment and write about things that you've *never* experienced. Test different genres, styles and voices. Delve into yourself and try to ascertain what you care about most. Listen to the stories of other people and incorporate elements of these into your own. And always carry a notebook to jot down snippets of conversations or stories that could be the fodder for future inspiration.

## Nothing worse than a blank page...

It all sounds so simple, but when faced with a blank page and an imagination awhirl with confusing possibilities, those stories don't always emerge when you want them to. There's nothing worse than staring at a blank page. There's nothing more frustrating than the absolute lack of a story and that abysmal feeling that you're not going to accomplish anything.

I stumbled upon an idea for finding stories when I was in a similar quandary. Nothing seemed new anymore. All of my ideas just appeared to be rehashed from the timeless and universal plots that surface in so many stories; they lacked that vital twist to make them unique. I was frustrated, reaching the point of writer's block. That is, until I took my eyes off that blank page for a few minutes and had a look around my house.

My house is my comfort zone, a place where I surround myself with "found" objects, reassuring relics from my past, each meaningful in itself, each with its own story to tell. It's a dust collector's paradise of comfortable clutter. But when I looked past the dust, when I took each object and studied it more closely, I realized that I *did* have stories — and plenty of them.

My eyes alighted on objects that have been passed down to me by my grandmother. I studied them, let my mind wander, let the memories wash over me. "Where can I go with this," I asked myself. And before long I'd found my way. Those objects evolved into an essay called "Old Things", which I eventually sold.

This process has served me well. The clutter on my son's bedroom floor, his "crow's nest collection" of trinkets that caught his eye, turned into a prize-winning poem. A nondescript grey rock found along the lakeshore eventually grew into a children's novel. Now I'm working on another novel based on an unusual object, and I'm amazed at the story that's blossomed just because I happened to be rummaging through the jumbled disarray of my desk one afternoon.

**Awaken buried memories...**

Found objects can provide you with a starting point, something tangible, something that you can handle, examine, fantasize about. They can awaken buried memories or suggest new directions of thought. And they can also murmur those two little words that are so instrumental in developing a story — "what if" — triggering countless questions that can only help to enhance a tale.

Look in your closet. Anything in there from Goodwill or a secondhand shop: a dress, a pair of pants, a sweater? Who wore it before you? How did it wind up in a used clothing store? Did the previous owner lose or gain weight? Or die? What story is that garment whispering?

Has an heirloom been passed down to you from a beloved relative: a piece of jewelry, fine china or furniture? Ask yourself why this object was important to someone in the past and try to shape a story around it. A hand-painted porcelain fruit bowl that my mother continues to cherish once cradled precious oranges at Christmas time when she was a child. That bowl, and the images it conjured of Depression-era Decembers, was a tale begging to be told. By fictionalizing my mother's family, borrowing some of her truths and mixing in a large measure of fanciful meandering, eventually a short story evolved in which the porcelain bowl became the focal point.

Look in your cupboards, at the clutter on the shelves. Explore your storage spaces, the attics and basements where musty old books, letters and diaries, knickknacks from ages ago, are tucked away for posterity. Why did they mean something to you then? What recollections do these mementos stir up, and why are you saving them? What part of your life are you unwilling to part with and is there a story behind it? And sometime in the future when your descendants unearth these treasures, what truths will they unearth about you? At the least, these found objects can offer a barrage of questions, maybe even some answers.

**Let your mind drift off in different directions...**

Be inventive when you interrogate yourself. What if someone lost this object? How important was it to that person, and how will it affect him? How will it affect the person who found it? Is there a moral issue here? Is the finder a keeper? Does she feel any guilt for keeping the object? Does she try to seek the person who lost it? What happens when they meet? The possibilities are endless and it even makes for an effective free-fall writing exercise, just for the practice. It's all a matter of letting your mind drift off in different directions, letting new ideas flow from that *thing* that you can touch whenever you want to. A talisman to inspire you while you work.

So take your eyes off the blank page for a while, look around and be creative. Who knows what stories are hidden in your most cherished possessions, thinly disguised as junk in your closet!

—

Deb Loughead is the author of numerous children's books, including *All I Need and other poems for kids* (Moonstruck Press, 1998) and *The Twisting Road Tea Room* (Ragweed Press, 2001). Her stories, poems and articles for children and adults have appeared in publications across the country.

# Walking into the Shadow

*by Claudia Carver*

My shadow journey began when I joined a dream group. After many months, someone in my group suggested I write a short story about one of my many food-themed dreams, as I obviously wasn't "getting the message." I had never written fiction in my life and believed I was totally lacking in creativity. But that week, for some very strange reason, I put my hands on the keyboard and a story came out through my fingertips. What surprised me most was that I, a very fussy person, loved it.

This does not mean that everyone loved it. Some (my daughters, for instance) seemed to enjoy it. Others (such as my husband) were polite. The publishers I sent it to were rather impolite. But whatever was I thinking — the short story had more than twenty characters, poorly developed ones at that.

Despite this initial rejection, the fact that I thought the story was marvelous has kept me writing more. Whereas dreams don't feature in every story I write, they often help me get started, flesh out a character, rewrite an important piece of dialogue, kick-start me when I'm stuck, or deliver an unexpected ending.

**Dreams relate to the *process* of creativity...**

Perhaps even more noteworthy is the way in which my dreams relate to the *process* of creativity. For example, I had a dream in which I was using a View-Master® to look at old photos. I had been told that when an object in a dream seems to have particular significance, it is helpful to use three adjectives to describe it, and then relate them to your waking life. I described the View-Master® as "old-fashioned, hand-held, and something to help me see better." So, what in my waking life was old-fashioned, hand-held and helped me see things better? The pen I use for morning journalling came readily to mind. Perhaps morning journalling will be a life sentence?

There are many reasons why it is important to record the *details* of the dream. Dream images are, of course, metaphors, and it is only when you write them down that you can begin to see how they are commenting on, challenging, or guiding your creative process. Seeing them in black and white helped me realize what some concrete dream images might mean — images such as writing between the lines, finding my way, a half-baked pumpkin loaf (half-baked idea), and picking letters out of alphabet soup.

The image in the dream I called "Alphabet Soup" was very intriguing. I was given a title for a story in a creative writing class. The title was, "The Alphabet from A to Z." I was about four or five (dreams are like that — four- or five-year-olds can go to creative writing classes) and I sat taking the letters out of some Campbell's alphabet soup. After I wrote the dream down and attempted to make some sense of it, it hit me that my "childhood soup" could be the inspiration for more stories.

**The power of synchronicity...**

This particular remembered dream also demonstrated the power of synchronicity — something that happens frequently when I'm writing. Several days after I had the dream, a horse named Alphabet Soup won the Breeder's Cup. He was a long shot and paid 20–1 odds. Sure wish I had heard his name mentioned *before* the race.

When synchronicity happens I know I'm doing something right. I realize yet again that Mulder's famous *X-Files* quote was right on the mark. "Dreams are answers to questions you haven't learned how to ask yet."

Dreams, with their metaphors, hidden messages, and shadow characters, might help you learn to ask the right questions. A character might step forward from the shadows of your dream, especially if you put out a casting call as you drift off to sleep.

—

Claudia Carver is a former social worker who writes on a wide variety of topics from gardening to sexual abuse to vegetarian cooking. She has won prizes for fiction in Waterloo County writing contests and frequently writes short humour pieces on the frustrations and absurdities of everyday life.

# Dialogue Demo

*by Margaret Springer*

Melissa chewed the end of her pencil. She wrote something, then scratched it out. She tried something else. She sighed. Thank goodness for Grandpa.

He was in his room as usual, writing the Great Canadian Novel.

"Grandpa, how do I get dialogue onto the page?" she asked him. "My characters have things to say, but I don't know how to write that down."

"Easy," Grandpa said. He had lived with this novel for a long time, long enough for six style manuals, four fat dictionaries and a thesaurus or two. "First rule: punctuation at the end of a phrase or sentence of dialogue always goes inside the quotation marks."

"OK," said Melissa, "I can handle that. But what about when a sentence of dialogue is split? I never know where to use capitals and where to use periods or commas."

"A sentence of dialogue interrupted by a tag line," said Grandpa, "is still a sentence. The capital letter goes only at the beginning, and the period goes only at the end."

"I see what you mean," said Melissa. She frowned. "But when two separate sentences are split by a tag line, there's a comma at the end of the first one. How come?"

Grandpa smiled. "It's still logical," he said. "Think of the tag line as part of the sentence. Ask yourself, what punctuation mark would be needed if the tag line were omitted? If it's a comma, use a comma after the tag line. If it's a period, use a period after the tag line. A period never goes before the tag line."

Melissa asked, "What if the tag line comes first?"

"You use a comma to set it off, same as always."

"And what about capitals?"

"What about them?" Grandpa was getting impatient. "You just use a capital letter whenever you begin a new sentence."

Hmm, thought Melissa. She sighed. It may seem easy to him, but he's been writing for a lot longer than I have.

"Well, what about thoughts?" she asked. "Do you put them in quotation marks, too?"

"No," said Grandpa. "Quotation marks indicate speech, at least with most publishers. Interior monologue is shown in other ways."

How can I get her to understand this? It sounds a lot more complicated than it is. But I can see from her face that I'm not explaining it very well. Let me think ... ok, I'll try this approach.

"Look, it depends on the publisher. Sometimes thoughts are printed in italics, and/or set off in a separate paragraph. So if you want to, you can use italics, or underline (which signals the printer to use italics). But it's easier to type normally, and just omit the quotation marks. The punctuation and capitals are the same as if the quotation marks were there. Does that make sense?"

"I guess so."

"Any more questions?"

"Well, we haven't mentioned paragraphing."

Grandpa reached over to his bookshelf and handed her a couple of texts. "The main thing to remember about dialogue paragraphing," he said, "is to give each speaker a separate paragraph, to avoid confusion. Now let me get back to my book."

"What's going on?" Mom had poked her head in the door. "You two look serious."

"No big deal," said Melissa. "Grandpa's helping me with my English assignment."

"Assignment!" echoed Grandpa. "You never told me this was your homework!"

Melissa grinned. "You didn't ask, Grandpa," she said.

—

Margaret Springer is a teacher and workshop leader as well as an author. Her fictional characters have been talking to each other since 1983, in dozens of magazine stories and three books. She is an instructor with the Institute of Children's Literature and a consulting editor for Boyds Mills Press.

# Creating a Believable World

*by Sharon Caseburg*

Any kind of speculative fiction — hardcore science fiction, time travel, horror, or fantasy — requires readers to put aside the conventions they have become accustomed to in the "real world" for the world the author presents in the story. For the most part, readers of these genres are more than willing to accept the environment an author has created. However, when the author does not provide a *believable* world, readers can become disenchanted with the author's realm and, in turn, the story itself.

Therefore the more the author knows about the world he or she is creating, the more confidently the author can write about it. If it is obvious to readers that the author fully believes in this alternative environment, then they will follow.

So how can the author successfully prepare for the creation of an alternative environment?

The answer is simple: work out *all* the details of your story before submitting your final draft to a publisher.

**Performing proper research...**

No "New World" can successfully come into being without the author first performing proper research. Whatever you do, don't make up your New World as you write. Map out everything you can possibly think of before you write about your realm. This activity will help make the actual writing about the environment much easier and will prevent any glaring inconsistencies (the bane of any speculative fiction reader) from occurring.

One easy way to get started on creating a believable environment for your story is to pick up a writers' reference book on world building from the local library or check the Internet for good sources of information. Use a variety of search engines when doing your research on the Internet. This will give you the widest pool to draw from. Be thorough in your background exercise and consider questions about your realm that may never come to figure in your story. You would be surprised how considering details that do not figure prominently in your story can enrich your storytelling technique and help you to create a lush and vibrant landscape for your readers.

Here are a few things to consider about the world you are creating. Answering as many of the following questions as you can will help you shape a strong, believable world; a realm you will be confident in writing about; a world that your readers can believe in. Don't limit yourself to this list. When you get down to it, there are thousands of other details you can consider, however the following can help you get started:

- Is the New World predominantly like the one we currently live in? Is it different? How is it different?
- What is the environment like on your New World? Is the air quality good? Is the air polluted? Is there an ozone layer? Do civilizations live in protected environments? How are these environments constructed? How are these environments controlled?
- Is there water on your world?
- How does the sun rise? How does it set? In fact, is there a sun?
- What are the life-sustaining factors of your world?
- What is the nature of your society? For example, is it predominantly agrarian or is it technological? Is it modelled after a real civilization that once lived on this earth? If so, research everything you can about that civilization. It will help you decide what is similar and what is different. If the world is technological, to what degree?
- Is your world contemporary, futuristic or alternatively historical? If it is futuristic, is it far-futuristic or near-futuristic?
- What year does your story take place in?
- What calendar does your civilization observe? In fact, does it even observe a calendar?
- What seasons exist in the realm?
- What is the plant life like in your realm? In fact, is there any plant life?
- What is the style of clothing worn?
- What currencies are used?
- What mode of transportation is used? If you are inventing one, how does it function? Is it petrol powered? Solar powered? Powered by another source? Describe the source in detail.
- Does the military exist in your realm? How is the military structured?
- Are there elected officials in the realm?

- Do they form some type of government? Is it a monarchy? A democracy?
- What is the hierarchy of the elected officials in the government?
- Do elders exist in the community? What role do they play? Is there a hierarchy that is adhered to with these individuals?
- If you are inventing new races of life forms, be prepared to make detailed notes about their societies as well.
- How do people communicate with each other? Is it verbal?
- Are there computers on the world? Are they the same as here?
- Do people read and write?
- Does telepathy exist?
- What is the same in the New World as in our world?
- What is different?
- What are the customs of your realm?
- How do people celebrate?
- How do people grieve?
- How are the young in society treated?
- How are the elderly in society treated?
- What is the average lifespan of your characters?
- What is the diet on your New World?

Remember that you are the creator of your New World, and you are all-powerful. You may choose not to answer every question on this list, or perhaps you will create new questions to consider. Knowing as much as possible about your New World will result in a more believable environment for your readers. The more intimately you yourself know your new environment, the more deftly you can convey its intricacies, even the unseen ones, to your audience.

—

Sharon Caseburg is an editor, poet, and freelance writer. She has a Master's degree from the University of Manitoba and currently works for a Western Canadian literary house.

# The Map of Charmangea

*by Ishbel Moore*

DunKhan, handsome hero, loses his argument with the lovely Princess Floranza. She won't leave her father's castle despite hearing that enemy forces are almost at the gate and are bent on killing her entire family. Unable to convince her that he only has her safety at heart, he rides across the landbridge and gallops off into the dark night, alone.

My fingers stop flying over the keyboard. The newly begun adventure — and DunKhan's horse — come to an unpleasant, jerking halt. Where exactly are we going?

I suffer dreadful embarrassment under DunKhan's unimpressed glare as he waits, struggling to control his impatient steed. I stammer my apologies. He's not impressed. "Hurry up, woman," he cries. "Give me some directions."

In a moment of inspiration I reply, "You can't leave Floranza. Go back and get her. Kidnap her if you have to. By the time you reach this spot again, I'll know what to tell you."

He kicks his horse and swoops back into Castle Cavernot. Whew! And while DunKhan is … em … convincing Floranza, I know I'd better get busy — drawing.

### Simply to satisfy a whim...

At first the thought of completely abandoning the project crossed my mind. I could hear my peers and teachers exclaiming loudly that I deserved this humiliating experience. I hadn't jotted down a rough outline of plot. No brief character sketches existed. Heck, I hadn't even seen this story coming. How dare I violate all I have been taught, simply to satisfy the craving to create on a whim? Perhaps it would be better to quit this insanity and return to a young adult manuscript I had underway.

Brave DunKhan and beautiful Floranza would brook no such betrayal. Theirs was a love story needing to be told. They had chosen me to tell it. Desperate to overcome the feeling of potential failure, I picked up a pencil. But where to start? I am no artist, and certainly not a cartographer.

I began with a blank 8.5 x 11 inch piece of paper. It stayed blank for some time while I chewed the end of the pencil. I prefer to think I was immersing myself in a writer's trance. The result of my meditation came as a further blow. With a certainty that settled in my gut, I realized I needed a much larger piece of paper. Out came the flip chart. More pencil chewing ensued. I reached for the atlas. Africa loomed before me. I traced it, then proceeded to reinvent the entire coastline. Meanwhile, DunKhan saves Floranza from a midnight marauder. While the physical attraction and personality conflicts deepen in Castle Cavernot, I have other problems.

I ask myself, what did I know about this story and the characters, and how would that affect the map and vice versa? For example:

- I knew: that Floranza was the first child of Ferrisan of Libona and Evelina of Belladiz.

I learned: that these two most powerful countries were at opposite ends of the "continent." The marriage of Ferrisan and Evelina resulted in the ending of bitter feuds, brought increased trade, and set in motion the ancient prophesy that one day a child of Libona would rule the entire continent (and, although the major players were of the opposite impression, that child would not be Floranza).

- I knew: that DunKhan was a member of an intelligence network called the Nongris.

I learned: Nongris functioned under the umbrella of the Brath; that they were not allowed to marry; that DunKhan was actually a crown prince of the legendary Paxarterra and in the Nongris under false pretenses; that the training ground of the Nongris was at Haidencrag Fortress; that DunKhan's current and temporary "camp" was in the Circle of Bradasha some 20 miles from Cavernot; and that the whole network was being systematically destroyed from within.

- I knew: that DunKhan had saved Ferrisan's life.

I learned: Libona is bordered by the Great Ridge Mountains, and the Soul and Three Step rivers; that there are other rivers, seasonal roads, vast forests, heavily guarded gatehouses; that Libona is primarily a farming/fishing country with a bull as its emblem; that Libona is also famous for its wrought iron; and that Castle Cavernot sat perched on a tiny protuberance of land, cut off at high tide; that Ferrisan considered himself invincible.

- I knew: that Floranza loved horses and did beautiful needlework, and was having great difficulty proving herself in the role of Princess Royal.

I learned: Ranzii province bred the best horses on its vast steppe; that her sister Phyllicia grew beautiful roses; that royal houses sent their children to the spiritual center of Brightly Castle and to a "university" at Benharlach for education; that these two places were in neutral territories; that Floranza was a bit short on true princess-like spunk but high on imagination; that she developed a secret female messenger system since the Brath seemed to be losing control.

- I knew: there would be weather interference in the plot.

I learned: (or rather, I had to relearn) how landscape both affected weather patterns while being sculpted by them; where and how mountain lakes were formed; which way the winds blew and why; tides, seasons, growth patterns for each country; that Ferrisan's despotism had resulted in a revolt.

- I knew: the map would enable me to give DunKhan his much-needed directions.

I learned: to trust the map completely; that I would be allowed to modify the map at any time; that if I ever didn't know what came next, all I had to do was look at the map.

**Conjured up a mythical world...**

My pencil scratched away for three wonderful days. Totally engrossed, grinning widely with the adventure of it all, I placed the warning/message beacons that surrounded the continent, named waterfalls and lakes, mines and capital cities, developed religious beliefs, located the mystical whirlpools, conjured up mythical beasts, established naval and army bases, determined ferry routes and dangerous shipwreck sites, made lists of characters and characteristics of people from each country, and finally unearthed the "bad guys." Africa became completely unrecognizable as it morphed into Charmangea with its eleven countries, rugged shoreline, varied geographical features and offshore neighbours.

My children and visitors appropriately "oohed and aahed" (as good supportive folk will do) when they paused at the kitchen table where I had my flip chart, eraser, sharpener and pencils spread out. I took the map to my romance writers group to whom I was reading this *Blood Tapestry*. But by this time I had to also hand out to those poor, long-suffering group members pages of characters' names and descriptions, plus information pages on the Brath, animals and foods of this fantasy land.

More importantly, I've discovered a marvellous, if somewhat psychologically dangerous, method for story development. I've never been much inspired by traditional outlines and character sketches. This map of Charmangea taught me to rely on my muse, to put myself right into

A portion of Ishbel Moore's hand-drawn map of Charmangea.

the setting and main characters much more than for any novel I have previously written. *Blood Tapestry* refuses to be rushed. It demands a precision I hope I can provide. This map of Charmangea has told me that the story of Floranza and DunKhan is only one of a trilogy of novels, maybe a quartet! Well, the manuscript of *Blood Tapestry* is now 275 pages long, and it is perhaps half finished. Wish me luck. And, in case anyone is wondering, I actually do know how this will all end. Happily Ever After — of course!

### "What are you going to do now?"

DunKhan and Floranza, plus two servants, *do* leave Castle Cavernot. This time when DunKhan reins in his horse, I know precisely where he'll be taking the princess. She's on a quest to find the truth behind the rebellion. She will learn what it takes be a good ruler. He's on a quest to find the people behind the cold-blooded murder of his father. His need for revenge dissipates as the danger to Floranza increases. They head south, aiming for Belladiz. It is rumoured the rebellion is being spearheaded by her Uncle Pertobus. DunKhan and Floranza are captured during a "momentary distraction" and hauled to the Carhoch Fortress and flung into separate dungeons. DunKhan is tortured. Both experience epiphanies during the confinement. Floranza's epiphany is easy enough. I know her and her background very well. But as DunKhan lies semiconscious in the dank cell, I have to ask him, "What are you going to do now?"

He opens one swollen eyelid. "I'm going to do what all good natives of Paxarterra do."

"Oh? What's that?" I'm almost afraid of the answer.

His lips twitch — in pain or annoyance, I can't tell. He says, "Have you studied my country, my upbringing, my beliefs?"

"Em ... no, not really."

He groans. "Hurry up, woman. I won't survive much longer like this. Find Paxarterra."

"You rest," I say. "I'll be back. I just have to sharpen my pencil."

—

Prolific writer and mentor, Ishbel Moore, thought she understood the writing process until she began work on *Blood Tapestry*, a fantasy romance novel. To move her story beyond chapter one, she required a map. While drawing "Charmangea," Ishbel discovered how much magic a writer could experience if willing to learn a different kind of "outline."

# A Writer as a Time Traveller

*by Kenneth S. Kalman*

Writing is an exercise of mind over matter. In order to provide the reader with a palette of tasty words, one must be *involved.* A reader can see through a narrow exercise in clichés and current chatter. Hence the author must be prepared to read widely and really know his subject. And once knowledgeable, the author must transport the reader to that period. Hence "time travel."

**The elements of time travel...**

There are three main elements: *period, place,* and *character.* Each of these is part of the writer's — and thus the reader's — time travel. It is because of this transfer that a reader enjoys his time away from home in a world created by the author. I will now discuss each of these, and then their combination, to illustrate how transport is created and what you, the writer, can do to improve your skills.

**Period...**

To create a special world for the reader, you must pick a time and read widely of that period. Books, period pieces, history. Become totally involved with it. Write a short story taking place in that period. See the time period come alive. Feel the comfort of being in that time — of its idiosyncrasies, its comforts or lack thereof, its science, its thought and speech patterns. Compel your story to be of that period. Study it and understand it.

As an example look at the following passage set in ancient Palestine, 20 CE.

Nazareth is a small village, set on a rocky hillside, protected by a string of mountains, north of the valley of Jezreel. We passed pastures, fields of barley, and olive groves. We could see farmers harvesting their barley with scythes, women and children dragging the stalks to their courtyards to let them dry.

Jay pointed to a hut in the distance, and I could tell it was his home. As we approached it, he began to weep. I held his hand as we walked forward. Everything and everybody seemed to come to a stop. From the group assembled in front of the house, a woman walked forward to meet us. She embraced Jay eagerly, holding him, and he, her. There was total silence. "I have returned, Mother," he said, "and I have brought..."

"Sara," she said, joyfully, "just as I told you."

**Place...**

The location for your story again must become a part of you. Visit the location(s) if at all possible. Read local books, written by local people. Read novels located there. Read travelogues. Watch video diaries of the area. Combining them will give you the character of the place. Write a short story taking place there, using local colour gleaned from your reading. Feel yourself on location in your story. Time travel in your mind to the location. Make the landmarks come alive for your reader and your characters.

As an example review the following:

April 28, 1948 — At long last, we are in Jerusalem, and I am in love. Oh, what a beautiful old city! Of course, I've seen pictures, but nothing compares to being here, touching the ancient stone buildings, some that, perhaps, Jesus, or his Apostles, or the Gospel writers touched. It is too much, my eyes amazed at every fragment of an ancient civilization, still standing, still breathing after so many battles, won and lost. Sensing the souls of civilizations come and gone...

Back to reality. We are staying in a small two-storey brick rooming house in the old city. Outside, everywhere you look the streets are lined with vendors, dressed in rags, scraping for a living, selling fruit, vegetables, meat, fish, pottery, notions, and supplies. The more prosperous men in their tailored suits sell guns, jewellery, and even slaves.

**Character...**

Research your characters well. Pattern them if at all possible on people you have met on location, on real living beings. Watch them, their facial, hand movements, their stride, their body language. Write a short story using some of these characters reacting to some specific event in their lives. Feel comfortable with the characters, with their movements, with their speaking inflections.

As an example see the following:

"I remember," Miriam said wistfully, "that first journey I made to Bethlehem with Joseph. It was the beginning of autumn and you, my son, were so big in my belly. I thought you would come out before we got there. Me, a frail girl of thirteen years, on a donkey. Joseph pulling us along, through the rough terrain, up and down the hills. I just wanted so much to be somewhere inside, in a warm place. There were early storms that year, rains and wind, and the journey was so difficult. It would have been hard for two able-bodied persons; I was far from that, almost ready to give birth."

"Mother," Jay interrupted, "you never told me why you picked that time to travel to Bethlehem."

"Oh, son," Miriam said putting her arms around her body, and breathing hard, "it was so, so, uh, terribly difficult here. For months, the elders of Nazareth were against Joseph and I. They argued it was not his baby. I knew it was, of course, but there was no convincing them. So finally we just had had enough, and we set out for the home of Joseph's parents. When we finally got there, with the wind howling and the rain and such, there was no room in the house. Well, you have seen how small it is. Some of your father's cousins had arrived for the holiday feasts, so we went to the Inn in the square. It, too, is very small, just three or four rooms, and was completely filled, so the owner took pity on us, and let us stay in the stable next to the Inn. And there, my son," she said proudly, "is where you were born. You were loved immediately. As soon as they heard the news, Joseph's whole family came to see you. There was so much joy!"

**Combining period, place and character...**

After you have achieved comfort with each of these you are ready to try combining them. You may pick any two or try for the three at once. Find a topic and again write a short story utilizing your characters in a place or period or both. You need to feel you are there. In that place. In that period. Be your character. Feel yourself travelling to that time and place. Time travel in your mind and write as you see it. Let your characters "freewheel" it a bit. Let them decide where to go and what to do. You will have travelled in time and have transported your audience as well.

As an example see the following:

October 3, 1948 — "The main Israeli camp is set up about fifteen miles west of here just south of Nazareth," Nathan said. He had been our driver since we left Jerusalem. A youngster, only seventeen, and wanting to contribute, he was wise beyond his years, keeping us away from the enemy on numerous occasions. We continued west and as we approached the camp, Jay's face went white.

"What happened to the homes and the fertile fields and orchards," he whispered. It was plainly a battlefield, bodies, jeeps, strewn everywhere. There was no sign of life on the hillsides we had known.

"That was two centuries ago, my love," I whispered back. "You cannot expect..."

It continues with:

"I want to go up on the hill and see the place where our home was," he said. "I just want to touch the soil and pray for them, our friends and family of so long ago."

So we left the tent, walked up the hill over the road, and continued into the hills to our ancient home. "The trees are young here, but I remember these rocks and, yes, there is that almond tree, the crooked one that was next to our house. It is still here," he cried. It was huge now. He went over and touched it and bent in front of it. He blessed the land that was there. And said Kaddish for his family, dead so long ago.

"So many memories, Father, Mother, oh where are you?" he cried. I knelt beside him, my arm on his shoulder.

As you can see from the above, if you transport yourself to the time and place of your story choice, your readers will also feel they are there. You will have succeeded in your short story form. Now you are ready to put your characters in a novel or novella. Keep the characters in your head, and even during your novel writing, use them in a short story, if a new idea comes to mind.

Every writer is a time traveller and every reader travels in time to the fantasy world of his author's dreams.

—

Dr. Kenneth Kalman is a poet and the author of several short stories on time travel. His poetry and fiction encompass the essence of both today and historical times. He is an observer and student of history and archaeology, whose life's passion is the study of first century Palestine, particularly the historical evidence for Jesus. His novel *Sara Church and the Jesus Diaries* is expected to be published in 2003.

# Confessions of a Rejected Romance Writer

*by Shirley Byers Lalonde*

I had come to the place in my career where I realized that my family didn't need a famous mother. They didn't need a literary genius. Good thing. I wasn't either.

What my family needed was a second income.

At that time, about ten years ago, I was selling fairly regularly to one or two newspapers, I'd broken into a few magazines and I'd had a children's book published. All well and good but stacked up, plumped up and puffed up as high as I could puff it, it still didn't pay the bills.

We needed some real money.

That's when I decided I would write a romance novel. Now there was a genre where I could make some real money and make it fast.

**Confession number 1:** I did it for the money. Just the money.

Now, I hadn't opened a romance since I was a teenager, so I picked up a few paperbacks. And found they had changed a bit in the interim. They were rather explicit.

That gave me pause. I don't do explicit. I don't do graphic.

Ever persistent, I poked around and found a line that was more to my taste. Harlequin's Intrigue novels were mysteries with a romantic component and according to the guidelines, the romances were sweet rather than sultry.

I set to work to create my masterpiece. I figured I could produce an Intrigue in, oh, about three weeks, a month tops.

**Confession number 2:** My heart wasn't really in it.

I called my book *Picture of Innocence*. The plot involved the disappearance of Mia, an eccentric young artist. My heroine, Paige, worked with Seth, an undercover RCMP officer to unravel the mystery.

I gave Paige and Seth lots of witty dialogue, plenty of clever clues and a total of two kisses. It took a little longer than I had calculated but when I shipped it off there was no doubt in my mind that it would be snapped up by the publisher. They would love it.

**Confession number 3:** It wasn't and they didn't.

Turns out my masterpiece "did not meet their requirements." Now, it's been awhile, and in a fit of pique I did throw the rejection letter away, but I seem to recall phrases such as "no chemistry between the protagonists," "lack of a plausible plot," and, "what ever made you imagine you could write a romance?" peppered throughout the missive.

They didn't ask for a rewrite. They didn't encourage me to try again. They just sent it back.

**Confession number 4:** A wiser and, yes, humbler woman, I stand before you and say, "In spite of popular opinion, in spite of what I believed for years, not just anybody can write a romance."

But, the initial problem remained. I needed to make more money.

I resolved to go with my writing strengths. I had sold stories to several kids' magazines and Sunday School papers. I liked to construct stories, starting with an incident or starting with a character. I didn't even mind "writing to a theme," which many children's publications require.

In short, I enjoyed writing kids' stories. I would do more of that.

I sold nonfiction previously to a variety of kids' and grownups' magazines. I enjoyed doing the research, interviewing people, and cobbling it all together into an article that could enlighten and entertain. I enjoyed writing nonfiction. I would do more of that.

I worked hard, disciplined myself to put in eight hour days, five days a week. The more I worked, the more ideas I came up with. And the more ideas I came up with, the more I wrote. My income gradually increased.

Today I am a self-supporting freelance writer.

**Confession number 5:** I am a more prosperous and definitely a happier writer when I write what I want to write. When my heart isn't in it, it shows.

And it doesn't sell.

—

Shirley Byers Lalonde lives near Kelvington, Saskatchewan. She is a contributing editor for *WITH*, a U.S.-based teen magazine and has also written for such periodicals as *The United Church Observer*, *My Friend*, *Brio*, *On the Line* and *Listen*.

# Developing Character and Conflict in Romantic Fiction

*by Laura Byrne Paquet and Yvonne Jeffery Hope*

Many people (wrongly) think that plotting a romance novel is simply a matter of Boy Meets Girl, Boy Loses Girl, Boy Gets Girl Back. While that may indeed be the romance plot laid bare, the way in which "Boy Loses Girl" provides endless options for conflict and character development. Master these two concepts and you'll be writing romance novels that capture a reader's heart and a publisher's attention, whatever your genre — from Regency to paranormal, category to mainstream.

**Make your characters real...**

At its most fundamental, a romance novel tells the story of the main characters' journey, or development, from the people they are at the novel's opening to the changed people they become at its closing. The author's objective is to guide the hero and heroine along the rocky path of romance until they can walk believably off into the rest of their lives — happy and together.

Conflict refers to the obstacles that each character faces along that path. If there's no conflict, there's no reason why the hero and heroine can't fall into each other's arms by the end of chapter one. Nice idea, but not much of a book. Instead, the conflict works against the attraction that the two characters feel, providing reasons for them to resist it.

**Conflict is not just a misunderstanding...**

A word to the wise here. Conflict is most definitely not just a misunderstanding. If the "conflict" can be resolved by a straightforward conversation between the characters, it's not strong enough. Trust us.

Instead, conflict arises from either external or internal sources. External conflict might see the character dealing with a situation (Julie is working to put herself through law school) or another person (Robert is fighting to bring a crooked politician to justice). Internal conflict — the most powerful kind — comes from within the characters themselves (Robert hates lies but must lie to Julie to protect her). As the characters resolve each obstacle, and eventually each conflict, they'll eliminate every reason to stay apart ... which provides the happy ending.

While external conflicts provide useful plot twists and motivations for the two characters to be either thrown together or pulled apart (Julie's job is executive assistant to Robert's crooked-politician target), internal conflicts more effectively sustain the emotional roller coaster that is romance.

That's because character development depends largely on how the characters react to the obstacles created by various conflicts, especially internal conflicts.

Characters begin their journey with a particular view of themselves. This view may not match the view that other people have of them, and the difference between the two often gives the reader the sharpest insight into the character growth to come. For example, others might view Julie as a confident, perhaps even cool, career woman; she, however, might see herself as too emotional, choosing to hide this "flaw" by acting confident and unemotional.

**Keep in mind that human beings tend to resist change...**

To achieve character growth, the story may force her to rely on her emotions (trusting Robert, even though he lied), thus creating an internal conflict and raising questions about how she sees herself. Keeping in mind that human beings naturally tend to resist change, the most powerful internal conflict arises when characters are finally forced to reassess who they believe they are (Julie realizes that she can, and should, trust her emotions).

So how do you create conflict strong enough to sustain the book?

The key is to deeply motivate your characters and your conflict, so that you — and your readers — understand the reasons for the characters' behaviour and the reasons characters change. You can achieve this with just one word: Why?

Many how-to-write-fiction books recommend drafting a background sheet for your characters, listing everything from physical attributes such as eye colour to key events in their pasts. This can help you develop your characters, but it's much more valuable if you ask, Why?

Imagine, for example, that Julie's favourite colour is azure. Why? Does she appreciate its calming, cooling effect? Keep going. Why? Does she feel her life is chaotic? Why? Has she taken on too many tasks in her drive to become a lawyer? Why? And why is she so driven?

As you answer each successive question, you'll delve deeper into your characters, gaining insight into their motivations, their fears and their flaws. All of these determine how characters react to situations, to other people and to conflicts within themselves. You'll see where characters need to grow, and you'll see exactly which situations and people will force them to reassess themselves and achieve that growth.

**Make your characters sound real...**

Once you've created deeply motivated characters, how do you make them live and breathe like real people? Through details. Describing a hero as a "successful businessman" sounds one-dimensional. But start adding details, and he can become unique, individual and memorable.

Perhaps the hero is a jazz fan who doodles during business meetings and needles his secretary to give up smoking. These details help distinguish him from other people in the book, but they can also reveal character. For instance, perhaps he grew up in New Orleans (jazz), wanted to be a cartoonist (doodling) and saw his sister die young of lung cancer (smoking).

**Reveal character through dialogue...**

Two of the most effective ways to reveal character details are through dialogue (which adds interest and energy to the story) and through narrative (which grounds the characters in a particular place and situation).

Let's look at this revealing dialogue.

"If you're gonna fly off the handle over every little thing, ma'am, there's about as much use talkin' to you as talkin' to a mule," Robert muttered.

"I did not 'fly off the handle', Mr. Carson," Julie replied. "I was merely stating the facts of the situation as I perceived them."

Robert's drawl ("gonna") and references ("talkin' to a mule") show that he's a down-to-earth guy, maybe a cowboy. Julie's more formal words ("Mr. Carson" and "perceived"), on the other hand, show that she may be better educated than Robert ... and, perhaps, a bit prissy.

Bring everything you know about your characters into the dialogue: their social position, their attitudes, their fears. It can be helpful to give each major character a verbal "tic," a word or way of speaking that only that person uses.

Think about Chandler's character on *Friends*. Fans familiar with his speech patterns would immediately recognize a line like, "Could I be any dumber?" as his. Not only does Chandler say, "Could I be..." often, but he is also the show's most self-deprecating character.

As well as differentiating characters, verbal tics help you avoid overusing dialogue "tags," or the text following a bit of dialogue, such as "Julie muttered," that tells readers who is speaking.

Consider this conversation.

"Where ya goin'?" Robert asked.

Julie mumbled, "It's none of your business."

"Don't be so sneaky," Robert said.

"Please stop interrogating me!" Julie cried.

All those tags get a bit monotonous and yank readers out of the story. They make reading more like watching a tennis game than listening to a real conversation. Word choice alone ("goin' " and "interrogating") can help your readers figure out who is speaking.

**Reveal character through narrative...**

But characterization involves more than dialogue. It also involves the way people act and the way they respond to their surroundings, which you can reveal in narrative.

Romances, more than most types of novels, are stories of emotions. Readers want to experience the story along with the characters. Showing your readers how a character feels is a much more effective way to help them do this than telling them. Consider these two passages.

Example #1: Julie was outraged that Robert had betrayed her, but she was terrified to discuss it with him.

Example #2: As Julie thought of Robert's betrayal, she had to force her hands not to clench into fists. With stiff fingers, she straightened a pile of magazines on the coffee table and adjusted the angle of a picture before turning to confront him.

In the first passage, the author tells us that Julie is "outraged" and "terrified." In the second passage, she shows us Julie's outrage (she wants to clench her fists) and terror (her nervous movements about the room).

**Use narrative to bring the setting alive...**

You can also use narrative to bring the setting alive, which helps make your characters more real by allowing them to react to their surroundings. By using all five senses, you can again draw readers into the emotions of the story. For example:

Julie inhaled the subtle, woodsy scent of his aftershave. His stubbled cheek was rough against hers.

"Do you want to talk about it?" he asked, his voice as comforting as honey. She heard a soft clink as he put his glass down on the table.

She shook her head, leaned back and looked at him, at the craggy, wind-worn face that had become so dear to her. Then she kissed him, slowly teasing the last drops of whiskey from his lips.

Concrete details in dialogue or in narrative, woven into a story with three-dimensional characters and believable conflict, can make your characters leap off the page and into readers' hearts.

—

Laura Byrne Paquet is an Ottawa writer/editor who writes Regency romances for Kensington Publishing in New York, as well as freelance magazine and newspaper articles.

Yvonne Jeffery Hope is a Canadian freelance writer/editor whose specialties include editing romantic fiction. Her current home is Cyprus, legendary island of Aphrodite, goddess of love.

# Getting Away with Murder: A Short Course on Mystery Writing

*by Janice MacDonald*

Here is a quick and easy introduction to the formula of mystery fiction in general. This is akin to a recipe for no-fail brownies. While you will turn out brownies each time with this formula, in order to win the bake-off, you're really going to have to add something of your own. The only warning is, don't tinker too much with the recipe. One or two tweaks per product will work, too many and you may end up with a bodice-ripping western, or (oh, the horror) a mainstream novel.

There are two ways to raise your genre novel out of the morass of all that has gone before. Create a believable and fascinating *detective* (your hero, and the character with whom your readers will identify) and conjure up a vision of a new *setting* in which to situate your plots. Plots themselves are secondary (when all is said and done, they've all been done before). This is not necessarily a bad thing. Your reader knows what to expect, is already halfway to becoming your "ideal reader" and is more able to jump right into your world as a result. What follows are some of the ingredients essential to the recipe.

### The detective

Your detective should be/have:

a) a loner

This is necessary to ensure the believability of your mystery. For one thing, the detective must necessarily be the "other" to allow him/her objectivity on the scene. There will also come a time when your detective will need to put himself in grave personal physical danger. You will lose your reader's sympathy immediately if your character is walking into a bullet at the same time she is supposed to be picking the kids up from an after-school program. If you *have* to give your detective a spouse, make sure the significant other has a good job, so that if your detective dies in the line of action, her husband will mourn, but not starve.

b) curious

The best way to show that your detective is the curious sort, the terrier type of person who just *has* to know the answer, is to put her in a job/career that seems to attract curious types. Make your detective a photojournalist, a scientist, a researcher, a librarian, a graduate student, a trained reader of some sort ... you get the idea. Not only will readers accept your detective as the sort who will pursue the quest; these jobs will also often lead to interesting plots.

c) abilities and resources

Consider your detective's *job*. Will it allow time out to go solve a puzzle? Is the mystery on site? Can the mystery take place over a weekend? Or a summer holiday? Is your detective independently wealthy? There is so much that is distinctly "unbelievable" in mystery novels (how many people trip over seven bodies a week?) that anything you can centre in reality is a great comfort for your readers.

Your detective has to be *strong*. She will be in great personal danger at some point in the novel. Make her strong, healthy, in shape. If you have her jogging regularly, or taking a dance course, the suggestion that she can endure a swim in icy water, or high kick a gun away, or wriggle out of constraints will be easier to absorb.

Think of hobbies and skills that will help. Is he a computer whiz? Can she read lips? Does he understand Latvian? Not all these traits will be necessary in each novel, but laying the groundwork now can be helpful.

Friends of your detective will be useful. All detectives should have one pal in either the police or Department of Motor Vehicles. Lawyers and research librarian friends also come in handy. If you want a really violent world, a doctor may be a good person to include.

d) a sense of morality

This doesn't mean they have to volunteer to teach Sunday School. However, in the words of Chandler, your detective has to be the "best man for his world, and a good enough man for any world." We have to know that, if offered a bribe by the bad'uns, she won't accept it.

e) needs to find the solution

To avoid your detective being seen as some sort of snoopy voyeur, you need to find a means by which he is impelled to find the solution. In police or private eye novels, this is easy: detectives are hired to do the job. They need the money, and have to move forward.

If your detective is a "gifted amateur," then the best way to have him continue is to make him either a suspect, or have someone he cares for be a suspect. If the police have determined that they have "who dunnit," then no one else is looking for the real culprit. Alternately, if the detective or someone she cares about is in danger, then she has to proceed with the investigation regardless of the danger.

f) intelligence

This character is going to solve a puzzle. Help people believe that he *can* do it. There is a curious paradox involved in reading mysteries whereby, while the readers want to solve the puzzle, they don't want to solve it themselves. If the detective is an idiot but solves a tremendously complex puzzle, it insults the readers' intelligence (this is *not* a good thing if you want to sell more books). This is often why there are side-kicks for the principle character, to give the reader someone to feel superior to (e.g. Watson, Hastings, Archie, Bunter).

**The victim**

There are three possible victims to create.

1. The victim should be someone the reader cannot stand. Snarky Uncle George who arrives at the family reunion, insults seventeen people in fifteen pages and then appears dead — face down in the fruit punch in chapter three. The reader can then say, "Tut tut, the game's afoot," and get on with the puzzle at hand. No mourning required.

2. The victim should be someone likeable but not too well-known. The reader isn't given time enough to identify with the victim, although she likes him/her enough to want vengeance/justice. Grief levels are moderately low.

3. The victim must never be a child. This is a mystery, not a slasher novel. If you want to write horror, kill seven children immediately and float them down a sewer drain. Kill a child in a mystery, and you risk losing your audience immediately. The concept of "game" goes out the window and your reader just gets sad. If your plot requires that you *must* kill a child, do it third or fourth in a long line. Ensure it comes well after your reader has identified with your detective and trusts him to return justice to the land.

**The villain**

In most cases, your villain will be the murderer. If by chance you decide that your murderer is a victim of society, give your detective someone else to truly hate in the narrative. An idiotic boss or overlord of some sort.

1. The murderer should be intelligent. He/she, after all, is presenting a seemingly insurmountable puzzle for your detective and reader. Make your villain worthy of the conundrum.

2. Decide early on whether your villain is amoral or immoral. This may dictate how many bodies you stack up. Remember, an immoral person knows that something is wrong, but decides to do it anyway. An

amoral person (serial killer, for instance) believes that rules are made for others, and just does whatsoever he or she pleases.

3. Somehow, you should present a flawed ego in your murderer. They might seem meek and mild, but they always press their trousers just so, or wear a flower in their lapel, or polish the undersides of their shoes. After all, it is the most egotistical thing in the world to consider taking another's life ... this has to appear somewhere in their psychological makeup to help the reader believe they are capable of the crime.

**The clues**

The etymology of the word "clue" comes from a Greek fable wherein Ariadne gave Theseus a "clew" of thread (one of those huge spools like they use on sergers) to tie to the opening of the Minotaur's labyrinth and reel out as he went in order to find his way back. That is what we give our readers, a maze to find their way through. However, we needn't (and this is a failing of novice mystery writers who are terribly intent on "playing fair") light the clues in neon for our readers. In fact, our readers really wish we wouldn't. The best place to salt a lot of clues is right at the beginning, when the reader is still trying desperately to find our rhythm, learn the characters' names and determine the "lay of the fictional land."

Dot clues sporadically, especially if your detective is communicating in the first person to the reader. Make it look like she is getting somewhere. The very best place to put a clue is upside down, hidden in a cluttered drawer, right next to a juicy "red herring" (see below). Remember though, play fair ... the clues should all be there.

**The Red Herrings**

Here is some more fascinating etymology that you can cast out at the next boring dinner party, where I can guarantee that you will be met with some amazing rejoinder like, "Pass the cauliflower, please."

Whatever. "Red herring" is the term used for false clues.

Centuries ago, when the gentry decided to call several dozen close personal friends down to their country estates, they would hold a Hunt as part of the lavish entertainment. Now, most of the countryside would be informed of this event beforehand so they could be hired in as extra help. The evening before the Hunt, reynardophiles (fox lovers) would wander about the countryside armed with three-day-old (or "red") fish, wiping said fish on trees, rocks, pathways, etc. The next morning, the hounds would get confused by the scent and go baying off in all directions, and the fox would be safe for another time.

Red herrings in mystery novels are either gloriously shiny and interesting "things" found next to rather drab real clues, or they are other suspects in the plot. Face it, everyone will have something to hide and, if pressed, at least half will lie about it. People don't lie just because they are murderers. Sometimes they just have something innocuous to hide, like a predilection for countryside animals. However, if a person is caught out in a lie, there is a very good chance your reader is going to finger that suspect as the murderer and follow his trail as your detective wanders off to corner the real fox ... I mean killer.

Red herrings can be a great deal of fun, but remember, you have to explain everything away to the reader's satisfaction by the end of the narrative, so don't get too carried away.

### The setting

This is the second-most-important part of your contribution to the genre. In mystery novels there are two forms of *setting* to consider. The first is the locale in which you situate your detective, the territory which you stake out as your own. (Hint: the Navaho Reservation, Alaska, and northern Alberta are all taken ... go find your own).

The second form of setting you need to consider is a closed environment. This is essential to a mystery novel and why so many have been located on trains, airplanes, cruise ships, and snowed-in ski resorts. You needn't limit yourself to these tired ways of corralling your villain though. Today, you can look to a specialized field of endeavour. If only seven people in the city could have committed the crime with their knowledge of a mass spectrometer ... and one of them has winged it to Brazil, chances are you know who the killer is. Closed environments make for a better read, giving the readers inside knowledge of a world they might ordinarily not be privy to.

And, most of all, never apologize or get flustered when someone accosts you and says, "When are you going to write a real book?" Agatha Christie, bless her li'l cotton socks, still outsells Saul Bellow.

—

Janice MacDonald's detective series set in Edmonton, Alberta features Randy Craig, whom some folks claim is very much like the author herself. Janice insists that she is slimmer, and, of course, Janice is happily married with two lovely children.

# Editing and Selling the "Scientist as Hero" Novel

*by Deborah Cannon*

Look inside any bookstore, and you will see a growing trend in popular fiction. Novels written by academics about academics. Witness Kathy Reichs' *Déjà Dead* or Elizabeth Peters' Amelia Peabody mysteries, the former a forensic anthropologist and the latter an Egyptologist. If you own an appropriate academic background, you may have already written this kind of book. But before you "Express Post" your submission to an unsuspecting publisher, learn to be your own critic. Scientists who write novels about scientists are compelled to be autobiographical, and autobiography doesn't always make good fiction. Assuming that the reading public is as enamoured of your subject as you are can also make the manuscript read like a textbook rather than a novel. So edit and re-edit your work. Don't presume your academic credentials make you an expert in writing fiction. Seek advice from creative writing courses, writer's groups and professional manuscript reading services. Judicious revision will minimize your chances of rejection.

As with any first novel, it is wise to check for verbiage. It is hard enough for an unknown writer to get the attention of a busy editor or agent without burdening them with extra reading. Unless you really need 300,000 words to tell your story, pare it down. I was asked to cut my first novel by 20 percent.

**What kind of novel is it?**

At one time I might have answered: an archaeology novel.

A mystery about archaeology, leaning towards a romance. Or was it a thriller? With a bit of the supernatural. If you write in a commercial genre, you must learn the rules of your genre — and the genre must be clear. When it comes time to sell there must be no doubt as to what kind of book it is. If you have trouble deciding, ask yourself: What is the story about? A novel pitting archaeologists against big business makes a better thriller than a romance.

During the process of revision, and with the help of a savvy agent, my manuscript was often returned to me marked, "Too much archaeology."

If you want to keep your readers gripped, eliminate dialogue in your writing that sounds like this:

"Deer?" Jake asked.

"Elk, I think." Angeline scrutinized the faunal fragment, twisting and turning it, put it down, and picked up another piece. "Here's a humerus."

"How about these?" He stirred some porous chunks of bone that lay on the counter. "Sea lion?"

"Too fragmented to tell. Could be, or could be harbour seal. This one's definitely a juvenile though. See?" She indicated the soft unformed distal end of a femur. "It's an unfused epiphysis. Seal pup."

The conversation is technical, and for such a short passage is loaded with jargon. Archaeologists may talk like this in real life, but real life is boring. It takes discipline to strike the perfect balance between stimulating and mundane. Science is not fascinating unless you have interesting characters in a compelling story (remember, this is fiction). On the other hand, don't overdramatize. Cultivate serious nuances in your writing. In Peter Benchley's classic thriller, *Jaws*, the author used a Great White shark to terrorize the folk of a small town, but he also embraced a universal theme: When people offend nature, nature takes revenge.

Beware of lecturing:

"I know what you mean," Katherine said. "Though I'm not a collector myself, I have several books on Native art."

"Holm's *Northwest Coast Indian Art*?"

Katherine lowered her wine glass. "Why, yes. Do you have *Native Arts of the Pacific Northwest*? If you're looking for a popular book, *Looking at Indian Art of the Northwest Coast* is easy reading."

**The middle of a novel is no place for a bibliography.**

If your plot is character-driven, make sure she (he?) is unforgettable. Draw on life. If your scientist is modelled on you, make her realistic, but give her an identifying trait. Temperance Brennan, Kathy Reichs' forensic anthropologist, is an on-the-wagon alcoholic. Elizabeth Peters' Amelia Peabody is a turn-of-the-twentieth-century Egyptologist, married with grown children, who takes her family on all of her expeditions.

The most popular stories are often those that strike at our darkest fears. Kathy Reichs hit a nerve with her avenging serial killer in *Déjà Dead*. Michael Crichton's *Jurassic Park*, superficially a tale of dinosaurs on the rampage, raised a global dilemma: Can science without ethics destroy the world? Ideas that are universally recognized have universal appeal.

An editor once sent me a rejection slip that said, "This story just doesn't work for me."

Analyzing films in your genre is a good way to see how and why stories work. *Raiders of the Lost Ark* and *Allan Quartermain and the Lost City of Gold* are action/adventure. *Raiders* grabs you from the opening with a strong character — Indiana Jones; an interesting story idea — the search for the lost Ark; tension — each encounter with the enemy brings him closer to his goal; and human drama — a sexually charged relationship with a female cohort. *Quartermain* bores you silly. It lacks suspense, interest, and emotion. *Raiders of the Lost Ark* is high entertainment, but at the same time, subtly suggests that some things in the world are not meant for human understanding. *Quartermain* sends its heroes off to be chased, shot at, and boiled in a giant pot by irate natives for no comprehensible reason. A story is more effective if it has a clear theme. And the plot must always make sense.

According to a British survey one person in ten thinks they can write a book, and one in fifty have already done so. Assuming this holds true in Canada and the U.S., the competition is formidable. Canadian presses rarely publish popular fiction. That means your best chance is south of the border. Most American publishers require the author to be represented by a literary agent, so if you already have a manuscript, look for an agent who sells commercial fiction and who will work in an editorial capacity with you. Agents who devote time to developing writers charge a fee, but if you find someone who will stick with you, it will be worth the expense. Valuable criticisms of your manuscript can be obtained from writers' groups, reading services, and writing classes, but it is an agent's business to know the market.

—

Deborah Cannon is an archaeologist and museologist. She is published by Simon Fraser University's Archaeology Press and the *Canadian Journal of Archaeology*. She has written several short stories, completed two novels, and is working on a third.

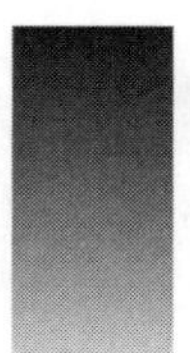

# Science Fiction

*by Robert J. Sawyer*

Science fiction is a genre in which Canadian writers are having international success, but unless you follow the rules, you're doomed to failure.

First, science fiction literature has nothing to do with what you see on TV and in the movies. For one thing, printed SF is a largely character-driven genre, devoid of the simplistic heroes and villains of *Star Wars*. For another, SF is a literature of *ideas*. Although there is a place for mindless action-adventure, good SF is usually *about* something (and often something very profound, such as whether or not God exists).

Second, science fiction and fantasy are radically different — indeed, antithetical — genres. There is always a way to get from our here and now to the setting of any science fiction story (usually by making reasonable advances in science and technology as time marches on); there is never a way to get from our real world to the setting of a fantasy story (magic simply doesn't work in our universe).

Third, science fiction is a largely pro-science genre. Although Vancouver's William Gibson is right when he says the job of the SF writer is to be "profoundly ambivalent about changes in science and technology," printed SF rarely takes the anti-science stance of Michael Crichton's *Jurassic Park*. Nor does it embrace the paranoia and credulous acceptance of the supernatural that underlies *The X-Files*.

### The science must be accurate...

Fourth, the science in printed SF must be accurate. In *Star Wars*, Han Solo could talk about parsecs as a unit of time (rather than distance), and about "making the jump to light-speed" (the one thing Einstein prohibits is traveling *at* the speed of light); those gaffes would spell instant rejection from a print SF market. Still, nonscientists write much of the best science fiction. To keep up to date, read the magazines *Discover, New Scientist*, and *Science News*, and watch Discovery Channel Canada's nightly science newscast, *@discovery.ca*.

Fifth, science fiction, although sometimes a medium of stylistic experimentation, is usually told in either third-person limited narration (following the point of view, and knowing the thoughts of, one character per scene), or first-person (unlike some fields, there is no taboo in SF against first-person narrative).

**Readership is split between men and women...**

Note, too, that SF is an *adult* literature: strong language, explicit sex, and graphic violence are acceptable if required by the story. Readership (and authorship) is evenly split between men and women.

Mystery writers complain that U.S. publishers are prejudiced against Canadian settings. That's not true in SF. The works of Terence M. Green, Nalo Hopkinson, Spider Robinson, and myself are all published by major New York houses, yet revel in their Canadian settings.

If you're scratching your head and saying, "How can SF possibly take place in Canada — isn't it all set on alien planets and spaceships or in the far future?" you haven't done your homework. The only way to write SF successfully is to read it. An excellent "SF 101" course would be to read all the Hugo- and Nebula-winning novels, as well as the annual reprint anthologies *The Year's Best Science Fiction* edited by Gardner Dozois (St. Martin's) and *Year's Best SF* edited by David G. Hartwell (Eos).

Not only do American publishers routinely buy Canadian-authored SF, but you should in fact turn to them as your first choice. Most major U.S. publishers have SF imprints (Ace and Roc at Penguin, Aspect at Warner, Del Rey at Random House, Eos at HarperCollins, and Spectra at Doubleday), and there are significant publishers that do nothing but SF (and fantasy): the giant Tor, and smaller Baen and DAW. Advances for North American rights to first novels usually range from U.S. $2,500 to U.S. $7,500; successful mid-career novelists can get between U.S. $20,000 and U.S. $50,000 up front; the biggest names slide into six figures per book.

The only Canadian publishers regularly doing SF are small, specialty presses, with advances in the Cdn $500 to Cdn $1,000 range, and little chance of earning royalties beyond that. Canadian presses that have had success with SF include Bakka, Edge, Pottersfield, Quarry, and Tesseract.

Although many unpublished authors have cracked the U.S. novel market with over-the-transom submissions, the standard career path is to first sell short fiction (at 5 to 8 cents U.S. a word) to the genre's digest-sized American magazines (*Analog Science Fiction and Fact*, *Asimov's Science Fiction*, and *The Magazine of Fantasy & Science Fiction*), or one of the "semiprozines" (semi-professional magazines, lower in pay and circulation), such as *Absolute Magnitude*. The only Canadian SF magazine whose contents are noted by American editors is Edmonton's *On Spec*.

Short fiction sales can help you land one of the two dozen New York agents who handle the bulk of SF (don't get a Canadian agent for this field). But even if you don't have an agent, your novel manuscript will be read by most publishers, although response time may be up to a year, and simultaneous submissions aren't allowed.

There is a lot of e-publishing at the fringes of SF, but almost none of it is taken seriously. And speaking of not being taken seriously, don't try to break in by doing tie-in novels based on SF TV shows, movies, or games. These are considered hackwork, and, besides, are generally open only to *experienced* hacks ...

**Online news sources...**

Canadian SF writers have two advocacy groups, neither overly effective. The Canadian Region of the Science Fiction and Fantasy Writers of America (SFWA) has more stringent membership requirements and offers several publications. SF Canada's main service is a listserve. Many pros do fine without belonging to either group; all the news you need can be found on the SFWA news site (www.sfwa.org/news) and at *Locus Online* (www.locusmag.com), the web counterpart of one of the field's two trade journals (the other is *Science Fiction Chronicle*).

Face-to-face networking is still the best way to meet SF writers and editors, and to hear industry gossip. There are annual science fiction conventions in most regions of Canada, including V-Con in Vancouver, ConVersion in Calgary, KeyCon in Winnipeg, Ad Astra in Toronto, Can-Con in Ottawa, and Con*Cept in Montreal.

Canada has two SF awards, the venerable Aurora (voted on by readers) and the nascent, juried Sunburst.

Information on Canadian SF can be found at Made in Canada: The Homepage for Canadian Science Fiction (www.geocities.com/canadian_sf); the SF Canada homepage (www.sfcanada.ca); and my own Canadian Science Fiction Index (www.sfwriter.com/caindex.htm). The principal reference works on Canadian SF are *Northern Dreamers* by Edo van Belkom (Quarry, 1998), and *Dictionary of Literary Biography 251: Canadian Science Fiction and Fantasy Authors* (Gale, 2001).

—

Robert J. Sawyer's 13 SF novels include the Nebula Award-winner *The Terminal Experiment*, the national best seller *Calculating God*, and the just-released *Hominids*. He lives in Mississauga, Ontario. Visit his website at sfwriter.com.

# Autobiography to Fiction: Getting There from Here

*by Barbara Turner-Vesselago*

"The real truth is one thing, and the literary truth is another, and there is nothing more difficult than to want both truths to coincide," writes Mario Vargas Llosa in *A Writer's Reality*. But why should that be so, beginning writers keep demanding. Why can't I just write about what I've experienced, as vividly as possible, and *call* it fiction? I can change the "I" to "he" or "she" if I have to. What's the difference? Isn't fiction often just thinly disguised autobiography? Aren't writers always being told to "write what you know?"

Those writers would be hard put to find practical answers to their questions in the essays that most well-known fiction writers write about fiction. Vargas Llosa is typical. Having asserted an absolute distinction between life and literature, he then rambles around throwing out equally forceful but oddly unconnected statements: "the truths that come out of literature are never the truths personally experienced by the writer;" "the novel is ... created out of fantasy;" "you must lie without any scruples;" and, "you must not shrink from the idea of distorting or manipulating reality." As if lying about or distorting one's experience were not a very different thing from refraining from using it at all.

### Let them meet and they destroy each other...

Virginia Woolf also made a point of insisting, throughout her writing career, on the distinction between *truth* and *fiction*. They are "granite" and "rainbow," "let them meet and they destroy each other." But when she too tries to pin down just how they differ for the writer, she becomes either contradictory (the two categories soon slide into each other, just as they did for Vargas Llosa) or coy: the writer must retreat to "that solitary room, whose door the critics are forever trying to unlock" and subject his experience to "those mysterious processes by which life becomes, like the Chinese coat, able to stand by itself — a sort of impersonal miracle."

As readers, we all know that autobiography differs from fiction. An autobiography is always primarily referent to life ("this really did happen," we tell ourselves as we read), while a work of fiction refers above all to itself (the gun produced in the opening scene goes off at the climax and our expectations are met — or not met — in ways that we find satisfactory, given what went before). We identify with the characters in a work of fiction differently. Instead of finding out about someone else's life as we read, we seem instead to become that other person.

But as writers, we still need a straight answer to the question: How do we achieve that "impersonal miracle?" How do we transcend our own experience and write fiction that does not have to be supported by the assumption that "this really did happen," but is fully able, as Virginia Woolf puts it, "to stand by itself?"

**Learn, through writing, to become detached...**

In my view, one of the best ways you can do that is to begin by writing about *your own* experience. Not only can you acquire many of the skills you need in order to create a fully absorbing and self-sufficient world in the process, but you can also learn, through writing, to become detached from that world in a way that is essential if you are to allow it to become a world that other people can inhabit.

My own understanding of how that process is best undertaken (and consequently of the whole relationship of autobiography to fiction) comes from 20 years of teaching "freefall" — a method of writing first proposed by W.O. Mitchell. This I have analyzed, streamlined, and to some degree reinvented as the need arose.

In this way of writing, writers are told to "write what comes up for them," without any preconception of what it is they're going to write about. Ninety-five percent of the time, what does come up for them is autobiographical. If they can observe Mitchell's "ten-year rule" (i.e. favour material that is more than ten years old); if they can muster the self-discipline not to change what they write (a task surprisingly more difficult than it sounds); if they can follow Mitchell's instruction to enter into all the sensuous detail that is in it — how things felt, tasted, smelled, looked, and sounded; and above all, I have found, if they can muster the courage to go *fearward* (to keep pushing the edge of what they *don't* want to write about), their work quickly begins to take on many of the qualities of good fiction. The predominant mode of writing shifts from referring to experience (telling) to evoking it on the page (showing), vivid and engaging scenes open up, and the reader becomes immersed in the perspective of one of the writer's past selves. Thus the "vivid, continuous dream," as John Gardner calls the fictional world, is created and sustained.

For writers, these skills are invaluable, and I believe that they are much more easily learned in this way than in any other.

But for those who want to write fiction, further skills still need to be acquired. Because their material has its roots in autobiography, writers who learn to write in this way must also be able to disengage from that material, or they will never let it find its own shape as fiction. For one thing, they must begin to allow themselves not only to identify with one character (inspired, quite possibly, by some past self or understanding), as they did in life, but also to function as the narrator — the one who has created and understands *all* the characters involved in the story. That kind of split focus is essential, since the point of view of any one character, however passionately held, can never function as more than a part of that greater whole.

**There is a new life to be served...**

Another essential skill is the ability to let go of the structure of events as they happened, in order to allow them to serve the needs of the narrative. For fully developed scenes to emerge and build to a climax, the fundamentally episodic structure of life ("this happened, and then this happened, and then this") will probably have to give way to a causal one ("this happened because of this, and led to this"). Instead of being important because they happened to the *writer*, events now become important because of their relationship to one another. Any desire on the writer's part to be seen and known must be jettisoned. There is a new life to be served now: the life of the story.

Fortunately for the writer, this *detachment* seems to arise, if we let it, not as the result of any arid, intellectual decision, but as a natural outcome of the experience of writing.

The "ten-year rule" yields the first experience of that kind of double-vision: it's not hard, in writing, to see the world from the perspective of a long-past self, yet remain aware, as we write, that we are not that person now. Add to this the necessity of "showing" in writing what in life we would "tell," and the engaging — though demanding — attention to specific, sensuous detail that doing so requires, and for most people, the larger viewpoint of the all-embracing narrator emerges unbidden. Thus another layer of detachment is laid down, almost without our noticing it.

Finally, and most important of all in my view, the more we write, the more the fundamental experience of "going fearward" evolves, too. What began as an inner imperative to choose (when the choice comes up) to write about experiences we don't want to write about, becomes the far more perilous one to write without knowing what will come up at all — writing in the state of creative willingness that Ursula LeGuin has called “the only thing that makes life possible” — “permanent, intolerable uncertainty: not knowing what comes next.”

It is then that the really startling magic of writing begins. Things that seemed random or absurd when they occurred, now show their logic: a dog, for instance, which turned up on page three proves vital to the action on page 10; the old sled we couldn’t make a character stop thinking of becomes a central symbol.

It is only at this stage that the kind of knowing which seems to come from some place larger than our normal thinking minds can begin to enter, and writing becomes a perpetual process of discovering what’s there. Perhaps it is in this place that what Vargos Llosa calls “literary truth” is generated. But “real truth,” in my opinion, is the best way to get there from here.

—

Barbara Turner-Vesselago is the author of *Skelton at Sixty* (Porcupine’s Quill), *Freefall: Writing Without a Parachute* (The Writing Space) and *No News But Kindness*, a finalist for the (cancelled) 2001 Chapters/Robertson Davies Book Prize. She teaches Freefall Writing Workshops in Canada, the United States, England and Australia. www.freefallwriting.com.

# There Is No Such Thing As Altruism!

*by R.G. Condie*

This always causes arguments in groups of listeners, but ask any advertiser. Self-gain is the single most consistently identifiable motivation. And the most manipulative.

Why would this be of interest to the writer? Because this is a fundamental human behaviour, it must be the cornerstone of character building. Good fiction requires unexpected human actions or reactions. It requires realistic reactions to unusual outside forces and stimuli.

When the heroine in a Romance novel throws herself at the hero, he must decline her offering for at least 200 pages. Hormones and glands and libido being what they are, the writer must provide a believable reason. The writer must identify and explain the hero's personal gain for flying in the face of natural inclinations. How well the writer succeeds, tells us how well the book will be received.

When our mild-mannered young hero turns to mass murder, we, as writers, had better offer an identifiable and acceptable personal gain for his actions, or our hero becomes a villain.

When our high-powered executive bows to corporate manipulation, the reader wants to know what he or she gains, even if only temporarily.

Good fiction requires that we take an identifiable human animal, place him or her in harm's way, and chronicle the results. The more the reader can identify and empathize with our hero, the better the acceptance of our story.

—

R.G. Condie, author, columnist, journalist, and editor, is a published writer whose nonfiction, fiction, and poetry has appeared in a wide variety of books, magazines, and newspapers. His *Psychology for Writers* was sold to America House Publishers. He was CAA's first Writer-in-Residence.

# 7. Children & Young Adults

# Reclaiming the Wonder: Writing for Children & Other Intelligent People

*by Alison Lohans*

*Writing is a reflexive activity that involves the totality of our physical and mental being. To write means to write myself, not in a narcissistic sense but in a deep collective sense. To write phenomenologically is the untiring effort to author a sensitive grasp of being itself — of that which authors us, of that which makes it possible for us to be and speak...in the first place.*

(Max van Manen, 1994, in *Researching Lived Experience*, p. 132)

Max van Manen, whose quote I've borrowed, is probably little-known in writers' circles. A professor at the University of Alberta, his speciality is phenomenological research methods in the field of education. Philosophical writings on research may seem way out of scope for those of us who write "creatively" — yet looking more closely, we may find we're talking about some of the same things. Van Manen considers writing a crucial aspect of coming to understand a "life question," a way of giving it voice. In this sense *all* writing, including literary exploration, becomes a form of "research." And isn't this exactly what we do as we find things out, as we grow during the writing process and emerge a changed person as the result of having written something?

## Connect with a feeling of wonder...

I think it's important for writers to be able to connect with a feeling of wonder — beyond that sense of excitement or delight which hits us with the initial *bang!* of an idea. Then we must continue to express the feeling as we proceed into the narrative. What I'm getting at is the spirit of *play* that each of us knows, and which keeps us at this peculiar occupation that gives very little in the way of financial reward for the huge amount of work that we actually do. So many barriers can stand in our way. Writing becomes a job; we come to the conclusion that we write because this is what we do, and we're good at it. And sometimes we remember that it's a lot of fun. How *do* we reclaim the wonder, that freshness, year after year?

## Barriers...

At times this whole business of writing feels like trying to break though a multi-layered wall. There's the rejection-slip treadmill we all know so well, and often not enough uninterrupted time to plunge deeply into the creative part of our work. With tangible success — a new book in hand — comes a new assortment of barriers. Our huge investment of time and self is subjected to the uncertainties of promotion. There are negative reviews or, worse, insidious quiet neglect — those ugly, blank silences when we wonder if we will "get our turn." Worse still is the roller coaster ride of marketing that is too often driven by central-office orders, by corporate powers that have the clout to put writers and publishers alike out of business. Royalties go unpaid; wonderful books that took years to write are too-quickly remaindered, or allowed to go out of print. This is brutal stuff, and it's sometimes hard enough to hang onto a sense of personal validity, let alone the wonder. If we try putting a dollar-value to the worth of our dreams, our craft and art, cynicism oozes into the mix. Things can get kind of messy.

They get even messier when "genre games" come into play. Childhood tends to be devalued in this society, and there is a common perception that our books, written for "less important" people, shouldn't be taken as seriously as those written for adults (after all, "it's just a little book; it can't possibly have been hard to write"). Two-time Governor General's Award winner Julie Johnston probably shocked polite literary society several years ago when she spoke up at the awards ceremony about "being allowed to read along with all the grownup writers;" however, her point is well made. Children's writers aren't the only ones who are given short shrift in this unevenly stacked deck. Nobody likes being pigeonholed as "lesser" on the basis of what we choose to write. Or what calls to us to be written.

## Creative stance...

Writing is about creating timeless moments, or, perhaps, *re*-creating those moments: the stilled sensory "experiencing" when we truly perceive or apprehend with an uncluttered mind. It's about evoking the authentic, the aesthetic, about calling up primal names (and the unnamed) from our innermost self, which is probably most accessible when left-brain thinking shuts off. Call it a willing suspension of disbelief; call it wonderment. W.O. Mitchell's *Who Has Seen the Wind?* comes immediately to mind as a powerful example.

Fictional writing is also about creating movement. It's about change and growth, about logic used as a tool to craft a convincing narrative by gathering, sorting, and re-clustering selected moments (and silences) in a skilled sequence which adheres to the rhythms of plot. Include in this mix a generous dose of human empathy, manifested in believable characters. And, of course, avid curiosity.

Good writing for children (and other intelligent people) includes all of the above.

Good writing for children is a multi-faceted process. I think the most crucial aspect is respect: respecting readers, and pre-readers, enough to approach them as equals, offering a face-to-face encounter with something that genuinely excites us. The late Ernie Coombs, perhaps better known as Mr. Dressup, provided a stellar example of this respectful, non-condescending approach toward his child audiences. This quickly excludes sermonizing with its hierarchical power dynamic, the "I-am-greater/wiser-than-thou" narrative stance. Rather, we invite readers to share a whimsical sense of delight, or perhaps to feel and come to better understand certain elements of the fears and pain that are necessary for the growth of the human spirit. Honesty and empathy are essential.

**So how do we see eye-to-eye with our child characters?**

Each of us has a continuing awareness of self that accompanies us throughout our conscious existence. This singular "self" may in fact be viewed as a cluster of multiple awarenesses and roles, or plural selves. We are both one and the "many" and, as such, we're offered exciting possibilities for literary voice.

As writers we're challenged to *be* the "other," who may or may not reflect our own personal experience or values. We see through those particular eyes; we resonate to that unique voice. In this way, we give birth to characters who live and breathe within the framework of the narrative. It's important to have more than a single question or challenge in our story, for each prompts levels of problem-solving that result in character growth and empowerment. Writing for children is all about letting child characters wrestle with imbalance to work out their own solutions.

There are other important aspects. Good children's writing is about active voice: using strong verbs to craft an image-packed presentation. It's about experiencing the world with *immediacy*, about articulating ideas without pedantic explanations or lengthy flashbacks. In doing all of the above, we can begin to write convincingly and with authenticity for younger readers. (And for plenty of older ones, as well.)

So how *do* we reclaim the wonder? Where do we find the stillness, the silence that we need in order to fully perceive? Where is the drive not only to nourish our rushed adult selves, but to access that inner self from which we re-create? From what part of our mind comes the willingness to dream a little?

We need to trust ourselves and the processes by which we practise our craft, yet we have also to remain open to growth for we can't keep living the same literary questions. We need to hold onto a basic faith that the market *will* provide opportunities for our offerings to shine, but we must also expect doors to slam closed. We need to develop a strong protective shell, and still remain open and vulnerable to fleeting moments which can translate into something of beauty.

**No universal recipes...**

I'm afraid there are no simple answers, no universal recipes. No step-by-step survival manuals. The act of writing, that "untiring effort to author a sensitive grasp of being itself — of that which authors use [and] ... makes it possible for us to be and speak ... in the first place," *demands* that we seek the wonder. That we stop to attend fully, with uncluttered mind. For without this pure "seeing," without the stillness which permits re-creation, we invite the risks of imitation rather than innovation, of jarring false notes when we could be singing in perfect pitch. Whatever the barriers, we owe it to ourselves, and to our craft, to do it well. In writing for children, after all, we always try to leave our readers with hope.

Of course, it's probably audacity to claim to write *for* anybody, child or adult. Rather, we write from and for ourselves, those works which demand to be written.

—

Alison Lohans published her first book in 1983. Since then, twelve more of her books have been published for people ages four through adult. Alison will be Writer-in-Residence at Regina Public Library in 2002–2003. Her newest title is *Waiting for the Sun* (Red Deer Press, fall 2001).

# Short Fiction for Children: A Ten-Point Checklist

*by Margaret Springer*

You've written a wonderful story for children. Before you send it off, evaluate it one more time. Ask yourself the following questions:

**1. The basics:**

- Who is this written for? Imagine *one* child.
- Age level: pre-school, early reader, 8–11, 12 plus?
- Intended publication: magazine, anthology, picture book?
- Word count, to the nearest 25? (Shorter texts for younger ages.)

**2. Main character:**

- Age? The same as, or slightly older than, the reader.
- Main character's viewpoint? Omit what s/he can't see or know.
- Viewpoint consistent? Keep the author out of the story.
- Person consistent? (Third person best for youngest readers.)

**3. Who or what is main character up against?**

- What is at stake? Avoid slice-of-life vignettes.
- Is this vital? If it isn't, the reader doesn't care.
- Conflicts: another person, self, society, time, nature, the unknown?
- Appropriate to age level? (I wish, I worry... for youngest.)

**4. What makes this story special?**

- Plot fresh/original? Read published stories, so you'll know.
- Humour? Editors and readers love a light touch.
- Rhythms and language? Listen for the *music* of your words.
- Values underlying the story? (Subtle, without preaching.)

**•5. Beginning:**

- Title pulls us in? This label must attract attention.
- Story jumps right in and hooks the reader?
- The reader *cares*? (A story is easy to put down!)

**6. Middle:**

- Events, characters, setting are believable?
- The story *shows*, rather than telling?
- Dialogue sounds like real people talking?
- Pace is fast, with unnecessary detail cut?
- Complications make things worse before they get better?

**7. Ending:**

- Main character solves problem, or is on way to solving it, by own efforts?
- Adults are kept in the background?
- Ending is unpredictable, but satisfying?
- Ending echoes beginning and/or title in some way?

**8. For picture books:**

- Writing is tight and lyrical, with rhythms and repetitions?
- Includes humour and/or a fresh twist for young children?
- Every segment picturable, with detail left equally to the illustrator?
- Strong emotional resonance?

**•9. Presentation:**

- Manuscript neat and legible, in correct format?
- Spelling and grammar checked; no tense shifts?
- Within the target word count?
- Within all the guidelines of your intended publisher?

**10. Last but not least:**

- Is this the best story I am capable of right now?

When you can answer all of the above questions to your satisfaction, send it out — and good luck with it!

Editors will be impressed.

—

Margaret Springer has written and published dozens of children's stories, a picture book and two junior novels. An instructor with the Institute of Children's Literature and a Consulting Editor for Boyds Mills Press, she developed this checklist for her own use, and for local workshops and courses.

# Breaking into Children's Publishing

*by Linda Aksomitis*

It isn't easy to break into the children's publishing industry these days. The Canadian marketplace is suffering the economic strains of big book chains and deep discounts. The U.S. market has the same challenges, and an anthrax mail scare to contend with as well.

So how do you sell that first manuscript?

Many children's writers are trying to find an agent, whether it's their first submission, or their tenth book. Various publishing houses through North America deal only with materials submitted through an agent. The reason? An agent has already gone through the "slush pile" and, often, has worked with the author to edit the manuscript first. This eliminates a couple of steps for overworked publishing staff. Plus, an agent negotiates the contract on an author's behalf, so there are fewer questions to answer.

## Agent often not *the* solution...

However, an agent is often not *the* solution. First of all, agents aren't typically interested in unpublished children's authors. There just aren't enough publishing houses focusing on children's literature to make them have to work that hard. So, what about letting a mediocre "general" writer's agent take your book? Unfortunately it likely won't do the author any good. Agents who do a good job of placing manuscripts have worked closely with editors so they know what types of material will best fit each market. An agent unfamiliar with the industry won't likely get much further than the author will.

There are some agents that a beginning author needs to be aware of. These charge large reading fees, provide expensive editorial consultative services (which they refer you to) and earn revenue from you without ever selling your work. You normally expect to pay the cost of copying and mailing materials out, but many agents may deduct those amounts from your royalty cheques.

So the question remains, how do you break into the children's market?

The first thing to do is to become a professional. That doesn't mean quitting your day job to write full-time, it simply means doing all of the research to find out how to present yourself as a professional.

You need to make a great, not a good, impression on the editor opening your submission package. This means your cover letter should:

- Be on standard white paper. The objective is to be business-like, not flashy.
- Have a simple letterhead if you use one at all.
- Be written in a standard business format. If you haven't written a business letter since you finished typing class twenty years ago, you'll need to locate a textbook or website that will help you brush up on your technique. Enter the phrase "business letter format" into your favorite search engine on the Internet and you'll likely find a sample with specific tips.
- Provide a hook to interest the editor in your work. That doesn't mean you should say your grandchildren love the story. It means you should open with something original and descriptive of your work. For example: "Folk tales have a unique appeal to beginning readers, as does the Old West. In my Gopher Gulch folk tales I have combined the motifs of traditional folk tales with an 1890s setting, to create a new North American approach."
- Keep the letter to one page, briefly including the most relevant information about you and the submission.
- Use spell-checker and check the grammar.
- Include a SASE, or self-addressed stamped envelope for a response.
- Include information about whether the submission is exclusive to this publisher, or a multiple submission. Remember you *must* follow the publisher's guidelines in this area.

**Join writer's groups...**

Professional authors also join writers' groups, particularly ones for children's authors. Canada has CANSCAIP, which is the Canadian Society of Children's Authors, Illustrators and Performers. Information for joining is online at www.canscaip.org. There is also a Canadian chapter of SCBWI, the Society of Children's Book Writers & Illustrators, the U.S. international organization. Make sure you include information about your memberships in your submissions.

This type of information, along with prior publishing credits (if you have any) can be inserted in your cover letter or on a professional curriculum vitae or CV. The CV should be sorted into categories outlining your publishing history and other relevant details for your writing. If you've been writing your town news for the local newspaper for the past five years, include it under a heading *Newspaper Publications*. If you're a member of writing organizations, include them under a heading *Professional Memberships*. If you have an English degree, include it under *Education*, along with any writing workshops you've attended. If you're a teacher's aide at the Elementary School, include that under *Related Work Experience*. You know what life details have made you particularly suited to write the piece you're submitting. Organize a brief outline in your one or two page CV, and show the editor!

Of course the big catch is choosing which editor to send your material to once you've got the package ready. The first rule is to be familiar with the publisher's line. Read, read, and read some more of their books, plus their publishing catalogues or websites. If they don't include anything similar to your material, pick a different publisher. Likewise, with style. If your writing is quirky and humorous, find a publisher who seems attracted to that style.

**Get submission guidelines...**

Get up-to-date information on each publisher's submission guidelines before you send out your packages. The Canadian Children's Book Centre (www.bookcentre.ca) website provides links to all publishers, or you can purchase a pamphlet listing Canadian publishers accepting unsolicited submissions, with editor's names and guidelines. For Canadian and U.S. markets you can purchase the *Children's Writers & Illustrator's Market*, which is released each December.

With the anthrax scare, many of the largest U.S. publishers are destroying unsolicited submissions rather than opening them. This policy will be re-evaluated, but in the meantime, if you are planning to submit to American publishers, there are some rules to follow:

- Always provide a complete return address.
- Use a postage meter if possible, instead of stamps.
- If you are not a member of SCBWI, so that you get regular updates on these publishing companies, telephone before submitting. Request the name of the editor of your area, so that you can address your submission to someone.

—

Linda Aksomitis is in her Masters of Vocational/Technical Education program, writing and teaching various online courses. She has taught over 20,000 students in her *Writing for Children* course. *Becoming a Library Technician*, her latest book, will be released in 2003. Linda's resource page for emerging children's writers can be found at www3.sk.sympatico.ca/aksoml/.

# Writing for the Very Young

*by Joanna Emery*

Books for the very young — picture books, concept books, and board books — look so easy to write.

But don't be fooled by appearances. Not everyone can write for children. Before you add the talent, before you stir the luck, and before you mull it all in an inexhaustible supply of perseverance, you need one important ingredient — passion.

Writing for young children is like having a baby; a tedious process at times, a thrilling adventure at others. What keeps you going is the result. The work you create for children is your baby.

Celebrities might like to show off their children's books. Publishing houses know that famous names sell, and profit, after all, is their bottom line. But the ordinary among us must strive against incredible odds to see our work published. We must have the passion, a deep, lasting desire that verges on obsession, a soulful urge to create words and stories that children will love.

## What do little children want?

And what do these little children want? You don't need a Ph.D. to guess the answers. Children want security. They want loveable characters. They want to see the good guys win. They want to see pictures and hear stories that make them laugh and help them make sense of this crazy world. They want sing-song rhyme and eye-popping prose. They may not understand every word but the exposure to language that books give young children is just as important to their growing minds as proper nutrition. We've all seen that exquisite picture book with wonderful illustrations, heart-tugging theme and lilting prose. But was it written for children? Did it lift their little spirits or was the book really one made by adults and for, well, other adults?

So before you send off that cute story to the address on the back of your son's favourite book, ask yourself one question. Do I have the passion to write for children? If you do, or even think you do, then don't put it to waste. Grab that community college calendar and sign up for a workshop on how to get published. Join a writer's group or professional organization such as the Canadian Society of Children's Authors, Illustrators and Performers (CANSCAIP), The Canadian Children's Book Centre or the Canadian Authors Association. Write for submission guidelines. Visit libraries. Read a slew of writing books. Check out the children's section of a bookstore. Talk to teachers, parents, and librarians. Find out how you can give young children what they want.

**Rejections can be painful...**

Word of warning: writing for children is usually not a lucrative calling. But you weren't in it for the money anyway, were you? The inevitable flurry of rejections in your mailbox can be a painful process. But if you stick with it and find those people who share your passion of writing for children too, you won't feel so alone. And when that baby of yours finally comes, there won't be anything in the world quite like it.

—

Joanna Emery's first picture book, *Melville Smellville*, was published by a small Nova Scotia Press, Small World Publishing, in December 2001. Her poems and articles have appeared in various children's magazines such as *Jack & Jill* and *Ladybug*. She lives in Dundas, Ontario, with her husband and three children.

# Writing Series Fiction for Children

*by Nikki Tate*

Children become great friends with the characters they read about, so if an author can write several books in a series, the sale of one book usually means repeat customers for additional volumes. But writing series fiction is easier said than done. It's hard enough to write one decent novel but there are all sorts of challenges facing a writer who chooses to spread a character's story over three or more books.

**Continuous storyline?**

Whether or not to continue the storyline from book to book is one of many decisions the series writer must make. Each novel might use the same characters and have a similar plot structure but there may be no overall continuity. There are some series where each new novel starts at the beginning of the summer or during a never-ending fifth grade. The characters do not get older or develop from book to book. Instead, each novel is a self-contained story that doesn't bring forward information from previous books. The advantage of this format is that the characters are not likely to outgrow their readers. Rather, the readers will eventually outgrow the characters. By choosing this format, the author avoids the prickly issues of what to do when protagonists hit adolescence, become interested in dating, or develop drinking problems.

**Not all linear development is equal...**

Another option is to structure the series so the books are sequential, the characters do age and develop over time, and some information is carried forward. If time passes from book to book, the author must decide what the pacing will be over the course of the whole series and how much development will occur for each character both within a title and across multiple novels. If the series covers a period of several years (or generations), where does the first story begin? And, where will the last one end?

Before starting to write the *StableMates* series, I knew I did not want my main character to age beyond the end of Grade Seven. If I decide to continue the books after that, I will either have to find a new main character, one closer in age to most of my readers, or begin a new series.

### Point of view...

Some authors prefer to stick with one main character and all the novels in the series are written from the same character's point of view. In other cases, each book in the series features a different character. The characters know each other, but of course, each has a unique perspective on the goings-on in the stories.

Since the young reader must be able to identify with the central characters in the books, lengthy, multiple-generation series often choose an appropriate child from each generation to become the main character for new stories.

### Historical context...

The author must also decide on the relative importance of the historical period in which the books are set. Obviously, in the case of historical fiction, it is critical to keep track of the changing historical context as time passes. However, for a generic contemporary series, it is not so important to identify the exact year in which the story takes place.

Beverly Cleary's "Ramona" books have been written over a period of many years, but because their focus is on the everyday interactions of a child and her family and friends, there is no need to identify specific political or historical events. Unless such events are critical to the novel's plot, their inclusion can date the book and make it more difficult to keep the series as a whole current and appealing to new readers.

### Seed planting...

One of the great advantages of writing series fiction is the way an author can plant the seeds of future story ideas in early books. Various minor characters can be set up to have full stories at a later date. For example, in all of my series, I've set the scene for various supporting characters to play larger roles in future books. These possible stories develop in a non-linear manner and are initially tangential to the main plot. The evolution from sidebar to main plot reflects the non-linear nature of story in society: life is, indeed, a web of interconnected stories.

By writing a very long piece (a story that may stretch over ten to twelve books), the author has a chance to explore many alleys, turnoffs, forks in the road that aren't possible to include in a shorter book. It just isn't practical to write a nine-hundred-page novel for eight-year-olds, but by the time a child has read six or seven books in a series, the author has had a chance to create and explore inner and outer landscapes far more complex and subtle than is possible within a single novel of 40,000 words.

## A cast of thousands...

Working on such a large scale, the author has access to a very large cast. While this certainly allows for many subplots and the ongoing exploration of all sorts of interpersonal dynamics, a cast of thousands can be hard to keep track of. I use a set of index cards — one for every character. Each contains some sort of visual reference (a picture from a magazine or a rough sketch), a list of characteristics, quotes with book and page references, and important family, friend, and pet relationships. Each animal also gets a card to ensure I don't accidentally change the colour of someone's cat between books three and seven!

When I begin work on a new book within a series, I pull out the cards of the characters to be involved in the main storyline and sit them around me on my desk. I physically arrange them in a way that makes sense in the story (Jack and Emma are best friends — they sit side by side — whereas Jessa and Cheryl, who are fighting at the beginning of the novel, sit as far away from each other as they can).

As the story develops, I add notes to the character cards so they are up to date when I begin the next novel.

## Keeping track of the details...

Keeping track of time is best done with a calendar. Banks are a great source of free calendars and I collect these for time-keeping in my books. Each new book gets a calendar where I record dates of final exams and Halloween dances, birthdays, travel days, and details like the number of days required for antidepressant medication to kick in (no point in having the depressed mother smile when she would still be hiding under the covers). Each series also gets an overall calendar that tracks the progress of the characters across books. This is particularly important to make sure all references to birthdays and other milestones are consistent.

Geography is another thing that must be consistent from one book to the next. The obvious solution here is to keep maps and make sure they are updated whenever new place references are made. Somehow, I forgot to write down the name of the street on which an important barn is located in the *StableMates* series and, as a result, the street name references made in two different books were inconsistent! The mistake was discovered when an artist was hired to draw an official map for the series. We had to move the farm so it is now flanked on one side by Street X and on the other by Street Y. Avoid embarrassing mistakes like that by carefully recording every place name on your master map!

In a fantasy series, the number of things to track grows exponentially as the author can assume no prior knowledge by readers embarking on a journey through imaginary lands. *The Estorian Chronicles* is a fantasy series steeped in a mythology and history all its own. I have a filing box filled with cards for mythological creatures as well as a hardcover journal where I carefully record all kinds of details about the flora, fauna, and landscape of my made-up world as well as many anthropological notes about the various tribes that live there. Though it may take many years to write a number of books, keen readers can devour them in a single long weekend and any inconsistencies become painfully obvious.

**Reader expectations...**

For better or for worse, readers bring expectations to the latest book in a favourite series. The series author treads a fine line between allowing well-loved characters to grow, change, develop, and face new challenges without reaching too far beyond what their committed readers will accept.

When a child picks up a *StableMates* novel, he or she expects plenty of horse-related action. Though many teachers, librarians, and parents feel that *Return to Skoki Lake (StableMates #6)* is a strong novel about facing the challenge of being diagnosed with diabetes, a number of younger readers have complained that the focus of the book strayed too far from the horse-centred adventures they were used to. Knowing this, try to develop central characters and a series premise in the first book that will allow plenty of scope down the line.

**So, how do you know?**

It's not always easy to know whether your juvenile or YA novel is going to be a one-off wonder or the first book in a new series. If you are the kind of author who finds that each main storyline spins off a dozen new plot ideas, if you are constantly cutting out subplots that are threatening to take over your novel, if you have no trouble writing a list of ten possible plots using the same characters, or if you never seem to get to the end of a particular character's story, then you may just have a knack for this particular writing niche.

If, on the other hand, you worry that you've put all the good stuff in the first book or keep being tormented by new characters who want nothing to do with the cast you've already created, then perhaps you are better off starting over, rather than trying to stretch your one really great novel into a less-than-satisfying series.

—

Nikki Tate is an award-winning author of three series for young readers: *The Estorian Chronicles*, *The Tarragon Island Series*, and the *StableMates* novels. A dynamic speaker, Tate visits thousands of school children each year to talk about the writing process and is much in demand as a writing workshop leader.

# Recent Trends in Picture Books

*by Margaret Bunel Edwards*

A disquieting number of editors are rejecting our picture books, the kinds we've always sold to them, with the words, "lacks an edge." The "edge" referred to deals with life's harsher side. Young readers are being introduced to civil unrest, as in *Smoky Night* by Eve Bunting, or the reality of the atomic bomb or Nazi concentration camps.

On one occasion, I reviewed books with "an edge" for the Children's Book Centre. Many were well written and plotted, and in some cases, included humour. They dealt with spousal and child abuse and alcohol addiction. I found the plots disturbing and wondered what a child's reaction might be if he/she were actually trying to cope with these problems.

Not every writer is capable of writing about these subjects and many do not want to. They protest that a child's view of the world is innocent for a short time and why shorten it even further?

James Cross Giblin, an author and editor, supports the view that children are aware of life's cruelties and their fears should be dealt with honestly and, if possible, with reassurance. He suggests that for a young child, the story may be set in a war-torn country but lengthy details about "savage ethnic rivalries" should not be included.

**Sees more beautifully illustrated books...**

Kathryn Cole, writer and publisher, writes of trends of a different kind in picture books. She sees more beautifully illustrated books being published, their stories often including historical and geographical information.

The adults buying these books are attracted by their educational value in addition to their interesting stories. She refers to *Emma and the Silk Train* by Julie Lawson and *Beethoven Lives Upstairs* by Barbara Nichol as examples of books which encourage the reader to find out more about the story's background. These books appeal to teachers and librarians, as well, since they often use them in discussion and while researching with older children.

We are constantly reminded how September 11, 2001 has changed the world politically, and it has brought about yet another trend in children's books.

It would seem that "harsh reality" has invaded our lives and is losing its fictional appeal. More reassuring stories are once again being published for young readers. As writers, we are fortunate to have this variety of choices as we contribute to the child's world of literature.

—

Margaret Bunel Edwards is an Ottawa writer with more than 600 stories and articles published in Canada and the United States. Her stories have appeared in anthologies by Holt, Rinehart & Winston, Ginn, Nelson, and Gage. She is the author of two picture books. Her young adult historical novel, *The Ocean Between*, was shortlisted for the Geoffrey Bilson Award.

# “Hey, Look at This!” Nonfiction for Children

*by Margaret Springer*

Shhh! Here’s a secret. A secret for success in writing for children. It will open more markets, expand your horizons, bring added satisfaction, and increase your sales.

Will you stop reading if I mention the word “nonfiction”?

Please don’t.

Current nonfiction for kids is lively, appealing, fun to write — and in demand by editors.

Think textbook? Think boring? Think again.

Take a look in a library or bookstore. Read the magazine articles and nonfiction books aimed at a young audience. They’ve changed a lot since your childhood — and you can write for this expanding market!

Begin with a subject you know well, or a subject that interests you. Nonfiction for kids is tightly written, so the key word is focus. Slice your subject in some way — by time, by place, by sub-topic, by slant.

Suppose, for example, your passion is golf. Not of interest to kids? Only for sports magazines? Consider one of these topics:

- History: Did the Romans invent golf?
- Unusual laws: Why was golf banned in Scotland in 1457?
- Language: What’s a mulligan, and a blind bogey?
- Equipment: How are golf balls made?
- Biography: One player, famous or infamous, or one golf course designer.

The list is almost endless, and any subject can be sliced in this way.

Forget the general, rewritten encyclopaedia piece. The adjective “encyclopaedic” is the kiss of death in kids’ nonfiction. By definition *your subject* interests you, so research it thoroughly, as thoroughly as if a college course demanded it. Your piece may well be a young reader’s first introduction to the topic. That’s a big responsibility, and accuracy is vital.

Use printed sources and the Internet, but be careful. Substantiate what you find, and evaluate its accuracy. Many errors are copied and recopied. Keep a detailed list of your sources as you go along, to be ready in case an editor or reader questions something later.

Most of all, find an expert or two. "Interview" is another scary word, but people love to chat about their enthusiasms. Experts can verify facts, suggest new angles, give you colourful quotes and bring your piece to life.

Look always for the unusual, the weird, the little-known. Try for that "Oh, wow!" factor, that "Hey, look at this!" and that "Cool!" You are competing with television, the computer, video games and other modern distractions for your audience's attention. Their magazines and nonfiction books are leisure reading, and educational publishers also reject the dry and boring. So fill your piece full of information, but make it fun.

Editors love ideas for small bites, sidebars, charts, and other tasty nuggets of information beyond the main "meat" of your piece. If you come across sources of photos, note them as well, for the editor's information. And yes, most will expect a thorough and up-to-date bibliography.

Where are these editors and these markets? Take a look at any market listing. You will find magazines and book publishers with a range of subjects for a young audience. Some list upcoming themes, others limit themselves to specific subject matter, and all mention required lengths and age ranges. More and more writers' guidelines are available online, updated as needed. Find a library, if you do not have other convenient Internet access.

So get busy. Start with a simple, step-by-step "how-to" on a subject you know well. Think about your own interests and skills, and make a list of other possible topics.

Writing nonfiction for kids is creative, flexes those writing muscles, and opens new worlds. It is also published in a ratio of at least 3 to 1 over fiction.

It's a secret well worth knowing about.

—

Margaret Springer began writing nonfiction for children after many fiction sales. Now she regularly rediscovers history, biography, the arts, and how things work for a young audience. An editor, teacher and author, her nonfiction has won two Arts Feature of the Year awards from *Highlights for Children* magazine.

# Naming Fiction's Children

*by Shirley Byers Lalonde*

Renowned author Phyllis Whitney keeps a notebook just for names. People's names she might some day use in her fiction. "Why?" I once naively mused. Then I became a writer of "kiddy lit." And now I know. Naming is hard work. Naming needs preparation.

And it's only fair. After all, names work hard for us. Perhaps no word or pair of words can give an impression that is as immediate and lasting. Consider these variations: Patricia Gallant — Patsy Craven. Leonard Lake — Lenny Leech. Constance LaPlante — Connie Weed. Francis Link — Frank Fink.

The name must fit with the time of the story. If your story is set in the present calling your characters Valerie, Marilyn, Ned and Billy yanks it back into the fifties. If your fiction is historical, do your homework, find out what names were used at that time, in that place. Currently favoured Hannah would fit nicely into the early nineteen hundreds. Equally popular Madison would not. If you're aiming for a classic stay far away from the very sticky-out and trendy names such as Calliope, Hawk, Jagger and Hecuba. As fast as Valerie, Marilyn, Ned and Billy, they will date your story (and make your readers think they've stumbled onto the set of a soap opera).

On the other hand, names such as Jason, Jack and Sean for boys and Patricia, Susan and Heather for girls seem to hold their popularity. Many Bible names also fall into this category. Adam, John, Joseph, Elizabeth, Mary, Sarah …

It's probably never a good idea to try to be clever with names or combinations of names such as Robin Tweet, Heidi Ho or Hy Gene.

I've learned to be careful not to give my characters names similar in spelling, sound or initial letter. Three friends named Casey, Lacey and Macey may be just so cute but they will also be very difficult to individuate — both for the reader and the writer.

Certain names are verboten simply by association. Of course you would never call a boy Adolf or Judas, Nero or Cain. Nor would you tag a child with same name as a notorious criminal. Less obvious to most Canadian writers are the names that would be taboo in the Jewish or Islamic community. Haman, for example, was responsible for an Old Testament plan (fortunately thwarted) to destroy all the Jews in the kingdom of Ahasuerus. Do your homework.

Also, be careful of unintended racial slurs ingrained in otherwise perfectly good names. You can't call a Black girl Jemima, a Black boy Tom. Don't christen an Irish youngster Mick.

Particularly if you are setting your story in an actual town or city — and particularly if your story is based on historical facts — always, always, always check the phone books and directories of that area and be sure you are not giving a character the name of a real person. Writing is fun. Litigation is not fun.

Remember that not all Canadian children carry an Anglo-Saxon surname. Every classroom has its Mary Eyolfsons, its Suzanne Lalondes, its Jason Squirrels, its Merlin Syroskis. Your fiction should reflect this diversity.

And finally, the cardinal rule for all children's writers who are also parents of teenagers is: you must never, never, never use your teen's name at any place, anywhere for any character in any story.

I know, I know, that practice was perfectly acceptable and indeed clamoured for when this same child was six years old. But you can't do it any more.

Get a notebook. Start collecting names.

Or ... if you want to speed up the process, there are scads of sites on the web devoted to supplying expectant parents, students of history and genealogy and writers such as thee and me with a plethora of names, name origins, favourite names, least favourite names etc., etc. A couple to get you started:

- www.geocities.com/Heartland/Meadows/2151
- www.babynames.com
- www2.parentsoup.com/babynames/index.html?babyname/

—

Shirley Byers Lalonde lives near Kelvington, Saskatchewan. She is a contributing editor for *WITH*, a U.S. based teen magazine and has also practised naming fiction's children in such periodicals as *The United Church Observer*, *My Friend*, *Brio*, *On the Line and Listen*.

# The Writing Process for Children and Beginners

*by Donna Gamache*

When teaching creative writing to beginners or school-aged students, it is important to have them recognize that writing is a process. Young people (and some older people) tend to dash off a story and submit it as is. They need to realize that writing involves several steps, and that missing one will result in a poorer final copy.

When I teach creative writing classes to beginners, I give the following two sheets as handouts, but I don t give them out at the first class. We spend our first few classes (depending on how many sessions I have), dealing with pre-writing aspects: we brainstorm; examine the world for topics; discuss the "what if " method of coming up with an idea; and discuss the frequent necessity of research. We spend a class dealing with the four Ws (who, what, where, and when) and the viewpoint/voice aspects of writing (even middle-grade children can learn to distinguish between first and third person, and can learn to decide which one will work better for their story).

Another class can be used to plan the beginning, middle, and end, and to figure out the setting and climax. By this time, the class should be itching to get to the actual writing. Then I give them the first handout, so they can begin to understand the process and realize how much they've already accomplished.

The second handout comes after the rough copy is written (and usually results in groans!) but it is important for them to realize the importance of rewriting. Younger writers, especially, will be eager to get to the "sharing" stage, but they must do some revising before they share, and final editing afterwards, too. If one can successfully lead beginning students through the writing process, the results will be worthwhile.

Note: The handouts are on the following pages.

—

Donna Gamache, from MacGregor, Manitoba, has published numerous short stories for both children and adults, as well as *Spruce Woods Adventure*, a novel for middle-grade children. She has also given classes in writing fiction to both children and adults.

## The Writing Process (Handout #1).

### 1. Pre-writing.

- Brainstorm: get ideas from the world around you and from your own life; choose your topic ("what if" method is one way); search for information, if necessary.
- Write the 4 Ws.
- Choose the viewpoint/voice.
- Briefly plan beginning/middle/end. Try to figure out the climax.
- Plan setting.

### 2. Composing (Write your first copy).

- Write quickly.
- Skip every other line; leave margins on both sides.
- Don't worry about all the details of spelling and grammar, but if you notice something that needs correcting, circle or underline it.
- Write the draft all the way through.
- Try to think of a title.
- If possible, put your story aside for a day or two (or a few weeks).

### 3. Revising.

- Rewrite your first copy. Do this several times, if necessary.

### 4. Sharing (with a partner).

- Read and discuss each other's stories.
- First, tell your partner what you like.
- Then, tell what you think needs to be changed, and why (look for the things listed on the Revising Sheet).
- Listen to the suggestions your partner gives you and decide if these changes should be made.

### 5. Editing.

- Go over your copy again before starting the final copy. Make any more changes.
- Check all the ideas in #3 again.

### 6. Making the final copy.

- Make a final, clean copy.
- Check it again for capitals, spelling, and punctuation.
- Make pictures to go with your story, if you want.

## Revising Your Story (Handout # 2).

- Check to see that the 4 Ws are answered near the beginning.
- Rewrite ideas to make them clear and easy to understand.
- Put in needed information.
- Take out unnecessary information.
- Make sure your story is divided into paragraphs (remember that when people talk, you need a new paragraph each time the speaker changes).
- Be sure you are writing in sentences.
- Change or correct words that are wrong or dull.
- Check for capital letters and spelling.
- Check punctuation (periods, question marks, quotation marks, commas, and apostrophes).
- Make sure that you have stopped at the right place.

—

# 8. Poetry & Lyrics

# How to Write Haiku and Senryu

*by Terry Ann Carter*

Haiku originated from *renga* of seventeenth century Japan (literally linked songs or linked verses — the word for poem and song in Japanese is the same). There writing haiku is an elegant literary pastime in which poets singly or in groups, improvised connecting stanzas to create long poems sometimes consisting of 1,000 verses. Renga were interlocking chains of seventeen syllables (three lines of five, seven, five) proceeded or followed by fourteen syllables (two lines of seven, seven) with each tercet and couplet producing a poem in itself.

By the sixteenth century, along with the traditional arts of Kabuki theatre and *ukiyo-e* (woodblock prints), *haikai-no-renga* became a national obsession. *Haikai*, from the two words meaning "sportive" and "pleasantry," meant unusual or offbeat and is translated as "comic linked verse." It was a reaction to the formality of the "language of the gods" used in the *waka/tanka* of Court poetry, written by mikados and later, as power shifted from the nobles to the military, by exalted shoguns and ruling warriors. Haikai spoke in everyday language and sometimes, in its exuberance, became little more than a display of wit.

### A twentieth-century term...

By the second half of the sixteenth century, the poet Basho and his followers elevated haikai to a level of great sensitivity and dignity, although the underlying humour and surprise often remained present. During this time, the opening stanza of renga, called *hokku* or "starting verse" became independent, what William J. Higginson calls the "stand alone verse." This hokku had to contain a seasonal word (*kigo*) and be an entity of itself. Basho probably never heard the word haiku; it has only come into use in the twentieth century. "Hai" in haiku means "unusual" and "ku" denotes strophe, lines, stanzas or verse. Recently, hokku and haiku have become interchangeable.

### Guidelines for haiku...

Haiku is simply what is happening in this place, at this time; it is a poetic form concerned with one particular event. Haiku works best when it is written in the present tense; it is composed within seventeen syllables in three lines with increments of five–seven–five syllables. Many modern and postmodern haiku poets, however, have moved away from this strict rule; thus in many haiku societies, it is a controversial issue and a subject always ready for debate.

Use an image from nature. Allude to a season. Time may "stand still" while the haiku poet paints a picture.

just then
snow from the pine bough
slips

A lesser known "rule" concerns the where, what and when aspect of haiku.

| | |
|---|---|
| (where) | stepping out on ice |
| (what) | my mother's cane |
| (when) | first |

or variations:

| | |
|---|---|
| (where/when) | winter dusk |
| (what) | in my mother's log cabin quilt |
| | my father's red shirt |

Haiku may also contain a hidden dualism: past and present, high and low, near and far, temporality and eternity. A few of these "dualities" are found in this single haiku written for my mother shortly after the Christmas season.

taking down ornaments
my mother tells war stories —
the hand blown glass

| | |
|---|---|
| (past) | war stories |
| (present) | taking down ornaments |
| (sound) | war |
| (silence) | glass |
| (eternity) | the effect of war |
| (temporality) | the glass ornament |

There is also the "hidden" idea of hand-blown glass and hands blown off from war.

The "when" of many haiku pre-assumes a time of year, month or day. The place in time of the poem is often conveyed by references to occurrences in nature or to specific flora and fauna. Haze connotes spring; wisteria blossoms in late spring; and morning glories in summer. Some *kigo* or seasonal words will change in different geographic regions. Ducks are a winter kigo in Japan, a fall kigo in Canada.

Although haiku are "songs to be sung in one breath," a "cutting word" introduces a short caesura or thought-pause for emphasis. In Japanese, it occurs often in the fifth syllable or twelfth syllable, and breaks the tiny poem asymmetrically. In English, translators sometimes convey this idea by punctuation marks (! , ... and :).

**Guidelines for senryu...**

Unapologetically populist, senryu demands the same brevity as traditional haiku and is written in the same format (three lines of seventeen syllables: five–seven–five). Senryu, however, allows the poet the liberties of expressing emotion and writing about topics other than the seasons. The latest fashion in Japan is "current events senryu" whereby poets (and everyday citizens) use a time honoured format to write about foibles of modern life: the heart break of a sick child, the loneliness of the long-distance commuter, or the cynical certainty that voters are being snookered by politicians. The editor of the current events senryu column for the *Yomiuri* newspaper has said that "the basic theme is anxiety." In a Japan gripped by new economic and moral uncertainty, senryu have tackled fear of firing and parents' laments over children.

**Confusion between the two forms...**

In North America, there is sometimes confusion between the two forms. Elizabeth St. Jacques in her article, "Haiku or Senryu? How To Tell The Difference" (first published in *Poet's Forum*, vol. 11:1, 1999), states that "in the past, humour and most particularly human nature, were excluded from haiku, reserved specifically for senryu. Now, however, both regularly appear in haiku."

She also writes, "Of course, when submitting work to editors, most poets don't bother to indicate haiku or senryu, but let the editors decide. Nevertheless, it's to your benefit to learn how to tell the difference between these genres ..."

Several of my senryu were published by *Haiku Canada* last year:

in the waiting room
the outdated magazine
gives advice

and

on the way to work
watching construction workers
watch the girls

There are an estimated one million haiku poets in Japan today, and in North America, societies and haiku gatherings, as well as small presses for publishing haiku, are popular. Seeking poetic inspiration, from landscape or the frenzied life that surrounds us, is a way of coping and surviving in the modern world. Composing haiku and senryu slows us down to see what is unfolding around us.

Take time to view the moon.

Take time to write a haiku or senryu today.

under the crescent moon
my heart
full

—

Terry Ann Carter is a teacher and poet working in Ottawa. After seven chapbooks, her first book of poetry *Waiting for Julia* was published by Third Eye Press, London, Ontario. She serves on the Education Committee for the League of Canadian Poets. Her paper on Chiyo-ni (18th century woman haiku master) was presented to the Annual Haiku Canada Weekend in Kingston and again at the International Haiku Festival in Montreal where her haiku *yesterday's rain* took first place.

# A Villanelle Need Not Be Villainous

*by Ruth Latta*

Writing, like clothing, has its fashions. Currently, non-rhymed poetry is in vogue. In fact, rhymed, metered verse has been out of style for so long that it seems to be coming back again. Since some poets like structured verse in traditional forms and others prefer freer forms, my local CAA branch has categories for both kinds of poetry in its contests.

Whatever style or form you are interested in, you should study the techniques of the masters of that type of poetry. Learning your poetic lineage through various ages and countries can add depth to your work.

In recent years, I have become interested again in rhymed, structured poetry, through the influence of some seniors with whom I work. At first, forms such as the villanelle filled me with trepidation. Now, however, I enjoy the challenge of blending instinct and intellect. You might like it too.

**Derived from peasant songs...**

A villanelle is a form derived from peasant songs. Remember the discussion of the feudal system in our history books and the serfs or "villeins"? This form of poetry is derived from their feast day songs. Clearly, it's a form especially suited for someone like me, who started life as a farm girl in Northern Ontario.

The villanelle first appeared in English verse in the second half of the 19th century, originally for fairly lighthearted poems. The obsessive repetition can, however, work well for a serious subject, as demonstrated by Dylan Thomas's famous villanelle, "Do Not Go Gentle into That Good Night," about a son's feelings for an ageing father.

It is a nineteen line poem, employing only two different end rhymes (in this case, words that rhyme with "night" and those that rhyme with "day").

The rhyme scheme is aba, aba, aba.

For instance:

> Do not go gentle into that good night,
> Old age should burn and rave at close of day;
> Rage, rage against the dying of the light.

Line 1 is repeated as lines 6, 12, and 18. Line 3 is repeated as lines 9, 15, and 19. The first and third lines return as a rhymed couplet at the end. The scheme is aba, aba, aba, aba, aba, abaa.

You will note, as well, that Thomas's lines are in iambic pentameter; that is, each foot or section is an iamb, a word with the emphasis on the second syllable. Each line is made up of five iambs. Each goes: daDUM/daDUM/daDUM/daDUM/daDUM. A villanelle need not be in iambic pentameter, but all the lines must have the same rhythm.

First, choose your subject matter, and begin as you would for any poem, jotting down words, phrases, and images. In my villanelle, below, I wrote out thoughts and feelings about my sister and I, celebrating middle age at the end of the millennium. At some stage, when you have a page full of words and phrases, begin making them into iambic pentameter lines, or, if you prefer, sentences with the rhythm: daDUM, daDUM, daDUM, daDUM, daDUM. This isn't hard, as the rhythm of many English sentences is often iambic pentameter.

**Make a nineteen-line chart...**

I accumulated statements ending in words that rhymed with "by," and another group that rhymed with "glow." I write at least ten lines for each of the rhymes I choose. Then, on lined paper, I make a nineteen-line chart, indicating with an asterisk and an ampersand, which lines repeat, and marking in the rhyme scheme: aba, aba ... to the end. I choose from my collection of lines or sentences the two that I think are most appropriate to be emphasized. These are the lines that will repeat. I write them in at the outset. Then I look at the rest of my lines and arrange them, both to fit the "aba" rhyme scheme and to show a logical progression of thought.

It can be fun to make a villanelle a group exercise. Students, or poets in a workshop, may find it too daunting to contemplate writing an entire villanelle all on their own. However, if the subject matter is established beforehand, each participant can usually contribute at least one or two lines on that theme. Later, these lines can be put together into a villanelle of which everyone is proud.

VILLANELLE FOR MY SISTER'S BIRTHDAY
ON THE EVE OF THE MILLENNIUM
by Ruth Latta © 1999

We'll talk and smile and keep our spirits high
Our days are just a twinkling — that we know.
We'll drink to life beneath the August sky.

We both hate ageing and we wonder why
Time flies when once it used to be so slow
We'll talk and smile and keep our spirits high.

I couldn't let this special day slip by
We'll marvel at the things we two now know.
We'll drink to life beneath the August sky.

And though we sometimes steal away and cry
For olden days and those who loved us so
We'll talk and smile and keep our spirits high.

And though some preachers say the end is nigh
Your candles in the dark will blaze and glow
We'll drink to life beneath the August sky.

We'll talk of young folk growing wings to fly
Of childhood birthdays of so long ago
We'll talk and smile and keep our spirits high.

We'll drink to life beneath the August sky.

—

Ruth Latta's poetry has appeared in a range of publications, from *Bywords* to *Whetstone*. She is the coauthor of two chapbooks of poetry, *Three's Company*, 1996 and *Polarities*, 2000. Her most recently published poem appears in the current issue of *The Grist Mill*, the Valley Writer's Guild's annual. To see some of her poems, please visit her website at www.cyberus.ca/~rklatta/RuthLatta.html

# Poets in the Slipstream

*by Eileen Kernaghan*

The latest catchword in speculative writing is *slipstream*: writing that defies categorization, that contains elements of fantasy, horror or science fiction, but takes a mainstream approach to its material. Slipstream writing deals with universal concerns, with universal images, and pays attention to craft and technique as well as to theme. Nowhere is slipstream writing more in evidence than in that thriving science fiction sub-genre known as speculative poetry.

Like speculative fiction, SF poetry draws its inspiration from many sources: scientific concepts, speculation about the future, folk and fairy tales, the supernatural, dreams and visions. Its history extends from *Beowulf* and *The Epic of Gilgamesh* through Coleridge and Poe, to modern Canadians, such as Gwendolyn MacEwen and Christopher Dewdney.

In Canada, we have two well-respected SF/fantasy publications, both of them Edmonton-based: the anthology series *Tesseracts*, from The Book Collective, and *On Spec* magazine. As well, Canadian literary magazines often announce a special speculative contest or theme issue. Browsing the Internet for "SF and fantasy magazines" will give you detailed guidelines for a host of genre poetry markets, both print and electronic.

The monthly *Scavenger's Newsletter* (Janet Fox, 833 Main, Osage City KS 66523-1241) is a source of small press SF/fantasy/horror markets.

Another excellent resource is *StarLine*, a journal of SF poetry and commentary published by the Science Fiction Poetry Association. Contact John Nichols, 6075 Bellevue Drive, North Olmsted OH 44070, e-mail him at bejay@worldnet.att.net.

For other outstanding examples of the genre, the long-established *Magazine of Speculative Poetry* is edited by Roger Dutcher at PO Box 564, Beloit WI U.S.A. 53512, e-mail sfpoetry@yahoo.com.

—

Eileen Kernaghan has published poetry in magazines ranging from *PRISM international* to The *Magazine of Gothic Vampire Poetry*. She is part of the BC women's poetry group Quintet, which published *Quintet: Themes & Variations* (Ekstasis Editions).

# Editing Your Own Poetry

*by Susan Ioannou*

If you think your poems are just naturally brilliant, you are probably a beginner. Good poetry isn't a flash of inspiration, but art. It's only after a series of rejections that the hard fact begins to sink in. You have to learn to edit your work if you want to get published.

Editing your own poems is much like readying a house to show to prospective buyers. You need to deal with the most public areas to the smallest detail. It works best if you can view your poems as if standing in a buyer's shoes.

First, of course, you must put out the trash. Mechanical errors in spelling, punctuation, grammar and usage are easy and painless to spot and discard. It's the clutter that requires more thought and judgement, and is often hard to let go of. Although it may be painful, you CAN throw away cherished phrases, penned in the heat of emotion.

Are you sabotaging yourself, trying too hard to impress? Instead of writing honestly, in your eagerness to create immortal lines, you may have over-decorated with sentimentality or bombast. Did you tassel your stanzas with adverbs such as "very" and "quite," or wallpaper with flowery adjectives, or drape melodramatic phrases everywhere to dramatize emotion? Clear out the lot. The simpler and more understated the writing, the truer are the lines of the furnishings (your thoughts).

**Check for clichés and needless repetition...**

Conversely, check where the language is worn thin from clichés and needless repetition. Do old-fashioned words like "O," "ere," and "thou" make the poem flake with age? Do picture frames hang empty, holding only the glass of abstractions and generalizations? Fill them with scenes painted from gritty, sensuous nouns and vigorous verbs. Good poetry is not flat and transparent, but sets the nerve ends tingling. An inventory should show a high percentage of words in the poem that make readers see, hear, smell, taste, and touch. On the other hand, don't get drunk on your palette. Good imagery is fresh and vivid, but should complement the whole, not overpower like a giant-screen television in a pantry.

Next, look at how your rooms are connected. Can the reader find his way? Do the passages lead unobstructed toward a conclusion, or do side corridors stray off here and there? Especially, check the front hall — your opening lines. Do they lead right into the poem, or are they just a sun porch where you are warming up? Could you even drop these first stanzas or shift them to a side door or the back? Are the rest of the stanza-rooms in easy-to-follow order, or do readers have to walk through a bedroom to arrive at the kitchen?

**Layout is important...**

If the poem is contemporary free verse, its layout on the page (like a floor plan) is especially important. It should help, not hinder, readers in finding their way. Like paragraphs in prose, each new stanza represents a separate room set aside for a different person or time or activity. Similarly, the way the stanzas are placed on the page in relation to each other — flush left, indented, or centred — can show if the ideas they contain are parallel (like a dining room next to a kitchen), or in contrast (like a den across the hall from the bathroom), or represent steps in thought (from an upstairs bedroom, to the main-floor breakfast nook, to a home office in the basement).

Study your arches and doorways carefully, where one line or stanza ends to open into another. Are such line breaks clearly and sensibly placed to move readers unimpeded through the house? If you divide with enjambment (breaking a line in mid-phrase or mid-sentence), does its surprise value enrich the journey or just slam the reader into a closet?

**Listen to the sounds...**

Listen to the floors. When you read the poem aloud, are the sounds of feet and the echoes created by the words so cushioned by carpet you can't hear them or too loud against bare hardwood? Perhaps you need scatter rugs here and there woven of softer vowels, or consonants' harder ceramic tile, to make the overall sound harmonize with the mood you want in the house.

If you meant to construct your poem in a traditional form, do the number of lines, refrain and other aspects of its plan and decor match the period you've chosen, or jar like mismatched drapes? If rhyme is part of the scheme, does it sound natural, and not too loud or overwrought? Does metre, like background music, slide over the ear on the normal pronunciation of the words, not thump like a rock band?

Despite your good efforts, sometimes a line, a stanza or even a whole poem still doesn't feel ready to show. To locate the source of the problem, you may need to get behind the lines and revise the blueprint. Lock the front door and let your mind go blank. Wander through the stanzas silently, letting their images dance across your mental screen. Whenever the picture greys out, that's a clue that something in the writing has turned abstract or general. It's time to bring in more sensuous words, or create stronger sounds and rhythms.

Suppose, instead, you suddenly find yourself flat on your face. A spelling error, cliché, or awkward line break may have tripped you. Or perhaps, like a castoff overcoat, an image lies crumpled inside out, or repetition blocks the path or an awkward phrase juts out like a rolled rug.

Maybe a line break would work better shifted further left or right.

Study the words' colours, sounds, textures, and connotations for hints of how to remodel. Try rearranging the various pieces this way and that. Often you just have to walk away for a while. Be patient with the slowness of the task. Given enough time, a solution usually lights up a bulb in your brain.

**What is the market?**

After you've sorted, uncluttered, repaired, straightened, moved, dusted and polished, step back.

Of course, because it's your poem, you love it.

However, try to see it through a buyer's eyes. Be realistic. Now that you've set everything in its best possible order, what is the poem's potential market? Is it really ready for a carriage-trade academic journal, or saleable as an avant-garde condo, or should your asking price be more modest, for a writer's-newsletter starter home? It makes sense to begin small, then gradually trade upmarket. With patience and effort, your edited poems can attract serious buyers, as fine new homes for the imagination.

—

Susan Ioannou's poetry, fiction, and essays have appeared in numerous anthologies and magazines across Canada. Her most recent of several books is the critically acclaimed literary study *A Magical Clockwork: The Art of Writing the Poem* (Wordwrights Canada, 2000). By day she works as an editor for ClearTEXT in Toronto.

# Submitting Poetry to Periodicals

*by Melanie Cameron*

As one of two poetry editors at a national literary periodical, I read hundreds of poetry submissions each year. I want to suggest some submission strategies that you won't find in most guidelines or market books. But first I'll reiterate the familiar, standard advice about how to submit poems to periodicals.

**First the basics...**

Everything you submit should be printed, typo-free, on one side of 8.5 by 11 inch paper and be bound by paper clips rather than staples. It's a good idea to use a header, indicating your name and a means of contacting you, on each page, even if the guidelines don't request it. The exception to this is contests with "blind judging" where neither your name nor your address should appear on your manuscript pages.

Six poems is a common maximum number accepted by periodicals (the submission guidelines of some periodicals state they will accept a few more, or a few less, than this number of poems). You can verify a periodical's stipulations by consulting its listing in market books, at its website, or by writing to its office and requesting submission guidelines.

Include a self-addressed, stamped envelope (SASE). If you're submitting poems to a periodical in another country, use International Reply Coupons or see if you can acquire stamps from that country for their response or to return your manuscript.

Include a cover letter that identifies the poems you have submitted.

Look at back issues before you send your poems, to ensure that your work is an appropriate match for the periodical, given its mandate and aesthetic inclinations. Also verify whether it accepts poems on any subject, or produces theme issues.

Research the conditions of publication before submitting your poems. For example:

- Is this a "legitimate" periodical? (You should never have to pay to have your poems published.)
- Will you be paid for your poems?

- Will your poems appear on the periodical's website?

Don't make simultaneous submissions to a periodical that doesn't accept them. (Making a "simultaneous submission" or "multiple submission" means submitting the same poem to more than one periodical at a time.) An editor might invest a lot of time in your poem, only to discover that you've sold it to another periodical: this situation can jeopardize the amount of time the editor's willing to invest in your next submission.

If you address the editor by name, make sure you have up-to-date information. You don't want to suggest that you haven't looked at the periodical recently by addressing your cover letter to an editor who left long ago.

**Additional strategies...**

Working as a poetry editor has helped me identify additional strategies that poets might use to further strengthen their submissions to periodicals. Note that these suggestions do not necessarily represent the views of other poetry editors.

Submission guidelines usually indicate *maximum* acceptable submission lengths, and it's important that you don't overload your submission. (If you do, you risk annoying the editor, having only the first several poems read anyway, or disqualifying your submission.)

However, on the other hand, don't "under-load." Even though the editor is likely to choose only one or two pieces from your submission, you still want to demonstrate that you can offer a number of solid poems and give the editor the opportunity to select the strongest pieces.

Many guidelines state *generally* that manuscript submissions must be double-spaced, with the implicit understanding that this rule *does not* apply to poetry. Unless submission guidelines are very clear on this point, I recommend laying out your poems exactly as you would like them to appear in the periodical. You can also contact the publication for its preferred presentation.

As you order the poems in your submission, consider placing what you think is your strongest poem first, your second-strongest poem second, and so on. This way the editor has the best possible first impression of your work.

Consider how the poems you're submitting work together as a group. Many periodicals prefer to publish at least two poems by one author. You can further entice an editor if your poems, published together, demonstrate your range by being significantly different in content and/or approach or, conversely, by being resonant companions.

Include all your possible contact information: your address, phone number, e-mail address, and maybe even a fax number. It's much faster and easier for an editor to confirm your permission to publish and discuss possible editorial changes by phone or e-mail than by writing you a letter. Also, if an editor is "sitting on the fence" about accepting your work, you don't want it to be rejected because it might be difficult to communicate with you.

**A biographical note can add credibility...**

Include, on your cover page, a brief biographical note suitable for publication in the periodical. In doing so, you're saving the editor the work of tracking down your information and matching it up with the right submission, should your poems be accepted. Also, the biographical note can offer a sense of your credibility. While many editors may not read a cover letter until they've made a decision about your poems, so as not to be influenced by your previous publication history, it can't hurt to make your publication and award successes known.

If you're an unpublished or newly published writer, consider stating that you're just beginning to seek publication of your poetry. Telling the editor this information can work to your advantage, as most periodicals are interested in publishing a range of new to established writers. You may include your biographical information in the body of your cover letter. I prefer bio notes set at the bottom of the letter: this presentation makes it easy for the editor to identify the information intended for inclusion in the periodical, and it also prevents your cover letter from sounding like a list of your accomplishments.

**Don't try to convince the editor...**

Think carefully about how flowery or anecdotal you want to be in your cover letters. I've read many a cover letter relaying the poet's discoveries in the garden earlier that afternoon, stories of dodging parking tickets by reading the officer a poem, and passionate rants about how poetry can save the world. Many of these letters are entertaining, and some are even delightful. But *none* of these approaches has ever persuaded me to accept someone's poem. To the contrary, some of them have made me apprehensive about an editorial relationship with the author.

Don't try to convince the editor to accept your poems by stating that your friends love them, you know this editor will like them, etc. Doing so can imply that you don't believe the poems' strength is self-evident, or that you don't believe the editor capable of making a judgement.

After you submit a poem, you might find yourself tempted to revise it further. If so, make sure you keep copies of the version you sent. If your poem is accepted, you'll need to know what, exactly, the editor wishes to print. Don't send updated drafts to the editor. Doing so makes more editorial work. It also gives the impression that you think your poem's not as effective as it could be. If you feel strongly that you have to make changes to the poem before it goes to print, wait to see if it's accepted. If it isn't, you can always send the new version to a different periodical. If it is, you *might* decide to suggest possible changes (keeping in mind that you risk irritating the editor), or you might realize that the poem was already effective in its previous version.

You can spare yourself and the editor this situation if you only send poems you're satisfied with and have finished redrafting.

—

Melanie Cameron is poetry co-editor of *Prairie Fire Magazine*. Her book, *Holding the Dark* (poetry, The Muses' Company, 1999), was shortlisted for the Eileen MacTavish Sykes Award for Best First Book by a Manitoban Writer, and she was shortlisted for the John Hirsch Award for Most Promising Manitoban Writer.

# Beware of Poetry Contests

*by Eileen Kernaghan*

It seems that every literary magazine and writers' organization in the country is running a poetry competition. In most cases, the sponsors are legitimate and the aims are worthwhile: improving a membership or subscription base, bringing recognition and financial rewards to deserving poets.

Usually, in order to cover prizes and other expenses, entry fees are charged. These may be nominal (a dollar or two) or, when large cash prizes and prestigious judges are involved, or if a magazine subscription is included, they can be considerably higher. If you're talented and lucky enough to win a major competition, the returns on that investment can be substantial.

**Beware of the vanity contests...**

Then there are the vanity contests: those money-grabbing schemes that pop up like weeds in print and on the Internet.

"World's Best Poetry Contest: Up to $20,000 in prizes! Become a Published Poet!"

How is the struggling writer to distinguish the reputable contests from the not-so-reputable?

Some warning signs:

- Expensive, high-pressure ads in mass-circulation publications. Legitimate writers' organizations are more likely to run modest announcements in publications read by the writing community such as literary magazines, writers' newsletters, etc.
- Very large cash prizes with no entry fee. Ask yourself how this contest is being financed.

If you submit to one of these pseudo-contests, your letter of acceptance, which you will almost certainly get, should also set off alarm bells. Every sentence oozes flattery; you've been selected for publication solely on the basis of your "rare and unique talent."

In a legitimate competition, you're judged by recognized professionals or, at least, by your writing peers. In the vanity contests, there's no discrimination. Good poems and deliberately awful ones receive the same lavish praise. The anthology itself will be described in glowing terms: "One of the most highly acclaimed additions to the pool of poetic literature," raves one promotional piece. They're selling books, not snake oil, but the language is the same.

There are no free contributors' copies. However, you will be asked to buy your author's copy and, they hope, several more for your friends and relatives, and your local library, at up to $150 each. You will be expected to attend a convention (registration fee: $495) or join their illustrious organization ($125) or attend a poetry camp where your name goes up in lights ($600 for 3 days).

Note, for example, that the National Library of Poetry anthologies extend to 600 pages with 10 poems per page. That's 6000 aspiring poets and I suspect that the organizers are sure that a fair percentage will buy the book.

**Do your research...**

If you're in doubt about the validity of a contest, take the time to do some research. Talk to your provincial writers' federation. Phone your library and your local bookseller to ask if they've ever heard of the sponsoring organization or its publications. Check with the Better Business Bureau. Easiest of all is a search for "Poetry Scams" on the Internet, where you'll find handy lists of the Worst Online Poetry Contests.

An August 2002 Internet search for the phrase "National Library of Poetry" using the AltaVista search engine turned up 2801 matches, including a long string of postings by disenchanted contest entrants. As one disgruntled "winner" remarked, "it seems there are one million unique poets out there."

—

Eileen Kernaghan is editor of the Burnaby Writers' Newsletter, and serves on the group's contest committee. She is the author of five novels and coauthor of two nonfiction books. (A shorter version of this article appeared in *WordWorks,* newsletter of the Federation of BC Writers, and on the League of Canadian Poets website.)

# Teaching Aspiring Poets

*by Anne Fairley*

"With me poetry has not been a purpose, but a passion."
*Edgar Allan Poe*

When teaching poetry, my first step is to discuss haiku. The reason? It is short, succinct and fun. Plus, it should be untitled, another challenge for the poet. Prose can function with plenty of words, but poets have to chose words well and express themselves in tight, waste-free language. In some cases it's quite a challenge.

I've taught students from ages 8 to 80. I encourage them to use their instincts to branch out into free verse, blank verse, couplets, quatrains, or rhyme if they wish. It is important to allow them an opportunity to find their own niche. Eventually they may want to try sonnets, ballads or odes. Or they may want to remain with free verse, which I personally prefer.

**Work with themes...**

I provide certain themes. For instance, I encourage them to write about plants and flowers in a less traditional way. When I was disheartened to find that all terrain vehicles (ATVs) had almost eliminated the Prairie Crocus in an area near our cottage, my poem "Survivors of Mechanical Predators" reflected this.

Students will equate certain flowers with death, happiness or love. Perhaps they will choose to reflect on what the scent of certain flowers brings to mind. Or the colour. The possibilities are endless.

**Work with the surroundings...**

The two topics that I like to combine are season and time of day. I ask the students to consider the changes in landscape created as the seasons shift from spring to summer, autumn and winter. Each day is further modified as it changes from sunrise to noon, late afternoon and sunset. Students discover and reveal, line by line, amazing details of their surroundings under these differing circumstances.

**Work with images...**

Photographs entice students to think poetically. As an instructor, I provide a photo, usually of a person or a group. Then I supply questions to stimulate students to use their innate curiosity. (No one who wants to write wouldn't be curious.) Questions usually include the person's (or persons') age, occupation, era, location, family situation and so on. Students are surprised at their own ingenuity. After they read the poems, and I reveal who the person is, their interpretations leave all of us with much to ponder. Some will have revealed much about the person or their own personality; others will have used imagination to create someone entirely different. It's fun and remarkable, too.

**Work with layout...**

Encouraging students to use layout to enhance their poetry often stimulates the creative aspect. For instance, I ask them to experiment with line depth and centering, circles or diamond shapes, slopes or whatever. With computers as tools, anything is possible.

This results in unique words (that's where a Thesaurus might be considered a tool) and line lengths as well.

**Work with words.**

Another idea I have found popular, is to provide several words and ask students to write a poem including all of them. You may want to chose a noun, an adjective and a verb. Or a word that can be used in various forms. For instance, love, lovely, loved. Possibilities, endless!

**Work with events...**

Supplying a news item and writing about it from their own perspective is always popular with students. For instance, one very well known poet used a tragedy to write about the problems of a love/hate relationship in a marriage. The result is a moving, emotional work. The events of September 11, 2001 have encouraged many to write poetry. Often it is the only genre to really express one's feelings.

**Work with location...**

At some point in our sessions, I ask poets to reflect on where they do their best work. Is it at a table, a chair by a window or in bed? Then I ask them to change location while composing the same poem and see what happens. For some, the results do not change, but for others location is everything.

A location that greatly changes perspective is an eating establishment. I encourage them to try to write a poem about someone they see and are curious about in a café. Then I request that they refrain from reworking the poem, just bring it to class the way it streamed out.

**Work with caesura...**

However, whatever the style or subject, since I discovered the value of the caesura, I've shared it with my students. Caesura, or "pause," is, in my opinion, a useful tool in poetry. Rather than three periods, backward and forward slashes, commas or dashes, the caesura encourages the writer to pause and make the most of each and every line and word. In my own work the caesura reveals so much.

For instance, in my poem "Gram's Lilacs" it proved invaluable:

"They were always there
in the yard    waiting
as she    unconditionally."

For me, as you can tell, teaching, writing and sharing the love of poetry is tremendously rewarding.

One of my older students told me that writing poetry has made her life more meaningful.

What more could an instructor want?

—

Although Anne Fairley has written many nonfiction pieces, she loves poetry as a reader and a writer. Through the years she has used her love of the genre to share the pleasure with children and adults.

# Writing Songs

*by Bruce Madole*

If you can write and you can hum, you can probably write a song. Whether you can write a great artistic or commercial song, is a different question. But I'd like to see you try. Really. More than that, I'd like to see you succeed, so I've written down a few helpful pointers.

An average commercial song is made up of about 18 lines. That's three verses times four lines each, which makes 12 lines; then add four more lines for a chorus (that makes 16), and two lines for a bridge. All in all: 18 lines to change the world. Then, or sometimes first, you need a melody that goes with your words like skin over muscle and bone. Something original, something powerful, and something so simple that any child could hum or sing it. Something so lasting that it leaves a space in the air and in your chest after it's gone.

That's what we, as songwriters, try for all our lives ... and we may never get there.

**Song lyrics need structure...**

Each part of a song lyric has a specific role. Verse, chorus, bridge — each one strengthens the effect of the other parts.

Verses are where you tell the main part of your story, that is, whatever you have decided your song is to be about. Is it about lost love? You might decide that verse one should be about how you fell in love, so that verse two can be about how you broke up, and verse three can be about how you want your lover to come back and try again (or not). By deciding what each verse does within your story, you have to write clearly in a confined space. There's not a lot of room for wandering around in a verse of four or perhaps six lines. Get right to the point. Say something that matters.

Song lyrics need a consistent structure, because they have to interface with the music. By consistent structure, I mean that your lines should be of approximately the same length, with the same number of syllables, and with approximately the same internal rhythms and stresses in each line. (If not in each line, try to create rhythmic and structural relationships within pairs or groups of lines.)

## Show, don't tell...

The language you use may be poetic, but it needs to sustain meaning. It shouldn't be flowery, overwrought or vague. When Mark Knopfler wrote about "prehistoric garbage trucks" in the lyric for *Your Latest Trick*, he conjured up a powerful image with one lean phrase. Aim for a style of language that flows conversationally, as though you had something you wanted to show, not tell, a very good friend. Draw pictures with your words. If you are in love, find ways to show it; if you are sad, write about how you act when you are sad, or how you look. Your listeners will catch the picture in their imagination and say, "Yeah, that's a sad person there, doing those things." They will identify with, and understand, and share more of the feelings that lie beneath the words.

Song lyrics need to rhyme because it helps listeners remember and follow along with a song. Songwriters are encouraged to use a different rhyme scheme in the verses than the chorus, e.g. if you rhymed pairs of lines in the verse, then try rhyming alternate lines in the chorus. It makes the chorus stand out from the verses.

## The chorus represents the lyrical and musical climax...

A chorus needs to stand out from the verses because it represents the lyrical and musical climax of the song. Unlike the climax of a story though, a chorus is repeated — often three or even four times. At the very heart of your chorus is the single most memorable, unique and powerful element of all: the hook. The hook is the single phrase or line that supplies the title and the meaning of your song.

If you study great songs, you will see how often the content of the preceding verse brings out new shades of meaning in the chorus that follows, even though the chorus itself hasn't changed. How is this possible? Verses often provide us with new knowledge, and that knowledge can change how we react to the words of the chorus.

## A musical bridge brings variation...

In addition to verses and your chorus, you may want to use a musical bridge. Not every song requires a bridge, but you should learn how to write one. A bridge is a short musical section — often two lines or eight musical bars — designed to bring new perspective and musical variation to your song. Typically, a bridge appears about two-thirds of the way through a song: after a second chorus or leading into a third verse. You can use it to reinforce the message of your chorus or to take a different point of view as a way to add contrast. Used well, a bridge builds additional lyrical, emotional and musical momentum to drive home the chorus.

Study musical form and lyrical structures of your favourite songs and the music. Understanding how a song works doesn't take away from its joy or power any more than understanding a heartbeat would diminish the pleasure of a lover's kiss.

If you don't play or write music yourself, get involved in songwriting workshops and seek out collaborators. You don't actually have to play an instrument; you can sing your melody ideas or record them on tape.

**Learn about the music business...**

Get involved in the organizations that focus on songwriting: the Songwriters Association of Canada (SAC), the Canadian Country Music Association (CCMA), the Nashville Songwriters Association International (NSAI), the Folk Alliance, and others. Take courses and attend workshops. If you begin to take songwriting seriously, you will need to learn about the music business — there is much to learn, it's complex, and some of it is not pleasant.

I won't recommend writing songs as a way to make extra cash or to build up a fragile ego. Commercial songwriting is fraught with difficulty and overrun with competition. Most of us labour for years without significant accomplishment. Your work will be rejected, most of the time. Get over it. Write a better song next time. If you keep trying, you will.

—

Bruce Madole is a member of the Canadian Country Music Association (CCMA), the Songwriters Association of Canada (SAC), and the Nashville Songwriter's Association International (NSAI), and is a co-coordinator of the NSAI's Toronto Regional Workshop. He has had nine songs cut by Canadian recording artists.

# Be Your Own Publicist

*by Kimberley Alcock*

A self-published friend of mine recently participated in a poetry reading featuring five poets. Of the sixty-odd people in the audience, over two-thirds were people that she had invited. How did she get such a great turnout? The answer lies in publicity.

Author publicity means getting media attention such as radio or television programs, or printed articles, which feature your book. If you're self-publishing your work, or if you have published with a small press that doesn't have a large publicity budget, you can take charge of publicity and the success of your book by being your own publicist. Here are some guidelines for creating your own publicity campaign.

**Make a plan...**

Every good campaign begins with a plan. It should include your contact list, dates to make contacts (lead time) and dates for sending out copies of your book and press kits. Remember to set goals for yourself. How many media interviews do you intend to get? Be realistic. If you're a new writer, you likely won't get interviews with top magazines. On the other hand, success never comes from lack of trying. Be assertive when pitching your work to the press, but also remember to be polite.

**The media list...**

The media list is essential for the publicist. A good list is the first step towards good results. Divide the list into names of programs for radio or television, and names of supplements or sections for newspapers and magazines. Then list contact names (writers, editors and producers) for every program, supplement, or section. Also include program times for radio and television. Then comes the contact information, which includes phone number(s), fax, e-mail, and mailing address. The contact list should also include any important details about the program or section, and upcoming editorial. For example, the food section of newspaper X is looking for articles about Canadian wine for the spring issue.

Even before you get published, you should start building your media list, as it takes considerable time to collect the information. You likely already have the building blocks of a media list in your file drawers where you keep guidelines and potential articles. Keep your eyes open for any publication, or television or radio program that's related to your writing field. For example, if you write history books then keep a lookout for any journals or programs that are related to history, as these are the people that will be interested in your book.

If your publisher doesn't have a publicity budget, they should still have a media list and be willing to give you contact information for your campaign as success with your book means profit for both you and the publisher. Also check with your fellow writers for suggestions.

**Lead time...**

Lead time is the amount of time that you need to contact the media prior to the publicity. Magazines have the greatest amount of lead time since they plan their publications far in advance. Daily publications usually have the shortest amount of lead time, and radio and television programs can vary. When you make up your contact list, ask what the lead time is and be sure to get them press kits in plenty of time.

**Press releases and media kits...**

The media kit is a package that your send out to solicit attention for your book. It should always include a press release, and may also include photographs and biographical information. And your book should always accompany it. The press release should be written in journalistic style and include the "who, what, where, when, how and why" of journalistic writing. It should be titled "Media Release" in capitals, followed on the next line by "For Immediate Release" and then dated. The release should end with the symbol " 30-" which signifies the end of the release or any information that can be issued in the press, and the bottom of the release should include your name and phone number for further contact information.

**Getting the media's attention...**

After you've got your contact list and press kits in order, the next step is sending out the press releases and/or media kits. Ideally, the press release should stir the interest of the person reading it so much that they call you and ask for an interview.

However, this is not always the case as editors and producers receive sometimes hundreds of releases a day on their desk. This means that you need to follow up the release with a phone call and offer your suggestions about why their publication should write a review about your book or interview you. Before you call, practice your pitch and story angle to make sure that what you pitch is reasonable for their publication. Who is their target audience? Why would a story on you and your book appeal to their audience or readers?

**Booking the interview...**

If you're booking a number of interviews over a short period of days (commonly known as the media tour), let the media know that you're on tour for those specific days. If you're booking interviews in your hometown, try to be flexible since media people have very tight schedules. Do not, unless absolutely necessary, change interview times as this creates a risk of losing the interview altogether.

**Before, during and after the interview...**

Before the interview, think about possible questions and responses, and if you're doing live interviews for the first time, practice taping yourself beforehand so you're comfortable with cameras and recorders. Be on time and be polite. Arriving late throws programming off schedule and you're more likely to be remembered as the late rather than the great writer. After the interview is over, thank the interviewer and follow up with a brief thank you note. Remember that whoever is interviewing you is helping your career. A little appreciation goes a long way in establishing good rapport.

**Publicity events...**

Readings and book launches are spring-offs for creating publicity for your book. The launch party or readings are opportunities for the press to meet you face to face. When planning readings, try and determine if there are other writers in the community that can do readings with you as this creates even more publicity. For example, if you've just written a travel guide to Vancouver, is there an author who has a restaurant guide that might want to read or launch with you? Ask your publisher and writing community for suggestions. In the end, the more press you have at your launch or reading, the more attention your book will receive.

—

Kimberley Alcock is a writer, teacher, editor and former publicist for several publishing houses. Her publicity work has included book launches, press conferences, and publicity campaigns for several prominent international and BC authors, including Nick Bantock, Farley Mowat, Andrew Morton, Lesley Forbes, Patrick Lane, and Linda Svendsen.

# Triple Filing for Poets & Lyricists

*by Bernice Lever*

Accurate record keeping is important for any business or professional endeavour, but professional poets and lyricists may wish to keep three types of chronological files: (1) Creative, (2) Publishing and (3) Financial records.

**Creative records** preserve one's growth as a writer as well providing a storage place for unfinished ideas and uncompleted inspirations. My first draft scribblers of dated poems and fragments — as short as a few phrases — span four decades. These provide an archaeology lesson of my writing life. Now (since mid-1980s), my computer files contain polished copies — third or further drafts — but the original wording may still be the best!

But do keep chronological paper notebooks as disks can become "unreadable." Technology evolves faster than a writer can revise old starter pieces or create new works from other fragments. Your biographer may appreciate these notebooks or journals, or you can choose to have your executor destroy them when they are of no further use to you.

**Publishing records** are necessary for accurate bibliographic listing or acknowledgments for anthologies, your own book collections, reprints as well as proper rights in various media and/or geographic areas. My marketing notebooks list which poems have been sent where each month, any contest fees or possible prizes and later, rejections or acceptances with expected publishing dates.

Poets and lyricists soon learn that rejections outnumber acceptances in "literary bingo." It isn't like nonfiction where potential markets can evaluated through query letters, but lyricists and poets *can* learn editors' and musicians' or producers' tastes and requirements from all those rejection slips. Rejection notices with added handwritten words can provide valuable instruction.

Publishing records stop me from sending the same five poems to the same editor in succeeding years. Once you have a few dozen poems or songs to market, only a marketing book or computer file will help you avoid duplications or omissions in your submission plans. It takes an organized filing system to track which poems or songs have been printed in magazines, newsletters, newspapers, websites, books, etc., or broadcast on radio and television, or recorded on cassette or CD, or performed on stages, and in which countries in English and/or in translation.

Some very efficient writers keep an index card for each poem and song. If this is daunting, think of Gordon Lightfoot (as a creator of hundreds of songs) who needs to keep track of the dozens of performers who record some of his songs each and every year!

**Financial records** organize your income tax information and track whether your annual writing accounts are in a negative or positive balance. Writers can maintain a "home office" with deductible expenses, but take advice from a good tax accountant.

You should try to keep receipts and bills for all expenses. These may include a percentage of your housing costs and utilities, monthly Internet connection, part of your car or transportation costs, phone charges, postage, office supplies and equipment, books, newspapers, journals, writer memberships and conference fees, stationery, business cards, contest entry fees, self-promotion ads or flyers, copying costs, workshop fees, and much more.

Your income list will probably record your Public Lending Right (PLR) and Access Copyright™ payments, reader, performance or speaker fees, royalties from all sources, direct sales of your broadsheets, books, cassettes or CDs, workshop leader fees, grants, awards, prizes, editing manuscripts or judging contests payments, and/or other writer generated monies.

Working with other creative people, such as musicians who may set musical notes to your poems, or dancers who may choreograph your lyrics, or artists who may paint or sculpt images for your words, will lead to entries of co-operative ventures in your files. So do not waste time and talent searching for forgotten or mislaid pieces of information. Consider these three sets of files, stored disks or computer files as keys for a successful writing life.

—

Bernice Lever, current President of CAA, Vancouver, has retired from teaching English at Seneca College (Toronto) to live on Bowen Island, BC. She continues to publish, to lead writing workshops and to give readings. A literary editor, her seventh book of poems is *BLESSINGS*, Black Moss, 2000. She is Literary Chair of the Bowen Island Festival of the Arts which is held each summer. Known as "Granny Grammar," her composition text and much more are listed on her website: www.colourofwords.com.

# 9. People & Places Past

# Writing a Biography

*by Cheryl MacDonald*

On some level, everything we write is about people. Whether it's a personal essay, a blockbuster novel or a newspaper report, what a person does and why is usually the underlying theme. Because of this, writing biography is, in many ways, just like any other kind of writing.

But writing biography is also different. A good biographer tries to distill the essence of a life and re-create a living, breathing person on the printed page. Done well, a biography can give the reader the illusion that, for at least a little while, he has been intimately acquainted with an outstanding individual.

**Pick your person...**

Whether you're writing a biographical article or a full-length book, you will be living with your subject for quite a while. You must either find that individual fascinating or so important that you'll be compelled to continue. You don't necessarily have to like the subject of your biography, but it helps to have some respect and admiration for the individual's accomplishments. I once tackled a biographical article of a 19th century literary figure whose work was widely admired. I knew relatively little about the writer when I started, but by the time I was finished, I absolutely loathed her. The piece was published, but it was definitely not my favourite project.

Liking a subject too much can create other problems. The day of biographer as publicist is pretty much past. In fairness to the reader, the biography you write should present a balanced portrait. If your subject is one you deeply admire, commit yourself to being as unbiased as possible in your writing. This may be doubly difficult if the subject is a friend or relative, but your work will be stronger and definitely more professional.

**Do your research...**

You have probably read several books or articles about your subject already. To make the leap from reader to biographer, you must read everything that's been written — the good and the bad. Examine scholarly works as well. If no full-length scholarly biography exists, delve into academic treatments of subjects that might be related. While a scholarly approach might not be suitable for the readers you are targeting, the analysis and list of resources will be extremely useful.

Personal papers, diaries and letters are excellent resources, providing you can find them. In addition to contacting libraries or large archives, try smaller museums and historical societies. It can also be helpful to write letters to newspaper editors or organizations with which your subject was involved. Interviews with your subject or colleagues, family and friends are another way of amassing the information you'll need to complete your project.

And don't overlook audio-visual records. Gather every photograph you can of the subject. You'll want some of these to illustrate your book or article. But you'll also want to examine them for clues to your subject's personality. After years researching the life of poet Wilson MacDonald, I knew he liked to dress well. But a shot of him in pants and a sports jacket when everyone else was in beach clothes underscored the fastidiousness that was so much a part of his character.

That particular shot was in an old home movie and was used in a video I scripted for a local historical society. Wilson's nephew David MacDonald, who handled the videography and narration, also located an old 78 recording of his uncle reciting poetry. Since I had never heard Wilson recite his poetry, I was absolutely delighted. Not only did the recording enhance the video, it also provided me with additional understanding about my subject. If you are writing a biography about a 20th century personality, make sure you explore the possibilities offered by film and sound archives.

### Refining and writing...

Research is often the most time-consuming aspect of writing a biography, and frequently the most costly and frustrating. You will find gaps: a diary discontinued for several months or years, papers burned by a relative concerned about the family's reputation. You will also find conflicting information. One of the biographer's most challenging tasks is to sort through various versions of a story and present a narrative that comes as close as possible to the truth.

A useful method for refining your research, as well as pinpointing some conflicts in the historic record, is the creation of a chronology or timeline. At the very least, you should have a detailed record of your subject's activities, starting with date of birth. Include locations as well, and make sure you note the source of your information. A good chronology can sometimes speed up the verification of a disputed fact.

Naturally you will question every fact you encounter, even those that sound most plausible. For instance, Wilson MacDonald Memorial School Museum was named because the well-known poet was born a short distance away. His grandparents ran the village store, his mother was buried nearby, and many people assume that he started his education in what was once McGaw's School. In fact, his first experience with formal education was in another village, although he later attended McGaw's for a few weeks.

Inevitably you will encounter quotations or anecdotes attributed to your subject. Again, verification is essential. Sometimes, legends spring up during a famous person's lifetime that have no basis or are wild exaggerations. Your task is to establish what information is accurate and what is not.

You must also immerse yourself in your subject's time period. Understanding an era may give you some insight into why your subject acted in a particular way, or why certain opportunities were closed to him. It will also give you a frame of reference for judging your subject's character. For instance, attitudes and language that are considered politically incorrect today might have been thought liberal in the past. The only way you'll know which applies to your subject is if you understand the times in which he lived.

**Writing...**

While you may have a general outline in mind during the research process, it usually is a better idea to wait until research is complete before you commit yourself to any one approach. A strictly chronological account may work for subjects whose careers tended to be linear, or where there's a discernible dramatic pattern. For my biography of Emma Albani, the choice was straightforward: early years of struggle, her career as one of the most celebrated operatic sopranos in the British Empire, followed by years of decline and poverty. But most people's lives are far more complicated, so a thematic approach might work better. Wilson MacDonald was simultaneously a poet, musician, artist, performer and a mentally tormented individual. It makes more sense to explore each of these areas of his life separately. If you opt for a thematic approach, you can always include an abbreviated chronology to help the reader stay on track.

Whichever approach you choose be sure to include lots of anecdotes and quotations. William Van Horne, the great 19th century railway builder, was also a talented artist with a puckish sense of humour. But simply stating this is nowhere near as effective as telling how Van Horne once dashed off a painting, framed it, then tried to convince his guests that it was a newly purchased European masterpiece. In the same way, your subject's actual words will be far more vivid than simply paraphrasing.

Writing biography requires just about every skill in a writer's repertoire. You need description to set the scene, exposition to explain specific events, careful plotting to make the narrative as interesting as a novel. To do this, you will probably discard more than half of the research material you've gathered, but like the back story in a novel, it is not wasted. All that research has given you insight that you might not otherwise have had, and your biography will be livelier for it.

—

Cheryl MacDonald has written several biographical articles and two full-length biographies, *Emma Albani: Victorian Diva* and *Adelaide Hoodless: Domestic Crusader*. She is now working on a biography of poet Wilson MacDonald.

# Writing a Family History

*by Betty Dyck*

I begin my workshops with an anecdote about the "Mennonite Game," a game I learned when I married into the Manitoba Mennonite community. At an initial meeting people trace back their lineage beginning with the East and West Reserve (east and west of the Red River where Mennonites settled in Manitoba), the year of emigration and thence to Europe. The game continues until you finally connect with a shared relative, no matter how distant. Once that's settled, you have established your place in the order of things. You belong.

My hope is that a written family history will give our children a strong sense of belonging.

Many people are attempting to leave a written heritage for their children. You will have a head start if, as parents, you kept looseleaf or scrapbooks of their activities. After our children left home, I gathered all the material collected throughout the years into individual three-ring binders. This included report cards, school pictures, Brownie, Beaver, Girl Guide and Scout merits, baptismal, musical and graduation certificates, plus captioned photographs. These books were indispensable in rounding out our family history.

**Begin with what you know...**

Time, patience and perseverance are the main ingredients, and are usually only rediscovered once your children have left home. Begin with what you know — and work backwards.

Genealogical charts play an important role in registering time frames for telling the story. We had one on the Dyck side and then we acquired others regarding my ancestors (one of which dates back to the 1700s when the first McLeod of our clan landed in Newfoundland). These are later incorporated into an appendix.

A family tree is much like a winter elm if it contains only names. Add the green leaves of summer by providing brief histories of each member. My father-in-law's obituary tells of his 47 years teaching in southern Manitoba. He sang in church choirs from the time he was 17. Grampa Dyck loved music and singing, and led a young people's band in which all his children played musical instruments. So teaching, the love of music and the ability to sing are part of our children's heritage.

In any project, memory plays a large part, so special family celebrations throughout the years can provide great clues. Once you exhaust memorabilia collections and interviews, the next step is usually a visit to your local genealogical society. It can direct you to available sources such as provincial and national archives.

Principal sources for genealogical research in Canada include census records, vital statistics (births, deaths, marriages), wills and records of land holdings, estates, military service and immigration. Baptismal and marriage certificates often lead to places where further information might be on record. Libraries have back issues of newspapers on microfilm. Through inter-library loan, microfilmed newspapers from most cities can be forwarded to your local library.

**Anecdotes can make for pleasant reading...**

Once your research is completed, write succinctly. The most important element is to record your story. Think about the words you are using — familiar words in short, simple sentences with active verbs. Consider the project a series of chapters or short stories, not a whole book. Liberal use of family anecdotes can make for pleasant reading.

An outline is my guide, but you may find the need to change it several times as you work with the material. Originally I planned to put published articles and poems drawn from family events in an appendix, but found them better suited for inclusion in relevant chapters.

I decided to tell our story in the first person, and acknowledged other sources. For instance, my grandfather kept a sparse diary of his Boer War service; I found a letter in the *Saint John Globe* written by a soldier travelling on the same troop ship. The letter gave an authentic account of the ocean voyage from Saint John, New Brunswick to Cape Town, South Africa. I also found journalists' accounts of the train trip and marches through the African countryside. Including these will give our children graphic descriptions of their grandparents' lives.

**A Proposed Chronological Outline for a Family History...**

Preface : Your reason for compiling this family history.

Acknowledgments: A mention of others who contributed to your compilation and family history.

Chapter 1: Paternal family background.

Chapter 2: Maternal family background.

Chapter 3: First twenty years of paternal grandparents' lives and how they met and married.

Chapter 4: First twenty years of maternal grandparents' lives and how they met and married.

Chapter 5: Birth and first 20 years of father's life or until marriage to mother.

Chapter 6: Birth and first 20 years of mother's life or until marriage to father.

Chapter 7: How parents met, where they lived, early married life including occupations and associations, travel and accomplishments.

Chapter 8: Family history up to the present. Possibly your own marriage, children and grandchildren.

Pictures: Inserted into the text or grouped as whole pages. It is popular to have a picture section (with captions) one-third and two-thirds through the book, to sustain focus on the story.

Appendix: Lists of names, dates and places of births/deaths as far back as you have researched. Also, maps indicating places of origins, especially if the towns have since disappeared or have been renamed. Certificates of births, baptisms, marriages, university degrees, other achievements, deaths, etc.

Bibliography: A detailed list of sources you used to round out your own family history.

Writing a family history is a personal project and there are as many ways to tackle it as there are people. There is always the chance that, once you have completed your family history, you can use the research to write another book like David Macfarlane's *The Danger Tree*, which won the Canadian Authors Association literary award for nonfiction in 1992.

—

Betty Dyck is the Winnipeg-based author of three nonfiction books, editor of two church histories, a published poet and freelance writer who conducts workshops on creative nonfiction and writing family histories.

# Writing a Community History

*by Cheryl MacDonald*

Writing a community history can be a great chance to learn about the past while exercising your writing skills. It can also be an enormous challenge, so careful planning is essential.

First off, let's define a community history. There are literally thousands in print. Most can be divided into three broad categories:

*Geographic* — focusing on a physical location, such as a town, county, or urban neighbourhood.

*Social* — here the focus is on people, often specific ethnic or religious groups.

*Organizational* — churches, schools, service clubs and other organizations are communities in their own right, with their own distinctive history and culture.

None of these categories is cut and dried. For instance, when I was hired to write the history of the Jarvis Lions Club, it quickly became apparent that the club's history was to some extent a history of the town. The approach you choose will depend on your interests, the material available and your publisher. It may also depend on whether you are writing the history on your own or working with a committee.

**Committee work...**

There can be advantages to a committee-driven community history. There is more opportunity to publicize the project and bring more material. Committees affiliated with nonprofit organizations may be eligible for publishing grants or tax breaks. And, since community histories often run several hundred pages, several people can share the workload.

There are, however, disadvantages, including politics, personality clashes and conflicting visions of what the finished book should be. Will stories be presented in chronological order? Or will different chapters discuss different themes? Will genealogies or farm histories be included?

As soon as possible, gather samples of community histories, note those that appeal, those that don't, analyze why, then make an outline of what your book will be like. If you're dealing with a committee, this may take hours of discussion, but it will avoid problems later on. And keep in mind that an outline can be changed as the book evolves.

Once you know your approach, it's time to gather material. Perhaps the local museum has an extensive archive, the organization has preserved all its minutes, or the town newspaper is available on microfilm. Use these. But also consider interviewing people or asking them to write down their memories. Individuals may also have historical documents — letters, diaries, minute books — that are not available anywhere else. An appeal in your local newspaper or historical society bulletin can bring in some wonderful material.

Don't restrict your research to local sources. Provincial and federal government reports, especially in the 19th and early 20th centuries, often contain interesting information. Newspapers from neighbouring towns can be valuable. I once ran across a report of a scandal involving a small-town doctor and an abandoned baby. The local newspaper ignored the story, but a city newspaper covered it in detail.

Your research should also include sources of photographs and other illustrative material. Think of maps, sketches, old newspaper advertisements and posters to add to the visual appeal of the book.

While you're gathering material, look for "hidden" stories. Too many community histories focus on dominant social or political groups, or people connected with the most prominent founding families.

**What about ethnic minorities? Women? Workers?**

Ten years after serving as editor and chief writer for a book on the history of Dunnville, Ontario, I stumbled across a fabulous story. In the 1960s, female workers, most of them French Canadian, went on strike at a local factory. To call attention to their cause, they marched to the provincial legislature in Toronto. This dramatic event should have made it into the book. But no one suggested it, apparently because mid-20th century labour disputes did not meet the committee's definition of local history.

Stretching the definition of local history means thinking of the big picture. Your main audience will probably be people from the community. Many of them may not be great history readers, and some will be young students.

Part of your task is to give at least some indication of how your community's story paralleled or differed from what was happening elsewhere in the province, the country and the world.

**Writing it down...**

Writing should begin fairly early in the project with a preliminary draft. As research continues, the drafts will be expanded, revised and refined. When a single author is involved, it is easier to produce a cohesive manuscript with a strong narrative voice. When several authors are involved, especially when many of them are inexperienced, producing a book can be a nightmare. If you find yourself serving as chief writer or editor for a book committee, insist on developing an editorial policy. If you ask the community for stories, what will you do if several people submit stories on the same topic? How will you handle unpleasant or controversial events, such as murders or political scandals? What style will you use when it comes to spelling and punctuation? Will you refer to people by surname after the initial reference?

Even if you are working on your own, a personal editorial policy is useful. If a trade publisher is handling the book, the publisher's house style will probably prevail. But if you are self-publishing, creating your own policy and style guide will help you avoid inconsistencies in the text.

Community standards also have to be considered if you want to ensure your book is read. Lurid descriptions of sex and violence probably don't belong, especially if there are plans to put the book into schools. But sex and violence are a part of history and sometimes need to be mentioned in passing.

**Bring people to life...**

The most important thing to remember about writing a community history is *people*. As much as possible, tell your story through the actions of people. Use anecdotes to bring them to life. Remember that there are no saints, so don't rely solely on a newspaper obituary or laudatory family history. If you can describe flaws and eccentricities, you'll create a much more realistic portrait.

Quotations also help bring history to life. You may not be able to interview long-dead local heroes, but you can use diaries, letters or newspaper articles to good advantage. Just be sure to present quoted material accurately. There can be no changes in punctuation or spelling, even if there are errors in the original, unless the reader is informed about the changes by such devices as square brackets or ellipses. The same applies to oral history, although writers usually eliminate verbal ticks such as "um" and "er."

You may also have to decide on how to handle language that is politically incorrect but perfectly captures a particularly time or place. I recall one instance where our book committee debated the use of a racial epithet. We could have paraphrased the quotation in which it appeared, losing some of the impact in the process. Instead, we put it into the book, preceded by a sentence that made it clear to readers that the committee recognized the objectionable nature of the word.

Charts can also be helpful, both as part of the research process and part of the final text. For one project, I created a chart showing when various schoolhouses were built, what material was used, when plumbing and electricity were installed. There were gaps, and the chart was not used in the book, but it did provide insight into the evolution of the county's education system. Charts can also save space and sustain reader interest when presenting quantities of similar information, such as a list of town politicians or the date when various churches were established. You can also use sidebars or box text to present material that's interesting but doesn't fit easily into the main narrative.

Think about maps, too. If you can't use a map, then be very careful when describing settings. Phrases like "across from Brown's bakery" or "two farms down from the red mill" mean nothing if Brown's bakery burned down in 1930 and the red mill is now a bed and breakfast. Street addresses, lot and concession numbers are far more useful to the reader.

**Include a bibliography and an index...**

Speaking of references, you should decide early on whether to include footnotes or endnotes in the published version. At the very least, you may want to have an annotated version of the manuscript on file, both to answer questions about your sources, and to assist future researchers. (You might also arrange to deposit all working papers from the book project at a local library or museum). And you should definitely include a bibliography and an index. I routinely included two indexes in community histories — a general index, listing all the topics covered and a personal names index. You'd be surprised how many people will buy a book simply because a family member's name is mentioned!

When the book is finished, congratulate yourself. There may be criticism from some readers who disagree with your version of the past, or who wonder why certain stories were overlooked. But if you've carried the project through from concept to published book, you've created a legacy that future authors and historians can build upon!

—

Cheryl MacDonald's community history books include *Port Dover: A Summer Garden*, *Memories of Van Wagner's Beach*, *Parkview Survey* and *Splendor in the Fall: Norfolk County Fair*. A heritage columnist with the *Simcoe Times-Reformer* and frequent contributor to *The Beaver*, she holds history degrees from McMaster University and the University of Waterloo.

# 10. Newspapers & Periodicals

# Ten Tips When You're Stuck at the Start

*by Mark Kearney*

A lead, a lead, my kingdom for a lead.

You may not actually hear news and feature writers crying out this pseudo-Shakespearean speech when they're stuck on how to begin an article, but they may be frustrated enough to think about making such a trade if they could just find a way to begin. After all, a good beginning is crucial in grabbing a reader's attention.

We've all come up against a mini writer's block at some point in our careers when we want to start a news or feature article, and fortunately there are some "formula" leads we can call on to get the creative juices flowing.

In the 10 years I've been teaching writing to adult students, I've encountered just about every possible way to start an article. But here are 10 (and I used a version of one of them to start this piece) that can kick-start you into writing the article you want.

They're not the only way, of course, but they can come in handy if you're stuck. Each example is followed by an explanation of why this particular kind of lead can work.

The basic facts used here are taken from an article I wrote for a business publication in 1996. It examined how bartering products and services among companies is becoming a growing trend rather than the traditional way of shelling out money each time.

The lead I used in my article was:

1. Your carpet cleaning company needs a computer, but you're short on cash. The computer firm has excess equipment but really needs some advertising that's beyond its budget. And the radio station has ad time it hasn't been able to sell.

In the bartering world of "I'll scratch your back if you scratch mine" — or the next person's for that matter — everyone's needs can be met without any exchange of money.

(This is the "you" kind of lead where you talk directly to readers in the second person and try to involve them in the article that way. I like this style and use it as much as I can get away with. This is also a type of colourful, descriptive lead where you give examples right at the start to illustrate what the article is about. They give the readers something they may be able to relate to. The downside is this style can be a bit long for many news stories because it takes two paragraphs to get to the point.)

Other possibilities:

2. Bartering trades and services is a hot new trend in the business world that's proving popular with companies short of cash.

(Straight news lead, bare bones, no flourishes. It's short. I don't like writing more than 30 words in an opening paragraph unless it's a longer feature, and this kind of lead gets the reader right to the heart of the matter. It's the kind of inverted pyramid style lead where you start with the most important thing right at the top and then work your way to the least important at the end. It can be dry and dull at times, but sometimes you don't want to sweat over an article too long. You ask yourself, "What is this article about in a nutshell?" and then write it. This works well for those readers who only want to read the opening sentences of an article and get the gist of the article.)

3. Bartering.

That's the latest trend in business circles for companies that prefer to share products and services rather than dip into their pockets to pay for them.

(Ahh, the good old one-word lead. I try not to use this one too much, but once in a while it works and you do see it often enough in newspapers. It's usually followed by a longer sentence that often starts with "That" and then explains a little bit more about the one word you used. It can look good on the printed page, and it probably shakes up the reader to see a one-word sentence starting an article. If a reader is shaken up a bit he/she may just keep reading.)

4. Bill Smith had a problem. He needed to buy computer equipment for his company, but didn't have enough cash on hand for the purchase. Fortunately, he found a customer who needed some of his product and also wanted to get rid of some excess computer hardware.

They agreed to swap products and joined a growing trend in the business world toward bartering.

(Okay, this might be tightened up slightly, but essentially this is the "putting a face or a name to the article" lead. You take someone you interviewed and how it worked for him/her and start the article with his/her specific situation. Saying that so-and-so has a problem that was solved by the new trend sets up a nice personal situation for the reader.)

5.a) When Bill Smith needed computer equipment, he traded some services from his carpet cleaning business to get it.

OR

5.b) When Bill Smith needed computer equipment, he didn't pay for it; he traded some services from his carpeting cleaning business instead.

(This is that kind of rhythmic lead you will see often in newspapers — read it out loud. It's hard to describe in print, but it has kind of a duh-dum, duh-dum, duh-dum rhythm at the start and then a duh-dum, duh-dum, duh-dum follow in the second. Especially the first example. It doesn't always start with "when" but that often sets it up. "When something-something-something happened, then something-something -something took place.")

6. Bartering among businesses is the hottest trend going now, and experts agree it will only get hotter.

(This is the kind of newsy lead that's almost an exaggeration by saying how big, hot, important, whatever something is so that readers have to keep reading. Of course, you have to be able to back that up and having one or two experts agree that it's the hottest thing allows you to write that).

7. When it comes to getting equipment for his business, Bill Smith has a barter idea than most.

He trades …

(The pun lead. Okay, this isn't probably the greatest example of a pun, but if you groaned a bit I'm on the right track. Sometimes using a pun or some other play on words is a nice way to start an article. You see these a fair amount in news stories. Another example I used not too long ago was an article on the world wide web and writing something like companies are "spinning" new business on the web. So you take part of the word and then make a pun related to it.)

8. "Life has loveliness to sell" goes the old poem "Barter," and many businesses are finding that trading goods and services is just as lovely as selling.

(Using some kind of famous quote and paraphrasing it to make it fit your story — as I did at the beginning of this article. This doesn't work too often, and I find it tends to be used more in longer stories, but it can work if the quotation or reference is right. It's always nice to add some literary touch whenever you can to something banal.)

9. What's a good way for companies to get products and services when their cash flow is low?

Bartering may be the answer, and if recent trends are an indication …

(The question lead. Posing a question to readers to tease them into the next paragraph. You always have to watch these teasing kinds of leads where you supply a bit of information in the first few sentences before delivering the payoff farther down. You can't be too cute with it because readers may give up if you don't pay off quickly enough. This kind of tease lead may work better in longer features where the reader is more likely to spend more time with an article.)

10. "Bartering has helped turn our business around. We think it can work for just about anybody."

Bill Smith knows what he's talking about. As the owner of a carpet cleaning business, he's traded his services into much-needed computer equipment for his own firm.

(The quotation lead. Not a bad one to fall back on especially if you've got a good one that tells something dramatic about an article. You then have to follow it up with who is saying it and why.)

Read these over the next time you're wanting to trade your kingdom for a lead. They may just inspire you to get writing.

—

Mark Kearney is an award-winning journalist who has had his work published in more than 60 magazines and newspapers in North America. During his 25-year career, he has also coauthored six books, three of them best sellers. Mark has taught writing at the University of Western Ontario for 12 years.

# Breaking into Newspapers

*by Donna D'Amour*

The great thing about writing for newspapers is that you have a big market with a hungry appetite. From local weekly papers to daily regional or provincial papers to national and international papers, the markets are there. The trick is to find the market that's right for you.

To do that you have to read the paper, not from a subscriber's viewpoint, from a writer's angle. Weekly papers have low budgets and need copy. Some pay $10 per story, or nothing at all. Provincial newspapers pay anywhere from $50–$100 depending on the length, they may pay more for assigned pieces. Read the paper, notice the business stories, sports, profiles of individuals or organizations, reviews of books or productions that happen in the area. Think of the newspaper as blocks of text on a page — this works for the big papers as well. There are blocks for advertising, big blocks usually; blocks for headlines, for major stories, minor reports, fillers ... a three-sentence report on an accident or arrest, which will be followed each week with an update. There are also regular columns, opinion pieces on all kinds of subjects from politics to practical advice on home repair.

**Some papers ask for articles by the inch...**

What do you enjoy most? Let's say it's people profiles. What is the word count? Some papers ask for articles by the inch, 30 words to an inch. I've had editors call and ask for 10 inches or 20 inches. Look at the writing style; most local papers prefer a friendly chatty style.

Think of the people you admire, those that stir your interest. If it's a local paper, call or drop in and ask the editor if he could use a piece on Mr. Barnes, the beekeeper who sells honey to the local stores.

If it's larger paper, e-mail a query to the editor of the section you choose. Have a few other names to suggest in case he's already had one on Mr. Barnes. Have an angle — not just the beekeeper but this aspect of his beekeeping: a home based business that has existed for years, a retirement occupation, a how-to keep bees if you'd like to start.

Editors like new angles. It appeals to readers. So you get a yes from the editor. You ask how long the piece should be, does he need a photo, what is the deadline, how do you deliver it? E-mail is popular now; ask if he prefers attachments and in which program, or if you should include it in the body of the e-mail. This is something many editors prefer since attachments can contain bugs. Some accept fax or snail mail submissions but most prefer the article they won't have to retype. Some may ask for it on computer disk, in Microsoft word or some other program.

Ask what and when you will be paid. Usually a photo is paid extra; don't forget to consider the cost of the film and developing. Some editors just want the film, black and white; they develop their own. Most pay a couple of weeks after the article has been published. Some require you to invoice them, stating the date of publication, title and page where it appeared.

**Sell first North American serial rights...**

Editors of larger papers will send you a contract to sign and return by fax. It states the rights you are selling. This is a whole other article. Briefly, you sell first North American serial rights, which means the paper can run your article once. If they want to run it in an affiliated paper they should contact you and pay you a percentage of the original fee.

They may also ask to add it to their web page edition. There have been battles in the courts over newspapers that ran articles without asking the author's permission or paying extra. Often the contracts will include electronic rights. You can agree at no extra charge, agree but suggest a fee, or take your article elsewhere.

Once the article appears in the newspaper, you are free to sell it again. You can shop for another newspaper in a different province or for a magazine. Now you would be selling reprint rights, permission for one-time publication of an article that has already been published.

You have the assignment, now you have to write the article. Think of the things that you want to include, make an outline or list of questions for Mr. Barnes. How did he learn beekeeping, what is involved, what are the cautions for a new beekeeper, how is honey harvested, what is his market, any good honey recipes he'd like to pass on?

Call him to ask if you can come over to talk beekeeping with him. It's really an interview but some people bristle at the word interview. A talk, chat or visit is less threatening. Take a tape recorder. Mention it to Mr. Barnes, but only once you are comfortable and are ready to start the interview. Tell him you want the story in his words, if you try to write notes or to remember you may not be as accurate. The other thing about recording his voice is that each person has a distinct vocabulary, often connected to his profession. It adds colour to your article. A person who is passionate about what they do has a wonderful way of expressing it. You don't want to replace that with a list of facts.

Don't overstay your welcome. An hour should be plenty of time to find out all you need. You can always call to clarify anything later. Take your photos; have him do something with the hives, wearing his protective gear. It's the atmosphere in a photograph that catches our attention. No one wants to see a posed portrait of a man in a suit if the story is about beekeeping.

I'm a slow and fussy writer so I transcribe interviews as soon as I get home. I also have a device you can get at any Radio Shack for under $10, it attaches to my phone and to my tape recorder so I can record interviews by phone. I always tell the person I am recording the information for an article. I find that by transcribing the interview I tend to mentally select the quotes and sections I will use. I also tend to mentally arrange the order of my article as I type the transcription. By the time I'm finished I start writing it.

**A line that grabs people...**

Begin with a hook; a crisp line that grabs people. Could be a quote from Mr. Barnes or from Winnie the Pooh. "How sweet it is!" (I don't know if Winnie said that, but you should check any quotes you use.) Note my first sentence in this article. Hooked you, didn't I?

Use lots of anecdotes from Mr. Barnes. Make any instructions easy to follow. Write brief paragraphs. Use active verbs. You may want to include a contact for a local beekeeping group or website with more info. Once you've finished the article put it aside for an hour or two. Read it again, to a friend if possible. Often when we read out loud, we pause at a difficult sentence structure or something that just doesn't fit. Edit for clean, clear writing, and correct spelling.

Check your word count. Editors want exactly the word count they ask for, not 100 words more because it's so good you can't cut it. Remember the blocks; your story is a block with very definite dimensions. Give him what he needs and he'll ask for more. Make his life difficult by making him cut your work and he won't be so willing to look at your work again.

Write an interesting cutline, the words that go under the photo. Often it's the first thing a person reads when they look at your article. Send it off to the editor. You may get a call from a staff reader at the newspaper who wants to clarify something in your piece. He may ask you to call Mr. Barnes for a little more info or a statistic. It's all part of the process. Some newspapers edit a lot, some edit little if at all.

Once you've answered the final questions, your piece appears with a byline. You collect your payment and save a copy for your files. Notify Mr. Barnes that his article has been published; a courtesy but I think it should be done. Now look for another market for the same story, maybe a magazine about country living, retirement, hobbies or healthy living. Have another few ideas to pitch to the editor of the original story when you send a thank you note for using your article.

—

Donna D'Amour was a freelance reporter for *The Chronicle-Herald* newspaper for several years. Her articles have appeared in *The Globe and Mail*, *Trade and Commerce*, *Saltscapes*, *50-Plus*, and *Reading Today*. Her book, *Colouring the Road*, was published in 1995 by Lancelot Press. In 2001 she directed a weekly writer's workshop.

# Writing the Tribute Column

*by Linda Jeays*

Few freelance writers make a living wage from their work, but one way to cover your writing expenses, and make a small profit by the end of the year is to write a weekly or monthly column for a local, franchised or city newspaper. While columnists generally need expertise in a specialized subject — gardening, finance, home renovations — anyone with a flare for interviewing and a strong grasp of profile writing can write the tribute column.

To use a simple example: you could write a tribute column for a newspaper for seniors. It could feature people 50+ who, over a number of years, have contributed their time, energy, and talents to making their community a better place. Have a column header such as "This Month's Achiever" and accompany your piece with a photograph of your subject (provided by your subject, or taken yourself). Since human interest is the keystone of most good stories, and this is the premise for the profile, you will rapidly build a faithful following for your column.

**Tight well-structured writing...**

Plan to outline the subject's life, to honour particular achievements and to highlight particular qualities needed to participate in community affairs. The editor is likely to ask for 600–800 words. The challenge of fitting a storyline, achievements and character qualities into this modest word count needs tight, well-structured writing, and ruthless focus.

Zero in on your theme from the first sentence. For example, show how a woman whose husband developed Alzheimer's disease channeled her anger and distress into founding a local branch of the Alzheimer's society. Stick to your theme throughout your profile and subordinate other aspects of your subject's life to it. Since your article is a tribute to your subject, and you do not have space for a lifetime of events and relationships, focus on the exceptional. Show your subject's best profile.

Long-term dedication to a particular cause is usually, in itself, worthy of being honoured. The president of a writer's club can be praised for taking on responsible organizational tasks and showing leadership skills. But a founding member of the group who has faithfully taken the minutes of meetings for a decade — and had dozens of poems printed in small magazines — may spark an equally interesting story.

**Profile subjects...**

Choose your subjects from both professional fields and volunteer activities in a wide variety of disciplines, for example: education, healthcare, recreation, sports, and charitable work. Balance entrepreneurs with community activists, tradespeople with artists, intellectuals with entertainers. As you build your portfolio of published columns, aim for a balance of male and female subjects, native-born Canadians and immigrants, and people from different social backgrounds.

Select figures that could inspire your readers: the leader of a steel band, the author of a cookbook, a professional Santa Claus, a war veteran. Show how these people applied professional skills to volunteer commitments, creative skills to practical situations, or simply used their life skills to offer caring and compassion to others.

**Never be short of material...**

One of the advantages of writing a tribute column is that you will never be short of material. Watch for newspaper and magazine listings of service awards and other special presentations given by associations, institutions and businesses. Local radio and television stations often do brief interviews with award recipients. Canvass your friends for ideas or talk to complete strangers. Visit the websites of well-known charities, service groups, hospitals, women's shelters, seniors' residences, museums, social clubs, and city hall. Get yourself on promising e-mail lists.

In addition to community and in-house presentations, keep an eye open for local people who win provincial or national awards, such as the scouting movement's Silver Acorn, the Prime Minister's Award for teaching excellence, and the Order of Canada.

Be alert for the names of people who have been nominated for an award but who did *not* win. They could be particularly interesting because they are less well known members of the community.

**The interview...**

Since you are writing a relatively short piece on just one aspect of a person's life, your interviews and any rechecking can be done by telephone. At the beginning of your interview ask for brief biographical information about the person's childhood, education, marriage, children or career. Then follow up with your prepared questions.

Here are some examples:

- How did you become interested in (for example) the Humane Society?
- What are the overall goals of the organization?
- What is the main focus of your work there?
- Describe a funny, tragic, or inspirational day?
- What sustained your commitment to this cause?
- When did you first get involved and how has your involvement changed over time?
- What are the personal challenges of dedicated service to a good cause?
- How do you juggle family and other commitments to make time for this activity?
- What support do you have during difficult times?
- Is there a sense of personal fulfillment from your work?
- What sort of people would you encourage to become involved in this activity?

In your initial contact with the interviewee, watch for any private or political agenda that is not your cup of tea! Remember that, as a reporter paying tribute to the person's work, you may be perceived as endorsing the work of any organizations mentioned in these stories. Always check out less-familiar organizations before contacting your intended profile subject.

**Conclusion...**

Writing a weekly or monthly tribute column can provide steady returns for freelance work, and can rapidly build a sizable portfolio of published articles. This should also result in a growing list of contacts that may provide other writing assignments.

Best of all, when your spirits are low, writing profiles of people who use their time and talents to contribute to the health and welfare of their community is sure to restore your faith in humanity.

—

Linda Jeays considers the tribute column she wrote for a franchised seniors' newspaper in Ottawa one of her most rewarding long-term assignments.

# Writing "Slice-of-Life" Columns

*by Sheila T. Paynter*

Do you want to write a "slice-of-life" column with a touch of humour? Prepare by reading newspapers and magazines that carry them. These columns will reveal an approach to ordinary happenings but with a comic spin. Very nearly always, the writer is the butt of any absurdities.

Choose a general theme. Look around. Sources abound: your family and your friends will all have anecdotes about their dogs, their cats, even their canaries, that you can convert into a weekly or monthly column.

Events in your own life are priceless. Readers are delighted when you are willing to confide a nugget that isn't common knowledge. In a column on "love and marriage" I reprinted extracts from journal entries describing the first months after our wedding. I complained then that my husband didn't come home on time for the meals I had lovingly prepared. The column went on to describe how, fifty years later, I am still trying to change him.

Keep files of newspaper and magazine stories that catch your attention. Seasonal columns are especially useful when searching for themes. Aren't we lucky that the spring-cleaning crisis arrives every year?

Work from the general to the particular. Use a colourful phrase to catch the reader's attention in the first sentence. Use examples. If it's about spring cleaning you may spend many hours sorting and you find yourself with just three neckties to discard this year. End with a reference that readers can relate to, suggest that they are not alone with the challenges they encounter in their lives.

In her book, *The Artist's Way*, Julia Cameron suggests "creativity heals myself and others." Use this healing process when your editor replaces your favourite line or a crafty subtitle with one of his own.

—

Sheila T. Paynter from Westbank, British Columbia wrote for *BC Farm and Garden* in the mid 1950s and a further guest column for *Valley Vistas* in the 1980s. She self-published three outdoors books in the 1990s. She is currently writing a monthly freelance column for *Westside Weekly*, an insert in the *Kelowna Daily Courier*.

# Become a Travel Writer

*by Katharine Fletcher*

Do you love to travel? Do you want to sell you travel stories? If you're like most people, this is a cherished dream. Whether extreme adventure, golfing, or cruise trips, there are readers who want to read your travel stories.

There is no other genre that inspires such desire among writers. How do you break into this genre? Let me share some tips with you.

I broke in without realizing it, actually, by self-publishing my first book *Historical Walks: The Gatineau Park Story*. Over thirty publishers rejected this history and guide to 25 trails of a park I located north of Ottawa in Québec. Since its publication in 1988 my book remains a unique guide to its trails, and also describes its human and natural history.

What's important in the above paragraph?

First of all, I'm noting that we writers can literally "fall into" new markets without recognizing it. Although I ought to have recognized that my book was a guidebook, and hence in the realm of travel writing, this fact somehow escaped me. I only realized it after hearing a colleague introduce me as a "travel writer."

### Don't pigeonhole yourself...

Which brings me to my first point: diversification is the best friend of all writers. Don't pigeonhole yourself by thinking that you are in a single genre. You are capable of much, much more.

This reveals other invaluable tenets of the writer's life: Write what you know. Write what you love. And, research your markets thoroughly prior to writing an article or book. When I proposed *Historical Walks* to publishers, I knew it was a unique book: in 1988 there was no guidebook to Gatineau Park and in 2002 *Historical Walks* remains unique.

Such tenets apply to all writing, but they are particularly important for travel writing. It might not seem glamorous, but start off with "what you know best." It might not seem glamorous to write about your neighbourhood park. "Hardly as sexy a topic as hiking Nepal," you yawn?

Possibly not, but how many books on hiking Nepal are there? Tons. How many books and specialists on Gatineau Park? A mere handful. And I'm one of them.

Get it?

If you are an unpublished travel writer, become a specialist on your city, your town, your region. Don't be shy: spin its history, its festivals, its funky museums and B&Bs. Create your niche and tell their stories. Sell them anywhere you can, and then, before you know it, you'll be a travel writer with solid clips (tearsheets).

Then you can build your business and expand your territory. In fact, your potential territory is the world, isn't it?

**Focus your energies...**

With such a huge potential, it becomes necessary to focus your energies and specialize. Are you a "foodie"? That is, a writer who writes about food and wine? Are you a golfer? A horseback rider? An art nut? A spa aficionado? A gardener?

Examine your personal interests. Then carve yourself a niche. Keep it focused, but not rigid. Here's what I've done.

*Historical Walks* addresses three of my main interests in life: human and natural history, and hiking. My second book, published by McClelland and Stewart, expands my interests. *Capital Walks: Walking Tours of Ottawa*, not only discusses the history and social growth of Ottawa, but also architecture and art. My third book, coauthored with my husband Eric, *Québec Off the Beaten Path*, (Globe Pequot Press, 2nd ed. March 2002) showcases my home province. In it, I cover everything from museums to art galleries, whale watching and many other things. My new book, to be published by Fitzhenry & Whiteside spring 2003, will introduce more outdoor adventures, human and natural history.

I also write magazine and newspaper articles, features, lifestyle profiles. My articles all reflect my curiosity with my natural world and our human role in it, and with art and architecture. These are the grand themes that capture my interest and sustain me in my life and travels.

Perhaps you can see where I'm heading with this? Travel writing can be one facet of your writing career that can interweave with your other interests and writing abilities. Are you a food writer? No reason you cannot spin articles on Northern Italian cuisine into a travel story.

But you must be targeted, focused, and pursue your markets and goals doggedly. Writing and publishing remain risk-venture businesses so there is no tried-and-true formula for getting published.

Take heart: there are markets everywhere. Travel writing comes in a multitude of forms which include everything from guidebooks to magazine and newspaper articles, websites and travel narrative (nonfiction) books. Even fiction and kids literature incorporate a strong sense of place which must resonate with authenticity. Travel journals, and even letters and postcards can be part and parcel of a travel writer's book.

Lets use my Gatineau Park book as an example. Gatineau Park has become a rich well of stories for me: I've sold hiking and skiing stories to newspapers across Canada; a story on mountain biking in the park to *Explore: Canada's Outdoor Adventure Magazine*; round-up articles of what to do in and around Ottawa for *Dallas Morning News* and for *Distinction: Elegant Living on Long Island*; countless weekend destinations for travel columns for *Ottawa Life Magazine*, *Forever Young* and *Capital Parents* ...

**Become a specialist...**

I have incorporated Gatineau Park in two Michelin guides and a Canadian travel anthology published by Reader's Digest. I have been interviewed many times on national and local media (*Global News*, *Morningside*, *Cross Country Checkup* and more). And, the park is frequently a topic for my environment column. I've designed custom hikes and become a tour guide, written scripts for themed bus tours, given innumerable slide shows and lectures. Want to know about the park? Just ask me ... people do, all the time.

So from the above, we can see that travel writing shares characteristics of all other freelance writing: it can be shaped into stories for many markets for which you will be paid or which directly promote you as a specialist. And that leads to more paying markets.

That's what this business of writing is all about. Getting paid for written, published works. My personal mantra is: become a specialist; love what you write about; then diversify, diversify, diversify!

Enough of how to look at opportunities. How do you find markets?

Go to your local magazine shop and look through the vast selection of magazines. Pick one and examine what constitutes a travel article.

Find *Writer's Digest*, that tome-sized compendium of markets for freelance writers. And don't just concentrate on travel magazines. Research different categories of markets. Business magazines want hard news stories about travel trends: these are travel articles.

Now that we all recognize that we can write travel articles for the City or Art section of our daily newspaper, not to mention *National Geographic Traveler*, we are ready to figure out how to break into this genre.

No matter how your mom gushed over your trip journal to her friends, you must prove yourself to an editor. It's rather different.

How to break in? Be realistic. Study your market. Know its audience. Analyze the magazines you want to write for: exactly how do *National Geographic Traveler* and *National Geographic Adventure* differ? If you don't know the answer, it's time for you to take another serious look and figure it out *prior* to pitching (querying) the editor.

Analyze the magazine thoroughly so you know its small departments, not just the features, well. Sad but true, unknown writers are unlikely to sell a feature first.

Then impress the editor to whom you are sending your query. Send your very best clips. Send a targeted query letter including up to three story ideas. Ensure your ideas will fit a small department, so offer a story of 500 to 800 words or so. This proves you know the business and don't expect a feature.

**Network, network, network...**

Attend conferences. Want to make money? You're in business, so you need to spend money to make money (within reason). I sold an article to another writer I met at a conference, who was also an editor. You never can tell where your markets are! Attend writers' groups and volunteer to become program coordinator — this way you can invite editors to chat to your group.

At one meeting of the Periodical Writer's Association of Canada, I told an editor of a brand new magazine that he needed a travel column. Could I be his columnist? He said yes. Since then I've been co-writing a column with my husband and business partner, Eric. Not bad.

It never ever hurts to ask the question. "Ask and you might receive," is another chorus of my mantra. All the editor/publisher can do is say no. What's stopping you?

Finally, although I know this is a challenge, learn to take rejection with grace, not as a personal slight. And then re-pitch: again and again and again.

—

Katharine Fletcher is a freelance writer who seeks the unusual, whether it be hiking Greece's remote Peloponnese or discovering a funky Glasgow museum. She telecommutes from her electronic cottage bordering Gatineau Park's wilderness sector, a landscape providing rich inspiration for her travel, environment and lifestyle columns, articles and books. Contact her at: chesley@netcom.ca.

# Travel Free as a Writer

*by Phil Philcox*

Travel writing sounds like fun. You head off to some exotic location, shoot some photos, take some notes. When you return you write a travel article that earns enough to cover your expenses and earn you a profit.

The reality is that only a few fortunate writers get to travel on expense-paid adventures and earn enough to wander around the globe looking for experiences to write about. Some magazines that rarely use travel articles might be interested in you as a "travelling writer," though. Using your imagination and devoting some time to marketing, can help you spend a few weeks or a few months in a North American city or an exotic foreign country. And you could return with enough pre-sold articles to cover your expenses, and turn a profit.

**Businesspeople want to know how other people operate...**

There are about 6,500 business trade journals published in the U.S. and Canada. They're described in detail in the *Writer's Market* books. These magazines feature everything from running a pet shop to selling TV sets and pizza. What they all have in common is they're in business and all businesspeople want to know how other businesspeople operate. Would a florist in Cleveland be interested in how a florist in Munich or Vienna maintains their fresh flower inventory? Would a dry cleaner in New Orleans be interested in how a San Francisco or Rome dry cleaning shop handles advertising? Would a print shop owner in Miami like to know how a print shop owner in Tokyo or Chicago prices business cards or reprographics? They certainly would and, if you can supply this type of information, there are hundreds of trade journal editors out there who might be willing to give you an assignment.

One editor I called said she often asks regular contributors to tell her about their upcoming travels so she can arrange some out-of-town pieces. "I'd certainly be interested in some profiles of foreign-based businesses or businesses around the country similar to those owned by my readers. For a thousand words and 2–3 good black and white photos, I'd gladly pay $150–$200."

Another editor said he'd be interested in articles on U.S.-based businesses of interest to his readers. "For a really interesting article on how they do it and turn a profit or keep from going out of business, I'd pay 15-cents a word and $10 each for three photos. I can supply the writer with the names and addresses of businesses in major cities I'd like profiled. How these businesses operate is of interest to my subscribers and I'd love to have some articles written on how they do it. If the first few articles worked out, I could use one profile article a month on a regular basis."

**Write different articles for other trade magazines...**

Fifteen cents a word, times 1500 words, times twelve times a year adds up. If you can produce a 1500-word interview to this editor's liking, you could earn $225 for the article, plus $30 for photos ($255), times twelve issues, or $3000 by profiling a dozen businesses. While you're in the neighbourhood, you could write different articles for other trade magazines and can earn a comfortable living.

Payment for articles at trade journals is usually lower than most consumer magazines, so editors aren't able to attract highly-priced writers to travel around the globe. That's where you fit in. It won't offer a career, but certainly enough to travel in reasonable style, paying your way by writing about the experience.

If you think this is your type of writing assignment and adventure, you can begin by contacting editors with a letter or by fax, phone or e-mail. Contact an assortment of magazines on different subjects so you can interview different businesses in one city. On a trip to London in England, for instance, you could profile (among other things) a motorcycle shop, a men's clothing store, a restaurant, a wholesale fish outlet, a garage, an auto parts store, a florist, a print shop, a shoe store, an independently owned hotel, a TV repair shop, a taxi company, a laundromat, etc. A mere $100 per article for that list would net you $1300. On any trip to a Canadian or American city, you could do the same.

Need a list of the types of businesses you might be able to profile? Check the Yellow Pages of your telephone directory. Use the "since-I'm-in-the-neighbourhood" approach and be reasonable about payment. Most trade journals can't pay that much, so you're offering them a low-cost alternative to a problem they probably can't afford to solve.

If you do go overseas, plan at least a two-week trip and try to get as many assignments as you can in advance. If they want you to do it on spec and you think you can do a great job, take the offer but get some commitments so you're not paying for everything yourself. Check with the destination country's tourist office and explain the project. Ask the tourism people for the names and telephone numbers of contacts at the overseas tourist office and business associations in the cities you plan on visiting. All of these sources can help, providing you with businesses to interview, making appointments and even acting as interpreters. If language is a problem, interview only business owners who speak English.

**Make a list of the questions...**

If you don't know how to write business profiles, ask the editors to supply you with tear sheets of previously published profiles and follow that style. Note what information was covered and put together a questionnaire to use at your interviews. Check other trade journals for profile articles and make a list of the questions those authors asked. If you're new to interviewing and profile writing, drop in on a local store, interview the owner, shoot some photos and see what your finished product looks like. If you can find editors to buy these profiles, you've passed the test and you know you can turn out adequate material. If they don't buy it, ask them what's wrong and try again.

Writing is a tough business and in order to earn a living you not only have to write but you have to know what to write about and come up with ideas other writers have overlooked, then find editors willing to pay you. This trade journal interviewing could open up a whole new writing career. The destination points range from your local town to any of the exotic overseas locations, so you get to travel, hone your writing skills and, best of all, get paid for it.

—

Phil Philcox and Beverly Boe are a husband–wife magazine- and book-writing team living in Panama City Beach, Florida. They have been freelance writers for over thirty years and have travelled around the world writing for book and magazine publishers in the U.S., Canada, Australia, England and Europe.

# Find a Spot in the Glossies

*by Donna D'Amour*

When you decide to write for magazines there are two things to consider: you and the magazine. Jot down a list of your interests, skills, experiences, and travels. Think of where you are in life — just starting out in the adult world, mid-life, or ready for retirement. What magazines do you enjoy and why? These may be the magazines to approach first.

I was involved with reading ceilidhs in Cape Breton. I had read at the gatherings and felt it was an exciting new form of entertainment. (Ceilidh, pronounced kay-lee, is a Gaelic word for gathering.) The ceilidhs I'd read at were an evening of music and readings and a lot of good food. I thought others might enjoy a story about them. I looked for the right magazine.

I had a subscription to *Canadian Living* and thought it might be the right place. I loved the back page section, a 400-word essay, "O Canada." So I wrote my piece for that. I emphasized that it is Canadian family entertainment, the Canadian multicultural aspect, that readers from Acadian, Mi'kmaq, and Scottish cultures took part. I called it "A Canadian Ceilidh" and mailed it.

**Study the market...**

When you have a good idea, study the market to find where you will fit. Pick two or three possible markets. Read with a "writer's eye." Who is the reader — age, social class, lifestyle? Check out the article titles, do they deal with self-improvement, how-to, people profiles, crafts, sports food, travel. Read several for the style — is it formal or relaxed, general or specific, does it seem to have a particular slant?

Check out the masthead, the list of editors, etc. who put the magazine together. Do they e-mail "in the body" or as an attachment and in what program, snail mail, or fax? They may ask for a brief bio or a sample or two of your published work. They will tell you if a query letter is required.

Most magazines prefer that you query first with an outline of your idea. If you go ahead and write the article first, the magazine may have published one recently on a similar topic, the editor may not care for the slant or approach and will ask you to rewrite it, or the word length or style may not be appropriate. Since my piece was brief and submissions were requested in the magazine, I sent the whole piece. I wouldn't do that for an article on the subject.

So you're wondering: if you have a great idea and know just what you want to say, am I asking you to forget about it? No. Write your idea in as much detail as you like. This is background for your pitch and hopefully for your article. You just don't submit this to the editor before you find out what she wants.

Try to pitch two or three ideas at once. Since you have her attention, multiply your odds by offering more than one suggestion.

**You must impress her with your idea...**

The query is the pitch you make to the editor. You must impress her with your idea and how you will deliver it. Your opening sentence should have just the same "grabbing power" as the article itself. The editor may like the idea but want a different approach. Adaptability and the ability to listen to what the editor wants is essential if you want to see your work in print.

Magazine writing can be an exercise in perseverance some times. Remember my reading ceilidh essay?

I got a call from the editor. She was intrigued by the idea of a reading ceilidh but did not want my essay. I promised to keep her informed when the next event was in the works. Several months passed when I e-mailed info and suggested I cover the upcoming ceilidh. She was once again all excited about the idea but chose to assign the piece to a well-known writer. The article appeared complete with professional photography and it was well done. But I felt left out of the picture, and the money.

The following year I pitched the idea to a new Halifax lifestyle magazine, *Saltscapes*. The editor liked it. I gave her a couple of ways I could write it; from the point of view of a reader in the event, or as a person in the audience. She chose the audience angle and I wrote, rewrote and finally sent off the article. I was told the editor was on vacation and the assistant editor would handle my piece.

He preferred the reader viewpoint and asked me to rewrite it and also extended the word count. Hesitantly, I did. It took time and I really wasn't pleased with the finished product but I sent it off. By this time the editor had returned and saw only the second version. She didn't like it either and was a bit puzzled since it wasn't at all what she asked for. She gave me an option, write it one more time from the spectator perspective, have them rewrite the entire article, or forget about it.

This is where perseverance comes in. I chose to rewrite one more time, which turned out to be very much like the original story I'd sent. It was accepted. I was paid and got lots of e-mail comments on it.

When I approached a U.S. publication to offer my writing, they asked for a sample of my work. I sent the reading ceilidh story. They asked if they could buy it as a reprint. This time it went to an even larger audience and I was paid in U.S. dollars. I also followed up with more story ideas and have since sold two new pieces to the publication.

**Back it up with a plan...**

If you have an idea which you believe is good, gather as much info as you need to write an interesting pitch. Open with a hook, very much like the article itself. Back it up with a plan: the focus, the interviews, a conclusion. Photos or opportunity for photos should be offered if possible. Some larger magazines deal only with professional photographers.

I once sold a travel piece and sent my husband's photos plus those I requested from the local tourist bureau. The article used a couple of each.

It's best to take direction from the editor before you write the piece. The word length, style, and approach are decisions she will make. You can also offer to write a sidebar, a list of facts or contacts, especially if it's a travel piece — how to get there, cost of rooms, attractions, best season.

Even after you've spell-checked, grammar-checked and read the piece aloud several times, don't be surprised if the editor wants minor changes. As you get more experienced, this happens less. They don't pay for rewrite time. The price, usually per word, that you are given is firm. Some editors allow for long distance calls or travel costs but you have to ask that before you begin. Many do not cover these. Those that do require receipts.

Seeing the finished article with your byline and a cheque in the mail a month or so later is your reward. By now you know you earned it.

—

Donna D'Amour was a freelance reporter for *The Chronicle-Herald* newspaper (Halifax) for several years. Her articles have appeared in *The Globe and Mail*, *Trade and Commerce*, *Saltscapes*, *50-Plus*, and *Reading Today*. Her book, *Colouring the Road*, was published in 1995 by Lancelot Press (Hantsport, NS). In 2001 she directed a weekly writer's workshop.

# Market to the Magazines

*by Hélèna Katz*

Many people seem to think it isn't possible to make a living writing for magazines anymore. They're wrong — I'm proof of that. For the first eight years of my freelancing career, I made my living almost exclusively from periodical writing. Here are eight marketing techniques that have worked for me.

1) Marketing and business development has to be done a little bit every week, even if you spend just half a day a week or one hour a day on it. Keep a business/market development file of information about markets you'd like to approach and try to send out a few queries each week. If you send out 20 a month, that's how many possibilities you have to get assignments. Write your queries at the time of day when you're at your peak — which might be first thing in the morning for some people. Sluggish moods create sluggish writing.

2) I landed one client — a small American news service — because I read about them in *The Globe and Mail*. When I cold-called the managing editor to ask if they bought Canadian stories he replied, "Nobody has ever asked us that but I am interested."

We batted around some ideas, as I'd taken the precaution of drawing up a list of six suggestions before calling him. Then I sent him a package of clips and ideas. I landed four shorter items and two feature-length pieces. Soon I was writing for them as much or as little as I wanted, depending on what other assignments I had on the go.

3) Read the masthead of magazines to see if there are any people you've met somewhere along the line to whom you could pitch ideas. That's how I landed (the now-defunct) Canadian Airlines *inflight* magazine as a client.

4) Write clear, concise query letters that shine and target the appropriate publications. If you can't clearly express your idea in a query, it will be hard to convince an editor that you are the right person to handle an entire article on the subject. If you send a query without first reading the magazine, it's quite possible you'll waste your time proposing an idea that doesn't fit their readership or one that has recently been covered.

5) Being dependable, reliable and a good writer is also a good form of marketing. It's called good customer service and that's what keeps editors coming back.

6) Once you've cracked a market that you like working with, keep the relationship going by sending more queries to them regularly. It shows that you want to keep writing for them and that you're keen with an endless supply of good ideas. Besides, it's more work to land new markets than it is to maintain current ones.

7) The most labour-intensive part of putting together a story is doing the research, not the writing. To make my research pay off, I frequently rewrite and resell stories. One piece, which I sold four times, netted me a total of about $1,500.

8) Volunteering for writers' organizations is also a good way to develop contacts among other writers who can refer work to you. Volunteering for the Periodical Writers Association of Canada, of which I am a member, has been great for my career. I've helped organize some local activities and chaired the annual general meeting held in Montreal in 2001. Now I'm chairing a national committee for PWAC. I do it because I enjoy it. But at some point I began getting calls from editors telling me that so-and-so (from PWAC) had given them my name. I've had at least a half-dozen referrals that way. The reality is, if other writers don't know you exist, or what kinds of stuff you write about and that you are reliable, how do you expect them to refer work to you?

—

Hélèna Katz is a Montreal journalist whose work has appeared in magazines and newspapers in both Canada and the United States. She has given workshops on marketing for freelancers, writing queries and recycling stories in Montreal, Ottawa, and eastern Canada. She can be reached at: hkatz@web.ca.

# Write for the U.S. Market

*by Albert G. Fowler*

"Large" and "lucrative" are terms that describe the American literary marketplace. It is estimated to include around 2,000 magazines and 1,200 book publishers. One can only guess at the number of electronic markets. A Canadian writer does not require special permission from the U.S. Immigration Service to sell south of the border, but should remember that many American writers are competing for the same jobs. To be a winner in the United States' market, a Canadian writer must carefully target an American magazine and then do just what would be done when writing a piece for a Canadian magazine.

To target the right magazine, begin with the current version of *Writer's Market* and/or search the Internet. You can find guidelines, hints and current requirements at several sites on the Web. Some of the more popular spots to look are:

- www.absolutewrite.com/freelance_writing/markets_online.htm
- www.fictionfactor.com/markets.html
- www.forwriters.com/
- www.writersmarkets.com/index-guidelines.htm and the *Writer's Digest's* own www.writersdigest.com/hotlist/index.htm

**Spell the editor's name correctly...**

When you have a target, find out everything you can about it. See if the magazine has its own Web page. Find the name of the current editor and remember to spell that name correctly in all correspondence. Get recent editions of the magazine and read them carefully. Look for an index of articles written in the past and determine which articles staff writers wrote and which freelancers wrote. What length of article is the editor publishing and is there a common tone or slant? Do they use photographs and who takes them? Look at the advertising. Who reads this magazine? Check the style: are the sentences short or long, and what about punctuation? Remember that you are writing for an American audience and spell accordingly. The editor has probably never heard of the

*Canadian Press Style Book*, but will have a copy of the *Chicago Manual of Style* close at hand.

Send your query electronically or by mail, whatever the magazine's guidelines demand. If the editor does not know you, send clips to show that other editors have trusted you to write for them. If you have no clips, an offer to complete the work "on spec" might be enough to convince the editor to give you a chance.

If submitting your query by mail, always enclose a self-addressed, standard size envelope (SASE). Because the reply will come from a United States post office, you will need an international reply coupon from your local post office. For details see:

- www.canadapost.ca/tools/pg/manual/d09-e.asp

Alternatively, you can purchase United States' stamps online at:

- shop.usps.com/cgi-bin/vsbv/postal_store_non_ssl/home.jsp

**Legal concerns the same anywhere in the world...**

Any legal concerns that you have such as libel, plagiarism and copyright are the same in the United States as they would be anywhere in the world. Check your facts, rely on public documents, and archive all written and taped interviews. Be discreet, but if you must be controversial, attribute quotes to an individual by name and keep all written or taped interviews. You may even want to consult a lawyer before releasing facts that may be private or embarrassing for your subject.

United States' copyright laws are more relaxed than Canadian copyright laws, but are written in the same spirit and are designed to protect your work. A few years ago, an American work had to be published before it was considered copyrighted but that has changed. As soon as your work is in some fixed form, such as on your computer, it is protected.

A similar leftover from the previous era is the notice of copyright. That is the © symbol, or the word "copyright" followed by the first year of publication and your name. For example, *Copyright 2002 by Albert G. Fowler.* Notice of copyright is no longer required to prove ownership in the United States, but many people still use it.

Of course, you can still register your copyright with the Library of Congress Copyright Office for a non-refundable fee of $30 per item. If registration is made within 3 months after publication of the work or prior to any infringements, statutory damages and attorney's fees will be available to the copyright owner in court actions. Otherwise, only an award of actual damages and profits is available to the copyright owner. To get the latest information on United States' copyright rules and prices, check out the Library of Congress website: www.loc.gov/copyright/circs/circ1.html#cr

You can expect to receive a cheque from a United States' market with no more or less difficulty than if you were an American. You will then have to report the income, in Canadian dollars, on your Revenue Canada tax return, along with amounts from Canadian sources. No tax money will be withheld by United States' publishers for articles contributed by Canadian or American freelance writers.

**All kinds of confusion in the tax system...**

That being said, there are times when an American publisher may withhold payment for taxes. If you become a contractor, which is almost like becoming a "temporary" employee, this can lead to all kinds of confusion in the tax system. Book writers may also have this problem if their works are published in the United States. Article XII of the Canada–United States Tax Treaty, covers rules concerning literary royalties. In both cases, details should be worked out between the writer and the publisher. Because you do not have a United States' Social Security Number, you will be required to obtain your unique Individual Tax Identification Number (ITIN). You can do this through any accounting firm that deals with American financial matters and acts as an "Acceptance Agent" for the Internal Revenue Service. They will ask for three pieces of identification, and at least two must have your photo on them. Shop around because the cost varies from $75 to $200 for the same service.

Next, you must then submit a completed W-8BEN or W-8ECI form to your employer to prove that you are a Canadian and to request that the taxes not be withheld, because you will be declaring the income to Revenue Canada. You can find the required forms and other details on the Internal Revenue Service Web page: www.irs.gov.

Remember that laws change, as do Web pages, and you should not take any written commentary as the last word on taxes. When in doubt, raise the question with your American publisher and then consult a Canadian accountant or lawyer.

Quality work is in demand on both sides of the border and Canadian writers *do* get published in the United States. Carefully analyze the market, thoroughly research your article, pitch the idea and, with a bit of luck, American dollars will soon be flowing into your pocket.

—

Albert G. Fowler, OMM, CD, a retired chaplain, military historian, and freelance writer, is author of the book *Peacetime Padres* and a wide variety of freelance articles.

# Tips for Literary Magazines

*by Shirley A. Serviss*

Acquiring publishing credits in literary magazines is an important step towards establishing yourself as a writer. Most book publishers will be more interested in your work if you have already developed a readership.

Understanding how the process works can improve your chances of success and make the inevitable rejections slightly less painful.

- Read the magazine before submitting. There's no point in sending articles on organic farming to *Grain*.
- Entry fees are a legitimate way for literary magazines to acquire prize money and increase readership. Even if you don't win, you get a tax-deductible subscription.
- Always include a self-addressed, stamped envelope (SASE) if you expect a reply or even a copy of submission guidelines. Most literary magazines operate on a tight budget.
- Include a brief biographical note in your cover letter in case your work is accepted. This can mention publishing credits or your pets and gives the magazine something to say about you under contributor's notes.
- If you're submitting poetry, send more than one poem, but no more than half a dozen. They might publish more than one ... or they might pick the one you threw in to make six. Don't send your entire life's work (unless you've written only six poems).
- Include your phone number or e-mail address in case an editor wants to invite you to read at a launch or propose editorial changes. Don't be surprised if you're asked to remove the last stanza/paragraph or to change the title.
- Keep an open mind when it comes to editorial suggestions. Do you want to be published or not? You can always put the last stanza/paragraph back later on.

- Read rejection letters closely for words of encouragement or constructive criticism. Any hint that your work has promise or suggestion that you submit again or try elsewhere should be noted.
- Don't write the editor a nasty reply taking issue with the feedback or the fact you were rejected. This tactic does not improve your chances of being published in this (or any other) magazine.
- Just because there is a piece on death, dementia or divorce in the next issue doesn't mean that someone has stolen your idea. Everyone is writing about death, dementia or divorce and the editors didn't want to dedicate a whole issue to these subjects so they kept one piece and sent the others back. The Muse tends to be a bit like Johnny Appleseed.
- If you've submitted the same piece(s) simultaneously to several publications, say so in your covering letter and inform the others if it is accepted. *Other Voices* is not going to publish the same piece as *Whetstone* because many of their readers are the same.
- Remember that a rejection doesn't mean a) you can't write; b) you're a total failure; c) you should pull the covers over your head and never get out of bed again; d) all of the above. A rejection means that this particular editorial board of this particular magazine chose not to publish this particular piece of writing at this particular time.
- Try the magazine again with other work. If your rejection letter said: "We all read your work and hated it!" you might want to wait until there's a new editorial board. Editorial boards change frequently so you can probably resubmit during your lifetime.
- Expect not to hear back for months, especially if you've missed a deadline and the publication comes out only twice a year. The editorial board probably won't meet again until after the next deadline. They have lives.
- Don't harass the editors. They are likely volunteers with children in soccer, ageing parents and day jobs. Join a fitness club. Read a good book. Go to a reading. Invite a friend over for dinner. Better yet, write something new and send it out. Then write something else ...

—

Shirley A. Serviss owned and operated a literary press for seven years and has served on the editorial boards of *Other Voices* and *Quest*. She currently edits *WestWord* for the Writers Guild of Alberta. She has two published poetry collections: *Model Families* and *Reading Between the Lines.*

# 11. Books

# Improve Your Book Queries

*by Julie H. Ferguson*

Query letters are a writer's ultimate writing showcase. They present a daunting prospect to aspiring authors; so much so, that many prefer to write a book than a query to a publisher. This formal request to submit your work for consideration takes hard work and research to produce but, most of all, it takes a critical eye that is not your own.

Key ingredients are outstanding writing, generation of excitement, and realism: no editor wants to hear about "the next best seller" from a first-time author. There are more, but here are six basic ways to improve your query letters so they rise above the fierce competition.

### 1. Remove all opportunities for rejection.

Editors and agents receive upwards of 100 queries a week and are likely to be intolerant of any unforced errors a writer may make. Today, these may include producing the letter on a dot matrix printer or a typewriter, choosing a fancy font in the hopes your letter stands out, or being too familiar; remember, this is a business letter from a professional. Other signals for instant rejection are sending the query as an electronic attachment to your e-query, sending it to the wrong editor or the wrong house, writing too long a letter (only 1–1.5 pages max), or omitting one of the required components. Don't give editors any reason to discard your query before they read it all.

### 2. Categorize your book.

The editor/agent needs to know what type of book your query letter is about up front: "I have completed a mainstream novel of 90,000 words called *Down Under* …"

Categorization refers to the shelf your book will sit on in the bookstore and it needs to be precisely identified for both fiction and nonfiction queries. Take the time to explore and grasp the nuances of the many categories and sub-categories and endeavour to slot your book into the right one. Sometimes books straddle categories and make it difficult to choose. To get the idea, read some books on how to get published and prowl the shelves of the big bookstores, the smaller independents, and perhaps a specialty bookstore or two. Some writers, who have a good relationship with their local bookstore owner, ask them where they would shelve the book. Get writer colleagues to assist too, especially if they have heard you read regularly at your critique group. An accurately pigeonholed book can mean the difference between rejection and a request for more material.

**3. Include all the required components.**

If you don't know exactly what publishers want in a query letter, find out by reading books on the subject or taking a course. Just like any letter, the query has a lead (or introduction), a body, and a conclusion. The lead for both fiction and nonfiction can be either businesslike with a simple statement describing your book or creative with a compelling hook. Novelists also commonly include their book's theme statement, as well as its period, setting, or milieu in the lead. Nonfiction leads may use a surprising statistic, an anecdote, or a provocative question to lure the editor to read further. The body for fiction contains the three to four paragraph synopsis of your story. For nonfiction, the query's body contains more details about your subject, what differentiates your book, as well as a discussion about its market and competition. The last paragraph in both bodies briefly covers the author's credentials. The conclusion of any query is the "call to action" to send your manuscript or proposal to the publisher. As sales experts tell us, we must ask for the sale: "May I send a long synopsis and three sample chapters of *Down Under* for your consideration?" Also editors/agents expect that you will send your query letter out to others (simultaneous submissions) so you need not mention in your letter that you have done this.

**4. Get rid of the passive voice and other *to be* verbs.**

Nothing dooms your query more effectively than sentences like, "John was seen at the murder site by his wife," or, "it was unfortunate."

If you do nothing else, scour your query for this weakness and replace the offending occurrences with concrete, action verbs. Then give your finely honed letter to some experienced writers and get them to critique and edit it — then rewrite it, several times if necessary, passing it back for comment each time.

**5. Format your query properly.**

Anything other than a standard business letter format will invite rejection. Your own, tasteful letterhead on white or ivory bond is fine and so is a plain text e-mail query, as long as you know for sure that a particular house accepts them. Times New Roman font, single-spaced, and sized at 12 points is easy to read and always acceptable. Margins should be a minimum of one inch on paper and left justified only. The synopsis paragraphs should be in the present tense and all others, in the past tense.

**6. Include appropriate enclosures.**

The most useful enclosure for an editor/agent is a table of contents (TOC) for a nonfiction book. If your author credentials are lengthy and distinctly relevant, you may enclose a one-page bio, having mentioned the most important points in a sentence or two in the letter itself. Some writers also attach a longer synopsis and/or copies of one or two short stories or articles that have been published. Indicate any enclosures in the normal way at the end of your query with "enc." While you can add the TOC at the end of an e-query, you can't attach tear sheets. So simply ask the editor if they would like you to snail mail them. This sentence at least shows you have been published!

Writers often spend twenty hours or more crafting their letter. If yours yields invitations to submit your work from 25% or more of the recipients, your query has achieved considerable success.

—

Freelance writer and author of two nonfiction books, Vancouver-based Julie H. Ferguson leads workshops that provide writers with the knowledge, skills, and confidence to approach publishers. Her website is at www.beaconlit.com.

# Prepare a Convincing Book Proposal

*by Katharine Fletcher*

How can you ensure your book will be published? There are no guarantees. But by doing scrupulous research and creating a targeted book proposal, you increase your chances.

## How do you decide which publisher to approach?

- Network and find a mentor! Find writers who are published by a publisher you think might be interested in your book and ask if you can talk with them about their experiences. Did they enjoy the process? If not, why not? While working on my first book proposal (for McClelland & Stewart), another M&S author agreed to be my mentor. He reviewed my proposal and showed me his contract.
- Use writers' networks such as the Canadian Authors Association, Periodical Writers Association of Canada, or The Writers' Union of Canada.
- Browse the Internet for publishers' websites. Locate the name of the acquisitions editor to whom you will snail mail your proposal.
- Examine publishers' catalogues. Has your idea been published? Is the nonfiction publisher likely to be interested in your niche or idea? Research your competition.
- Review guidebooks and markets listings.

## What is a book proposal?

A book proposal is a comprehensive marketing tool that sells your product concept — your book — to the publisher.

Your book is a product that needs a market. As such, it needs an audience that is clearly defined. Your prospective publisher must have a clear idea of exactly what your book is about and who will read it. Your well-crafted, well-researched book proposal reveals this.

## What does a book proposal contain?

Not all book publishers want exactly the same type of proposal. Some want the entire book written (in the case of fiction, so I understand). Others want one to three completed chapters and a full TOC (Table of Contents) outlining the structure and contents of your entire book.

Therefore, your preliminary research is crucial. However, based on my successful proposals to McClelland & Stewart, The Globe Pequot Press and Fitzhenry & Whiteside, here are some tips:

*Covering letter.* Write to the specific acquisitions editor who will be responsible for reviewing the type of book you propose. Ensure you spell his or her name perfectly and be sure to use that person's correct title, along with the correct company name and full address. The letter should succinctly describe your book project: its working title, its theme, and its scope in an introductory paragraph. In another paragraph, briefly introduce yourself and mention why you are the best author for the project. (Yes: the book is a project and publishing it is a process.)

*Tone*: Don't forget that your book will require editing. The editor is your ally, with whom you will spend a considerable amount of time while your manuscript is edited and shaped into its final draft. The editor/publisher and the writer must form a cohesive team. Your introductory letter can convey valuable information about your perception of your role as a team player in the publication process.

- Working title/subtitle of book. What is the title? Keep it short, targeted and give it a hook.
- Author(s), illustrator(s), photographer(s) names and addresses. Are you the only author? If not, list your coauthor(s) and the illustrator(s), photographer(s). Be sure to include your full name, address, telephone and fax numbers, website and e-mail addresses.
- Synopsis. This is an overview; a brief description of the book that, in paragraph form, establishes your book's main goals and themes. Why do you want to write it? Why will readers be compelled to buy it? What does it contain? What insights will readers gain from it? Does it have a market as a course prerequisite? What are your primary and secondary markets? The primary market for my first book, *Historical Walks: the Gatineau Park Story* is active outdoors people who want to hike, mountain bike or ski in Gatineau Park. The secondary market is "armchair hikers" and historians who want to know about the human and natural history of Gatineau Park, located 20 minutes north of Ottawa, Canada's capital city. My book represents an indispensable guide, and since 1988 I've led guided hikes in the park to people who buy it as part of my course curriculum. Such details should be included in a book proposal.
- Table of Contents. List a full table of contents, including all sections you want to include. What are normal sections of a book? Look in *The Chicago Manual of Style* to find out. Components of a book are:

Preface, Acknowledgments, Introduction, Chapters, Conclusion, Endnotes, Bibliographic references/other reading, Glossary, Index.

- Sample chapter(s). In the case of my second book, *Capital Walks: Walking Tours of Ottawa*, McClelland and Stewart advised me that they did not need sample chapters, because they had a good understanding of my writing capabilities from my self-published book. You may be in the same situation. However, do not assume this will be the case. Publishers generally want to see sample chapters. This not only proves that you can write; it demonstrates that you can stay on target — and maintain both your theme and the reader's interest. Continue with a detailed list of subsequent chapters and their relevant sub-headings, if applicable.
- Competing books. What is currently published in your chosen field of interest? Go to your local bookstores and research current titles. Ask the bookshop managers for help. They know what new releases are coming — and from which publishers. Also use the Internet and other tools such as *Books in Print* and your library catalogue system. Thoroughly research what is both in and out of print that covers your chosen topic. Don't be discouraged if there are several books already in print, you may just have come up with the definitive work. Now you are ready to list the competition. List them in bibliographic format, sorted alphabetically by surname of the author (again, refer to *The Chicago Manual of Style* for this information). In addition to the name of the author, book title, etc., I also added a brief comment describing the focus of each competing title, mentioning why my book would be different. *Tip*: Don't denigrate the competition. Point out their good (and bad) points, highlighting where it fails to deliver — but where yours won't. Some measurements are: Is it too technical? Out of date? Incomplete? Or, is it very popular? Be fair. Your comments speak volumes about how you assess others' work, and how you think.
- The market. What is the target audience? What are the demographics: "the educated layperson," professional group(s), the health-conscious senior's market? Describe this for the editor/publisher to demonstrate that you understand your book's purpose, market and marketability.
- Promotion campaign. What are the sales handles? What are the sales opportunities? Is the book seasonal — if it is a hiking book, can you expand it to include skiing and canoeing, thus widening its appeal? Is your book politically sensitive? Will it have a brief window of

opportunity for sales, as in a political exposé to be printed in the few months leading up to an election?

- Your curriculum vitae. Stress your special credentials as well as your promote-ability. Why are you the perfect author for this book? Are you a specialist? Have you been interviewed on television or radio? Are you well known in the area, across Canada, or internationally? Have your won awards? Do you teach? What associations do you belong to? What are your publishing credits?
- Appendix. Here's where you include supporting material. Are you already a published author? If so, include at least a list of titles and better still, include a complimentary copy of the book that you think best represents you. Do you have book reviews, tear sheets of magazine or newspaper articles, samples of brochures, photographs that you have produced? Send copies.

**Some general pointers...**

Here are some final words of caution:

- Copyright your proposal. Insert the copyright symbol © and your name and date as part of the footer on every page. An idea cannot be copyrighted, but you can discourage efforts to steal your proposal. Don't be paranoid. Do be smart, protect your rights.
- Include generous margins. Use about an inch (72 points) along the top, bottom and sides so that the editor can make notes.
- Include a header and footer on every page. The heading should contain the working title and your name and date. The footer should include the page number (page x of x).
- Keep a complete copy of the entire proposal including the Appendix's tearsheets, reviews etc.
- Be patient. Expect a response to take several months. In your covering letter, ask for a reply by a specific date.
- Consider simultaneous submissions. Should you send the proposal simultaneously to more than one publisher? Many writers do this because getting published is so difficult.
- Consider your alternatives. If you decide to self-publish, you should still write a detailed book proposal for your own use.

—

Katharine Fletcher is a freelance writer who seeks the unusual. She telecommutes from her electronic cottage bordering Gatineau Park's wilderness sector, a landscape providing rich inspiration for her travel, environment and lifestyle columns, articles and books. Contact her at: chesley@netcom.ca.

# How to Negotiate Your Book Contract

*by Marian Dingman Hebb*

When you are offered a contract by a publisher, the temptation is to sign it without careful consideration of its contents. Contracts are not written in stone, even the ones which appear to be a standard printed form with little or no space for amendments. Editors and publishers are not surprised to be asked to make changes. In fact, most probably expect this. Many authors, the agents, and the lawyers who represent some of them, ask for and very often get important changes in the contracts offered. The discussion itself with the publisher about the contract is often useful, whether or not it results in changes to the contract, as it makes clear to both author and publisher the expectations of the other and reduces the risk of later misunderstandings.

**Protect your copyright...**

When looking at a contract for publication of a book, first ask yourself these two basic questions: What are you giving (and what aren't you giving) to the publisher? And when will you get it back?

Don't give copyright. In a few situations it may be appropriate to do so, but these are limited. The usual grant to the publisher is an exclusive license to publish throughout the term of copyright. It may be limited to Canada or to the English language, and it may also be limited to publication in book form. Occasionally the licence is limited to a specified number of years. Before requesting such limitations, you should endeavour to find out the publisher's track record in licensing publishers outside Canada or in selling or licensing film and other non-print rights. Will the publisher actively seek deals or just react to inquiries? You should also consider whether you have alternative ways of placing these rights yourself. In other words, retaining rights to exploit them yourself may not always be a wise decision. But, do bear in mind that the opportunity to acquire a film or multimedia deal usually only arises when a producer approaches you or your publisher, so you are probably better off keeping these rights to deal with by yourself with advice from a lawyer or other person with related expertise, should occasion arise. Another possibility is to give the publisher the right to exploit certain rights for several years following publication of its own edition and, if it hasn't successfully done so, to reclaim the right to do so either yourself or with the assistance of an agent. This is often done with respect to rights outside Canada and translation rights.

It is smart to have a clause which says that "all rights not specifically granted to the publisher" are retained by you as author. Then, if there is uncertainty later over what you actually granted to the publisher, a dispute is more likely to be resolved in your favour. But, if the contract seems unclear to you at the outset, do not rely on this outcome, and specify also that you are keeping certain rights "including but not limited to all motion picture, sound recording and electronic rights" (for example).

**Don't lose control of electronic rights...**

Unless the publisher is an electronic publisher and you intend to grant electronic rights, it is wise to specify that you are keeping "all electronic rights." It is reasonable, however, for the book publisher to want electronic database rights which would allow (subject to your written approval and a payment to you of a percentage of revenues received) customers of the book publisher or another publisher licensed by the book publisher to download and print out the verbatim text without adaptation or added elements (music, other sound, graphics, animation, links to other text, etc.). Some book publishers ask for these "verbatim electronic rights" (often referred to as database storage and retrieval rights) because they fear that you might grant these rights to a competing publisher who might provide your text to its customers on demand and undercut sales of the original book. Alternatively, it would be reasonable for the contract to contain a prohibition against your granting such rights to another publisher or a requirement that if you are going to offer these rights to any publisher they must be offered first to your book publisher.

Interactive CD-ROM or similar multimedia electronic rights are very different from verbatim electronic rights and, unless you reserve all electronic rights, should be dealt with separately and differently. An electronic product with added elements does not usually compete with the original book. Rights to produce such enhanced products are frequently referred to as "multimedia rights." You might easily have to undertake a great deal of further work if you were to become involved in an adaptation of your book for a CD-ROM, although you might just be asked for permission to allow others to adapt your work or part of it. Or your work might be one of a large number of other works incorporated into an electronic product.

No one yet knows all the possibilities for electronic publication and keeping electronic rights yourself preserves your flexibility to deal with them. If you do grant any electronic rights to the publisher, be specific about which electronic rights you are granting. Make it clear whether the grant to the publisher is for verbatim electronic rights only (recommended!) or also for electronic rights including multimedia rights. If you grant multimedia rights, try to be very specific about what you are granting (for example, English-language CD-ROM, Macintosh platform, for North America only) and what you are retaining. Insist on approval over any use of the rights either by the publisher or someone licensed by the publisher. A word of caution: if you grant verbatim electronic rights to the publisher and retain multimedia rights, be sure that the publishing contract does not preclude you from using your text in unadapted form in a multimedia product.

**Preserve the right to regain control of your rights in certain situations...**

Although you will not have assigned your copyright to the publisher in most cases, the contract will still determine the control which you and the publisher will each have over your material. The difference between "assigning" copyright and granting a licence is rather like the difference between selling and renting your house. If you license certain rights — as when you rent your house — you retain ownership. However, retaining copyright and granting a licence to the publisher does not mean that you can grant permission to others to use your material in different ways unless the contract between you and the publisher permits this.

The most important reason to retain your copyright is that in certain instances you will be able to regain control of your material at a later time without having to obtain a reassignment or written transfer of the copyright back to you from the publisher. For example, you may (and should) seek to negotiate that all publishing rights revert to you automatically if the publisher becomes insolvent or bankrupt.

There are a number of other situations where all publishing rights should revert to you — not automatically, but if you so wish. You will probably want your contract to provide that rights may revert to you in the following circumstances:

- The book is not published within, say, eighteen or twenty-four months of delivery of the manuscript, or within a much shorter time if the success of the book depends on its timing.
- The book is out of print and is not reprinted within a specified period, usually six or nine months, following your request that the

publisher reprint. Negotiate as short a period as you can. Contrary to what many authors think, you are not usually entitled to take a book away from the publisher simply because it is out of print, unless the contract makes it clear that you can.

- The publisher fails to send royalty statements and payments, if any are owing. This clause — becoming a common one — is worth its weight in gold on occasion! Either the publisher finds it can pay you after all — or you become free to take your book to another publisher. It may save you from further losses as well as the complications that always develop if you should have the bad luck to have to deal with a receiver or trustee in bankruptcy.

**Clarify the publication date...**

Another basic question to be resolved is when the book is to be published. It is surprising how many contracts are completely silent on a date of publication. An obligation to publish may be implied, and if so, publication should be within a reasonable time after delivery of the complete, final manuscript. How long is "reasonable"? Eighteen months is usual, but it would depend on the circumstances. Avoid this uncertainty by checking your contract for a publication date before signing! It should at the very least specify that your book will be published within a specified number of months, often twelve but sometimes eighteen.

**Establish a consultative process...**

When you enter a contract with a publisher, you give the publisher the power to do a number of things for your mutual benefit. Usually most of the decisions other than on content become entirely the publisher's, unless you write in clauses that require the publisher to obtain your approval or at least to consult you at certain points. Many publishers — the good ones — do consult their authors, whether or not it is in the contract. But there are oversights. People forget or make mistakes — and if there is a formal requirement to consult or obtain approval, it seems such oversights happen less often! If you ask for consultation or approval, it is clear to the publisher that you are interested and want to be involved in particular aspects of the publishing process which are sometimes considered not a legitimate concern of the author. Certainly you should have the opportunity to approve the copy-edited manuscript before it goes for typesetting. You should see the cover artwork and any illustrations and may wish to see the page layout and design. You should check the biographical blurb and any other text on the book jacket or paperback cover. Publishers are usually appreciative of an author's input and are always grateful when an author has saved them from making an embarrassing and sometimes costly mistake. You may also want the right of approval on foreign publishing or other sub-licenses granted, although a few publishers regard this requirement as a hindrance to them.

**Negotiate a "no assignment" clause...**

A wise author knows his or her own publisher. Try to ensure that a contract has a "no assignment" clause, so that it will clearly be necessary for the publisher to obtain your consent before selling or otherwise disposing of your contract — and hence, control of your book — to another publisher. If your contract is a license only (and not a copyright assignment), you can probably stop your publisher from assigning or disposing of your contract to another publisher, unless there is a clause — as there sometimes is — expressly permitting the publisher to sell off your contract as a business asset, along with the computers and desks of the publishing company. You made a personal choice of whom you wanted as your publisher initially. Take care that a subsequent publisher is not foisted on you. You may not hit it lucky, or be compatible with the publisher someone else has "chosen" for you in such a situation.

**Additional clauses to consider...**

Some additional clauses to look for in your contract — and to bargain for if you don't find them — are listed below:

- When you sign a contract you should receive an advance that is not returnable. This should be clearly stated in your contract. Otherwise the publisher has obtained, at no cost, the right to see and consider your manuscript when you have completed it. The publisher can then decide that your manuscript isn't "satisfactory" and reject it. The wording of most contracts makes this a subjective decision by the publisher, rather than an objective assessment of the manuscript. (An advance should only be repayable if you default on delivery of a complete manuscript.)
- If your contract gives the publisher the right to reject an "unsatisfactory" manuscript, there should be safeguards to protect you from an arbitrary rejection — for example, a clause requiring the publisher to give you written reasons for its dissatisfaction and an opportunity to revise the manuscript to meet its requirements. If you don't think that the publisher's criticisms or requests for revision are valid, you should be able to keep the advance (but only if the contract permits this) and take your manuscript to another publisher who finds it satisfactory in its present form!
- Royalties! This is probably the first clause you look for. Most publishers offer 10 percent on the suggested retail price of a trade book (that is, a book which is not for the educational or technical

markets) on the first five thousand copies sold, 12½ percent on the next five thousand copies sold, and 15 percent on all copies sold thereafter.

- Most publishers pay royalties twice a year and many will pay you your share of any revenues received from sub-licenses within thirty days of when such revenues are received by them.
- Most contracts have a clause that permits you or your accountant to inspect the publisher's financial records relating to your own particular book.
- Your contract should contain a clause that permits the Canadian Copyright Licensing Agency (Access Copyright™) to authorize photocopying and similar forms of reproduction of your book. Access Copyright™ and its Quebec sister, Union des écrivaines et écrivains québecois, are collective societies which license copying on behalf of authors and publishers in Canada and through similar, sister organizations outside Canada, throughout the world.
- Warranty and indemnification clauses should always be read with great care. The publisher is entitled to a warranty from you that your book is not plagiarized or copied from the work of another author. You should not have to give an unqualified warranty to a publisher that your work contains no libellous material, although as author you should be prepared to stand behind the professionalism of your research and it is clearly not fair to depict your landlady, for example, in your novel. However, if you are writing on a controversial subject and about contemporary persons, to take one example, you and the publisher should share the risks of any libel action and the publisher should not ask you to indemnify it for any financial loss in respect to an action or threat of action. If you anticipate a possible problem of this sort, you and your publisher should discuss the advisability of insurance coverage. If the publisher already has libel insurance, this can probably be extended to insure you as well. But you should be sure that any commitment from the publisher to provide you with insurance is included in your contract. If you are giving any warranty on libel, whether or not there is insurance, you should limit any promise to indemnify the publisher to costs resulting from actual breaches of your warranty, and not to all costs resulting from mere threats and claims. If an unknown glory-seeker claims to be one of the characters in your novel, your publisher should neither blame you nor collect its defence costs from you!

- Your life will be simpler if you don't give your publisher an option to publish or make an offer on your next work. A publisher is usually content to rely on your goodwill to give it the first opportunity to do so. But if the contract does contain an option clause, be sure that the publisher must make its offer or decision to publish within a specified period, say, thirty days, of receiving an outline and sample material.
- If the publisher decides that the time has come when it is no longer economic to keep your book in stock, it should first offer you an opportunity to purchase any or all remaining copies at the same low price as it is prepared to sell them to a remainder dealer or book jobber. Authors sometimes become apoplectic when they see their books selling for a dollar or two on a discount table, especially when they have a yen to go into the mail-order book business themselves. And if a publisher decides to pulp or destroy excess stock of your book, you should have the right to purchase these copies for the cost of shipping them to you.

Most of the above suggestions are likely to cost a publisher financially very little. But in certain circumstances, it may cost you a lot if you do not have these protections in your written contract.

—

Marian Dingman Hebb spent ten years as a book and magazine editor before becoming a lawyer and specializing in arts, entertainment and copyright law. She has advised authors on contracts for more than two decades and has written self-help guides entitled *Help Yourself to a Better Contract*, *Ghost Writing*, *Writers' Guide to Electronic Publishing Rights* and, together with Maggie Siggins, *From Page to Screen — Negotiating Film and TV Contracts for Original Literary Works*, all published by the Writers' Union of Canada.

# Are Literary Agents Essential?

*by Julie H. Ferguson*

"You must get an agent!" Is it true?

Canadian publishing statistics demonstrate this is a misconception caused by the influence of American material pouring over our border. In Canada, literary agents represent only ten percent of our published books. Canadian authors successfully submit the majority of the 14,000 titles published every year directly to editors. U.S. writers face tougher odds. Eighty percent of all American books published are represented.

Do you need an agent? Well, try answering these questions:

- Do I want to publish in the United States and Canada?
- Is my book international in scope?
- Will it sell tens of thousands of copies?
- Is the topic interesting to everyone?

If you answered "yes" to them, you will need an agent to break into one of the six publishing conglomerates in the U.S., which work solely through literary agencies. In Canada you might succeed without an agent, but you would benefit from one.

**The math tells the story...**

If your book is more modest, the chances of attracting representation are slim because of the bottom line. Agents are paid out of the author's advance and royalty payments and the math tells the story. An author makes 10 percent on each book sold. On 4000 copies sold at $25/copy, the author earns $10,000. With a commission of 15 percent, an agent earns $1500 on 4000 copies.

Agents spend over $1000 to market a first work, typically take a year to sell it, and only then receive their first commission. As first books usually sell less than 4000 copies in Canada and only one in four earns out its advance, agents are cautious. For example, my book *Through a Canadian Periscope* (Dundurn, 1995) had a print run of 3000 and was considered a success. But no agent would have been interested because it couldn't earn enough. The figures, of course, get better for the agent as the sales go up. At 10,000 copies, an agent would earn $3750; at 50,000 copies, $18,750. In Canada, sales of 50,000 are the exception and unlikely for a first time author.

If you have the next blockbuster, you need an agent. Your agent will help you prepare an outstanding proposal or synopsis and even improve your manuscript. A good agent exposes your work to editors at all the right houses and increases the chances of gaining its acceptance because the publishers know and trust their judgement. After receiving the offer to publish, an agent negotiates your contract and often achieves better terms than a fledgling author can ever hope to do. She/he will also sell subsidiary rights if they have been retained.

**Agents are fewer in Canada...**

Where do Canadians find a literary agent? This guide is a reliable print source for agents and is updated every few years. Another source is the web — try a search for canadian +literary +agents on Google and you'll hit many of them. Agents are fewer in Canada than in the U.S., though lately new Canadian agencies are appearing. Most Canadian agents have connections to American publishers. If you want to publish your book down south, there are hundreds of agencies and the best listing can be found in Jeff Herman's *Writer's Guide to Book Editors, Publishers, and Literary Agents* (Prima Publishing, 2000).

Authors submit to agents in the same way as they do to editors — with a sales pitch, your query letter. If an agent offers to represent you, find out what he has sold and who's on his client list. Get permission to talk to his authors. Ask if he attends major book fairs and what his connections are in the publishing industry.

The rest of us writing books of lesser stature or regional interest have to become our own literary agents. So take courses that will teach you where to market your work and how to write your own query letters, nonfiction proposals and fiction synopses. Understand clauses in publishing contracts and how to negotiate them and, last of all, develop the skills to promote your book to increase sales. Remember, in Canada the odds remain in your favour without an agent.

—

Freelance writer and author of two nonfiction books, Vancouver-based Julie Ferguson leads workshops that provide aspiring authors with the knowledge and confidence to professionally approach publishers. Her website is at www.beaconlit.com.

# Self-Publishing: A Viable Option?

*by Barbara Florio Graham*

Traditional forms of book publishing have been transformed by the electronic age, giving authors the option of publishing their work solely on the web, or dealing with publishers much further away than would have been possible in the days when manuscripts had to be delivered in paper form. And self-publishing — once considered a taboo indulgence of those with inferior quality work — has moved into the mainstream.

But self-publishing is still risky. Hiring an editor and designer and finding a printer are the easy parts. But after the book has been published, how will you distribute it? Who will handle the publicity essential to lead potential purchasers to buy the book?

A trade publisher published my first book, my second was a co-publishing venture, and my latest book was completely self-published. I'm aware of the advantages and disadvantages of all three approaches.

**Should *you* venture into self-publishing?**

1. Do you have a body of work that has won acclaim by publication otherwise, or through winning awards and contests?

2. Is there a clear target market for this kind of book? Have you researched carefully to ensure that your book will be sufficiently different from others available? Will you be able to produce it at a competitive price?

3. Do you have sufficient funds to invest in this kind of project? Ideally, this money should come from savings and not in the form of a loan.

You need to include design, layout, publicity, postage, distribution and other costs in your budget. Publicity is one of my areas of expertise, so I didn't hire someone to handle that for me. I also relied on colleagues in various writing organizations to help in getting the word out.

4. Are you prepared for the time it will take to bring this kind of project to fruition? My production manager and I worked for many hours refining the layout of each page, and because *Musings/Mewsings* is a "flip"

book, we had to ensure that the two sides matched equally. This was more time-consuming than we expected.

5. If you plan to include photographs, where will you obtain them? Do you have access to photographs of high-enough quality to reproduce well? Do you own the rights to these, or will you have to add the cost of a photographer to your budget?

6. How will you market and distribute this book? Hiring a distributor can be expensive, but distributing a book yourself can take a great deal of time and effort. Are you prepared to travel in ever-widening circles with cartons of books in the back of the car? How good a salesperson are you? What might this cost in time, gasoline, food, or accommodation?

7. Everybody seems to have a website, and it certainly makes sense when you have a book to sell. Do you have the expertise to design your own website? If you hire someone else to do this for you, will you then be able to maintain it on your own without having to pay a webmaster every time you want to make a small change?

In one of the most popular pieces in *Musings/Mewsings*, my coauthor Simon Teakettle advises readers to "Grow Your Own Fur Coat." Do I advise you to publish your own book? Maybe, maybe not.

—

The process of publishing and distributing *Musings/Mewsings* is on Barbara's website: www.SimonTeakettle.com. She and her cat, Simon Teakettle, can be reached at simon@storm.ca. Barbara's other books include *Five Fast Steps to Better Writing* and *Five Fast Steps to Low-cost Publicity*.

# Tips for Typesetting

*by Cheryl MacDonald*

The computer revolution has resulted in many writers becoming part-time typesetters and publishers. If you're starting out in desktop publishing, following these tips will make you look a bit more professional.

**Keep it simple...**

Don't use every feature or fancy font just because they're available. The most impressive looking books are often the most simply designed.

**Watch those fonts...**

For books and articles, choose a serif font, such as Times New Roman, rather than a sans-serif style (Helvetica, Arial). Choose 11- or 12-point fonts for maximum readability.

**Spaced out...**

Narrow margins or tightly spaced lines make reading difficult. If you must save space, use a smaller typeface and slightly wider spacing between lines.

**Go with the flow...**

Make sure the reader can easily follow the flow of text in multiple-column layouts. A carelessly placed graphic or box in the middle of a column can be confusing.

**Justified or not?**

Getting the right margin perfectly flush means extra spaces are added between words, sometimes resulting in unsightly "rivers" of white space. A ragged right margin is perfectly acceptable and often makes text easier to read.

**It's symbolic...**

Use the right symbols. There is a difference between a hyphen [-] and an em-dash [—], between a zero [0] and a capital O. If you make the wrong choice then translate something from one computer program to another, unwanted symbols may appear.

## Forget tradition...

Typists were once told to put two spaces after periods. Now, only one is required. With an ellipsis [...] a space on either side is recommended, especially if your right margin is justified. Otherwise, you may get odd line breaks.

—

In addition to writing, Cheryl MacDonald has handled design and typesetting on several projects, including two books for the Port Dover Board of Trade, *Port Dover: A Place in the Sun* and *Port Dover: A Summer Garden* (for details or to read an excerpt visit www.heronwoodent.ca/dover/).

# Ten Tips for Promoting Your Book

*by Cheryl MacDonald*

Promotion is a big part of writing. Best selling authors aren't best sellers just because they're great writers. Think about it. When you buy a book, you usually buy a title you've already heard about, or a work by a familiar author. Even if you've never read a particular writer's work before, if you know the name, you're more likely to make the purchase.

As a writer, part of your job is to promote your own work. If you have a contract with a book publisher, you'll soon discover that your book may not get the promotion it needs. Budget limitations, staff shortages and the number of titles published each year are the main reasons. So a wise writer gets involved in publicity right from the start.

Learning to promote your work effectively is even more important if you self-publish or your book is published through an organization whose main endeavours have little to do with writing or publishing. As a writer of historical nonfiction, I've done all three. While I'm still a long way from achieving fame and fortune, I've actually had better success, in terms of media coverage and remuneration, with the second and third approaches. In my opinion, that's because I've invested a lot of time in promoting the books.

One of the main reasons for this is the nature of my work. Much of what I do focuses on local history, especially the history of Haldimand and Norfolk Counties in southern Ontario. Most trade publishers have never even *heard* of these places, let alone expressed any interest in publishing books about their history. Yet there is a small but healthy market for local history books, and over the past dozen years, I've been deeply involved in publishing and promoting these. The skills I've learned are transferable to any kind of book (the one caveat being that if you have a contract with a publisher you should talk to them to coordinate your promotional efforts and avoid duplication).

The following tips are based on the assumption that your book is the absolute best you can produce, and that you have a firm publication date. Timing is crucial to many aspects of promotion, and if your book is not available on the date promised, you've wasted a lot of time and money.

**1. Announce the imminent publication of the book.**

Two to three months before the delivery date, send out a media release. Make sure it includes the title, number of pages, price, and a very brief synopsis of the book. If you have any pre-publication reviews, quote from these, and if you're planning a book launch, mention the date and advise readers to keep an eye out for further information. Send it to every newspaper within 100 miles, radio stations, magazines that your target audience may read, your alumni magazine, organizational newsletters and appropriate Internet sites.

**2. Offer a pre-publication discount.**

I partner with the Port Dover Board of Trade to publish local history books. So far we've produced two, with two more in the works. On the last one, we offered a 20 percent discount if books were ordered *and* paid for at least three weeks prior to publication date. By the time *Port Dover: A Summer Garden* rolled off the presses, 20 percent of the books had been sold.

**3. Use direct mail.**

There's a bit of cost involved, but the returns are worth it. Some books have a narrowly targeted market; model railway buffs, historical re-enactors, or dog breeders are some examples. Look for clubs or professional organizations, and see if you can borrow or rent membership mailing lists or insert a flyer in their regular mailing. If your book will be of interest to people in a particular geographic area, consider Canada Post's "unaddressed ad mail." For less than 10 cents an item, you can send a flyer or other literature to all the addresses in a particular area.

**4. Advertise in your local newspaper.**

It is safe to assume that newspaper subscribers are interested in reading, although not all of them will necessarily buy books. Furthermore, if your book has a local connection, your ad will reach people who have left the geographic area but are still interested in the community. Costs will vary depending on circulation, but in smaller centres newspaper advertising can be effective. One approach is to take out a display or classified ad, although I have some misgivings about this. It can be costly, and advertising works better if you repeat, repeat, repeat. In my experience, an insert works far better. Yes, they may annoy some readers when they fall out of the newspaper, but they also tend to get more attention. If you include an order form, you're far more likely to get a response.

**5. Set up a website.**

If you don't have a website, contact your Internet server. Sometimes, free Web pages are part of your package. If you already have a personal website, update it to include an announcement of your forthcoming book. Better yet, add a page promoting the book. Include the title, page count, price, a cover shot, and, if there's room, brief excerpts. Make sure there's contact information so prospective customers can order the book. Include an order form even if you aren't set up for e-commerce, by providing a form that customers can print out and send to you with a cheque. If feasible, link your site to others with common interests. And be sure to include your website address in all publicity.

**6. Arrange for speaking engagements.**

Publishing a book makes you something of an expert. If yours is a nonfiction book, that's the topic you should be speaking about. If it's fiction, you might want to talk about your experiences as a writer, or what you know about the genre you've chosen. Whatever your decide, contact appropriate groups, offer to speak to them, and to have your books available for purchase when you do.

**7. Print business cards that include your book title.**

My business card is printed on two sides. The front lists the usual contact information, including my e-mail address and website. The back lists all the books I've written. I have to update this periodically, but it's a quick way to remind people of both my latest book and all the previous titles.

**8. Schedule a book launch.**

This doesn't have to be a major social event with caviar and champagne. Coffee, juice and doughnuts are just fine. This is the date your book is officially revealed to the public. If you've arranged pre-publication sales, this is the date people will come to pick up the book, to chat and to get autographs. The launch needn't be a stand-alone event depending on your subject, it could be part of a museum Christmas party, or the opening of a sporting goods shop. But plan carefully if you're considering a multi-purpose event. Not everyone who turns out will be a book buyer, and some that are interested may choose not to purchase if it means carrying a book around for hours.

**9. Partner with a bookstore or other business.**

If a major chain is carrying your book, contact local outlets to see if they're interested in a book signing. (Your publisher may handle this. If not, it's up to you.) Don't overlook independent bookstores, especially if you have self-published or published through a small press or another organization. If possible, schedule your appearance in November or early December, traditionally the time of year when most books are sold. Also consider having your books available in other retail establishments that your readers are likely to frequent. If you've written a book on dog training, would your local veterinary clinic display it? Would the shop at a local trailer park or campsite stock your book on area nature trails?

**10. Keep plugging away.**

Don't stop promoting when the initial interest in your book dies down. While it is important to begin promoting early, most books are still of interest for many years after publication. Mention your book from time to time in news releases on other topics, or in biographical blurbs when you publish articles or short stories. Offer your book as a prize at select community events. Make sure retailers always have at least a couple of copies on hand, and if your budget allows, advertise the title from time to time.

Above all, stay optimistic. At the very least, promoting your book will be a learning experience, an opportunity to hone the skills that may very well turn your next one into a best seller!

—

Cheryl MacDonald's articles have appeared in such publications as *The Beaver*, *Harrowsmith* and *Canadian Living*. A columnist with the *Simcoe Times-Reformer*, she has written more than a dozen books, including *Port Dover: A Summer Garden*, *Emma Albani: Victorian Diva* and *Who Killed George? The Ordeal of Olive Sternaman*. She can be found at www.heronwoodent.ca

# Five Book Promotion Truths

*by Denyse O'Leary*

Promoting a book in Canada is not easy. I am a non-celebrity who did it, with moderate success, and I have distilled what I know into five "book promotion truths." Read them over and see if they will work for you.

**1. You must plan your strategy carefully.**

Most authors and publishers in North America are Americans. Their presence and promotional energy in the Canadian market is overwhelming. You must plan your strategy carefully to come out ahead. Many programs, including those offered by the Canadian Authors Association, exist to help you, but it is up to you to recognize what you are up against and take advantage of them.

**2. You must put time into promoting your book.**

Your publisher will put some time into the effort, but you probably know much more about your intended market than the publisher does. For maximum success, long before you start submitting your manuscript, start making lists of things you can do to promote your own book. These might include preparing publicity materials, giving talks at local relevant-interest groups, and appearing on radio or TV shows. Preparing for these events takes a lot of research time. My book has been in print for 13 days as I write this, but I have already spent 125 hours promoting it, not including a five-day book tour.

**3. You must put money into promoting your book.**

You will need items that you cannot ask your publisher to pay for. Here is an example from my own experience:

I set a budget of $1000 (the vacation I did not take) and made a point of keeping track. I do *not* claim that my experiences are any kind of a standard, but they do help you know what you might prepare for.

a) $350 for bright-coloured suits for TV appearances and author signings. Personal tastes may favor earth tones and denim, but personal tastes are not relevant. One must be *seen* on TV and in large bookstores.

b) $350 for new stationery that advertises one's writing career. Your first book is not the time to borrow stationery from a spouse's roofing business. Think for the long term.

c) $50 for books by professionals on book promotion. Spending this money was wise because reinventing the wheel is *never* time well spent.

d) $250 for special bookmark for my book, showing the cover design and a number of useful Internet sites to "bookmark," as well as my own website address.

Well, that accounted for $1000, but it turned out to be worth every penny, especially the suits and the bookmarks. Even though I was a newbie, in the bookstores I looked like a pro! And that sold a lot of books.

**4. You must network with other authors.**

Canadian fiction authors Nancy Lindquist and Linda Hall were invaluable sources of advice on book promotion. Granted, you must be alone in order to write. But once you start to promote yourself as an author, working with others gives you the oomph you need!

**5. You must cross promote, to build momentum for all.**

I wanted to provide gifts for people who had gone out of their way to assist me in getting published. Appropriate books by other Canadian authors turned out to be a wise choice. In fact, even if you think you are years away from publication, you might want to get into the habit of supporting other Canadian writers by giving their books as gifts. If the trend catches on, the market will still be there when you need it.

—

Denyse O'Leary is a Toronto-based freelance writer and the author of *Faith@Science* (Winnipeg: J. Gordon Shillingford, 2001). O'Leary writes regularly on science and faith issues. She also teaches workshops on business practice for writers and editors. She has two adult daughters, three gardens, and a website (www.denyseoleary.com).

# Help! I'm Going to Be on TV!

*by Barbara Florio Graham*

The "free" in freelance is one of the most attractive aspects of being a writer. When you work from home, you can sit at the computer in sweatpants, a T-shirt and your bunny slippers. So panic is common when writers are asked to appear on an arts segment of a local television program, or to be interviewed in connection with a new book or a writers' conference.

After many years as a public relations consultant, I find writers tend to fall into one of two categories. There are those who proclaim they are free spirits, not constrained by other people's rules; along with poets who appear at public readings with scraggly hair, bare toes poking out of their sandals, and faded jeans with fashionable tears at the knees. The others — liberated from an office environment — obsess about the fact that they no longer fit the stereotype. "Do I have to wear a tie?" the men ask. "My old office clothes no longer fit!" exclaim the women.

No wonder the public doesn't take them seriously as professionals! In a "visual medium" the focus is on how you look rather than what you say.

**First things first...**

It's absolutely essential to prepare some key remarks, and rehearse them thoroughly.

Enlist a colleague or close friend who admires your work, and ask him or her to describe what sets you apart from others in your genre. Skim through favourable reviews of your work for additional statements. Don't be afraid to describe yourself in positive terms. The most glaring mistake most individuals in the arts make when introducing themselves is to undervalue their importance.

Remember that the first few seconds make the most lasting impression. For that reason, you must have a clear, positive statement to make right away. Followed with your most engaging smile.

If you begin with an apology, make some kind of excuse for why you "don't belong" on the program, or claim that your work is less than wonderful, the audience will be turned off before you get a chance to show them what you're capable of.

**Dress is important...**

Someone else — usually the host — will be the focus of attention at the beginning of the program, so the first impression you make on the audience will be primarily visual. For this reason, you must give a lot of thought to dress and body language.

Artistic individuals tend to extremes of dress. Either they pay little attention to their clothing, dressing in all black or in jeans and a T-shirt, or they lean in the opposite direction toward unusual and elaborate costumes.

Neither of these will present you at your best on television.

If your "working uniform" tends to be jeans or drab colours, you should invest in one or two special pieces to wear just in case a TV producer calls. They needn't be expensive. In fact, no audience — stage or television — can tell if you're wearing silk, wool or polyester. What they will notice is colour, whether it fits you properly or if it appears rumpled.

The heavier you are (male or female) the more you need a long jacket. Whatever you wear underneath will be imperceptible particularly if it's dark.

Stage and television lights are hot. Nervousness makes most of us perspire even more. Select a lightweight jacket in a fabric that doesn't wrinkle and wear something under it that is cool and absorbent.

Women can express artistic flair in bright colours, unusual colour combinations, or a single accessory or piece of jewellery. Make sure your shoes are polished (avoid running shoes), and match socks or hose to your slacks or skirt.

Before deciding to wear a skirt, consider the view the audience will have of your lower body. Do you want your legs to be a focal point? Maybe you do, but more likely you be more comfortable in a longer, fuller skirt that doesn't need to be tugged and tucked in place!

Women should only wear boots with slacks long enough to cover all but the toes and heels, or with a mid-calf skirt. A man in boots looks ridiculous on TV unless the boots are the same dark colour as his pants.

Colours for both sexes to avoid include bright red (unless you have an excellent complexion), white (which creates too much contrast for TV cameras) and "muddy" colours such as khaki, mustard, avocado green or brown.

Women have more choice of colour than men do. Most shades of blue are flattering for everyone. Other good choices include coral and aqua. Those with dark hair look good in bright green, deep burgundy, and bright purple. Blondes can look wonderful in gold or rust. Grey hair requires a strong focal colour that isn't too harsh. Medium blue, violet, soft rose, and turquoise work well.

**Don't refuse TV make-up...**

The bright television lights wash out facial colour, and make even the healthiest person look pale and ill. On a small local or cable TV station (where make-up is usually not provided), women should use a foundation make-up in a neutral shade, blusher, clear red lipstick, a matte grey or taupe eye shadow, and mascara.

Men should shave with a blade, apply aftershave (which removes excess oil), and consider a light application of pressed powder in a neutral shade to oily areas of the face, as well as to high foreheads and any bald spots.

**Body language is important...**

In addition to what you say, and how you dress, don't forget body language. The best way to avoid distracting movement is to sit well back in your chair, cross one leg over the other (at the knee or at the ankle, not one ankle over the opposite knee), and rest your arms either on the arms of the chair or on a table.

If your hands tend to move nervously to your face, hair, or pockets, give them something to do. Take a "prop" with you to hold: a book, notebook and pen, something relating to your work or something to show the audience. Remove all temptation from your grasp including rings you tend to twirl, bracelets, and change in your pockets or dangling necklaces.

Just before you go "on," stretch your neck toward the ceiling, open your mouth in a big yawn, and consciously lower your shoulders. This will relax you, open your throat, and help you appear composed.

Then, smile!

—

This article was adapted from *Five Fast Steps to Low-Cost Publicity* which is described in full on Barbara Florio Graham's website: www.SimonTeakettle.com. Barbara is also the author of *Five Fast Steps to Better Writing* and *Musings/Mewsings*.

# Surviving Criticism

*by Ruth Latta*

"I want constructive criticism. Come on. I can take it." I've heard this remark in several writers' workshops, but I never entirely believe it. "Constructiveness" like beauty, is in the eye of the beholder.

Peer criticism came up in the movie *Henry and June*. In one memorable scene, novelist Henry Miller and diarist Anaïs Nin are sitting together, reading each other's latest manuscripts. Each praises the other. Suddenly Henry takes out a pencil and slashes down Anaïs's page. She gasps.

"You've got to take a few taps on the chin," he tells her. "Writing is like prizefighting." He tells her that she has to get knocked down occasionally to acquire the necessary ring tactics, and won't get anywhere shadow boxing in your room. "You wouldn't last two minutes if you stepped into the ring," he adds.

"I'm not interested in getting in the ring with you," says Anaïs. "The world will give us plenty of beatings. What we need is each other's support." And she picks up her manuscript and goes home.

**Failed creative artists...**

I agree with Anaïs Nin. So does Julia Cameron, author of the well-known creativity booster *The Artist's Way*. She warns budding writers against subjecting their first clumsy efforts to anyone expecting perfection in the first draft. Often academic people are failed creative artists and are jealous of those actually engaged in making something new. They excel in pulling things apart, but not in putting them together.

In a similar vein, author David Ray (*Writer's Digest*, July 1992) says that his method of teaching creative writing has changed. "The one great gift we can give anyone is to believe in them," he writes. Early in his career, full of confidence in his own judgement, he had two categories for student manuscripts: junk or gold. Eventually, though, he began to find hidden power in work he would classify as "junk," and to have doubts about technically competent, trendy stories.

"Somewhere along the line," writes Ray, "I began to think of my students as victims of vast networks of abuse in our society. They were seeking sanctuary in my classes, not just a place to compete and be evaluated anew." He considers that it is his role to help people confront the serious material in their lives and to steer them towards a knowledge of form and technique. His classes are a safe place for writers to produce new work and share it without fear. If only I'd studied writing with him!

Meanwhile, I have self-protective techniques. "Silence, exile and cunning," self-prescribed Stephen Dedalus, hero of *Portrait of the Artist as a Young Man*. Wise words. I show my unpublished work to a couple of people who love me, respect my writing, and know and love fiction.

Writers need human response. Those without kindly spouses are drawn to classes or workshops. Try to determine in advance whether the class will be conducted "Henry-style", or "Anaïs-style." Some years ago I walked out on an adversarial, abrasive workshop instructor. For me, the best training has been reading books like Natalie Goldberg's *Writing Down the Bones*, and Bernays and Painter's *What If: Exercises for Fiction Writers*.

**Does not fit our needs...**

At a later stage, when sending work out to publishers, you encounter another level of criticism — editorial feedback and reviews. Your self-addressed stamped envelopes come back to you with printed notes saying: "Sorry, not for us," or, "Does not fit our needs." Editorial comments on your work are a sign that it stood out enough among the influx of manuscripts to warrant individual feedback.

But don't overanalyze rejection notes.

"Does not meet our present needs," the writer agonizes, "what does that mean?"

Occasionally, you get a handwritten note. Messages such as, "characters wooden, plot improbable, wording clumsy," are hardly favourable, but if you decide to accept the editor's assessment, at least you know what to fix.

Rejection never ends. It is part of the process of being a writer.

Once you get that first book published, you may be rejected by an unenthusiastic reading public who fail to buy as many copies as you would like. Established writers get rejected by movie producers or foreign publishers and the like. Rejection can be a sign that your reach temporarily exceeds your grasp, and that you are trying to grow as a writer. Give yourself credit for having high aspirations and taking on new challenges.

Mystery novelist Lawrence Block urges writers not to let little slips of paper have too much power over them. "When I buy one brand of soapflakes instead of another," he writes, "I'm not rejecting the brand I don't buy — nor is the manufacturer likely to burst into tears as a result."

Rejection by one publication gives you the opportunity to try somewhere else, possibly a magazine that will pay you more than the original one, or advance your reputation. If an editor who intends to publish and pay you wants some changes, then revise! Go for it, unless the suggested modifications would grossly distort your work.

Reviews, I'm told, are necessary to publicize books. Some people believe that all publicity is good publicity, that there is no such thing as a bad review, but Julia Cameron (and I) would disagree. Cameron says, "Truth is good. When a well-aimed arrow hits its mark, the creative person will say, 'I can see that. I can change that.' "

Unjust criticism, however, leaves the writer feeling bludgeoned. "It is withering and shaming in tone, ambiguous in content, personal, inaccurate or blanket in its condemnations. Nothing can be gleaned from it."

Some years ago, in a local alternative tabloid, a reviewer called my book "drivel." He didn't understand the title, condemned the style as "too quiet," and accused me of not telling the "real story." I fretted for a while, but finally, a truth dawned. Not all reviewers are objective. Some people don't like stories that go against their view of the world.

**Condemned by critics as too realistic...**

John Steinbeck's novel, *The Grapes of Wrath*, was condemned by many critics as too realistic — a wallow in life's sordid side. Some claimed he had missed part of the story. They didn't like the story he told. His sympathetic depiction of migrant workers in Depression-ridden California presented the wealthy ranchers in a bad light. Historical research has vindicated Steinbeck, and his book lives on, still in print, read by people in all walks of life.

Margaret Atwood was once accused of presenting men in a negative light in her fiction. To paraphrase her response, "If the shoe fits, wear it."

Will a reviewer be frank about his dislike of the content? Or will he criticize the style, the structure, or say that you missed the "real story"? If a work strikes a nerve, it's easy enough to find justifications for condemning it.

In the face of ambiguous, blanket criticism, Cameron says, "Let yourself feel the criticism fully. Then analyze the review. Does the criticism remind you of something you were shamed for in the past? All the humiliations of a lifetime tend to descend at such times. Share your hurt with someone who loves and supports you, but don't tell too many people about the review. Why spread negative information about yourself?"

Finally, "Get back on your horse." Start writing immediately.

Nurture yourself by reading a good review or recalling a compliment. I was lucky; my book had received two positive reviews. I also went to "visit" my book at a local library, only to find that it was out in circulation. I looked myself up in the catalogue, admiring the three titles to my credit.

**How many remember a bad review...**

Next I searched for works by my reviewer, and drew a blank.

Only one person mentioned my bad review to me. Perhaps other friends were too polite. Maybe they didn't see it! Typical readers of the tabloid were students, then busy starting a new school year. How many picked up the rag and read the review? How many remember it?

Since I don't believe everything I read, why should I assume that others do? Ever since a certain reviewer trashed a wonderful book by a friend of mine, I have taken her recommendations with a grain of salt. Recently she dumped on a novel that received excellent reviews elsewhere, and a nomination for a literary award. Sometimes when she pans a work, I seek it out, knowing that if she hated it, I'll love it.

A mean-spirited review says more about the reviewer than it does about the book. "What does he have against that poor writer?" someone may say. "Can her book be that bad? I must buy it and see."

—

Ruth Latta's latest work is a biography of Grace MacInnis, coauthored by Joy Trott, and published by Xlibris, 2001. Visit her website for further information about her published work at www.cyberus.ca/~rklatta/RuthLatta.html.

# 12. Theatre, Screen & Radio

# Playwriting

*by Keith Slater*

Playwriting is an art that can be mastered by anyone willing to work at it. The important thing to remember is that you're writing words to be spoken by somebody else who wants to grip the attention of an audience.

**Work on emotions...**

The way to do this is to work on people's emotions, so it's your task to develop emotional experiences by your choice of words. The simplest way of doing this is to write dialogue that produces a conflict between two (or more) characters. You give them words that allow them to "top" each other's comments in turn, so that the emotional tension rises, carrying the audience with it. That emotion can be love, fear, hatred, jealousy, anger, sexual arousal, or any other human one, as long as it changes in the scene.

Obviously, the characters can't continue to increase the emotion, or the play would end up in a shrieking match, so what you need to do is provide a resolution of the conflict. This can be a pleasant one (lovers fall into each other's arms, one character agrees with the other, etc.) or a less happy one (one character is killed, or storms off stage, etc.), to let the actors (and audience) come down from their emotional high. In addition, the resolution should provide the beginning of the next conflict (perhaps of a different type) so that another emotional climb can take place. In this way, people watching the play won't get bored and will enjoy it.

**Convey information by dialogue...**

A challenge for novice writers is the need to convey all information by dialogue only, because the audience doesn't have the background to understand what's happening on stage. Words spoken by characters have to tell the story, develop the plot, and differentiate between characters. If it's vital to have the piece set in spring, have a character look out of a window and comment that trees are beginning to bloom. If you're writing a mystery and need it set in a big, old house, make somebody scared of shadows explain how he got lost in the third-floor wing.

As in all writing, you should begin with the characters and get to know them intimately. Then you can give them words that make sense for them in the circumstances in which you place them. You can't describe setting, moods, emotions, character traits, etc., so you must give actors words to allow (force?) them to portray these features as they speak. You can provide all the stage directions you want, but there's no guarantee that the director, designer, etc., will follow them.

**Establish the setting...**

In planning your work, establish the setting in your own mind very carefully, even if you don't use every bit of information in your notes. Know the time period, the social class of your characters, their financial status, their hopes and fears. Plan to have grouped scenes, rather than continuous action, so that less interesting developments in your plot can take place between scenes and can be omitted from your work.

Arrange the play into rough sections, set out in point form with all events, people, plot developments, conflicts, etc., noted. Put them into logical order (or rearrange them to end up that way) and provide a variety of types of conflict to enhance interest. Then write a scenario, a summary of all that's going to happen from beginning to end of the piece and use that as a guide for writing. This will help control characters, so they don't take over and change the direction of the play to dissipate all that lovely focus you've developed.

When you begin the writing process proper, choose words that express your intentions as succinctly as possible. Make each character speak in the way expected of that person in that situation, taking into account all the traits you've provided for that character. Write so that each character is always consistent in speech pattern, vocabulary, rhythm, cadence, tone or level of excitement. Avoid unnecessary duplication of information (unless it's part of the plot), and don't give mixed messages to the audience by having two incompatible versions of the same event (unless, again, it's to show characters being duped, etc.). Make words provide impact to reinforce the emotions you're trying to engage. Lady Macbeth didn't say "I'll never be able to forget what I've just done," but "All the perfumes of Arabia will not sweeten this little hand."

**Keep the audience guessing...**

As a scene develops, remember to build it to keep audience members guessing, tense, laughing, scared, etc. Vary impact to give them a rest between intense emotions, by balancing scenes (e.g. follow a harrowing one with a humorous one, and so on). Always use words to allow a character to tell the audience how he's feeling, because there's no descriptive material in the script to do that. Avoid over-exaggeration, unless it's to show how a character is pompous, hesitant, etc., to make sure the emotion you're trying to get across is a genuine one.

As you write, avoid the temptation to rewrite before the end of the play or section. Take notes of changes that strike you, but don't implement them until the piece is complete. This allows you to judge the balance of the play as a whole, rather than being distracted and going off on a tangent. Improvise if you feel you can't follow your scenario precisely, but don't feel you have to include a resolution for every single conflict in strict order, especially for short scenes. When you've finished the first draft, check each scene against your original scenario, and explain to yourself why deviations have appeared. Ask yourself if they've improved the play as a whole, then note changes you might need to get back to your original scheme if you feel the improvisations have worsened the piece.

**Time to rewrite...**

Then it's time for rewriting. Alternate your attack, starting first with scene-by-scene revisions, then revisions to the whole play. Then work on scenes again, and then on the whole play, repeating this two-step process as often as you think it's needed. Check for inconsistencies; do your characters say one thing about an event in Act I, but something entirely different in Act II? Are there inconsistencies in the way characters behave? Have you allowed time offstage for a character to accomplish something that's supposedly happened during his absence? Are all events consistent with the time period in which you've set the play? I once had a student writing a medieval piece have a character telephone a doctor, who arrived immediately — actions that destroyed the entire credibility of a tense scene he'd built up very carefully!

Once you're satisfied that the play is as good as you can make it, it's time to put it to the test. Get together a group of actors to give it a workshop reading, bribing them with free beer if necessary. If that's not possible, have friends over and ask them to read it aloud. Listen to the rendition, taping it for reference if possible. Try to decide how an audience, hearing the piece for the first time, will feel about it. Are the characters, events, actions, etc., believable? Does the plot develop as you wanted? Have the readers (and audience, if you have more friends than characters) discuss the work. Ask them to write comments anonymously, to avoid any sycophantic praise that's not a genuine expression of how they feel about it.

Start a discussion, asking specific questions about any aspect that you're unsure about after hearing your words spoken. Then digest the information they give you, and ask yourself if you agree with it (and, if you don't, why?). After waiting for a few days to let details sink in, begin the process of rewriting again with all the comments in mind. Use the same technique as before, scene-by-scene followed by the whole play, until you're satisfied that all the changes you feel were justified have been made. At that point, you have a play that you can submit to a local group to consider for their next season.

**Start with amateur theatre...**

One final word of advice — don't submit your first effort to a professional group. They won't even bother to read it. An amateur theatre company is always open to new work, because it gives them an edge on other groups nearby, and a good new play is a treasure for them. Let them read your play, listen to the director's suggestions (and make recommended changes), then sit back and let them take over the job of bringing it to the stage. Letting your "baby" go may be the most difficult part of the entire process, but the rewards at the end will be well worth the sacrifice.

Good luck. Or should I say, "Break a pen!"

—

Keith Slater has been involved in theatre as a playwright, actor, director, or member of the technical crew for over 27 years. He has written about 15 full-length plays and a number of one-act or shorter pieces. He has received several nominations or awards for his theatre work, and has conducted many acting, directing and playwriting workshops.

# Script Formats

*by Keith Slater*

So you've got a piece that you'd like to submit for performance? The first task is to format it in such a way that a publisher or director is willing to take a look at your script. You may not realize it, but there's a different way to present a manuscript for performing arts, depending on whether it's for stage, radio, moving pictures or television. If you don't have the right format, then, no matter how good the piece, you run the risk of having it discarded or returned without being read.

**Stage scripts...**

Let's look at stage scripts first. There are two formats, the so-called "standard American" used by Samuel French and the alternative one (which I prefer, as an actor) used by Dramatic Play Services and Playwrights Canada.

In the former one, character names are capitalized, bold font, and indented from the left margin, with no line spaces between speeches and a period after the name, followed by two character spaces and the dialogue. Stage directions of one line begin at the left margin, but are indented if they take more than one line. They are italicized. There is a line space between stage directions and dialogue, as follows:

*ENTER RALPH, carrying a large silver salver in both hands, with a huge lid covering it. It is obviously heavy or fragile.*

**MAGDA.** Ralph, darling, what have you got in my best silver salver?

**RALPH.** A special gift, mother. I picked it out just for you, seeing as you're fifty years old today.

*As MAGDA speaks, RALPH removes the cover*

**MAGDA.** Darling, how thoughtful! What is ... Oh!! Charles!! It's ...

*EXIT MAGDA in haste.*

**CHARLES.** What the devil do you think you're playing at, you damned fool? Another of your stupid jokes? Put the damned lid back on. You know your mother's a vegetarian and can't stand the sight of meat at the table. Especially not a … bird with its bloody feathers still on!

**RALPH.** Really? Sorry. Thought she'd like it. It's a birthday pheasant.

In the alternative method, names are printed bold face at the left margin, followed by a colon. Speeches are indented, and stage directions (again italicized) are double indented. Single line spacing is used between all speeches and stage directions. The same scene in this format would read as follows:

*ENTER RALPH, carrying a large silver salver in both hands, with a huge lid covering it. It is obviously heavy or fragile*

**MAGDA:** Ralph, darling, what have you got there?

**RALPH:** A special gift, mother. I picked it out just for you, seeing as you're fifty years old today.

*As MAGDA speaks, RALPH removes the cover*

**MAGDA:** Darling, how thoughtful! What is … Oh!! Charles!! It's …

*EXIT MAGDA in haste.*

**CHARLES:** What the devil do you think you're playing at, you damned fool? Another of your stupid jokes? Put the damned lid back on. You know your mother's a vegetarian and can't stand the sight of meat at the table. Especially not a … bird with its bloody feathers still on!

**RALPH:** Really? Sorry. Thought she'd like it. It's a birthday pheasant.

**Radio scripts…**

For radio, you have to tell the audience what's happening by using sound effects (SFX) in the script. Character names are again capitalized, and (as are all stage directions) are printed at the left margin, with stage directions underlined and capitalized. Dialogue is indented as in the second stage format. Our scene now reads:

SOUND: DOOR OPENS. FOOTSTEPS CROSS A ROOM.

MAGDA: Ralph, darling, what have you got in my best silver salver?

RALPH: A special gift, mother. I picked it out just for you, seeing as you're fifty years old today.

SOUND: A HEAVY LID IS REMOVED FROM A SALVER.

MAGDA: Darling, how thoughtful! What is ... Oh!! Charles!! It's ...

SOUND: FOOTSTEPS AND DOOR SLAM AS MAGDA EXITS IN HASTE.

CHARLES: What the devil do you think you're playing at, you damned fool? Another of your stupid jokes? Put the damned lid back on! You know your mother's a vegetarian and can't stand the sight of meat at the table. Especially not a ... bird with its bloody feathers still on!

SOUND: THE HEAVY LID IS REPLACED.

RALPH: Really? Sorry. Thought she'd like it. It's a birthday pheasant.

**Motion picture scripts...**

In motion pictures, you have to ensure that the page and scene numbers appear at the correct place. The page number is placed top right, and the scene number is at both the left and right edges of the first line in the scene. Each scene is numbered to correspond with a detailed description given at the beginning of the script, with an indication of where it takes place (INT for interior and EXT for exterior). The word "continued" (in capitals) is placed at the top left and bottom right of each page if the scene goes over that page break. Character names in capitals are placed at the centre of the page, and dialogue (double indented) follows with no line space. Scene directions are single-indented from the scene number column. If we assume that the dining room scene runs over two pages, then the script reads as follows:

18

5 CONTINUED

(The end of the previous scene would appear here on page 18.)

6 INT DINING ROOM WITH TABLE SET FOR DINNER. 6

ENTER RALPH CARRYING A COVERED SALVER

MAGDA

Ralph, darling, what have you got in my best silver salver?

RALPH

A special gift, mother. I picked it out just for you, seeing as you're fifty years old today.

CONTINUED

(A page break is supposed to be needed here.)

19

6 CONTINUED

AS MAGDA SPEAKS, RALPH REMOVES THE COVER.

MAGDA

Darling, how thoughtful! What is … Oh!! Charles!! It's …

EXIT MAGDA IN HASTE.

CHARLES

What the devil do you think you're playing at, you damned fool? Another of your stupid jokes? Put the damned lid back on. You know your mother's a vegetarian and can't stand the sight of meat at the table. Especially not a … bird with its bloody feathers still on!

RALPH

Really? Sorry. Thought she'd like it. It's a birthday pheasant.

**Television scripts...**

For television, there are several formats that can be used, depending on the type of show. Space limitation does not allow me the luxury of describing all of them, but two of the most common ones (for sitcoms and live variety/comedy shows respectively) are very similar to the moving picture one above. The major differences are the addition of the word TRANSITION at the right hand side of the page where one scene changes into the next one. In addition, for a comedy script only, dialogue lines are double spaced and both the margin scene number and CONTINUED are omitted (though there is still a need to identify the scene by naming it at the top right of each page, as shown later). Thus, the sitcom script is:

18

5 CONTINUED

(The end of the previous scene would appear here on page 18.)

TRANSITION

6 INT DINING ROOM WITH TABLE SET FOR DINNER. 6

ENTER RALPH CARRYING A COVERED SALVER

MAGDA

Ralph, darling, what have you got in my best silver salver?

RALPH

A special gift, mother. I picked it out just for you, seeing as you're fifty years old today.

CONTINUED

(A page break is supposed to be needed here.)

19

6 CONTINUED

AS MAGDA SPEAKS, RALPH REMOVES THE COVER.

MAGDA

Darling, how thoughtful! What is … Oh!! Charles!! It's …

EXIT MAGDA IN HASTE.

CHARLES

What the devil do you think you're playing at, you damned fool? Another of your stupid jokes? Put the damned lid back on. You know your mother's a vegetarian and can't stand the sight of meat at the table. Especially not a … bird with its bloody feathers still on!

RALPH

Really? Sorry. Thought she'd like it. It's a birthday pheasant.

The live variety/comedy script would read:

ACT I. SC. 5

18

(The end of the previous scene would appear here on page 18.)

TRANSITION

ACT I SC. 6

(The names of all characters appearing in this scene should be printed at the right hand side of the page.)

INT DINING ROOM WITH TABLE SET FOR DINNER.

ENTER RALPH CARRYING A COVERED SALVER

MAGDA

Ralph, darling, what have you got in my best silver salver?

RALPH

A special gift, mother. I picked it out just for you, seeing

as you're fifty years old today.

CONTINUED

(A page break is supposed to be needed here.)

19

ACT I SC. 5

AS MAGDA SPEAKS, RALPH REMOVES THE COVER.

MAGDA

Darling, how thoughtful! What is … Oh!! Charles!! It's …

EXIT MAGDA IN HASTE.

CHARLES

What the devil do you think you're playing at, you damned fool? Another of your stupid jokes? Put the damned lid back on. You know your mother's a vegetarian and can't stand the sight of meat at the table. Especially not a … bird with its bloody feathers still on!

RALPH

Really? Sorry. Thought she'd like it. It's a birthday pheasant.

Well, that's the lot, in very condensed form. There are other minor needs, such as indicating fades in or out and the exact number of spaces needed for the indented parts, but I suspect you'll get away with a submission where these aren't indicated. If your material's good, you'll be forgiven as a new writer. If not, you can always try the excuse that you thought the director might like to make those decisions! Good luck!

—

Keith Slater has been involved in theatre as a playwright, actor, director, or member of the technical crew for over 27 years. He has written about 15 full-length plays and a number of one-act or shorter pieces. He has received several nominations or awards for his theatre work, and has conducted many acting, directing and playwriting workshops.

# A Beginners' Guide to Writing for Radio

*by Elizabeth Ruth*

Remember those old radio dramas such as *The Green Hornet* and *The Shadow*? As a child I listened to them with my grandfather, chewing my nails, sitting on the edge of my seat as the plot unwound, mysteries were solved, and sometimes the world was saved. It was my first exposure to creative writing. For my grandfather, who fell asleep each night with a short-wave radio under his pillow, the beauty of this medium lay in its immediacy. I'd like to think that he was still somewhere out there listening when I wrote and produced my first piece for radio.

Have you tuned into the CBC lately? Shows such as *Out Front*, and *Definitely Not the Opera (DNTO)* are mandated to solicit work from freelancers and, in some cases, assist us to learn the skills necessary for writing and producing. There are a number of incentives to write for radio, not the least of which is that your work will reach a new and wider audience (unless of course, you're already a Governor General's Award-winning author, in which case you can probably ignore the rest of this article). Writing for radio will impart valuable skills, which can translate to work you produce for the printed page.

**Research your market...**

Now, if your interest is peaked, the first thing you need to do is research. It's the same as the review of literary journals and publishing houses before submitting your manuscript — you'll have greater success with your radio proposal if content and tone compliments the show's mandate.

Listen. Get a clear sense of their material and target audience. Do they prefer documentaries? Personal narrative? Are they experimenting with sound? If they have a website, spend time downloading and listening to old shows.

Once you've made a shortlist of programs, you'll need a well-written proposal. Clear and direct is best. And generally no longer than one page, typed and double-spaced. This is the producer's first impression of you, so take time to polish it. Producers look for unique ideas, or an old idea that could be reworked — and they want to know why you're the best person to execute it.

My proposal was for *Out Front*, a show of interactive, human interest stories, and those traditionally not heard on radio. *Out Front* was recorded with my own equipment, matched with a producer who offered technical support. She guided and advised without dominating the process or compromising a story's integrity. Like a good editor, the producer is there to hold you accountable for your writing choices. Perhaps more importantly, they explain why those choices will or won't work.

**A different process...**

The process of writing for radio is inherently different than writing for the two dimensional page. You simply cannot work the same way. On the radio you don't have time to explore issues, use lingering phrases, or ask the listener to get tangled up in your metaphors, as you sometimes hope to do with readers. Listeners have only one opportunity to "get" what you're saying. They cannot peruse your story over and over again, mining its thematic nuances and structural brilliance. They can't reread the last paragraph. But, like a reader they want to be entertained by well-crafted text. Remember to keep in mind a singular focus, idea or theme. In radio parlance this is your "through line." Everything else gets cut.

I arrived at my first production meeting with a tightly woven piece of prose in hand, eager to use it as the centrepiece for the rest of my documentary. This is the way I usually work: Write the skeleton of the piece, edit, rewrite, then layer, adding meat to the bones of the story. With radio, I quickly realized there are additional considerations, such as spaces between voices and sound. Interviewees project speech patterns, tones, and pacing that sometimes cannot be sewn together. To write for radio successfully, you must begin by *hearing* the piece. Each voice a fiction writer creates on the page, however differentiated, belongs to them. In radio, space is shared with others and the surroundings or environment. In short stories, for example, no one drops a pitcher of water in the background unless we plan for that to happen. When recording material for radio, though, we give up absolute control and if we're lucky, an unplanned siren blaring in the background might just enrich the story.

**The sound studio...**

So, after you've had your work approved by the producer, you head to the sound studio to record your segments. Most writers like the sound of their own voices, but not *literally*. Suddenly the sound producer and associate producer are listening across from you, directing you through every crack, unintended "um," and hesitancy. You spill your guts with no page to hide behind.

After recording, you create, add, and edit in sound, so the body of the writing shifts once more. Does the music you've selected distract from the piece? Does it flow, is it seamless?

I had a very clear idea (in my mind) of the sound I wanted and tried my best to convey that to the sound producer while he experimented on the keyboards. "Imagine what a black hole sounds like," I said, "pretend you're being sucked in." Needless to say, it was a lengthy process.

**For love or money...**

At one of our first meetings, my associate producer told me that those who write for radio don't do it for the money, but for the love of radio. I believe that's generally true. However as much as I love this, I *adore* paying my rent. In comparison with the honorariums most emerging writers are accustomed to receiving — a cash dividend perhaps, a free one-year subscription, or better yet (my personal favourite) two free back issues — I have to admit I was initially encouraged by the prospect of $800–$1000 for a single piece.

Beware! Payment for radio work may be higher than for other writing styles, but when you break down the time spent — writing, editing in studio, interviewing, transcribing, recording, meeting with your executive producer — you will discover that you're probably not even making minimum wage. As for other commercial issues, it's possible to be paid about half on signing your contract, and another half on completion of the project. If your piece doesn't go to air, you are normally paid a "kill" fee.

**Read the "fine print"...**

Always read contracts over carefully. Words such as "copyright" and "residual/repeat rights" should catch your eye.

It's worth noting that shows featuring personal issues are more likely to help beginners get started but this may be prohibitive for fiction writers. I was passionate about my proposed idea, but equally apprehensive about broadcasting anything personal. Nevertheless, the skills I gained are transferable and experience can make a better, more diverse writer. For some shows you are paying dues, working your way into the industry, sending your "manuscript" to a smaller "press", which will give you more currency if you later approach other, larger radio programs.

The potential for interaction with your audience on the radio is great.

People across the country will listen and send e-mail or write in. You might be able to request that this feedback is forwarded directly to you.

Listeners, like readers, are the other half of any writer's craft. Without them we might as well remain tucked away in obsessive seclusion. Writing for radio is another way to connect.

**It pays to listen...**

One final comment: It pays to listen. Just as you expect good fiction writers to be avid readers, tuning in will improve your ability to tell a good story. Seek out those who've been doing it for a while and listen to their shows. I purchased state-of-the-art recording equipment and then proceeded, against professional advice, to conduct several hours of taped interviews, using five different individuals.

Did I mention that it was a fifteen-minute documentary I was putting together? You see my mistake.

If you think you'd like to try your "ear" at writing for radio, go for it. Be prepared to be addicted. I was. I'll be writing for radio again very soon. But next time not for money.

—

Elizabeth Ruth's 2000 CBC radio documentary, *Quantum Father*, was selected as one of the year's best. Her debut novel, *Ten Good Seconds of Silence* was published to critical acclaim in 2001. Elizabeth is a graduate of the Humber School for Writers. She teaches at George Brown College, and edits *Fireweed*. Visit www.elizabethruth.com.

# The Radio Commentary

*by Marjorie Doyle*

Passionate about something? Feel you're never hearing your point of view on a particular issue? Write a radio commentary. The short shelf life gives it an urgency and immediacy that's quite appealing in the often-amorphous world of writing. Also, you'll get immediate feedback, and it pays!

Have three points, and make them clearly. Remember, a reader can turn back to a written piece again and again, but a listener doesn't get a second go. If it's possible to deflect criticism concisely, or take the juice out of an opposing argument, do it. And end with a punch. Don't start a new idea that won't be developed, and don't give a précis — the piece is too short for that. Instead, leave the listener with something definite to reflect on.

**Avoid convoluted sentences...**

Forget writing as you would for print. This commentary is going to be heard, not read. Write it out loud. Talk it. Make your sentences short, and keep word order straightforward. Avoid convoluted sentences and subordinate clauses. If you want to make a point within a point or add clarification or examples, it's best to do it in a separate sentence. Paragraphs should be short, just a sentence or two.

The ear can't make the connections that the eye can make: anything hanging between the subject of the sentence and the verb pushes the two apart and makes it hard for the listener to follow. What looks clean and clear to the eye can be amazingly cluttered to the ear. If you want to say, "the Better Business Bureau, the Home and School Association and the town councillors all feel that ..." better to say: "The Better Business Bureau feels that ... So do the Home and School Association and the town councillors." This example is simplistic, I know, but the point is crucial.

The ear has a strong tendency to tune out and certain things aid that process: dates, numbers, statistics and lists. They simply don't work on radio. Find another way to say what you want to say. On the other hand, there are things that catch the ear and bring the listener in, such as aural pictures and images. It's possible to create a scene or paint a picture in a single sentence, and the ear loves it. A vivid image will linger long in the mind of the listener. Once when I wanted to describe on radio just how windy Newfoundland can be, I said that one day when I was on a picnic, the tea had blown out of my cup (it had). Ten years later, I am still meeting people for the first time who say, "Was that true about your tea?"

Performance is a huge part of a radio piece. Many great pieces of writing fall flat on the radio, or don't even make it to air, because of the "read." Sometimes a producer will ask you not just to fax the piece you're selling, she/he may ask you to read it on the phone. You may feel self-conscious doing it, but in this vetting process, read your work as you would on air. The producer's decision to accept the piece is based not only on the content and how well you express your points, but also on how it will sound as part of a radio show.

**Make your pace right...**

Take your script and block it; that is, take a coloured marker and draw a line across the page after every paragraph, even a one-sentence paragraph. Train yourself to look up for a second, just a glance, every time you come to one of these lines. You'll probably feel you're pausing unnecessarily long and spoiling the flow. In fact, you are giving the ear a chance to digest what you're saying. Doing this — blocking and looking up — will make your pace right.

Practise your delivery. Read the piece out loud, taking into account where you'll breathe, where you'll turn a page. And don't be halfhearted. If it's worth saying, it's worth saying with conviction and energy. One huge difference in writing for print and writing for radio is that in print your words alone convey an idea; in radio your voice, too, is an integral part of it.

Always *time* a radio piece! Most people believe they know what "three minutes worth" looks like on paper, but it's deceptive. Read your piece aloud, exactly as you would on air, and time it with a second hand. Editors can be sticklers about word count but producers are much more exacting because there is less flexibility with radio — entire programs and individual items within the programs are timed to the second, literally. If there is a slot for a three-minute commentary or review, that's it folks! If you arrive at the studio and have to make a cut, you'll be flustered, sitting there with a producer and a technician, desperately trying to shave five seconds. It's hard to do. Timing a radio piece precisely, keeping in mind the tone and pace you will actually use, is essential, and saves grief.

In many ways, a radio commentary or review is the same as a column or op-ed piece in that it is short, clearly thought out and tightly written.

But style — writing for the ear — can make or break a radio piece. So can tone. Not just the tone of the writing, but the tone of the delivery: it can result in a piece that grabs the listener or drives the finger straight to the dial. To hit the right tone, consider that you're not preaching a sermon, or giving a lecture. You're talking to someone.

**Listen to the credits...**

Have an ear on the radio for openings and opportunities you can fit into: national commentary perhaps, or a review or commentary for *Definitely Not The Opera*. There may be similar spots on local noon or drive-home shows. Know the spots you're aiming for. Call your local station and get the name of the appropriate producer. If it's a national show, also get the name of the network producer, the person who works in your local station but is a liaison with national shows. Listen to the credits at the end of a program (given once a week only on daily shows) to get the name of the right contact person. Voice menus have made it almost impossible to reach someone if you don't know a particular telephone extension, but almost everyone at the CBC can be reached via e-mail using this formula: first name, underscore, last name @cbc.ca.

Writing for radio forces you to make your prose clean, clear and direct. Your piece gets a public life more quickly than most print pieces and the cheque will probably come faster, too.

—

Marjorie Doyle worked as a broadcaster from 1988–1999. Her commentaries and reviews were aired regionally and nationally on CBC Radio. She also hosted a national CBC radio show for six years. She's published two books of nonfiction and is working on her third.

# 13. Non-Traditional Markets

# "We Need a Speech ..."

*by Colin Moorhouse*

Whether you are a freelance writer offering writing services to a variety of corporate clients, or you work in public affairs, communications, or public relations within a corporate setting, inevitably you will be asked to write a speech. You want to be able to say yes to such a request.

Speech writing is part craft, part art and — when things go right — part magic. Without knowledge of the craft, the art and magic rarely happen. What follows are suggestions that speak to the craft of speech writing.

The very moment you say yes to a request for a speech there are two non-negotiable mantras you must keep front and centre.

**First mantra...**

Speeches are about engagement. Not information. Although information may well be a desired byproduct of a speech, without engagement — without a connection with the audience — all information will be lost on an unengaged audience.

Engagement usually comes from *story, humour, event, language*, or *oratory*. For most writers, it is next to impossible to write humourously for someone else. And you have limited control over the oratorical skills of your speaker. That leaves you with *event, language*, and *story*.

**Second mantra...**

The form and function of a speech should be primarily driven by the texture of the event and the needs of the audience, and not by the political or corporate needs of the speaker to deliver a favourite message. Sometimes, a very hard sell to your client.

Keeping these two mantras in the forefront of your preparations, you should next consider the following checklist.

**Speech checklist...**

1. Insist on seeing the letter of invitation. It will contain vital contact information and sources for further research.

2. Similarly, get the agenda that outlines who is speaking when, and other event-related activities. Try to negotiate your speaker to go first. If not first, then last.

3. Discuss expectations with the speaker ahead of time. At the very least, negotiate the messages the speech is to convey. And limit those messages to two or three only. Discourage your client from trying to include the kitchen sink.

4. Research. The client should provide subject- and message-related information. You should undertake supplementary research that might provide insight, story, and clarity.

5. Limit outlines to the extent that you keep in mind that certain messages have to be presented, and to keep you on track. But don't get obsessive about it. Outlines should just be a guide. They should not dictate the flow. Other than that, just …

6. Write. Without editing. Just get the words, stories, and thoughts down on paper. It's called the "puke draft" for a reason.

7. Make sure your speech has a strong opening. A story or anecdote usually will get you off to a good start. Remember that *showing* is always better than *telling.*

8. The secret is in the rewriting. Less is always more. Simple is better than complex. Omit words that are better read than spoken. Vary the length of sentences. Are your words interesting? Do they engage? Don't pontificate. Lean towards conversational language.

9. Remember that this is an aural medium. For the ear. Read your drafts out loud so you can check for rhythm, tone, and cadence. Listen for the silences between words/thoughts. Listen for the logic.

10. Visuals. Unless you are very good at designing, and your speaker is very good at using visual supplements, such as PowerPoint — avoid them. It is easy to "do visuals" badly, and difficult to use them well.

11. Don't let your speaker hand out anything before or during the speech.

12. Make sure *you know* what you expect the audience to do as a result of listening to your speech. And make sure they do, too.

**A word or three on openings...**

Effective openings set the level of engagement. Three approaches …

1. Storytelling is an extremely effective way to engage an audience right from the start. Good stories almost automatically catch attention, and create a personal link to the listener. And a well-chosen story can also introduce the overall message. So, where do we get story ideas?

Read newspapers and take a cue from the headlines. They can provide topical and timely subjects that can be spun off into personal or social storytelling commentary.

One-on-one interviews with experts in the subject of the speech can usually lead to fascinating and unique stories.

2. Take a cue from the opening lines of novels, not with the objective of using them literally, but rather to give you ideas that suggest tone, humour, tragedy, or thoughts about the human condition.

"It was the best of times, it was the worst of times …" From Charles Dickens, *Tale of Two Cities*.

"They shot the white girl first." From Toni Morrison, *Paradise*.

"Maybe I shouldn't have given my number to the guy who pumped my stomach." From Carrie Fisher, *Post Cards From the Edge*.

3. Understand why the audience is attending the event, and craft your opening accordingly. If you know the audience might be hostile to your message, acknowledge the validity of their anger, and what your speaker proposes to do about it.

—

Colin Moorhouse provides speechwriting services to public and private sector clients across Canada. Senior members of government and industry have delivered "his" speeches, numbering over 1000, all over the world. He teaches a two-day speech writing seminar at Simon Fraser University in Vancouver, and is in demand to give his two-hour workshops for those who want to touch up their skills. He can be reached at Colin_Moorhouse@telus.net.

# Eleven Tricks of the Speechwriter's Trade

*by Matt Hughes*

**1. Make an impression.**

Nobody remembers speeches. Listeners may remember a catchy phrase, a joke or a particularly startling fact, but no one can recall a full twenty minutes of continuous monologue. Instead, people retain an *impression*, a sense of what was said and what it meant.

A business speech audience will remember no more than two or three new facts from a twenty-minute talk. Crowd the text with facts and figures, and the listeners will remember only that they were bored. Ruthlessly pare the "fact load" down to the essential information that the audience must take away with them.

**2. Three times is the charm.**

The best structure for a speech is the "tell them three times" model. Begin with a brief introduction that tells the audience the subject of the speech and why it is relevant to the listeners. Then lay out your facts and arguments, and close with a recapitulation of the message.

**3. Plain English.**

Never call a spade an "excavation implement." Plain Anglo-Saxon English is usually clearer and more easily understood than a string of jargon and ten-dollar words. More important, it is the language of emotion. "I'm mad as hell and I'm not going to take it any more," has a lot more impact than, "I am extremely choleric and I encompass no intention of enduring any supplemental experience."

Using Anglo-Saxon English also puts you in good company. From Lincoln's "Government of the people, by the people and for the people shall not perish," to Churchill's "We shall fight on the beaches, we shall fight on the landing grounds," to Kennedy's "Ask not what your country can do for you," the best speech is plain English.

**4. Get active.**

The rules of English grammar allow for an active or a passive voice. In the active voice, you might say, "We have decided." In the passive voice, it comes out as, "A decision has been reached."

Bureaucrats and other haunters of committees love the passive voice. Because it is totally neutral, it lets them say things without having to take responsibility for saying them. But it puts an audience to sleep.

Some speakers believe that the passive voice adds a refined tone to their utterances; these are the same hopeless droners who consider "at this particular point in time" an elegant phrase. To infuse a speech text with life and emotion, always use the active voice.

**5. Picture this.**

All of us have small screens inside our heads where we can look at pictures that come to us in spoken or written words. Speech audiences need to have those screens filled regularly, or they start to nod off.

Try to make points and deliver information with word pictures. If your message is a warning of difficulties ahead, try something like, "We're climbing a hill that's getting steeper, and there are rockslides across the road."

If you want to tell them that the medium-term future is promising, you can use something as simple as, "Another mile or so, and we're out of these dark woods and back into open meadows."

Word pictures need only a few broad strokes; your audience's brains will fill in all the details. In the above examples, I did not specify the kind of road or the species of trees in the wood. Your mind did that for me.

**6. Can we talk?**

When you're writing it, a speech is words on paper. When it's given, it is one human being speaking directly to others. If you are more used to writing reports and memos, take care that their impersonal tone doesn't creep into your speech.

Don't be afraid to use the words "I," "you," "we" and "us," and except for occasions of truly high and mighty circumstance, strive for the comfortably informal tone that is standard issue for network news anchors.

**7. Say it again, Sam!**

Back in high school, your composition teacher blue-pencilled words, sentences and whole paragraphs, crossing them out and writing "redundant" in the margin. In reports, letters and memos, repetition is a writer's vice; in speechwriting, it's a virtue.

Your audience can't stop tape and replay your last remarks. They hear you live, and if they miss a key point, the rest of your speech may make no sense to them. So if a thing is worth saying, it's worth saying two or three times.

Of course, you won't just repeat the same words over and over; rephrase the point, perhaps giving two or three examples that leave your listeners in no doubt about what you're saying.

**8. Adjust the facts, Ma'am.**

What's a business speech without a lot of statistics? A better business speech. Figures and numbers and ratios are great in black and white, and no self-respecting report writer should leave them out. But unless each member of your audience has total recall, most statistics pass right through their heads.

When you have to use statistics, always simplify and always round off. Replace "68.2 percent" with "over two thirds," and "a 112 percent rise in production" with "our output more than doubled."

When dealing with big numbers, look for word pictures that convey size, but avoid the hackneyed images of this many football fields, or that many times around the world. Let a little imagination seep in, then reach for your calculator and work out whether you produced enough widgets last year to cover Nathan Philips Square to a depth of six feet.

The more novel and arresting the image, the more likely your audience is to remember the information you're trying to give them. Nobody knows how many billions of burgers McDonald's has sold, but if it were enough to make a cow five miles high, people would surely remember that cow.

**9. Laugh it up.**

People also remember jokes, so if you can find a way to make a point with humor, you've improved the odds of making your message stick. For example, if you want to warn of an expected tax increase, say, "Well, the government has finally decided how to divide up the pie; trouble is, we're the pie."

Humor can also relax an audience (and sometimes a speaker) and help conjure up the interpersonal bond that is the carrier wave beneath the impression. But don't open with one of those hoary chestnuts cribbed from a handbook of after-dinner humor. Make the joke fit the substance of your remarks.

**10. The ins and outs.**

Amateur speech writers lead off with tired old jokes because they don't know how else to begin. But the simplest way to open a speech is just to tell the audience that you are glad to be there.

You may start out with "I am honoured to have this opportunity," or, "When [whoever] invited me to be your guest speaker, I was delighted," or just, "I am very glad to be here tonight." The main thing is to let the listeners know that this is a positive experience for you; no one wants to watch a fellow human being in pain.

After telling them you're glad to see them, the next thing to do is to tell them why: because they are good people and well worth talking to.

If you're addressing a Chamber of Commerce, mention the Chamber's good works. If you're addressing the Bar Association, try to find something nice to say about lawyers.

The end of a speech is the most important part, because it's the part most likely to be remembered by your listeners. Put your best writing here — active voice, Anglo-Saxon English, word pictures and all — and lead the audience into a vision of the future, as it develops from the message in your speech.

If you have a "hard-news nugget" to announce, the place to put it is just before the finale. If you have a slogan or catch-phrase you want them to remember, put it at the end and find a way to repeat it a few times. If you've thought of a joke that perfectly encapsulates your message, use it for the last line and leave them laughing.

### 11. She sells seashells.

Let's say you've followed all the rules in this article, and you now have twelve or thirteen pages of neatly typed, double-spaced speech text on your desk, chock full of compelling imagery, fascinating facts and unforgettable humor. There remains one crucial thing to do.

Read the text out loud. Don't rely on that silent little "reading voice" in your head, because it won't be there to help you when you are delivering this text to your peers and colleagues. That little voice can easily read "the Leeth police dismisseth us" in black and white, but try to say it with an ordinary set of lips and teeth. If you find any such verbal potholes in your text, fill them in with a rewrite.

—

Matt Hughes writes speeches for politicians and corporate executives. He has published three novels — *Fools Errant and Fool Me Twice*, Warner Aspect 2001, *Downshift*, Doubleday Canada 1997 — and *Breaking Trail: the Memoirs of Senator Len Marchand*, Caitlin Press 2000. His suspense fiction has appeared in *Blue Murder*, *Alfred Hitchcock* and *Storyteller*.

# Cooking and Writing with Spicy Results

*by Vera Jones*

Cookbooks, newspapers, magazines, home-delivered flyers, Internet sites, and pamphlets all carry a myriad of cooking recipes for their readers. This array of reading materials with feverish activity from writers gives the impression that cookery writing is an easy subject to master. This can be the case sometimes, but more often than not, it can be as difficult to write the methodology of a recipe as it is to compose regular articles on seemingly more involved topics. I once submitted a recipe for publication that contained the sentence, "... Cook pasta in boiling water and salt in a large pot for 10 to 12 minutes." Competent editing would have got it right: "... Cook pasta and salt in a large pot of boiling water for 10 to 12 minutes."

Mistakes are often hard to pick out so the text needs to be scrutinized — often more than once — to correct errors. Place yourself in the same category as painters, woodcarvers and sculptors, and other artisans too numerous to mention, who skillfully create beautiful handmade products. As writers, we are craftsmen in the same way.

**A keen sense of humour...**

Not only are writing skills required for cookery text, each recipe must be kitchen-tested so that the results are exactly as is intended. In addition to writing, you'll need to test every recipe. They don't always work. Often, it can be helpful to have family or friends with a keen sense of humour.

I once made *Gadogodo*, an Indonesian dish of vegetables with a spicy peanut sauce. The recipe required "two teaspoons brown sugar," but when it was time to add the brown sugar, I mistakenly measured out two tablespoons. This gave the dish a pronounced sweet, dessert-like taste (think of peanut butter pie), which was not bad — except for the vegetables in it.

Another time I planned to make some Oriental dishes to serve to friends at a dinner party. The day before the dinner I prepared a lemon-ginger marinade for the fish dish, and an Oriental-style dressing for a cold noodle salad. I thought I marked the contents plainly on the covers of each container before putting them in the fridge. The next day, while arranging our meal, I unknowingly poured the oriental-style dressing over the fish, and the zesty lemon-ginger marinade was used as a dressing for the noodles.

"Very refreshing!" my friend commented after she finished her portion of noodle salad. It was only at the end of dinner that I explained to her why the salad tasted so pungent.

—

Vera Jones wrote a popular cooking column in the *Comox Valley Record* newspaper for seven years. Presently working as a freelance writer and editor at her home in Courtenay, British Columbia, her articles have recently appeared in *BC Outdoors* and *BC Sport Fishing*.

# Write Technical Material

*by Paul G. Cormack*

A Scottish friend of mine works as a schoolteacher for an oil company in Oman. Arriving home for the Christmas break she brought us a small, brown wicker pot of Frankincense from the Omani Heritage Gallery. It was a tremendous gift, but the small printed card tied to the basket quickly became more important than its contents.

Beyond the text encouraging support for local artisans, there were no instructions. Nothing to specify the process to heat or burn Frankincense, no safety precautions, and nothing to suggest that these small brown crystals aren't to be stirred into your coffee on a cold Christmas morning. Like demerara sugar.

For me, this was vivid confirmation that technical writing is a symptom of Western culture. As life became increasingly complex, we stopped believing that all of the skills required to survive in this world could be passed from parent to child or from teacher to student. Step-in-step with the evolution of product liability, technical writing became the first new writing style to appear in one hundred years.

**Its soul is investigative journalism...**

The heart of technical writing is a mixture of scientific research and advertising copywriting, but its soul is investigative journalism. Sharp text, research, drafts, deadlines, publication. It's all there. Its fundamentals are shared with any good writing, considered by Stephen King (*On Writing: A Memoir of the Craft*, 2000) as "vocabulary, grammar, the elements of style." Unfortunately, prose and passion are sacrificed for accuracy and precision. But, while technical writing may not yield the pathos of the romantic novel or poetry, it must still interest or elicit a performance from its audience. William Zinsser (*On Writing Well*, 1985) provides a particular insight into the effort required:

"Nowhere else must you work so hard to write sentences that form a linear sequence. This is no place for fanciful leaps or implied truths. Fact and deduction are the ruling family."

The comparative features for technical writing and journalism lie in levels of research required in both styles. Considerably more time is spent in interview, research and experimentation than "keying the screen" or putting pen to paper. Whether you are defining assembly instructions for a mountain bike or detailing maintenance and inspection routines for an oil rig far offshore in the Atlantic Ocean, the need for a defined linear sequence is still the same. The only variance is the cost of failure.

**Provides safety...**

Product liability is the gateway for technical writing. David Smith (*Reliability, Maintainability & Risk*, 2001) provides an insight into Western "consumer protection" legislation and how it considers that "a producer ... will be liable for damage caused wholly or partly by defective products ... 'defective' is defined as not providing such safety as people are generally entitled to expect, taking into account the manner of marketing, *instructions for use* ..."

**Varying backgrounds...**

Many technical writers have "drifted in" from engineering, specializing in construction project literature, operating instructions or guidance for equipment maintenance. Others are past quality or safety professionals (sometimes themselves engineers). Some can be found studying technical writing through distance learning or at their local college while in daytime employment at factories, oil installations or chemical processing plants (who then take up much of the update or revision effort in these same organizations). The rest are journalists with an interest in mechanics or "how things work," grasping opportunity where it presents itself.

**Never involves unsolicited manuscripts...**

A "mechanical bias" and a curious nature may be the skills that keep a technical writer employed, but the route in is almost always as a result of a manufacturer's quality assurance initiative or one relating to occupational safety. Providing technical guidance is a means of addressing corporate and personal risk, and endeavours to comply with a myriad of statutory requirements and industry standards. For these reasons, technical writing never involves unsolicited manuscripts.

Technical writing can take a number of different forms: product notes, assembly or task instructions, maintenance routines, operational procedures, quality or safety manuals, safety notices, management system or site overviews, Intranet sites or informational handbooks. All of these can require considerable "facilitator" skills, and experienced technical writers can often find themselves leading workgroups.

Some assignments are short hourly-rate arrangements, but considerable writing work is assigned through long-term contracts that can extend two years or more. The latter can involve diverse and complex assignments based on the expertise of a particular individual or a pool of writers within a single organization. Many contracted assignments include the editing of documents created by others: engineers, site technicians, safety or quality advisers, other technical writers or consultants.

**Author often a "ghostwriter"...**

Some of the most exciting technical writing assignments include research (sometimes in remote locations), development, influencing design elements, publication, and implementation — then the opportunity to describe the resulting process (where successful) in subsequent trade articles or industry conference papers. The drawback here is that the author is often a "ghostwriter" whose name rarely appears alongside the text. Some companies now insist that the technical writer is included in the names listed (at very least in the research credits). Most companies insist that the writer's name appears on any document resulting from the initial assignment.

**Writing in committee...**

The most challenging aspect of this style is "writing in committee," where a series of persons (known and unknown) contribute to an editorial process to validate the text and make it more precise. Sustaining "flow" through this process — which may last for months — can be a considerable endeavour. It can be a significant frustration for writers who may only be familiar with trained editors or experience publishers — especially when the only amendments suggested after weeks of review relate only to vocabulary or style!

Following on from agreeing to commercial terms and receiving a "project brief," the technical writer has to identify "cultural norms" within the organization. Most companies, especially those pursuing international quality standards, have detailed procedure or publication formats including standard document layouts with mandatory software specifications, fonts and corporate images. This guidance will also set out review and approval sequences.

Once this is complete, every assignment begins with a flowchart.

Whether hand-drawn on a flipchart or constructed through modern flowcharting software, the key to a sound description is identifying the steps involved and then linear progression. If it can't be flowcharted, it can't be described and then it surely cannot be followed.

Once the process has been mapped, the next step in the process is interview and research. Managers, engineers and site personnel may all contribute to the research effort, but this often needs to be supplemented

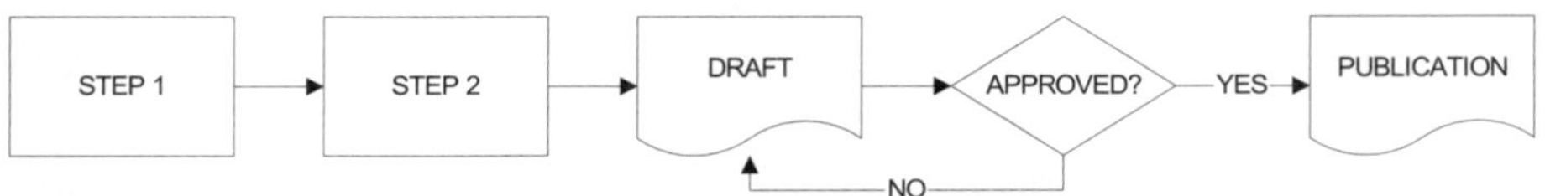


by observation or other active participation by the technical writer himself. By observing the task at the workplace or experimenting with the equipment (under site supervision), the writer can gain valuable experience about the task, the equipment, the operating environment, and the future audience.

Some technical writing assignments result from product failure, or investigations into personal injury or property damage. The information included in these investigations can provide considerable insight for any subsequent guidance, and can identify where additional information can be found.

Company risk assessments or reliability studies can also provide a valuable source of information. Unlike incident or product failure investigations though, risk assessments suggest only a probability of failure based on industry experience elsewhere or with similar equipment. The writer's efforts are often intended to prevent product failures or personal injuries where these can be anticipated. Most product notes or labelling is developed this way, although a considerable amount of this seems to be generated by advertising copywriters (i.e. the people who write "lather, rinse and repeat" on shampoo bottles probably have more of a marketing imperative than scientific or engineering requirement).

Information from national or other legislation, standards libraries, professional associations or Internet sites is often used to balance the information available from the company. Sometimes these can provide significant detail on associated risks and acceptable practice.

**Detailed reviews required...**

Before anything can be published, a detailed review through discussion or distribution is required to ensure the published document will be valid and rigorous. At least one formal review cycle is usually required prior to publication, and this is normally coordinated by a company representative. This review cycle is in addition to any proofreading or other process used to check technical accuracy.

With technical writing, formal review requires a traceable process so that the review process itself can be validated (e.g. did the writer involve the right people?). The writer is often required to archive letters, electronic mail, marked-up versions of the draft, facsimile transmissions, or meeting transcripts. Technical writers rarely have to incorporate all of the amendments suggested, but they do have do be able to demonstrate that the suggestions have been considered.

The review process needs to be sufficiently rigorous to ensure technical accuracy, and to ensure that the published work can provide clear and sufficient guidance to achieve its design purpose. The writer may also be required to identify the most practical means of communication and implementation. This may include the identification of other related manuals, procedures or other guidance that may be affected by the publication — and an agreed upon process to achieve any subsequent change in the company's management system arrangements.

This "management of change" process often creates its own work, and the writer sometimes continues from assignment to assignment for several years for the same or associated companies.

—

Paul Cormack holds a Master's Degree in Labour Economics from Aberdeen University. A former Toronto radio journalist and award-winning safety professional, he's had extensive experience as a technical writer for several multinational oil exploration companies operating in the North Sea.

# An Introduction to Minute-Taking

*by Gill Foss*

Do you belong to an organization that keeps regular meeting records? If so, you could add to your writing repertoire by offering to take the minutes. Or you could add minute-taking to your résumé when making job applications. The first suggestion may mean you offer your services as a freebie, but that will be useful from the practice angle, although payment may be negotiated. If you intend to include this on your résumé, I suggest you charge a starting fee of at least $15 per hour, including time attending the meeting, time preparing however many drafts are required and travel time if that is necessary.

Too often minute-taking is assigned to someone not conversant with the topic of the meeting or, equally inappropriately, to someone who will be taking an active part in the discussions. The former may well have difficulty following the gist of the debate and picking out which points need to be included while the latter may, however inadvertently, bias the final output towards the agenda he/she had in mind when coming to the meeting. Therefore, someone independent of the participants, but who is conversant with the subject under discussion, will make the best recorder.

## Correct, complete and unbiased...

Minutes are the official record of a meeting admissible in a court of law should the need arise. Therefore they must be correct, complete and unbiased. For the best results use simple, clear vocabulary and uncluttered sentence construction. Keep the tone businesslike and, where possible, use the *active* voice. If numbers figure in the discussions, make sure you have them correct. Ask to have them repeated if you are not sure. The finished minutes should be easy to read and digest for someone in a hurry (and who isn't nowadays?). To achieve this, both the writing and formatting are important.

Minutes are so called because they are intended to be brief, but they should contain all the important points raised. This doesn't mean you have to write down everything like a play script. What is needed is a good ear for listening and a mind that can select the gist of a discussion from the chaff of over-wordy participants. It certainly helps to develop your own version of shorthand. Alternatively use a tape recorder with a universal microphone that will pick up voices from a full 360 degrees. If you use tapes to back up your notes, don't forget to turn them over and number each one as you remove it. This avoids problems when time comes to transcribe.

If you are unfamiliar with the topic and have advance notice, pick up some background information so you have an idea what is relevant. If it's a meeting where a lot of acronyms will be used, make sure you know what they mean for the same reason.

When a *motion* is proposed, it is helpful to have the person proposing it pass it to you in writing. If this is not the norm, ask the chair if he/she will make this a rule. This way, there can be no argument when you come to prepare the report. The chair can then ask you to read it again prior to the vote so everyone is clear exactly what they are voting for.

The most important part of the minutes is the recording of *motions*. These are the decisions taken at the meeting that have an important bearing on the future direction of the committee or group.

The name of the person who introduces, or "proposes" the motion must be recorded as must the person who "seconds" the motion. Immediately following these two names come the motion, e.g. Motion: "That a committee be established to review the membership requirements."

**Make the motions stand out...**

It's a good idea to make the motions stand out. For those who missed the meeting, a quick review of these alone will give a good idea of the decisions that will lead into future meeting discussions.

Once the vote is taken on a motion, the result is recorded by one of the following:

a) Carried.

b) Defeated.

c) Tabled.

Where the decision is close it may be necessary to add the vote count for and against. In the case of *abstentions,* the number should be noted and, if requested, names included. Where the decision is unanimous, that can be indicated. The word *tabled* indicates that the motion has been deferred for further discussion at a forthcoming meeting.

When an action is decided, the name of the person assigned to undertake the task should be noted. After the minutes are prepared, a separate page listing all the actions to be taken, the names of those assigned to them, and the date by which each is to be done should be compiled. When the minutes are circulated, this list should be placed on top as a visible reminder to those involved. The chair can then check whether the tasks are complete, ahead of the next meeting.

Formatting your minutes:

It's a good idea to print the first page of the minutes on the appropriate group's letterhead as this marks them as *official*. Next you need to put what meeting it is, (monthly, annual etc), where it's being held, and lastly, the starting time of and date. For example:

Tumbleweed and District Council

General Monthly Meeting

City Hall, Room 213

7 p.m. March 4, 2008

The minutes should start with a list headed *Present* for those in attendance, including the position they hold at the meeting. For example:

M. Grand — Mayor.

P. Inkpot — Secretary.

Joe Doe — Director, Parks & Recreation.

Below this list should be one headed *Absent* with the names of those who were unable to attend. When the minutes are circulated everyone on both lists should receive a copy.

At this point the minutes begin to follow the headings as they appear on the meeting agenda.

1. Opening remarks.
2. Acceptance of the agenda (this needs a motion of acceptance).
3. Acceptance of minutes of last meeting (this needs a motion too).
4. Business arising from minutes of last meeting.
5. Report on ... etc.

When a speaker provides a document it should be handed to you after being presented. Be sure to number each one in order — Appendix 1, Appendix 2, etc. — and append them to the finished minutes for reference. Indicate at the appropriate point in the minutes that the report is included as Appendix 1, 2, etc. This way only a brief mention of the contents need appear in the relevant section of the text.

The last item on the agenda will be *Adjournment*. Remember to include the time the meeting ends.

When the first draft of the minutes is prepared it should be submitted to the chair for approval. Both you as minute-taker and the chair should sign the final draft. With that signature, the chair accepts responsibility for the accuracy of the document should it ever be challenged.

My personal preference is to have the minute-taker seated beside the chair. This makes it easier to remind him/her should a point of order be missed. Having been, on different occasions, a minute-taker and chair of a meeting, I can attest to the usefulness of this arrangement.

You now have the basic pointers for taking and preparing minutes. Remember, it's practice that makes perfect!

—

Gill Foss has taught one-day workshops on minute-taking for an Ottawa consulting company. She writes a regular profile column for a seniors' publication and articles and advertorials for two Ottawa newspapers. At the time of publication, she was National President of the Canadian Authors Association, which kept her busy with writing and administrative duties.

# Proceedings: Have Laptop, Will Travel

*by Heather Ebbs*

I wrote my first proceedings just a half-dozen or so years ago, but since then such work has become about half of my business. A niche market, the writing of proceedings can be not only profitable, but fascinating.

**What are proceedings?**

Proceedings are records of the presentations, discussions, decisions and recommendations of a meeting or conference. The meeting can last from one hour (as in a teleconference) to five days, and the client's specific expectations and needs can vary tremendously.

Conference records must be maintained for a number of compelling reasons, not the least of which is a reminder of the recommendations put forward. Those reminders may be needed internally (as checklists of things that participants have to do) or externally (such as the Krever Commission recommendations). Descriptions of presentations are important as records of the roles and findings of different partners. A common reason for recording discussions is to prevent repetitive, time-consuming rehashing of issues in later meetings.

On the other hand, clients may decide not to include discussion points in their proceedings. For example, some of my government clients prefer "records of decision," which barely touch on the discussions and instead focus heavily on the decisions and recommendations. Proprietary information from an industry partner could be mentioned during the course of a discussion; if such information were recorded, rival companies could discover it under access-to-information laws.

The need for proceedings is clear. The person who prepares them is required to be intelligent, quick thinking and a skilled writer. During a conference, detailed, highly technical information is often presented and discussed. Acronyms and abbreviations run rampant. Difficult-to-understand accents are almost a given, as experts come from not just across Canada, but around the world. Despite everything, the proceedings writer must be able to understand the information and capture it instantly while moving on mentally to the speaker's next point.

**The writer's role...**

If you are contacted about a proceedings assignment, the questions you should ask include when the conference is scheduled, how long you will have to produce the proceedings and what type of document is desired (length, inclusion or exclusion of graphics from presentations, degree of detail, etc.). I always ask for an agenda, a list of participants and any background material or presentations available. You should also ask how many drafts you are expected to work on; typically, I am asked to produce a first draft and to make one set of revisions, if necessary.

On the day of the meeting, arrive at the meeting place early to ensure an appropriate place to sit. The best seat is one having a clear view of all screens and flipcharts, a direct line of sight to the speaker's podium and a nearby electrical outlet for your laptop. I take along an extension cord in case the outlet is more than a few feet away, as well as duct tape to cover the cord and prevent anyone from tripping over it. A seat near the front of the room enhances your ability to hear the speaker and lessens the likelihood of distractions from whispered side conversations.

During the meeting, I find it simplest to try to capture everything said by every speaker. Later, I'll whittle the presentations and discussions down to the core. In the midst of a discussion, that core might not be readily apparent. In addition, there are few gaps in which to pause, synthesize and recast information — the speaker is moving on to her next point or the participants are on to another area of discussion.

I save the material frequently and back it up on diskette. On the way to and from the meeting, I keep the diskette and computer separate, so that if one should be lost, damaged or stolen, the other would still be available.

Writing the proceedings can take up to twice as long as the meeting itself. You may have to do some further research to clarify technical issues, define terms or acronyms and elaborate on topics that were covered elliptically. As with any job, you must identify the primary audience and write with that group in mind. Meetings tend to have a significant amount of repetition, which must be weeded out of the proceedings, and the variety of presentation styles must be made consistent. The degree to which presentations and discussion are summarized varies by job. I have one client who requires a day-and-a-half meeting to be condensed to about 7 or 8 single-spaced pages. Another prefers detailed summaries that result in a 25- to 30-page document. For both, I have about 45 to 55 single-spaced pages of raw notes.

Proceedings formats differ depending on the client and job, so identify client preferences in advance. Generally, proceedings for meetings that are more than one day in length include a title page and a table of contents. The bulk of the content follows the same chronological order as the meeting itself. The headings and subheadings used should match what the speakers used — proceedings are not an appropriate place to exercise your flair for snappy headlines — and the presenters are usually identified. Sections may or may not be numbered. Appendices might include a list of recommendations pulled from throughout the meeting, a copy of the agenda and a list of the participants with their contact information.

**Making money...**

I live near Ottawa, but have covered meetings in cities across Canada. My clients cover the costs of travel, meals and accommodation in addition to my fee for the hours spent attending the meeting and writing the proceedings. A friend expressed surprise that someone would pay such costs — surely, she said, there must be someone in the host city who could "type up the minutes." There may well be an appropriate person in the city, but proven writing abilities and familiarity with both proceedings and a given subject area make it a much less expensive proposition — in terms both of time and of money — to send that person to a meeting than to try out someone unknown.

Clients pay for this work either by the word or by the hour. I advocate the latter, because the end length of the proceedings has more to do with client needs than with the overall time spent on producing the final document.

Regardless of the payment formula, the writing of proceedings can be a profitable and intensely interesting line of work. Clients invariably offer sincere appreciation for a clean, coherent précis of what is often a repetitive, elliptical and highly technical conference.

—

Heather Ebbs writes proceedings for government departments, non-governmental organizations, national associations and industry on subjects ranging from West Nile virus to new drug products. In addition to her writing, Heather is also an indexer and an award-winning editor. She is a past-president of the (Freelance) Editors' Association of Canada.

# What Does an Archivist Do?

*by Walt McConville*

What does an archivist do? I guess that question is the one I am asked most frequently, along with, "Is it pronounced ar-KIGH-vist or ar-KIV-ist?" To which I always reply disarmingly, "Neither, actually. It's called AR-ki-vist." Oh, the joys of our devious English language when we put the em-PHAH-sis on the wrong sy-LAH-ble!

Anyhow, let's get back to our opening question demanding what it is that an archivist does. The dictionary definition states that an archivist is "one who is in charge of archives." Archives are defined as "an organized body of records pertaining to an organization or institution," or, "a place in which such records are preserved." To make it easy to remember, I then explain that an archivist does "G-I-R-L-S, *girls*," an acronym for:

Gathering,

Identifying or classifying,

Registering and recording,

Labelling, and

Storing.

These are the five links in every archivist's chain of office, and omitting any of them could lead to certain disaster.

## Gathering

Let's start out with gathering. An archivist should build up his or her memorabilia by requesting assistance from many different people. In any group or organization this means members, particularly those of long standing. There's no telling how many informational treasures could be stashed in attic boxes. Old diaries, photos, magazines, news clippings, newsletters, minutes from long-ago executive meetings, slide presentation commentaries — the possibilities are enormous!

During my own five-year stint, I remember missing parts of a series of newsletters. I put a notice about it in our newsletter. At our very next meeting an elderly member produced them. "Years ago I borrowed these," she said apologetically, "but I kept forgetting to return them."

But these obvious sources are only the beginning. Other less conspicuous areas can also yield a surprising amount of material. How about the public library? Books, periodicals and microfiche files of newspapers and periodicals can yield a wealth of data to the diligent researcher. Municipal, provincial, and university archives must not be overlooked, either. Then when these sources have been exhausted, classified ads just might yield something long-borrowed or stored away.

**Identifying**

Identification or classification often creates problems, especially if historical data such as origin, source, category or intrinsic value are immediately unavailable. Identical-looking objects can differ substantially in characteristics or backgrounds, and care must be taken not to lump them together without first ascertaining relevance.

The key word here is *research*.

As for items that *do* belong together, we simply need to classify them according to a prearranged plan: alphabetically, numerically, chronologically, or by type. This depends upon experience and can be frustrating and time-consuming. A sense of humour can lighten the task, but patience and perseverance are extremely important.

**Registering**

The registering and recording process can take many forms. Archivists may choose card files, ledgers, loose-leaf notebooks, computer databases, spreadsheets, or other software.

The operative word is *simplicity*. Don't get into long descriptive statements for articles in your list. Use few words, but ensure each term is both accurate and adequate.

A book title, as an example, should be followed by author, International Standard Book Number, publisher's name, and year of publication (e.g. *Syllables of Recorded Time*, Lyn Harrington, ISBN 0-88924-112-0, Simon and Pierre, 1981). Magazines should be listed by volume or folio number and year (e.g. *Canadian Author & Bookman*, Vol. 28, No. 4, 1952/3). Memorabilia items need only be listed by type and date of commission or acquisition (e.g. *Photo,* CAA Past National President, Dr. Don Thomson, 1960).

**Labelling**

Labelling should be done, preferably, with self-adhesive or gummed commercial labels like those used to affix prices in stores. Either colour-code according to category or type, or use an alphabetical or numerical prefix in the register's identification number.

It doesn't hurt to use both methods — then you have a double check if someone new inherits the registration list in the future. Identifying numbers should be neatly typed (to be readily and clearly legible) in a consistent, uniform, and sensible manner. Avoid obscure or fancy type fonts that may lead to error or confusion later.

Examples of prefix coding are:

a) *Canadian Author & Bookman* — CA001, CA002, etc.

b) *Canadian Poetry Magazine* — CP001, CP002, etc.

c) *National Newsline* — NN001, NN002, etc.

The two-letter prefix, provided it is always consistent, may be imaginative or simple — an easy reference tool.

A question arises. Somebody has brought in a previously missing item. What identity number do we assign to it in our alphabetical or chronological list? This is not a problem, really. We simply affix the next number in the particular series, incorporating its description in the proper list order. To access the item we must always refer first to the listing, since the identity number merely indicates its file location.

If you opt for colour-coding, such as blue for books, green for magazines, pink for pictures, etc., always stock enough labels for colours to be uniform. Replacing certain colours with slightly different shades invites confusion. In a small operation, mistaking one colour for another is not likely, but as the enterprise grows the possibility magnifies.

## Storing

Finally, we need a facility to keep all of our patiently accumulated treasures where they can be accessible at all times. It is one thing to amass great quantities of material, but quite another to arrange for their availability, even on a limited basis.

Steel (and preferably fireproof) filing cabinets provide the best protection for magazines or pictures, and their storage location can be easily catalogued with labels. Care should be taken to ensure that the storage building is not subject to sudden or extreme temperature changes, and is not likely to suffer from flooding or water damage.

Books should be stored in portable cases or shelves and classified (alphabetically, numerically, and chronologically) using methods similar to those used in public libraries and bookstores. This will take time, but the resulting convenience is more than worth the trouble.

Rules must be drawn up covering lending or removing a stored article, especially to ensure the security of more valuable materials. A decision needs to be made as to which articles can be loaned out. A reasonable duration should be established for each category. Always insist on signatures by recipients for security reasons. Various stored items may be virtually irreplaceable, and these should be insured against loss, theft, and destruction.

The *AR*-chivist's role needs not be onerous. Through sensible plans for gathering, identifying, registering, labelling and safely storing materials we can preserve history that would otherwise be lost forever.

—

Walt McConville has served the CAA Victoria and Islands Branch as newsletter editor, archivist, and vice-president. He's written six books, three musicals, two plays, and over 500 poems, technical articles and short stories published in Canada, Peru, the United Kingdom and the United States. He currently tutors a CAA poetry group and composes *Canauthword* crossword puzzles for the CAA National Newsline.

# 14. World Wide Web

# Protect Yourself While Online

*by Russ Harvey*

Today's writer increasingly needs to be connected to the Internet for e-mail and for Web-based research. This same worldwide interconnection of computers that proves so beneficial can put your computer at greater risk for virus infections and other vulnerabilities.

If you are connected to the Internet, you must purchase and maintain a current antivirus program. Keeping your virus program up to date should be part of your regular weekly maintenance program of backups, system maintenance, and archiving. If you are on a continuous Internet service you should check more regularly. You should also maintain the emergency recovery disks provided by your antivirus program since many viruses can destroy your ability to get to the antivirus program's website once you are infected.

The trend has been for viruses to become both more destructive and to spread themselves more quickly. In addition to your antivirus program you can follow these steps to reduce your vulnerability:

- Do not open attachments unless you are absolutely sure the attachment has been checked for viruses and that you require the attachment. Recognition of the sender's address means nothing since many viruses will forward themselves to everyone in the infected computer's e-mail address book without notifying the sender.
- Pay no attention to virus warnings e-mailed to you by your friends. Most are hoaxes, which waste Internet bandwidth and distract writers from their writing.
- If your e-mail program forwards mail as an attachment you should change this so that the forwarded mail is quoted in-line with the body of the message. Many recipients, including editors and other submission sites, will delete unsolicited attachments unread as a matter of policy.
- Outlook Express will open many attachments by default without asking you and uses scripting to share information between

Microsoft Office, Internet Explorer and other Windows programs. This may be convenient for you but is exploited by many viruses.

- Install and maintain a firewall product, especially if you are continually connected to the Internet. A firewall is a hardware or software product that places a barrier between your computer and the Internet. There are many such products available, but ZoneAlarm provides an excellent program free for personal use in addition to their commercial product.
- Be aware of the existence and nefarious purpose of spyware: software that monitors your online activity and reports this information to a third party. Your Web browser will also reveal much information about you as you visit various websites. Ad-Aware is an excellent product for detecting and removing spyware from your computer.
- Ensure that you have a weekly maintenance session scheduled where you regularly backup your work, preferably with a second copy for off-site storage in case of fire or theft. While insurance will replace your computer and programs it cannot replace your writing.

CD writers (CD-RW or "burners") are affordable for almost anyone. Blank CDs cost around $1 for 650 MB of backup space (or the equivalent of about 450 floppies) so this format faces no current file size limitations. Additionally the CDs can be shared with most current computer users. The CD-RW unit can be installed as a replacement for your CD-ROM or as an additional device if you have room for it in your computer. USB versions are available for Macintosh and laptop users although they are priced higher.

For more information about these issues and for the software mentioned in this article visit my Preventing Unauthorized Access website at: www.russharvey.bc.ca/rhc/security.html.

—

Russ Harvey is a west coast computer consultant and writes on computer and Internet issues. He routinely helps clients recover from the effects of virus infections on their computers. Check out his website at: www.russharvey.bc.ca/rhc/rhc.html.

# Search Engines Made Easy

*by Mark and Linda Jeays*

"I can't find anything on the Internet."

It's a common complaint and a frustrating situation for the writer with a deadline to meet. When in-depth current research material is only a mouse-click away, familiarity with a variety of search engines is a must for the successful writer today.

Here are a few hints to help you move quickly and productively through the several billion documents on the World Wide Web.

Broadly speaking, search engines are divided into five kinds: site directory, plain-text search, news search, meta-search and vertical portal. To get the best results, match the type of search engine you use with the type of information you need.

The most popular *site directory* is Yahoo! (www.yahoo.com), developed in the earliest days of the World Wide Web back in 1994. It now serves millions of Web pages a day to its Net-savvy users. A site directory, like Yahoo!, is a list of websites available worldwide. Company employees use their own judgment and client suggestions to rank listings, putting the most worthwhile ones first. Yahoo! features easy-to-use point-and-click formats attractively presented.

**Use Yahoo!'s classification system...**

Let's suppose you need information on Canadian author Margaret Atwood. Simply go to Yahoo! and type *Margaret Atwood* into the box at the top of the page. All directory entries matching this author's name will appear. Click on the one that sounds most promising to you. Yahoo! also offers a more sophisticated search method. What if you can't recall Atwood's name or are not sure which particular author you need? Use Yahoo!'s narrowing classification system that moves you step-by-step from the general to the specific. For example: Go to Yahoo!'s home page. Click on the Literature link. Click on Authors. Click on Literary Fiction. Now click on Complete Listing (of names) and choose Margaret Atwood. Note that each category further refines the previous one. Practice this way of searching until it becomes intuitive.

Choose Yahoo! as your search engine if you need information on a well-known person, place, company or item. Because of the large size of Yahoo!'s files, you will probably find several entries on your chosen subject, and as a worst-case scenario, at least one or two listings. In addition, Yahoo! keeps up to date with its links to other search sites, so it is a good departure for many journeys of discovery.

You may get addicted to Yahoo! since the site also features friendly and free services such as e-mail, games, personalized news, weather reports, stock quotes and auctions.

*Plain-text search engines*, such as Google (www.google.com) have multiplied faster than other types of search tools because they are easy and intuitive to use. The key to searching with Google, for example, is to use several relevant, and where possible unusual, words to refine your search. Common words such as *rhyme* and *rhythm* will provide you many thousands of web page listings to consider. In fact, at present, *rhythm* returns 2.45 million entries, *rhyme* 592,000 and *rhythm rhyme* 78,100. Typing in *Shakespeare "iambic pentameter" sonnets*, returns only 1,640 listings. The trick is to be specific enough to get adequate information (and a limited number of relevant listings), but not so nearsighted that you miss out on useful resources. Bear in mind that search terms are insensitive to the difference between upper and lower case letters.

**Enclose your search terms in quotation marks...**

Entering several words separated by spaces is a technique that returns only web pages that contain *all* of your chosen words. Enter as much specialized vocabulary as you can think of which relates to your search query. If too many listings appear and you need to narrow your search, add another relevant word or phrase. Also, try to anticipate a phrase or word-group that you think will appear in the document you want to reach. For example, searching for a scientific article on birds, use Latin terminology if you know it: *American Robin, Turdus migratorius*. To tell Google that you want to look for a phrase, rather than single words, enclose your search terms in quotation marks. Entering *"writing resources"* brings back many links to high-quality writing sites.

Here is another search technique supported by many search engines, including Google. To find Web pages that contain either one of two particular words (or both of them), you can separate the words with *or*. For example, searching for *Toronto or Montreal* returns all pages with either "Toronto" or "Montreal" in the text. Another important command is the minus sign, which excludes documents containing a given word. For example, searching for *Hamlet -Gibson* returns pages containing the word "Hamlet," but not "Gibson," which would be appropriate if you were not interested in the movie version of Shakespeare's play that starred Mel Gibson.

Within the last couple of years, Google has become the most efficient search engine on the Internet. As of early 2002, over two billion pages were indexed and re-indexed monthly, so that very few dead links persist. In addition, Google keeps a record of every page indexed in its archives, so that even if the link you choose no longer works, you can still access a recent version of the page. Google also features a site directory similar to Yahoo!'s, a news search engine, and image searching (enter "wolverine" or "Mario Lemieux" or "CN Tower" for pictures).

Be aware that even the most complete plain-text search engines have indexed only about 15% of the Web, so be prepared to try different search engines if you strike out first time. Other popular plain-text search engines include Lycos (www.lycos.com), Hotbot (www.hotbot.com) and AltaVista (www.altavista.com). Different search engines have different syntax for doing advanced searches, so choose one you like and become familiar with its particular syntax before moving on to other search tools.

**Over 700 million messages...**

At present, there is only one popular *news search engine*: Google Groups (groups.google.com). This site is particularly useful for finding answers to straightforward questions. It draws its information from Usenet, a system that allows users to post and read messages in public forums called newsgroups. Begun in 1981, the Usenet database includes over 700 million messages. Much of the traffic is in the form of questions and answers, so chances are that your particular question has been asked before and there are answers on file.

Let's say you are planning a summer vacation in Bermuda and want to know what weather to expect. You can type in a query in plain English: *What is the average summer temperature in Bermuda?* Or, since the search engine ignores grammatical facilitators such as conjunctions and prepositions, simply type in *average summer temperature Bermuda*. Either way, you are headed for twenty-five degrees and sunshine.

A *meta-search engine* uses the results of several search engines to provide you with the answers you need. The most well-known meta-search instrument is Ask Jeeves (www.ask.com), founded in 1996. It is another innovative site that allows you to enter a query in colloquial English. Simply type a question into the box provided: "What famous novels did Robertson Davies write?" The operators of Ask Jeeves combine the results of other search engines with their own knowledge base, so have huge resources to draw on for your answer.

A *vertical portal* such as About.com (www.about.com) can be the springboard for many hours of surfing, since the links are usually of very high quality and have been chosen by experts in the specific topics listed. Pages have a clear focus and you can target your search quite accurately. While your initial contact with About.com will click you through, for example, Arts and Entertainment to gradually narrowing subject areas, once you find a favourite destination (maybe freelancewrite.about.com) you can go straight there.

Search technology is changing rapidly. New companies frequently claim that they have more of the web indexed than any search engine established previously, or that they deliver the most relevant results. In the fast-paced world of the Internet, a new-name company may well arise at any moment and surpass the massive popularity of Yahoo! and Google. Meanwhile … happy hunting!

—

Mark Jeays is a computer programmer specializing in World Wide Web applications. He currently works at Transport Canada and has his own one-man business, Capital Computer Solutions. He inherits his word skills from Linda Jeays, an experienced freelance writer.

# Wikipedia: An Online Collaborative Encyclopedia

*by Mark Jeays*

Have you ever dreamed that people around the world were reading your words? Wikipedia (www.wikipedia.com) may be just the project for you. It's a great place to practise your writing skills, while helping to create a valuable free resource that is available to anyone in the world.

Wikipedia's goal is nothing less than to create a better encyclopedia than the *Encyclopedia Britannica*. This may seem like a lofty goal, and it may never be attained, but there are already many articles of comparable depth and quality. Since space is not a limitation online, many topics can be covered that *Britannica* doesn't have room for.

The Wikipedia website is a "wiki," a site whose pages anyone can edit. This is done by browsing to a particular page, and clicking on a link called "Edit This Page." This brings up a web form showing the contents of the page. You can make any additions, corrections or deletions you wish. Click on a "Save" button to make your changes visible to others. You are on an equal footing with all other visitors to the page.

**Articles are generally linked to related articles...**

Although no special syntax is required in order to be productive, there are a few special text sequences that add to the richness of the page you are working on. For instance, enclosing a word in two sets of square brackets, like this — [[Canada]] — creates a link from the current page to the article entitled "Canada." Articles are generally linked to related articles, which makes it easy for encyclopedia users to broaden their knowledge on a topic. Other commands can be typed to create lists and tables or to add images or Greek letters. HTML syntax can also be used to mark up a page.

Every part of the writing process can be practised on Wikipedia: writing outlines for large topics, writing new articles from scratch, editing for style and copy-editing for spelling and grammar. A "Talk" page is associated with every article, in which Wikipedians discuss the contents of the article. A virtual community has sprung up around Wikipedia, and there are many animated discussions on the process of building an encyclopedia.

Often one can receive feedback from other users within minutes of posting an article. To enjoy your participation fully, take criticism constructively and forget the concept of ownership of the text. One of the most important philosophies of the site is "be bold in updating pages." This means that everyone is encouraged to take responsibility for all articles that could use improvement. This constant refinement leads to high-quality text in a surprisingly short period of time.

To get started, browse the special pages on Wikipedia, which show ongoing activity, including "Most Wanted" (articles that are linked to by other articles, but do not yet exist), "Orphans" (articles that exist, but are not yet linked), "Most Popular" (pages that have been viewed the most times) and "Stub Articles" (very short articles that could use expanding). A stub article, for example, could be expanded, or a wanted page could be created. In addition, links to other pages show up in different colours depending on whether or not the page exists, providing a visual cue as to what needs to be done.

**You never have to face a blank page...**

New articles can be written on any topic that would be suitable in an encyclopedia. As this is written, five articles on the "Recent Changes" list are: Swedish Monarchs, Malcolm X, Mammalia, Red Shift and World War I. If you need an idea for something to write, try writing an article on your hobby or hometown. You could even write a plot synopsis of a movie or book. With Wikipedia, you never have to face a blank page, since you can always contribute to an article started by someone else.

Articles must be written from the "neutral point of view," which means that the writing must be impersonal and non-biased. For those writers wishing to state personal opinions on issues, a "Wikipedia Commentary" section is available. Many controversial issues are written about, however all major theories are presented, and writers do not draw conclusions about matters of opinion. As might be expected, there have been heated debates on such topics as abortion, religion and gun control. Over time, a consensus develops on how to present these issues fairly. There are several "meta" articles (articles about Wikipedia itself), which collectively define Wikipedia's policies on all sorts of issues. These are recommended reading for those who wish to participate fully.

Some people are skeptical that the wiki process will work at all. Two of the biggest potential problems include the possibility of vandalism, and the possibility of incorrect information. Pages may be vandalized, since any Internet user can edit them. However, the system keeps old versions of the pages, so if vandalism is noticed, another user can simply revert to a previous version of the page. There is a list of "Recent Changes," or most-recently edited pages, which many users habitually scan. The second objection is more substantive, but is still not a critical problem. As more people read a page, there is a greater chance of an error being detected. Since correcting errors can be done very quickly, the general accuracy of pages increases over time.

**Open licensing of the content...**

The website itself is owned by Bomis, a dot-com Web portal and search engine, although they do not own the information due to the open licensing of the content. The project was started on January 15, 2001, and after one year, over 22,000 articles had been created. A positive feedback cycle helps to ensure that Wikipedia continues to improve: as more articles get written, more people come to the site. A percentage of those people contribute to the site, in turn adding more content.

Note that all material added to Wikipedia is released under the GNU Free Documentation License (www.gnu.org/licenses/fdl.html), which gives other people the right to copy, distribute and modify the information. All writing is done on a volunteer, uncredited basis. Wikipedia is endorsed by the Free Software Foundation, a group that promotes free (non-proprietary) computer software and information.

If you are looking for a fun and potentially addictive way of doing some stress-free writing, head over to www.wikipedia.com and write an article or two. See you there!

—

Mark Jeays is a professional computer programmer by day and a regular contributor to Wikipedia. His website, http://jeays.net/, features a popular page on the Rubik's Cube.

# Running a Nonprofit Website

*by Russ Harvey*

As is the case for business, not-for-profit organizations must provide their information where people can find it. The Internet provides a very cost-effective way to inform others about your services and to communicate with your volunteers and members.

Your website should be part of your overall image and therefore needs to conform to any existing organizational image. Visitors should see the same concepts projected in your letterhead, brochures, business cards and your website. If your image needs updating, the process of creating an online presence may be an opportunity to do that.

The purpose of an Internet site will indicate how the site will be structured since the design must take into account the interaction of the various pages. Some sites are designed in a linear fashion where the viewer follows a logical progression of pages from beginning to end while others are designed with the idea that the viewer will branch off at various points depending upon the interest of the visitor. Both designs must take into account the ability for someone to find a particular piece of information on the site without too much trouble.

**Accessibility of the information is key...**

Whatever you decide, the accessibility of the information is key. In various studies to determine what draws people back to particular websites, *ease of navigation* heads the list. If viewers can't find what they are looking for, they will not return. The information is always key. Design elements should enhance the display of the information on the site, not replace it.

One page that will make it much easier for others to navigate your site is a site map or navigation page. By listing all the pages on your site in a logical order, the viewer can always use this resource to locate items on your site. This page should be designed simply since those with older browsers may have trouble with Java-based menus or frames elements, but could find their way around your site from the links on this page.

Maintenance of a site requires some knowledge of HTML language to know how code changes will affect the way the pages display in the various Web browsers — even if the site was professionally designed. Recent Web design programs have made this easier, however your ability to massage the content of a site to load more quickly or to provide better navigation will make your website a more desirable place to visit.

If others are involved in the decisions about the layout and content of your site you will need to educate them about the possibilities and limitations of the HTML language. Your website will also need to indicate how to get in contact with those that can answer queries or resolve issues. A contact information page or FAQ (frequently asked questions) page can be used to reduce the unnecessary traffic to the website developer by providing answers to common concerns.

Once the site is up and running you will need to ensure that the content remains current. Often you need to obtain information from others. It will help you if you set a policy on the nature and structure of submissions to make it easier to maintain a more uniform look and feel for your site. Ask for information in a plain-text e-mail to avoid issues with attachments or formatting conflicts with your HTML code.

You need to take care if you include advertising on a nonprofit website. The payment rates for banners are not usually very high and these can detract from your site by slowing down the loading process and irritating your viewers. The use of reciprocal links to similar sites with relevant content will do far more for your site than banner advertising.

One of the most frustrating things about the Internet is that pages continually appear and disappear without warning. If you maintain links to other pages you will need to revisit those links continually to ensure they are still valid and relevant. You should ensure that you do not create similar problems for those that link to your site by renaming your pages unnecessarily. Links bring traffic to your site so you do not want to short-circuit that process.

A properly designed and maintained website can be a valuable asset to any nonprofit organization. Providing timely and accurate information on demand can reduce the need for more frequent newsletters and other communications that are more costly in terms of postage, printing and labour.

—

Russ Harvey is a west coast computer consultant and writes on computer and Internet issues. Russ maintains a number of nonprofit websites including the Canadian Authors Association site.

# Five Reasons Why You Need a Website

*by Carol Matthews*

It used to be, you needed a simple business card to make marketing easier and show you were businesslike. Then an answering machine was mandatory to stay on top of communications. Now a website has become another of the expected requirements of the profession. Here are five reasons why every freelance writer should have one.

**1. Image & credibility.**

It's the professional thing to do. Show prospective clients and editors that you are a perceptive businessperson, knowledgeable about new technology, and in step with the times. Particularly when you want to query an editor about writing for their website, it's more convincing if you have your own presence on the medium.

**2. Convenience.**

Before you had to send out your query and clips (one week), wait for the editor to go through the mail and get back to you (another week — if you're lucky), wait for the contract to come in the mail (third week). With a website this procedure can take place in a single day!

**3. Marketing.**

A job many writers hate can be made easier with a website. Whether an editor is searching for a writer or you are querying them, your professional, informative website can do the selling and convincing. With a simple click on the URL or Internet address the editor has your data available — not only the specific information relating to the query, but your other accomplishments as well. This often results in a job in another area of your expertise.

**4. Make money.**

Yes you can, by selling reprints, your books, courses, newsletters, services, or by booking presentations, workshops and speeches. Canadian writers have made $10,000 and more annually, selling from their websites.

**5. The Equalizer Effect.**

Whether you live in Toronto, Ontario, or Elderbank, Nova Scotia, your website is just as accessible to an editor. Whether you've published 20 books and write for international magazines or write for your local media, your website is, again, just as accessible. A professional website indicates you're in business with the best.

Before you begin designing your own website, check out examples from other writers. This can be done through www.writers.ca or through Internet searches using the writer's name. Decide what makes one more impressive than another and make a list of how you can incorporate that into your own.

The primary elements to include are: education, experience, and expertise. Include a list of your clients, including magazines and corporations, as well as testimonials from editors who like your work (e-mail your favourite editors and ask for one, most are more than happy to help). Include samples of your work. If you have several specialties, use different pages for each. If you are uncomfortable placing complete articles online, use only the first few paragraphs or pages, noting where and when the rest of the work appeared.

There are many options to choose from once you're ready to start building your website.

You can go the "do it yourself" route using free page design templates available from various online providers such as www.pwac.net or www.myownweboffice.com. A web search would provide more possibilities. Many public libraries offer free or low-cost courses on how to create your own website. For a minimal fee you can hire community college students to build one for you. If you want it done by a professional, check the Internet or try the telephone yellow pages under Internet — Web Page Design, and ask to see samples of their work.

Compared to other forms of advertising and marketing, a website is a bargain. It is inexpensive and relatively easy, it saves on postage and time, and changes and additions are quickly made. Think of what it would cost to run a full-page, full-colour ad in print media for 365 days a year! Take it from someone who has experienced the benefits, you won't regret it.

—

Carol Matthews does not profess to be a computer whiz, but she built her own website in 2000, and has been reaping the benefits ever since. She is a freelance writer specializing in gardening, nature, and travel, and has written for several online websites and e-zines, along with print media. Carol lives in Yarmouth, Nova Scotia.

# Write for the Internet

*by Paul G. Cormack*

The Internet has the largest appetite for text of any medium this millennium. A mid-2001 survey by the Internet Software Consortium identified the existence of over 125 million domain hosts, an increase of almost a thousand percent in the past five years!

The millions of pages that populate these Internet sites offer both opportunity and disappointment for the writing community. The Internet has little "named text," so there are few *popular* authors. "Vanity presses" and cyber-babble often swamp the few that exist. As in radio and television commercials or corporate press, the people who create Internet "classics" revel in obscurity.

Writing for the Internet is not a classic style — it differs from bibliography, from stage plays, and from poetic verse. And it doesn't represent just another form of anthology — as CDs are for cassettes, as DVDs are for videotape. Writing for the Internet (or the Intranet or the Extranet) is an entertaining mix of advertising and radio copywriting. All three forms comprise the deployment of text to fill a defined space — in advertising, the magazine ad or billboard; in radio, the news interval or the commercial; in the Internet, the 15- or 17-inch screen.

In comparison books are as large as the story; movies are as long as the script; songs are as long as the verses. Poetry, stage plays, and popular fiction are unhindered by the size of the page. But Internet pages are nominally 150 to 200 words per page without graphics, and 50 to 100 words with graphics. Generally, there is more *image* than *imagery.*

There is a marketing bias in virtually every aspect of the Internet, from e-commerce to the Canadian Authors Association (i.e. "If you are looking for the type of support only a large national association can give you … then the CAA is for you."). It is a short, staccato style intending to grab, and then hold, readers attention as they "surf" from site to site to site. On the best sites, the visuals are intense with crisp zone titles, headlines and rolling footnotes. You can almost visualize the storyboards that guided the site's creation.

But people often forget that page content needs to be *written*. Every part of every page needs carefully developed text, especially if the page incorporates newer software that enables text scrolling. A common error in writing for the Internet is "redeployment of book or newspaper text as an Internet page." Unless you are CNN, there is very little chance of "keeping the reader."

In recent Internet page trials for a client, we experimented with script lengths and page sizes. Older audiences tended to view Internet pages as separate entities (as if turning pages in a book), whereas a younger audience (under 25 years old) viewed pages with a "mouse" as if they held a magnifying glass over part of the page. It was a fascinating experiment, but we concluded that our primary audience — those who could afford a computer *and* the time to surf — were of the older demographic. Interestingly, they also seemed to have a larger disposable income and responded better to text than graphics.

**Too little imagery...**

A common error in this writing style is a perceived lack of experimentation. There is often too much emphasis on the sales pitch, and too little imagery.

A few years ago I was writing an Internet site for a mountain bike shop in England. We researched site after site and the same formula repeated itself. Photos of mountain bikes, photos of mountain bike riders, photos of mountain bike clothing. And prices, very significant prices. It was surprisingly easy to convince the shop owners to experiment with the site, and to research "mountain bike culture." That research turned up an obscure mountain biking site that offered translations for mountain bike terminology heard amongst the shop's customers.

The site that was eventually commissioned included the usual photos of mountain bikes, photos of mountain bike riders, and photos of mountain bike clothing. But it also included *links* to international mountain bike events, mountain bike manufacturers (playing the Macy's card from *Miracle on 34th Street*) and original prose with mountain bike colloquialisms (Cormack/ManicMountain.com, 1999):

> *Cold steel in my hands, shifting up. The bike's dialed in and there's a glint from the midwest sun off my lid. Manic! I'm clipped in, rhoid buffing and heading for the zone. Looking for big air in a Colorado downhill. Twinges from last week's bear traps — should be no mud diving on this half-track.*
>
> *Death Cookies!*

> *I'm endo on skid row just past the washboard — rag dolly. Done a digger, pruning trees on my way past. Giblets everywhere! One less tooth and the front wheel's taco'd. Sacrificed to the cheering vultures and some sad Fred in white calf socks.*

That Internet site yielded great excitement and some fantastic posters, but the business closed down just two years later. I am unsure if this is perceived as a failure in the bicycle industry, but it was a significant success for the writing community. Here was an Internet site that was *written*. It wasn't just page after page of lists; the words weren't just inserted to fill in the space between the graphics or photographs. It was *written*. There was active debate on every line, even for the text that simply identified future mountain bike events in Europe and North America.

**New copyright questions...**

But what about copyright issues? The World Intellectual Property Organization (www.wipo.int, 2001) agrees that the "dissemination of works via the Internet is but the latest development which raises new questions concerning copyright."

WIPO is actively involved in the debate to agree upon new standards for copyright protection in cyberspace. But the debate continues, which means there is little protection from copyright infringement on the Internet. This is exacerbated by a widespread failure to credit the people writing for the Internet. It is the greatest anonymous medium since the scrolls of ancient Greece.

The best defence for any Internet writer is to ensure that the rewards are immediately evident. There will be little opportunity for reprint or paperback release. That can take courage, but a book published by a *vanity press* is somewhat cheaper.

The other advantage of writing for the Internet is the rate of dot-com failure. The pace of change in e-commerce has fostered a market that mandates completely rewritten Internet (and Intranet, Extranet) sites for successful companies — as well as new sites for the many "Phoenix" companies that rise from the ashes of failed dot-coms.

The Internet may not have the allure of Dickensian readings from hardcover classics. But if a person wants to write, then this can be a wonderful medium.

—

Paul Cormack has developed various Internet and Intranet sites on commission from multinational corporations, small businesses and local interest groups in the past five years. A former broadcast news editor from Toronto, he relocated to the north of Scotland (see also www.TucsonNorth.com ) in the early 1990s.

# Write an E-Book

*by Bryan M. Knight*

An e-book is a publication designed to be read on a computer screen or on a hand-held electronic device such as a dedicated book reader.

E-book writing has some similarities to writing a regular book:

- Content should be clear and paragraphs should cover a single topic.

E-book writing is also similar to newspaper or magazine writing:

- It can include sidebars.
- Sentences are usually short.

E-book writing has unique features:

- Hotlinks.
- Brief paragraphs.
- Bulleted or numbered lists.
- Instant updating.
- Multiple storylines.
- Inexpensive publishing.

Hotlinks take the reader instantly to elsewhere within the e-book, or to a website. They also offer the reader an interactivity that is not available in a printed book. Each chapter can end with a list of links that the reader can click on to go where she chooses.

Fiction or nonfiction, you can swiftly update your e-book.

E-books can be printed but they are designed to be read on computers. To avoid eye fatigue they have to be written in snappy prose and laid out in a clear, logical sequence.

What a great opportunity for writers who want to communicate!

—

Bryan M. Knight, MSW, PhD, is the author of several e-books, including: *Hypnosis: Software for Your Mind; SELF-HYPNOSIS: Safe, Simple, Superb; How To Avoid A Bad Relationship; Easily Hypnotize Anyone;* and, *Marketing Action Plan for Success in Private Practice*. His website, Hypnosis Headquarters, is at www.hypnosis.org.

# Sell Your Writing Using the Internet and E-Mail

*by Phil Philcox*

People around the world read newspapers, magazines and books and they're interested in basically what we North Americans are interested in: how to have a happy life, how to raise kids, how to buy a house or TV, how to save money or take a vacation.

Lots of people are interested in a good fiction novel. So how come more of us aren't tackling the foreign markets? One reason might be that foreign publishers are just that. Foreign. Before the Internet and e-mail, you had to find their address, print out your letter, query or article, stuff it in an envelope, address it, attach postage (about $1 airmail to Europe per letter) and wait weeks for an answer.

Today you can send an article, short story or book outline to a publisher in Mexico, Scotland, France or China just as easy as around the corner. Just open your e-mail program, insert their address, write your message and click on the mouse. Tomorrow they'll open their mailbox and read what you have to offer. That editor could be anywhere! Amazing! Considering all the publications in the world, those editors out there must require tens of millions of words every single week!

I've sold over 1200 articles and 46 nonfiction books to publishers here in the United States and around the world. I've written about skin diving for *Skin Diver* (U.S.), *Plunge* (France), and *Aqua* (England). I've written about vacationing in California for magazines in Japan and Australia, motorcycle touring for a magazine in Hong Kong, boating for marine magazines in Germany and articles on everything from health to self-help to magazines in the United States. My book subjects have ranged from computers to travel.

You may not appreciate this but publishers in foreign countries, even those who publish in other languages, are interested in North American writers like yourself. If the subject is of interest to their readers, the translation costs won't put them off publishing your work. Of course, the majority of your sales will be with North American magazine and book publishers, but if you're interested in selling your writing, don't overlook the overseas market.

And don't overlook online magazines either. There are thousands out there, scattered all over the world and they need material for their online pages. I received an e-mail one day from an online magazine that covered the e-mail marketing of products and services. They asked me to write 2,000 words on the subject and paid me $450. With the e-mail addresses of magazines, you can make multiple sales as long as the magazines don't have an overlap in readership. I send a specific article, something on vacationing in northwest Florida, for example, to a travel magazine, a senior magazine, a general interest magazine, etc., and let the editors know what I'm doing. I either sell it to one magazine or several magazines. All of this through e-mail.

For book proposals, I send manuscript information to a series of editors via e-mail and hope someone will reply. In this day and age, sending a proposal to one editor and sitting around for six months or more for a reply is not the way to succeed in the writing business. But while you are waiting for a response, you can keep yourself busy writing for the thousands of Internet-based magazines, e-zines and websites around the world. Check it out.

—

Phil Philcox and Beverly Boe are a husband–wife magazine and book writing team living in Panama City Beach, Florida. They have been freelance writers for over thirty years and have travelled around the world writing for book and magazine publishers in the U.S., Canada, Australia, England and Europe.

# E-Mail Submissions That Endear

*by Lois J. Peterson*

E-mail and the Internet have made life a lot easier for writers. Once, we relied on Canada Post, print guides, and word of mouth to share publishing and marketing information, and to send submissions and queries.

Now it can all be done with a few keystrokes.

But while it's easy to reach out and touch someone electronically, it's also easy to alienate an editor by overusing e-mail. These guidelines might help ensure editors continue to welcome your e-mail submissions.

**1. Prepare.**

The best advice is to prepare well *before* contacting an editor by e-mail. Then use practices that give you a good chance of getting the response you need.

(a) Closely study guidelines and submission information. If the periodical listing says the publication doesn't accept e-mail submissions, DON'T send them.

(b) If it does welcome them, and you have a further question, send a brief, business-like note.

(c) Use an informative subject line. "*WORDS query re: word length*" gives me an immediate idea of what you need. Specific subject lines also help the recipient filter your message into an appropriate folder.

(d) Use the editor's full name, rather than opening *Dear George* or *Editor.*

(e) Don't get chatty. Talking about the weather and your latest hip replacement is unlikely to positively affect the disposition of your submission.

(f) Make your questions clear and concise.

(g) Include everything in one e-mail so you don't have to send an "*I've just thought of something else*" follow-up. I've often received as many as three e-mails from one contributor before they've sent the actual submission.

(h) If the editor's response is unclear, look elsewhere for clarification. If you're told they *don't accept genre work*, or that submissions must be in *standard manuscript format*, don't ask the editor for a tutorial. Refer to a writing how-to book or another writer. Few editors have time to serve as writing mentors.

(i) Don't suggest the editor review your website for material. Demonstrate that you've studied their market by sending them what work they need and want.

**2. Submit.**

Few editors review submissions on-screen. Some print them out and file them separately from cover letters. Others delete the original e-mail, and rely on contact information on the manuscript. Your job is to make it easy for the editor to file your work, consider it, and respond.

(a) Use an informative subject line. "*WORDS short story submission from Selma Glutz*" allows me to filter this message into the appropriate folder.

(b) Include the same information in e-mail as you would in a regular mail cover letter. The genre, title, word length, and your full contact details (name, address, phone number, e-mail address, etc.) all are useful in reconciling manuscripts with cover letters.

(c) Including your full e-mail address in the cover letter helps the editor get back to you if he doesn't keep the original e-mail in his computer.

(d) Submit the work in the specific format the publication requests; some want it in the body of the e-mail; others want it as a specifically formatted attachment. If you don't know the difference between a Microsoft Word and another type of document, look in your computer manual.

(e) Remember to send everything in one e-mail. If you do need to update a submission, resend the original including the omission so the editor has it all in one.

(f) If it's not stated in the guidelines, you might want to inquire about response time when you send your submission.

Just as with regular mail submissions, few editors will let you know if you've not submitted your work properly. Many discard incomplete and improperly formatted submissions without a further glance. I try to contact the writer to give them a second chance, but increasing numbers of e-mail submissions might soon make that too time consuming.

**3. Respond.**

The ease of e-mail might make you think it's quick and easy to get into a continuing exchange with the editor. Avoid it unless they're the one to initiate further dialogue. In general, e-mail submissions and queries take up at least twice as much of an editor's time as snail mail letters.

(a) Few editors will acknowledge receipt of your work. Don't bother to enquire next day if they've received your material.

(b) If the guidelines don't state response time, and you didn't ask about it when you sent your work, wait at least four to six weeks before sending a note. "*Is it too soon to enquire about the status of my short story '__________' sent to you on _______?*" should generate a quick response.

(c) When the editor responds, a brief *thank you* note might be polite, but don't expect a further exchange.

(d) If you don't agree with what the editor has to say about your submission, think twice about debating the issue. If you feel inclined to call them on it, draft the e-mail, then file it for a day or two before you decide whether to pursue the matter.

I was recently challenged on how quickly I responded to a submission — surely I hadn't even bothered to read the work? I imagine that writer soon regretted his hasty action. Unfortunately for him, I haven't forgotten his name!

Your goal is to get the information you need so you can submit work to which an editor can respond with a resounding, "Yes!" Identifying appropriate markets is a first step; submitting only your best, well-crafted work is the next. But learning to communicate well might just make or break your chances of publication.

—

Lois J. Peterson is a published short story writer, and editor of *WORDS literary journal*, www3.telus.net/345/ljp/words.html. About seventy percent of submissions to *WORDS* have been by e-mail; not all of them have conformed to the guidelines noted in this article.

# Cures for the E-Mail Time Sink

*by Denyse O'Leary*

Having trouble managing your e-mail? If you're like many writers, you get personal messages, electronic newsletters, electronic news service bulletins, press releases, and daily or weekly listserves (proceedings of informal writing-related discussion groups). Added to these are spam (Internet junk mail), perhaps occasional flames (Internet crank mail) and then the occasional virus hoaxes.

Some people find that e-mail can consume as much time scheduled for productive activities as chatting on the telephone. Or more. For some, it's the electronic time sink.

Well, here are two possible solutions: You can abandon e-mail, or you can check to see if your program permits mail filters — if not, quickly abandon the program for one that does. Filters are a valuable tool that can effortlessly organize your electronic mail and, more important, prevent you from getting distracted from more urgent tasks.

**How mail filters work...**

A mail filter is an option (perhaps on the Edit menu in your Mailbox, for example) that enables you to forward mail without seeing it to a subfolder of your Inbox. You must create the subfolder before you ask for a mail filter. You can do that by creating a New Folder under the File options.

At the Mail Filters menu, you can classify your mail by sender, subject matter, a message that might always appear in the body, the recipient, or a number of other options. Then, all mail that fits that description goes directly to the subfolder.

Mail filters are useful for many types of e-mail communication, not just list-serves. If you are working with an editor on chapters of a book, you may wish to filter chapters coming back from an edit into a subfolder so that you will not be distracted while working on your current chapter. You need to agree with your editor that the chapters will always have "Edited Chapter" in the subject line so that the filter can pick it up. You will know that the mail has come in because the name of the subfolder will be highlighted. But if you don't have time right now, you don't go there.

Filters also prevent the problem of hastily skimming through material and deleting it impatiently, just to get it out of the Inbox — and deleting something you will later wish you had kept.

**Mail filter caution...**

Don't select a subfolder for messages that could be urgent, for example, from your editor cancelling a meeting, or an emergency message from your family overseas. Similarly, don't use a term that might appear in any post as a filter (such as "vacation in Florida").

**Spams, flames, and hoaxes...**

Just think ... spamsters, flamesters, and hoaxers need only try it on you once. You can select a specific phrase that routinely appears in their subject line or body, such as "Valuable Land in Florida," "hypocrites like you," or "this virus will delete your," and filter them unread to Trash.

Alternatively, if you are getting a lot of hoax virus messages from friends, you can go to www.symantec.com and search for the hoax in the virus library. Chances are you will find it there. Most hoaxes are old news. You can politely invite your friend to start using the library too.

Of course, if you find that you are not reading the mail from listserves that you have filtered into a subfolder, you may need to evaluate their importance. What is the cost they represent in time versus the value of belonging? A filter can help you see where they fit on your true priority list.

Mail filters won't solve all your e-mail time problems. But, first thing in the morning, you will look forward to seeing an Inbox with just the priority messages in it. And everything else neatly organized away from your view.

—

Denyse O'Leary is a Toronto-based freelance writer and the author of *Faith@Science* (Winnipeg: J. Gordon Shillingford, 2001). O'Leary writes regularly on science and faith issues. She also teaches workshops on business practice for writers and editors. She has two adult daughters, three gardens, and a website at www.denyseoleary.com.

# 15. Writer's Reference

# The Future of Publishing

*by Rowland Lorimer and Richard Smith*
*Advanced Publishing Research Lab*
*Simon Fraser University*

In 1985, when the first desktop computers began to arrive on the desks of a few authors, the role of the book publisher began to change. Within five years there was talk of desktop publishing, by which the computing community meant the ability to produce pages on a desktop computer that were indistinguishable from those of the printed book, at least to the untrained eye. The developers of computers and computer-assisted technology have never looked back. With each year has come increased capacity, delivered by both hardware and software, so that it is now commonplace for digital files to be sent electronically to printers who then use those files to go directly to press. Indeed in the scholarly journal and magazine industries, publishers are increasingly going to press and making online versions of their publications available simultaneously and in some cases abandoning print altogether. In short, there is no doubt that desktop computer technology has changed the face of publishing and that the role of the publisher has been substantially transformed.

But desktop computer technology has not done so alone. In the early 1990s, use of the Internet was beginning to expand its user base from the science community to the general scholarly community. Within seven years it would advance from a rather crude text- and data-based system though the capacity for communication of formatted text, then text with images, to, most recently, a full platform-independent multimedia system able to handle the exchange of any type of digital information sufficiently robust to support reasonably secure commerce.

The combination of desktop and Internet technology has given the world dramatic new capacity for information access and exchange. So dramatic is this combined capacity that computer purchases and Internet access have driven a vast expansion of the economy. Most notable is the presence of computers and Internet access in homes. Market penetration into homes in developed countries is well beyond 50 percent and the technology is commanding a growing and significant share of leisure time — to say nothing of on-the-job use.

Whereas desktop technology brought the possibility of producing professional looking documents (an enhancement of production technology), the Internet brought a new distribution system — the capacity for easy circulation of those documents, in other words, worldwide instantaneous and continuous access provided all the infrastructure is in place.

These combined technologies also brought a second major change, a change in the medium of the delivery of information from print on paper to computer screen. While such a shift is significant in itself, the properties of computer communications as opposed to print are also significant. They make the communication of colour and images both possible and feasible, and add the third dimension of sound and movement.

These technologies also brought significantly greater flexibility. That greater flexibility derives from the nature of the final form in which a document resides. If the final record is a digital file rather than a printed page, it is far easier to enable change. Not only can changes be made right up to the point of publication, they can still be made afterwards. In addition, with digital files as the foundation for printed documents, a publication need never go out of print. It can either be made available electronically to the consumer for printing or used to create a print-on-demand version of the original printed text. Commentary can also be more closely connected to documents, whether in electronic or print form. In scholarly journals, for example, a link can be created to reviews. In the book world, online bookstores offer reviews as part of the information package that is intended to encourage consumer purchase.

Do these developments mean that it is only a matter of time before the publisher is obsolete, an unnecessary mediator in the communication process between the author (a desktop document creator) and the public?

There are many who would argue yes. Probably many of the same people who believe that copyright is obsolete and information should be free. There are others who see the publisher as essential in his or her role selecting and investing in intellectual property, organizing authors, designers, editors, production and printing or online display and therefore unthreatened. Still others see publishers and publishing changing quite fundamentally. Machines will fulfill an ever-increasing number of publishing functions and the ever-expanding capacities of machines will result in publishers becoming increasingly concerned with access to credible information and significant creativity and also with interactivity.

## The evolving role of the publisher...

Rumours of the demise of publishers derive mainly from a concentration on a simplified vision of the material activities of a publisher rather than a richer understanding of the organizational activities.

Publishers are, more than anything, the creators of information systems and the full body of writing encompassed by what we call the literary arts and the provision of information in written form. In the simplest terms, they are the gatekeepers that decide on what is presented to the public eye.

Publishers have two modes of operation. The first the public understands and is common in fiction publishing. On reviewing a manuscript, publishers make a fundamental decision: does a manuscript warrant an investment of their resources or not? The second mode, in many cases a more common way of operating, especially in nonfiction publishing, is that the publisher decides that there is a need for publications dealing with a certain subject in a certain way. She or he then seeks an author to develop the manuscript and the publisher gives approval at various stages. Behind the publicly understood model, involving a decision to invest in a presented manuscript, is an assessment of the amount and kind of resources the manuscript will require to bring it to a point where it can be satisfactorily presented to the public. A second assessment is focused on whether the publisher or publishing house is appropriate to bring forward a particular title. A scholarly press is unlikely to succeed with a romance title. A Canadian publisher is an unlikely vehicle to bring a new German writer to the attention of the world. Behind the second model, typified by a nonfiction publisher seeking an author for a certain type of publication, these investment decisions are already made and the matter is more one of coming to an agreement with an known author on treatment, length, payment, and delivery time. Of course there is always a risk that the manuscript will be a poor one, but editing can do much more for nonfiction than fiction and the ever-present clause in the contract concerning "a manuscript satisfactory to the publisher" can always be invoked.

Behind these two models is the knowledge the publisher has of the capabilities and position of his or her firm, how manuscripts can be transformed into appealing publications, the nature of marketing, and the tastes of the reading public. This knowledge allows the publisher to make a decision on the likelihood of his or her firm succeeding in piquing the interest of the reading public with a particular manuscript.

Publishers also play the role of informed distributors and marketers. Seasoned publishers are well aware that keen readers of historical tomes are unlikely to look for them in big box bookstores partly because they will have already learned that such stores rarely stock anything beyond a wide range of mass-market items. Alternatively, publishers know that people will purchase publications at certain types of events. Publishers also know that consumers will purchase certain other types of publications in certain types of venues. In short, part of the publishers' function is to get the right publication in the right place at the right time.

The results of these many different decisions by publishers are a social information system and our literary heritage. A publisher is not just a printer and distributor of printed books and magazines but, rather, the developer and marketer of intellectual work. The significance of understanding this role of publishers is to see how it applies in the context of desktop publishing and the Internet.

The Internet is not a social information system but rather a crudely organized source of information of mixed quality, not unlike a publicly available dump of many things written in many places for many purposes. It is left to the user to organize. Yet, paeans to democracy aside, users rarely want to, nor do they have the skills to evaluate the credibility and the significance of information, analysis, and works of literary merit. We need publishers, as organizers of our social information system, to find ways to re-establish themselves not by shunning the Internet but by understanding its potential.

Publishers will evolve into credible nodes of organization not restricted to bringing forward manuscripts that they have been able to acquire directly from the author but pulling together literature, information and analysis that, as a whole, has value.

The knowledge formation that takes place may be in real time or not. A real time example of such knowledge creation is the website slashdot.com, which offers up information from credible, volunteer contributors who are involved in that of which they speak. The result, often enough, is that groundbreaking information appears on the site well before newspaper readers or television watchers hear of it. The slashdot team are Internet era publishers, in their creation of the site, in designing the opportunities for comment and thus an open system of knowledge creation, in privileging certain contributors, and so on. An over-time example would mine existing archives of knowledge as well as bringing new elements forward. For example, a publisher of social commentary on the ethics of society might combine work he or she is publishing with commentary and citations of other complementary work. The publisher might organize events as well as real and virtual symposia with the view of creating a steady flow of writing available to the market.

A working example of this publishing role can be found in John Willinsky's Public Knowledge Project (www.pkp.ubc.ca). If you go to his demonstration of his Research Support Tool from the home page through Demos and Downloads you will get a sense of Willinsky as online educational publisher. The Research Support Tool allows the site user into the structure of the paper through its metadata — the author, title, keywords, etc. The site provides an easy way for users to access related studies from free scholarly abstract services and electronic journals as well as studies for which one must pay to gain access. The user can then look into the background of the author and the terms the author has chosen as key to his or her article. Discussion groups on the topic are also made readily accessible, as are public sites that contain related policy or popular articles. The possibilities include alternative actions that the user can take, such as e-mailing the author, adding a comment, or e-mailing a colleague about the information found. This site is a working model of the state to which online educational publishing will be evolving.

Obviously, in such a world, payment to authors will have to be reconstructed. Such payment systems are possible, because everything on the Internet can be tracked. All that is required is people of good will to set in place a fair and reasonable system for doing it.

—

Rowland Lorimer is the Director of the Master of Publishing program at the Canadian Centre for Studies in Publishing at Simon Fraser University. He is Professor of Communication and the past editor of the *Canadian Journal of Communication*, of which he is now the publisher. He is honorary President of the Association for Canadian Studies.

Richard Smith is an Associate Professor of Communication at Simon Fraser University (SFU). He is also Director of the Centre for Policy Research on Science and Technology at SFU's Harbour Centre campus in downtown Vancouver.

# Managing Your Rights Through Collective Licensing

*by Access Copyright*

As a writer, you make sure your copyright and any royalties from publication are recognized in the contract you sign with a publisher. That's all you need to worry about, right? Wrong.

Since photocopiers became cheap and easy technology in the 1980s, your books, articles, photos and illustrations have been photocopied regularly, often without your knowledge or permission. To recognize this, the government introduced the concept of collective licensing in the Copyright Act to enable creators and publishers to recoup lost revenues as sales gave way to illegal copying. Access Copyright, the Canadian Copyright Licensing Agency (formerly CANCOPY), was established in 1988 by Canadian publishers and writers to license access to copyright works. The legal and easy licensing solutions Access Copyright offers to governments, schools, libraries and corporations now bring in millions of dollars in revenue each year, and that amount continues to climb.

Access Copyright's members include 33 national and regional publisher and creator organizations. It represents the vast international repertoire of more than 5,100 writers, artists and photographers and 450 Canadian newspaper, magazine and book publishers.

Access Copyright's mandate is to protect and advance the rights of copyright owners, promote public awareness and understanding of copyright law and collective administration of copyright, offer licences to copyright-protected works, and enforce the rights it represents.

In 2001, Access Copyright distributed over $18.5 million to rightsholders. This collective licensing approach has proven to be incredibly successful and will be applied to the digital copying of works as demand for this service grows.

**Become an affiliate of Access Copyright...**

It's easy and it's free. Contact Access Copyright at the coordinates listed at the end of this article, or go to the Access Copyright website to print a copy of the affiliation agreement. You must sign the basic grant of right, which allows Access Copyright to license *print-to-print* uses of published works. Optional grants of right include Digital Right — Conversion, which entitles Access Copyright to license *print-to-digital* uses of published works, and Digital Right — Importation, which entitles Access Copyright to license *digital-to-digital* uses of published works.

The benefits of affiliation are substantial, and include:

- The ability to set the price and terms of use for each individual work licensed on a transactional basis.
- Transparent reporting of all activities concerning your works. Online access to Access Copyright's new rights management system allows you to review the information maintained on you and your works and to review all transactions performed on your behalf. You will no longer need to be concerned about which rights or whose rights are being licensed.
- Better monitoring of compliance around digital uses of your works — Access Copyright's compliance program will include trained staff and the latest technology for monitoring digital infringement on the Internet, Intranet and password-protected sites. It is much more cost-effective, thorough and efficient than trying to do this yourself.
- Access Copyright will pursue infringement cases in its own name in court without your participation. When it wins a "wide injunction" case, the infringer will be prevented from copying other works in its repertoire, not just those of the copyright owner or owner whose works were actually infringed.
- Access Copyright will license those digital uses that are most vulnerable to copyright infringement, and to arguments for exemption from copyright protection.
- Access Copyright will not license digital uses that would compete with your economic exploitation of the work.
- More money for you — a new revenue stream from collective digital licensing.
- Inclusion of your works in the largest-ever searchable database of Canadian works.

For more information contact:
Access Copyright
1 Yonge Street, Suite 1900, Toronto, ON M5E 1E5
E-mail: affiliates@accesscopyright.ca
Web: www.accesscopyright.ca
Phone: 1-800-893-5777 or 416-868-1620

# Guidelines for Writing Groups

*by Shirley A. Serviss*

Writing can be a lonely and discouraging business. However, meeting regularly with a group of other writers can provide the incentive and encouragement you need to keep writing. These meetings can also offer opportunities to exchange information and provide constructive criticism. Writers' organizations in your community may have lists of groups open to new members. Groups may form from a writing class or you may want to start your own with a group of friends who write.

The format of writing groups can vary significantly. Participants may meet to critique, bringing copies of their work to the meeting or circulating work in advance for comment. If this is the objective, be sure to keep the group to a manageable size (eight participants is probably ample) to ensure that everyone has a turn. Some groups meet to write and share what they have written on the spot. Members take turns finding passages to share, bringing objects or offering exercises to inspire writing.

**Ensure that participants set aside the time to write...**

Other writers meet to work independently and may or may not share what they are working on. Although this is a more common format for longer retreats, it can also work well for short periods as it ensures that participants actually set aside the time to write.

Meetings may take place in libraries, coffee shops, members' homes or at retreat centres. The least desirable option is meeting in members' homes as the host may feel obligated to do housework or bake rather than write! Meeting outside the home sets a more business-like tone that keeps the focus on the work rather than on socializing. Some bookstores also have meeting spaces you can use.

If the objective of the group is to provide critical feedback, it's important to have certain "understandings" in place. Knowing how to ask for and accept criticism is as essential as knowing how to provide it.

Let other members of the group know what kind of feedback you want. This may be the first time you've shared your work with others and you may want to know if you're off to a good start or on the right track.

Or you may have a specific question about a particular aspect of the writing.

Don't attempt to respond to criticism immediately. The tendency is to become defensive and try to justify what we've written, but there is nothing to be gained from a debate on the merits of your piece. The words on the page will have to speak for themselves; you won't be there reading over the reader's shoulder waiting to explain yourself.

Make sure you understand what is being said about your piece. Listen carefully, make notes and ask for clarification. We tend to focus on the negative, so make sure you hear the positive comments as well as suggestions for improvements.

Don't feel you have to make all the changes that are suggested. Remember that you are the writer. Take the comments into consideration, but ultimately you are the only one who knows what works for you and your writing style. Readers often disagree amongst themselves, so learn that you can't please everyone.

**You are not a failure...**

Don't confuse yourself with your "writing." Sharing our writing offers a huge risk. It's easy to identify with our work and feel discouraged when it is criticized. Try to remember you are not a failure just because someone suggests that an article could use a bit more work.

Providing constructive criticism is a responsibility that should not be taken lightly. Treat each piece of work carefully and respectfully. We all have our own way of expressing thoughts and feelings or telling our stories. Don't try to impose your style on someone else.

At the same time, remember that your reaction is as valid as anyone else's. You don't need a degree to have an opinion on whether or not a piece of writing speaks to you as a reader. Make notes as you listen or on the copy provided so you can offer specific feedback on what you liked about the work and what you feel could be improved.

Talk about the work not the writer. Don't assume it is based on personal experience even though it is written in the first person. Refer to the persona in the piece or the main character, not the writer. Keep the focus on the work under discussion. This is not the time to share similar (or contradictory) experiences or opinions.

Begin with what you liked about the piece of writing. It is as helpful for the writer to know what works and what doesn't. That way the writer will know what to leave untouched and what to rewrite. Echo lines or images that stood out for you. Share the feelings you experienced from the writing. Let the writer know if the piece or characters seemed believable.

Point out places where the writing could be stronger. Perhaps it was unclear or confusing. There may be opportunities for the writer to be more specific, using an example rather than making a generalization. Point out clichés, inadvertent repetitions or grammatical errors. These don't have to be discussed, but can merely be noted on copies of the work that you return to the writer.

**The writer hasn't risked enough...**

Let the writer know if you feel it takes too long to get into the piece or if it is unfinished or goes on too long. Maybe you feel the writer hasn't risked enough. The piece may be so interesting that you want to know more. Or you may feel the writer has written past the ending and told you things you had already figured out for yourself.

Maintain a "nurturing spirit." It is always easier to find fault with something once it has been written than it is to write it in the first place. The purpose of *constructive* criticism is to help the writer build a better foundation, not destroy it.

—

Shirley A. Serviss has participated in numerous writing groups and retreats. She teaches creative writing workshops, works as a freelance writer and editor and has published two poetry collections: *Model Families* (Rowan Books, 1992) and *Reading Between the Lines* (Rowan Books, 2000).

# Organizations of Interest to Writers

*by Jennifer Crump*

Confused over payments, rights, and contracts? You're not alone. Writers today are finding it increasingly important to band together. Belonging to a writers' group or organization can help you navigate these issues. They can also provide you with vital technique and market information as well as companionship.

Before you sign on, though, determine what benefits you need. Some organizations excel at education, others at networking and still others at providing market information. Next, consider the criteria for acceptance. Some are open to all authors while others have more stringent membership criteria.

There are a number of national organizations geared to multi-genre writers in Canada. These include the Canadian Authors Association, The Periodical Writers Association of Canada and The Writers Union of Canada. Many of the national U.S. writing organizations such as the American Society of Journalists and Authors and the Writers Union boast many Canadians among their membership.

Regional writers' organizations are wonderful sources as well. Nearly every region of Canada can boast of several such organizations. We have listed several below.

Finally, there are organizations geared to specific genres. We have assembled a list of genre-specific organizations below that is followed by a list of organizations arranged alphabetically.

Note: We have included e-mail and Web page addresses whenever they where available. However, we would like to point out that the volatile nature of the Internet and the World Wide Web means that these could have changed by the time you read this publication. Be particularly careful with your address entry, but if you still fail to get through, use a search tool such as AltaVista — www.altavista.com — to find the new address.

—

## Organizations By Genre

### Automobile

Automobile Journalists Association of Canada

### Children

Children's Writers & Illustrators of BC
Canadian Association of Children's Authors, Illustrators and Performers
Canadian Children's Book Centre, The
Society of Children's Book Writers and Illustrators

### Business

International Association of Business Communicators

### Horror

Horror Writers Association

### Journalism

Canadian Association of Journalists
Society of Professional Journalists

### Magazines

Periodical Writers Association of Canada

### Medical

American Medical Writers Association, Canadian Chapter

### Mystery/Crime

Crime Writers of Canada
Mystery Writers of America
Sisters in Crime

### Outdoors

Outdoor Writers of Canada

### Poetry

Canadian Poetry Association
League of Canadian Poets, The
Poets & Writers

### Romance

Alberta Romance Writers Association
Canadian Romance Authors Network
Romance Writers of America

### Science

Canadian Science Writers' Association

### Science Fiction/Fantasy

Science Fiction and Fantasy Writers of America
SF Canada

### Screenwriters/Playwrights

Canadian Screenwriters Alliance
Playwrights Union of Canada

### Travel

Society of American Travel Writers
Society of American Travel Writers — Canadian Chapter

## Alphabetical List of Regional, National, International and Genre-specific organizations:

Alberta Romance Writers Association
223 – 12th Avenue S.W.
Calgary AB T2R 0G9
Phone: (403) 282-6676
E-mail: altaromwrtr@home.com
Web: albertaromancewriters.homestead.com/files/arwa/

American Medical Writers Association, Canadian Chapter
40 West Gude Drive, Suite 101
Rockville MD 20850-1192, U.S.A.
Phone: (301) 294-5303 - Fax: (301) 294-9006
E-mail: webmaster@amwa-canada.ca
Web: www.amwa-canada.ca

American Society of Journalists and Authors
1501 Broadway, Suite 302
New York NY 10036
Phone: (212) 997-0947
E-mail: execdir@asja.org
Web: www.asja.org

Asian Canadian Writer's Workshop of Canada
311 East 41st Avenue
Vancouver BC V5W 1N9
Phone: (604) 322-6616 - Fax: (604) 322-6616

E-mail: acww@vcn.bc.ca
Web: www.vcn.bc.ca/acww/welcome.html

Assoc. acadienne des artistes professionelles du NB
140, rue Botsford, Pièce 10
Moncton NB  E1C 4X4
Phone: (506) 852-3313 - Fax: (506) 852-3401

Association des Auteures et Auteurs de L'ontario Francais
(Association of Franco-Ontarian Authors)
5255, chemin Montreal, bureau 202
Vanier ON  K1L 6C4
Phone: (613) 744-0902
E-mail: aaofmtb@on.aira.com

Assoc. des écrivains acadiens du NB
140 rue Botsford
Moncton NB  E1C 4X4
Phone: (506) 856-9693 - Fax: (506) 857-3070

Association des journalistes independentes du Québec
4034 av. de Lorimier
Montreal QC  H2K 3X7
Phone: (514) 523-9845 - Fax: (514) 523-1270
E-mail: ajiq@cam.org
Web: www.ajiq.qc.ca/

Association of American Publishers
71 Fifth Avenue.
New York NY  10003-3004
Phone: (212) 255-0200 - Fax: (212) 255-7007
E-mail: amyg@publishers.org
Web: www.publishers.org/index.htm

Association of Book Publishers of British Columbia
#107 – 100 West Pender St.
Vancouver BC  V6B 1R8
Phone: (604) 684-0228 - Fax: (604) 684-5788
E-mail: admin@books.bc.ca
Web: www.books.bc.ca/

Authors Guild, Inc., The
31 E. 28th Street, 10th Floor
New York NY  10016

Phone: (212) 563-5904 - Fax: (212) 564-8363
E-mail: staff@authorsguild.org
Web: www.authorsguild.org

Authors League of America
234 West 44th Street
New York NY 10036
Phone: (212) 564-8350

Automobile Journalists Association of Canada
PO Box 85528, 875 Eglinton Ave. W.
Toronto ON M6C 4A8
Phone: (800) 361-1516 - Fax: (416) 785-1377
E-mail: autojourna@aol.com
Web: www.ajsa.org

Burnaby Writers' Society
6584 Deer Lake Avenue
Burnaby BC V5G 3T7
Phone: (604) 435-6500
E-mail: info@bws.bc.ca
Web: www.bws.bc.ca

CAN:BAIA
Black Artists in Action
54 Wolseley St., 2nd Fl.
Toronto ON M5T 1A5
Phone: (416) 703-9040
E-mail: canbaia@passport.ca

Canada Council for the Arts, The
350 Albert St., PO Box 1047
Ottawa ON K1P 5V8
Phone: (800) 263-5588 - Fax: (613) 566-4390
E-mail: michelle.legault@canadacouncil.ca
Web: www.canadacouncil.ca

Canadian Association of Children's Authors, Illustrators and Performers
c/o Northern District Library, Lower Level
40 Orchard View Blvd.
Toronto ON M4R 1B9
Phone: (416) 515-1559 - Fax: (416) 515-7022

E-mail: office@canscaip.org
Web: www.canscaip.org

Canadian Association of Journalists (CAJ)
Rm 316B, 1125 Colonel By Dr.
Ottawa ON K1S 5B6
Phone: (613) 526-8061 - Fax: (613) 521-3094
E-mail: caj@igs.net
Web: www.caj.ca

Canadian Association of Photographers and Illustrators in Communications
100 Broadview Ave., Suite 322
Toronto ON M4M 2E8
Phone: (416) 462-3700 - Fax: (416) 462-3678
E-mail: administrator@capic.org
Web: www.capic.org

Canadian Authors Assoc. – Alberta Branch
Allison Kydd
PO Box 52007
Edmonton AB T6G 2T5
Phone: (780) 433-9645 or (780) 451-3611
E-mail: caa@ecn.ab.ca
Web: www.ecn.ab.ca/caa

Canadian Authors Assoc. – Manitoba/Saskatchewan
Ishbel Moore
529 Chelsea Ave.
Winnipeg MB R2K 1A4
Phone: (204) 663-0605
E-mail: ilmoore@mb.sympatico.ca

Canadian Authors Assoc. – Montreal Branch
Aniko Koranyi-Bergman
3328 Troie Avenue, Apt. #908
Westmount PQ H3V 1B1
Phone: (514) 738-4108
E-mail: brotherbranch@yahoo.com

Canadian Authors Assoc. – Niagara Branch (ON)
Mike Keenan
64 Confederation Drive

Niagara-on-the-Lake ON  L0S 1J0
Phone: (905) 468-5517 - Fax (905) 468-5314
E-mail: keenan@vaxxine.com
Web: www.canauthorsniagara.org

Canadian Authors Assoc. – National Office
Alec McEachern
320 South Shores Road
PO Box 419
Campbellford ON  K0L 1L0
Phone: (705) 653-0323 - Fax: (705) 653-0593
Toll-free: 1-866-216-6222
E-mail: canauth@redden.on.ca
Web: www.CanAuthors.org

Canadian Authors Assoc. – Nova Scotia Branch
Murdena Skinner
85 Collins Grove
Dartmouth, NS  B2W 4G3
Phone: (902) 434-5658
E-mail: raemacpub@ns.sympatico.ca

Canadian Authors Assoc. – Okanagan Branch (BC)
L.B. Greenwood
1815 Maple Street
Kelowna BC  V1Y 1H4
Phone: (250) 763-4968
E-mail: morrwood@shaw.ca

Canadian Authors Assoc. – Ottawa Branch (ON)
Roma Quapp
2468 Clementine Blvd, Apt. #1
Ottawa ON  K1V 8E4
Phone: (613) 286-3017  (w) (819) 994-0783
E-mail: bluekelp@rogers.com

Canadian Authors Assoc. – Peterborough Branch (ON)
PO Box 2134
Peterborough ON  K9J 7Y4
Phone: (705) 745-0830
E-mail: clarified2000@yahoo.com

Canadian Authors Assoc. – Temiskaming Branch (ON)
PO Box 5180, RR #2
New Liskeard ON P0J 1P0
Phone: (705) 647-5424 - Fax: (705) 647-8366
E-mail: caa-tem@wmpub.ca
Web: www.wmpub.ca/caa-tem.htm

Canadian Authors Assoc. – Toronto Branch (ON)
Firdaus Bilimoria
221 Balliol Street, #1825
Toronto ON M4S 1E8
Phone: (416) 482-1603
E-mail: fbilimoria@hotmail.com
Web: www.tacob.org/

Canadian Authors Assoc. – Vancouver Branch (BC)
Bernice Lever
RR1, B69
Bowen Island BC V0N 1G0
Phone: (604) 947-0017
E-mail: blever2@hotmail.com
Web: www.canauthorsvancouver.org/

Canadian Authors Assoc. – Victoria & Islands Branch (BC)
Albert Fowler
1346 Lang Street
Victoria BC V8T 2S5
Phone: (250) 382-7871 - Fax: (250) 382-7872
E-mail: iwrite@islandnet.com
Web: www.canauthors.org/island/homepage.html

Canadian Authors Assoc. – Waterloo-Wellington Branch
Sandra Stewart
203 – 35 Flamingo Drive
Elmira ON N3B 1V3
Phone: (519) 669-3949
E-mail: stewartont@yahoo.ca

Canadian Children's Book Centre, The
40 Orchard View Blvd., Suite 101
Toronto ON M4R 1B9
Phone: (416) 975-0010 - Fax: (416) 975-8970

E-mail: info@bookcentre.ca
Web: www.bookcentre.ca/

Canadian Copyright Licensing Agency (Access Copyright™)
1 Yonge Street, Suite 1900
Toronto ON  M5E 1E5
Phone: 1-800-893-5777 - Fax: (416) 868-1621
E-mail: admin@accesscopyright.ca
Web: www.accesscopyright.ca

Canadian Ethnic Journalists' and Writers' Club
24 Tarlton Road
Toronto ON  M5P 2M4
Phone: (416) 944-8175 - Fax: (416) 260-3586
E-mail: canscene@home.com
Web: members.rogers.com/canscene/club.html

Canadian ISBN Agency, National Library of Canada
395 Wellington St.
Ottawa ON  K1A 0N4
Phone: (819) 994-6872 - Fax: (819) 953-8508
E-mail: isbn@nlc/bnc.ca
Web: www.nlc-bnc.ca/

Canadian Magazine Publishers Association (CMPA)
130 Spadina Ave., Suite 202
Toronto ON  M5V 1L4
Phone: (416) 504-0274 - Fax: (416) 504-0437
E-mail: cmpainfo@cmpa.ca
Web: www.cmpa.ca

Canadian Music Publishers Association
56 Wellesley St. West, Suite 320
Toronto ON  M5S 2S3
Phone: (416) 926-1966 - Fax: (416) 926-7521
E-mail: cmpa.inquiries@cmrra.ca
Web: www.cmrra.ca

Canadian Poetry Association
PO Box 22571 St. George Postal Outlet
264 Bloor Street West
Toronto ON  M5S 1V8

E-mail: writers@sympatico.ca
Web: www.mirror.org/cpa/

Canadian Romance Authors Network
1067 St. David Street
Victoria BC  V8S 4Y7
Phone: (250) 592 6337 - Fax: (250) 592 7578
E-mail: lsimmons23@home.com
Web: www.canadianromanceauthors.com/

Canadian Science Writers' Association
PO Box 75, Stn. A
Toronto ON  M5W 1A2
Phone: (416) 928-9624 - Fax: (416) 960-0528
E-mail: cswa@interlog.com
Web: www.interlog.com/~cswa/

Canadian Screenwriters Alliance
24 Watts Avenue, West Royalty Industrial Park
Charlottetown PE  C1E 1B0
Phone: (902) 628-3880 - Fax: (902) 368-1813
E-mail: evie@isn.net

Canadian Theatre Critics Association, The
405 Hamilton Avenue
Ottawa ON  K1Y 1C9
Fax: (613) 728-2028
E-mail: ruprechtalvina@hotmail.com
Web: www.canadiantheatre.com/ctca.html

Children's Writers & Illustrators of BC
3888 West 15th Avenue
Vancouver BC  V6R 2Z9
Phone: (604) 435-3108 - Fax: (604) 435-8499
E-mail: polestar@axionet.com
Web: www.swifty.com/cwill/list.htm

Crime Writers of Canada
3007 Kingston Rd., Box 113
Scarborough ON  M1M 1P1
Phone: (416) 782-3116 - Fax: (416) 789-4682
E-mail: info@crimewriterscanada.com
Web: www.crimewriterscanada.com

Editors' Association of Canada
502 - 27 Carlton Street
Toronto ON M5B 1L2
Phone: (416) 975-1379 - Fax: (416) 975-1637
E-mail: info@editors.ca
Web: www.editors.ca

Federation of British Columbia Writers, The
Suite 905 – 626 West Pender Street
Vancouver BC V6B 1V9
Phone: (604) 683-2057 - Fax: (604) 608-5522
E-mail: fedoffice@bcwriters.com
Web: bcwriters.com/

Federation of Canadian Artists
1241 Cartwright St.
Vancouver BC V6H 4B7
Phone: (604) 681-2744 - Fax: (604) 681-2740
E-mail: fcaoffice@artists.ca
Web: www.artists.ca/

International Association of Business Communicators
(Numerous Canadian Chapters)
One Hallidie Plaza, Suite 600
San Francisco CA 94102-2818, U.S.A.
Phone: (415) 544-4700 - Fax: (415) 544-4747
E-mail: service_center@iabc.com
Web: www.iabc.com

International Women's Writing Guild, The
Box 810, Gracie Station
New York NY 10028-0082
Phone: (212) 737-7536
E-mail: iwwg@iwwg.com
Web: www.iwwg.com/

Island Writers Association (P.E.I.)
PO Box 1204
Charlottetown PE C1A 7M8
Phone: (902) 566-9748 - Fax: (902) 566-9748
E-mail: Creative@peinet.pe.ca

League of Canadian Poets, The
54 Wolseley St., Suite 204
Toronto ON M5T 1A5
Phone: (416) 504-1657 - Fax: (416) 703-0096
E-mail: league@poets.ca
Web: www.poets.ca/

Literary Translators' Association of Canada, The
SB 335 Concordia University
1455, boul. de Maisonneuve ouest
Montréal PQ H3G 1M8
Phone: (514) 848-8702 - Fax: (514) 849-6239
E-mail: ltac@alcor.concordia.ca
Web: www.geocities.com/Athens/Oracle/9070/

Manitoba Writers' Guild Inc.
#206 100 Arthur St.
Winnipeg MB R3B 1H3
Phone: (204) 942-6134 - Fax: (204) 942-5754
E-mail: mbwriter@mts.net
Web: www.mbwriter.mb.ca/

Mystery Writers of America
17 E. 47th St., 6th Floor
New York NY 10017
Phone: (212) 888-8171 - Fax: (212) 888-8107
E-mail: mwa_org@earthlink.net
Web: mysterywriters.org/

National Writers Union, The
873 Broadway, #203
New York NY 10003
Phone: (212) 254-0279 - Fax: (212) 254-0673
E-mail: nwu@nwu.org
Web: www.nwu.org

Ottawa Independent Writers
PO Box 23137
Ottawa ON K2A 4E2
Phone: (613) 841-0572
E-mail: oiw@storm.ca

Outdoor Writers of Canada
10 Sugar Maple Street
Kitchener ON N2N 1X5
E-mail: lfridenburg@outdoorwritersofcanada.com
Web: www.inside-outdoors.com/

PEI Writers' Guild
115 Richmond Street, Box 1
Charlottetown PE C1A 1H7
Phone: (902) 961-2345
E-mail: brinklow@upei.ca

Pen International, Canadian Centre
#309 – 24 Ryerson Ave.
Toronto ON M5T 2P3
Phone: (416) 703-8448 - Fax: (416) 703-0826
E-mail: pencan@web.apc.org
Web: www.pencanada.ca

Periodical Writers Association of Canada
54 Wolseley St., Suite 203
Toronto ON M5T 1A5
Phone: (416) 504-1645 - Fax: (416) 703-0059
E-mail: pwac@web.net
Web: www.pwac.ca

Playwrights Union of Canada
54 Wolseley St., 2nd Floor
Toronto ON M5T 1A5
Phone: (416) 703-0201 - Fax: (416) 703-0059
E-mail: info@puc.ca
Web: www.puc.ca

Poetry Society of America
15 Gramercy Park
New York NY 10003
Phone: (212) 254-9628
E-mail: eve@poetrysociety.org
Web: www.poetrysociety.org/

Poets & Writers
72 Spring St., Rm. 301
New York NY 10012

Phone: 212) 226-3586 - Fax: (212) 226-3963
E-mail: info@pw.org
Web: www.pw.org/about.htm

Quebec Writers' Federation
3 – 1200 avenue Atwater
Montreal PQ H3Z 1X4
Phone: (514) 934-2485
E-mail: qspell@total.net
Web: www.qwf.org

Romance Writers of America
3707 FM 1960 W. Suite 555
Houston TX 77068
Phone: (281) 440-6885 - Fax: (281) 440-7510
E-mail: info@rwanational.com
Web: www.rwanational.com
Note: Canadian chapters in Vancouver, Manitoba, Atlantic Canada, Toronto, Ottawa, Vancouver Island.

Saskatchewan Publishers Group
#100 2505 11th Avenue
Regina SK S4P 0K6
Phone: (306) 780-9808 - Fax: (306) 780-9810
E-mail: bniskala@saskpublishers.sk.ca
Web: www.saskpublishers.sk.ca

Saskatchewan Writers Guild
PO Box 3986
Regina SK S4P 3R9
Phone: (306) 791-7740 - Fax: (306) 565-8554
E-mail: swg@sasktel.net
Web: www.skwriter.com

Science Fiction and Fantasy Writers of America
PO Box 877
Chesterton MD 21620
Phone: (410) 778-3052
E-mail: execdir@sfwa.org
Web: www.sfwa.org

SF Canada
106 Cocksfield Ave.

Toronto ON M3H 3T2
E-mail: micigold@sympatico.ca
Web: www.sfcanada.ca/

Sisters in Crime
PO Box 442124
Lawrence KS 66044-8933
Phone: (785) 842-1325
E-mail: sistersincrime@juno.com
Web: www.sistersincrime.org

Society of American Travel Writers
1500 Sunday Drive, Suite 102
Raleigh NC 27607
Phone: (919) 787-5181
E-mail: nshore@satw.org
Web: www.satw.org

Society of American Travel Writers – Canadian Chapter
135 Crescent Road
Toronto ON M4W 1TB
Phone: (416) 925-9286 - Fax: (416) 925-0116
E-mail: gdhall@astral.magic.ca
Web: www.satw.ca

Society of Children's Book Writers and Illustrators
8271 Beverly Blvd.
Los Angeles CA 90048
Phone: (323) 782-1010 - Fax: (323) 782-1892
E-mail: scbwi@scbwi.org
Web: www.scbwi.org

Society of Graphic Designers of Canada, BC
ArtsCourt – 2 Daly Avenue
Ottawa ON K1N 6E2
Phone: (877) 496-4453 or (613) 567-5400 - Fax: (613) 564-4428
E-mail: info@gdc.net
Web: www.gdc.net/

Society of Professional Journalists
3909 N. Meridian St.
Indianapolis IN 46208
Phone: (317) 927-8000 - Fax: (317) 920-4789

E-mail: questions@spj.org
Web: www.spj.org

Union des écrivaines et des écrivains québécois
3492 avenue Laval
Montreal QC H2X 3C8
Phone: (514) 849-8540 - Fax: (514) 849-6239
Web: www.uneq.qc.ca/

Victoria Writers Society
E-mail: poetic@telus.net
Web: www3.bc.sympatico.ca/poeticart/vws/

West Coast Book Prize Society
#902 – 207 West Hastings Street
Vancouver BC V6B 1H7
Phone: (604) 687-2405 - Fax: (604) 669-3701
E-mail: info@rebuscreative.net

Western Writers of America
1012 Fair St.
Franklin TN 37064-2718
Phone: (615) 791-1444
E-mail: webmaster@westernwriters.org
Web: www.westernwriters.org

Writers' Alliance of Newfoundland & Labrador
155 Water Street, Suite 102, Box 2681
St John's NF A1C 5M5
Phone: (709) 739-5215 - Fax: (709) 739-5931
E-mail: wanl@nfld.com
Web: www.writersalliance.nf.ca/writers.html

Writers' Federation of New Brunswick
PO Box 37, Station A
Fredericton NB E3B 4Y2
Phone: (506) 453-1366 - Fax: (506) 459-7228

Writers' Federation of Nova Scotia
1809 Barrington St., Ste. 901
Halifax NS B3J 3K8
Phone: (902) 423-8116 - Fax: (902) 422-0881
Web: www.writers.ns.ca/

Writers Guild of Alberta (Calgary)
#305, 223–12 Ave. S.W.
Calgary AB  T2R 0G9
Phone: (403) 269-8844
Web: www.writersguild.ab.ca/

Writers Guild of Alberta (Edmonton)
11759 Groat Rd., 3rd Fl.
Edmonton AB  T5M 3K6
Phone: (403) 422-8174 - Fax: (403) 422-2663
Web: www.writersguild.ab.ca/

Writers Guild of America
7000 W. Third St.
Los Angeles CA  90048
Phone: (800) 548-4532
E-mail: info@wga.org
Web: www.wga.org

Writers Guild of Canada
1225 – 123 Edward Street
Toronto ON  M5G 1E2
Phone: (800) 567-9974 - Fax. (416) 979-9273
E-mail: info@wgc.ca
Web: www.writersguildofcanada.com

Writers in Electronic Residence
300 – 317 Adelaide St. W.
Toronto ON  M5V 1P9
Phone: (416) 504-4490 - Fax: (416) 591-5345
E-mail: wier@wier.ca
Web: www.wier.ca

Writers' Trust of Canada, The
40 Wellington Street East, Suite 300
Toronto ON  M5E 1C7
Phone: (416) 504-8222 - Fax: (416) 504-9090
E-mail: info@writerstrust.com
Web: www.writerstrust.com/

Writers' Union of Canada, The
24 Ryerson Ave.
Toronto ON  M5T 2P3

Phone: (416) 703-8982 - Fax: (416) 703-0826
E-mail: info@writersunion.ca
Web: www.writersunion.ca

Writers' Union of Canada, The (Vancouver Chapter)
3102 Main St., 3rd Fl.
Vancouver BC V4A 3C7
Phone: (604) 874-1611 - Fax: (604) 874-1611
E-mail: twucpacific@shaw.ca
Web: www.writersunion.ca

—

Jennifer Crump is a freelance journalist whose work has recently appeared in *Reader's Digest*, *Canadian Geographic*, *Today's Parent*, *Writer's Digest* and *Worth*. She is also the author of the recently released Frommer's *Toronto with Kids* (Wiley, 2001). Jennifer lives in northeastern Ontario.

# Awards and Fellowships

*by Gill Foss*

The following list is a selection of the Awards and Fellowships available for writers in Canada, verified at the time of publication. As these are subject to change, it is best to verify the details before submitting material for consideration.

**Ruth Schwartz Awards for Children's Literature**

Guidelines: The writers and illustrators must be Canadian citizens or landed immigrants and the book published in Canada. The award is unique in that the juries for each category are made up of children chosen from a different school in Ontario each year.

*There is no application process*. A panel of children's booksellers selects two shortlists of five young adult and five picture books from children's trade books published in the previous year and generally sold in bookstores. The winners are announced in April; the awards are presented at the Canadian Booksellers Association annual trade book fair in the early summer.
Prizes: $3,000 (shared writer/illustrator of picture book); $2,000 to author of young adult book. Deadline: To be announced.

For further information contact:
Ontario Arts Council
181 Bloor Street West
Toronto ON  M5S 1T6
Phone: (416) 969-7450 - Fax: (416) 961-7796
E-mail: info@arts.on.ca

**Anne Szumigalski Editor's Prize**

Guidelines: The Anne Szumigalski Editor's Prize is an annual award for the best poem or group of poems published each year in *Grain*. Poets will automatically be eligible for the prize when their poems are published in the magazine. The *Grain* Editor and the Poetry Editor will decide on the winner. The prize will be awarded in April.
Prize: $500. Entry fee: None. Deadline: n/a.

For further information contact:
*Grain* magazine
PO Box 67
Saskatoon SK  S7K 3K1
Phone: (306) 244-2828 - Fax: (306) 244-0255
E-mail: grain.mag@sk.sympatico.ca
Web: www.skwriter.com/grain

**Confederation Poets Prize**

Guidelines: The Confederation Poets Prize is a contributor's award given to the best poem published in the two annual issues of *Arc: Canada's National Poetry Magazine* from the previous calendar year. Only those poems published in those issues will be considered; therefore no other poems may be entered. The winning poem and its author are announced in *Arc*'s Summer issue.
Prize: $100. Entry fee: None. Deadline: n/a.

For further information contact:
*Arc* Poetry Society
PO Box 7219
Ottawa ON  K1L 8E4
E-mail: arc.poetry@cyberus.ca
Web: www.cyberus.ca/~arc.poetry

**The Lina Chartrand Memorial Award**

Guidelines: The award is given for best poetry by an emerging woman poet whose submission was printed in the previous year's issues of *Contemporary Verse 2*, as selected by the editors. All poetry submissions printed in *CV2* from the previous year are considered. Winner is usually selected in June, and prize sent in September.
Prize: Approx. $250–$300 provided by the Lina Chartrand Memorial Fund. Entry fee: None. Deadline: n/a.

For further information contact:
*Contemporary Verse 2*
207–100 Arthur Street
Winnipeg MB  R3B 1H3

**Marian Engel Award**

Guidelines: Honours female Canadian writers in mid-career. Juried by three Canadian writers (including a past winner). Announcement date and location: March.
Prize: $10,000. Deadline/submission process: n/a.

For further information contact:
The Writers' Trust of Canada

40 Wellington St. E., Ste. 300
Toronto ON M5E 1C7
Phone: (416) 504-8222 - Fax: (416) 504-9090
E-mail: info@writerstrust.com
Web: www.writerstrust.com

**Southam Fellowships for Journalists**

Guidelines: Open to full-time news or editorial employees with at least five years experience. Freelance journalists who have been working consistently in the media over a five-year period will also be considered. Tenable for one academic year, Sept.–May, at the University of Toronto. No credit or degree is granted.
Prize: Eight months salary to a maximum of $4,900/month, all university fees and travel expenses for Fellow and family to and from Toronto.

For further information contact:
Southam Fellowships for Journalists
Attn: Anna Luengo
Massey College
4 Devonshire Place
Toronto ON M5S 2E1
Phone: (416) 978-6606 - Fax: (416) 971-3032
E-mail: southam.fellowships@utoronto.ca
Web: www.utoronto.ca/massey/southamfellowships

**The Alcuin Society Citation Awards**

Guidelines: Books published in Canada during the previous year are eligible for submission. Each title must represent the exclusive work of a Canadian book designer. Publishers may submit as many books in as many categories as they wish. Only limited editions will be returned. Each book should be assigned to a category that must be specified with each entry. Judging is based on the suitability of design concept in relation to the intellectual nature of the content and the intended audiences. Use of colour, type, and illustration and photography styles when applicable are also considered. The stock used in the text block, the binding, covering, and overall finish are judged in the context of the book's purpose. Entry form required. Publishers of winning entries will be requested to submit additional copies to allow for exhibition commitments.
Categories are: Prose – fiction; prose – nonfiction; prose – nonfiction – illustrated; poetry; pictorial; children's; reference (how-to, DIY, cooking, travel); limited editions.
Prizes: 1st; 2nd; 3rd place hand-calligraphed certificates (plus national exposure). Honourable mentions may be awarded. Entry fee: $15/book

as a cheque or money order payable to the Alcuin Society. Deadline: March 15.

For further information contact:
Alcuin Book Design Awards
Benwell-Atkins Ltd.
Attention: Jennifer Weber
901 Great Northern Way
Vancouver BC V5T 1E1
Phone/Fax: (604) 733-6484
E-mail: yandle@interchange.ubc.ca
Web: www.alcuinsociety.com

### Greg Clark Internship Award

Guidelines: Open to working journalists employed by newspapers, magazines, radio, television, news services and electronic news operations. Freelance journalists whose primary source of income comes from photographing, writing or editing news are also eligible. The selection committee is looking for innovative proposals from journalists interested in expanding their knowledge of key issues with the aim of promoting better journalism. The Greg Clark Internships are innovative professional development opportunities offering working journalists a chance to gain insight and meet key decision-makers in a sector or issue they regularly cover. The successful applicant(s) will get a chance to spend several days behind the scenes as a "fly on the wall" observing the inner workings of an organization. Please contact the CJF for further submission information.
Award: An internship. Deadline: March 15.

For further information contact:
Canadian Journalism Foundation
117 Peter St., Third Floor
Toronto ON M5V 2G9
Phone: (416) 955-0394 - Fax: (416) 955-0394.
E-mail: cjf@on.aibn.com

### The Atkinson Fellowship in Public Policy

Guidelines: Open to full-time Canadian journalists in any of the print or broadcast media, either English or French. The successful candidate will pursue a year-long research project on a topical policy issue and publish the results as a series of newspaper articles which the journalist is then free to develop into a book. Application form required. For complete details check website.

Award: A $75,000 stipend and may receive up to $25,000 for research expenses. Deadline: March 18.

For further information contact:
Elizabeth Chan, Coordinator
Atkinson Fellowship Committee
One Yonge Street, Suite 1508
Toronto ON M5E 1E5
Phone: (416) 869-4034
E-mail: echan@thestar.ca

### Sheldon M. Chumir Foundation for Ethics in Leadership Media Fellowships

Guidelines: Open to staff or freelance journalists working in print or electronic media or in an academia for a 3–4 month Fellowship working full-time on a project related to the theme of ethics in leadership. It is expected that appropriate background work will have been completed prior to taking up the fellowship so that, by the end of the period, the Fellow will produce a publishable paper, a series of articles or broadcasts on the project topic, and will provide several days consulting to the Foundation. Stipend for the Fellowship period will be $5,500 CDN per month plus an amount for research expenses not to exceed $5,000 CDN in total. In the case of regularly employed applicants, the recipient's employer will continue to pay the employer's portion of any benefits during the fellowship period. Application requirements available on the website. Deadline: March 22.

For further information contact:
Sheldon M. Chumir Foundation for Ethics in Leadership
Media Fellowships
200, 850 – 16th Avenue Southwest
Calgary AB T2R 0S9
Phone: (403) 244-6666 - Fax: (403) 244-5596
E-mail: mediafellow@chumirethicsfoundation.ca
Web: www.chumirethicsfoundation.calgary.ab.ca/pages/mediafellow.html

### The Pierre Berton Award

Guidelines: Open to individuals or organizations that have helped broaden the reach of Canadian history, through such means as publications, film, radio and television, theatre or volunteer service. In addition to the name and address of the nominee, nominations must be accompanied by detailed information in support of the candidate. A biography or curriculum vitae, newspaper or magazine articles, or letters of support outlining the achievements of the nominee would be welcome. There is no nomination form.

Prize: $5,000 and a medal. Entry fee: n/a. Deadline: May 24.

For further information contact:
Canada's National History Society
478 – 167 Lombard Avenue
Winnipeg MB R3B 0T6
Phone: (204) 988-9300 - Fax: (204) 988-9309
E-mail: cnhs@historysociety.ca
Web: www.beavermagazine.ca

—

Gill Foss is a freelance journalist and an award-winning poet whose work has appeared in several anthologies. She is National President of the Canadian Authors Association, a professional member of the Periodical Writers Association of Canada and an Associate member of the Editors Association.

# Canadian Contests for Writers

*by Gill Foss*

The following listings cover only those contests and awards offered in Canada. All information has been checked for accuracy at time of publication but may change without notice due to relocation, market fluctuations and sponsorship cutbacks.

Although this section includes many more entries than the previous edition of *The Canadian Writer's Guide* it in no way represents all available contests or awards. Sources carrying updated information include *Quill & Quire* magazine, E. Russell Smith's CanLit Contests listing at www.ncf.ca/~ab297/contests.html, many other websites and bulletin boards, and the reference section in public libraries.

The information included for each listing does not necessarily carry the full entry requirements due to space limitations. In all cases requesting a complete set of rules would avoid disqualification due to failure to comply with all criteria.

Common submission information:

- Entries must be typed or sent as computer/word processor printouts.
- Paper should be standard 8.5" x 11" (or metric equivalent).
- Prose submissions should be double-spaced, single-sided.
- Poetry submissions single-sided but spacing/formatting at discretion of the poet.
- Title should be repeated on top of each page subsequent to title page.
- Pages should be numbered consecutively.
- Entry fee must be included with submission as cheque or money order.
- Multiple entries usually require multiples of the entry fee.
- Deadline date is usually "as postmarked."
- One-time publication rights only granted (if applicable).
- Copyright remains with contestant.

- "Blind judging" means manuscripts must be anonymous. Entrant's name, address, phone number, e-mail address, word count and titles/categories of submission should be included on a separate sheet enclosed with the material entered.
- SASE (self-addressed, stamped envelope) must be included if requesting further information, winners' list etc.
- UNESCO definition of a book: 48 pages of literary content excluding front and back material. Chapbooks do not meet this standard.
- All contests/awards listed are offered annually unless otherwise stated.
- Prize money won should be included in taxable writing income that can be set against related expenses. Awards named on a résumé increase a professional profile.

Beware: Occasionally, contests offer prizes for amateur contributions but send back non-winning entries saying the piece (usually poetry) will be included in a proposed deluxe (expensive) anthology if the author agrees to purchase a copy. Make sure you think the benefit is worth the expense.

## Open or Variable Deadlines.

### Poems of the Month

Guidelines: No limits but poetry only.
Entry fee: $1 for up to four poems. Deadline: Ongoing. Prize: Publication online.

For more information contact:
*Prairie Journal*
PO Box 61203
Brentwood PO
Calgary AB T2L 2K6
Web: www.geocities.com/prairiejournal

### Barclay Prize for Writing ... Brief Moments in Time

Guidelines: Open to previously unpublished prose poems and postcard stories. Maximum word limit is 500.
Entry fee: $10. Deadline: Call for information. Prizes: $100; $50; $25.

For more information contact:
Canadian Mental Health Association (Saskatchewan Division) Inc.
2702 12th Ave.
Regina SK S4T 1J2
Phone: (306) 525-5601 - Fax: (306) 569-3788

E-mail: cmhask@accesscomm.ca
Web: www.cmhask.com

**The Great Canadian Story Contest**

Guidelines: Open to Canadian citizens or writers resident in Canada for original works of short fiction between 2,000 and 6,000 words containing a uniquely Canadian element (theme, setting, history, institution, politics, social phenomenon, etc.). Genre fiction is welcome. Stories judged on literary merit and entertainment value. Type the word count, your name, address, and phone number in the upper left-hand corner of the first page. No simultaneous or e-mail submissions.
Entry fee: $5 (may change). Make cheque/money order to: Tyo Communications. Deadline: Varies. See website for details, or send SASE. Prize(s): Vary with sponsorship.

For more information contact:
*Storyteller, Canada's Short Story Magazine*
858 Wingate Dr.
Ottawa ON  K1G 1S5
Phone: We do not accept telephone or fax queries.
E-mail: info@storytellermagazine.com
Web: www.storytellermagazine.com

**John V. Hicks Memorial Award**

Guidelines: Open to Saskatchewan-resident writers for a manuscript of poetry that exemplifies the spirit and skill of the late Price Albert author. We strongly suggest that those interested read John V. Hicks' work before submitting to ensure that this criteria is met. Manuscripts must be marked as submissions to this award, and include a CV, publishing history, and SASE. If no manuscript is found suitable the award will be deferred to the next publishing year.
Entry fee: None. Deadline: Open. Prize: Manuscript published in book form.

For more information contact:
Thistledown Press
Jesse Stothers
633 Main St.
Saskatoon SK  S7H 0J8
Phone: (306) 244-1722 - Fax: (306) 244-1762
E-mail: edit@thistledown.sk.ca
Web: www.thistledown.sk.ca

### Canadian Political Science Association Awards/ Prix de l'Association canadienne de science politique

Guidelines: For all contest information see website.
Entry fee: None. Deadlines: See website. Prizes: Various: Donald Smiley Prize; C.B. Macpherson Prize; Vincent Lemieux Prize; John McMenemy Prize.

For more information contact:
Canadian Political Science Association/
Association canadienne de science politique
#204 – 260 rue Dalhousie St.
Ottawa ON K1N 7E4
Phone: (613) 562-1202 - Fax: (613) 241-0019
E-mail: cpsa@csse.ca
Web: www.cpsa-acsp.ca

## January Deadlines.

### The John Hirsch Award for Most Promising Manitoba Writer

Guidelines: Open to Manitoba writers of poetry, fiction, creative non-fiction and drama. Eligible authors will have been resident in Manitoba for three of the last five years as well as one of the past two years. A jury of senior members of the Manitoba writing and publishing community will make the selection.
Entry fee: None. Deadline: January. Prize: $2,500

For more information contact:
Winnipeg Arts Advisory Council
207 – 180 Market Ave.
Winnipeg MB R3B 0P7
Phone: (204) 942-6134 - Fax: (204) 942-5754
E-mail: mbwriter@escape.ca
Web: n/a

### Western Ontario Newspaper Awards

Guidelines: Open to reporters and photographers of 31 participating member papers in Ontario.
Entry fee: None (member papers contribute based on circulation figures). Deadline: First week of January. Prizes: $100 in 35 categories. $500 each to Journalist and Photojournalist of the Year.

For more information contact:
Western Ontario Newspaper Awards
225 Fairway Rd. S.

Kitchener ON  N2G 4E5
Phone: (519) 894-2231 - Fax: (519) 894-3829
E-mail/Web: n/a

**The Carol Shields Winnipeg Book Award**

Guidelines: Open to books that evoke the special character of and contribute to the appreciation and understanding of the City of Winnipeg. Entries must be published between January 1 and December 31 of the award year. There is no residency requirement.
Entry fee: $25 per title (with 5 copies of book). Deadline: January (to be confirmed). Prize: $5,000 to author, certificate to publisher.

Winnipeg Arts Advisory Council
207 – 180 Market Avenue
Winnipeg MB  R3B 0P7
Phone: (204) 943-7668 - Fax: (204) 942-8669
E-mail: waac@escape.ca
Web: n/a

**Annual National Magazine Awards (over 30 categories)**

Guidelines: Magazine publishers, editors or freelancers may submit articles published in previous year. Editors are encouraged to make submissions on behalf of writers. For more information visit the website or e-mail Pat Kendall, Executive Director, National Magazine Awards Foundation.
Entry fee: $50 per entry payable to the National Magazine Awards Foundation. Deadline: January 14. Prizes: Gold awards $1,500; silver $500. President's Medal worth $3,000 awarded to an article considered "best of the show."

For more information contact:
Annual National Magazine Awards
109 Vanderhoof Avenue, Suite 207
Toronto ON  M4G 2H7
Phone: (416) 422-1358 - Fax: (416) 422-3762
E-mail: nmaf@interlog.com
Web: info.sources.com/fandf/fandf59.htm

**ReLit Awards for Novel, Short Fiction and Poetry**

Guidelines: Open to Canadian authors only. Books must have been written by Canadian authors while living in Canada and published between January 1 and December 31 in the preceding year. There is no limit on entries submitted by any one publisher. Send 4 copies of each book. Organizers of the ReLit Awards will not be eligible.

Entry fee: None. Deadline: January 15 (but sooner if possible). Prize: $1 and a specially designed, handmade ceramic award for each category.

For more information contact:
ReLit Awards
Burnt Head
Cupids NF  A0A 2B0
E-mail: ReLit@canada.com
Web: n/a

**Canadian Authors Association Conference Prize**

Guidelines: Open to Canadian citizens or residents of more than five years standing, over 18 years of age. Send a previously unpublished and un-contracted short story of 1,000-1,500 words. The prize is the opportunity to attend a stimulating conference of workshops and seminars on many aspects of writing. All expenses incurred, with the exception of food, drink, gifts and other non-conference expenses, will be reimbursed on presentation of receipts to a total of $1,500. Should the amount claimed be less than $1,500, the difference will be presented as a cheque. The winner is expected to make his/her own travel and accommodation arrangements. See website for complete information.
Entry fee: $20/non-members; $15/members (may change). Deadline: January 15. Prize: $1,500 to cover conference expenses, a public reading of story and Web publication.

For more information contact:
Canadian Authors Association
320 South Shores Road
PO Box 419
Campbellford ON  K0L 1L0
Phone: (705) 653-0323 - Fax: (705) 653-0593
Toll-free: 1-866-216-6222
E-mail: canauth@redden.on.ca
Web: www.CanAuthors.org

**The Writers' Trust of Canada/McClelland & Stewart Journey Prize**

Guidelines: Open to Canadian literary publications. Entries submitted directly by authors not accepted. Each eligible publication may submit up to three stories or excerpts from fiction works in progress written by a Canadian citizen or landed immigrant to Canada. See website for complete guidelines.
Entry fee: None. Deadline: Mid-January. Prizes: $10,000 to the winning

short story, and $2,000 to the Canadian literary journal that first published the winning story.

For more information contact:
McClelland & Stewart
481 University Avenue, Suite 900
Toronto ON M5G 2E9
Phone: (416) 598-1114 (ext. 341) - Fax: (416) 598-7764
E-mail: journeyprize@mcclelland.com
Web: www.mcclelland.com/jpa

**The Maeve Award for Nonfiction**

Guidelines: Alternates annually with Cecily Rose Award for Fiction (below). Open to essay(s) on personal experience; women's experiences in society, either contemporary or herstoric based on auto/biographical research. Length 100–250 pages, typewritten, double-spaced. Hardcopy only. May comprise one essay or collection.
Entry fee: $20. Deadline: January 15 (odd number years). Prize: $100 plus publication.

For more information contact:
Ride The Wind Publishing
PO Box 965, Stn. A
Campbell River BC V9W 6Y4
Phone: n/a - Fax: (250) 830-1447
E-mail: admin@ridewind.com
Web: www.ridewind.com

**Cecily Rose Award for Fiction**

Guidelines: Alternates annually with The Maeve Award for Nonfiction (above). Open to novels, short story collections. Length 100-250 pages, typewritten, double-spaced. Hardcopy only. Genres: adventure, a good yarn, whimsey, suspense, mystery, herstory, science fiction, contemporary. The central hero(s) must be a woman of courage and humour. She can confront adversity/change using her own wits. Manuscripts not returned.
Entry fee: $20. Deadline: January 15 (even years). Prize: $100 plus publication.

For more information contact:
Ride The Wind Publishing
PO Box 965 Stn. A
Campbell River BC V9W 6Y4
Phone: n/a - Fax: (250) 830-1447

E-mail: admin@ridewind.com
Web: www.ridewind.com

**Poetic Licence Contest for Canadian Youth**

Guidelines: Open to young poets writing in either English or French. First prize national winners in each language and age category will have their winning poems printed on National Poetry Month Posters. Over 10,000 copies distributed across the country and internationally for display during April (National Poetry Month). Check website for complete guidelines.
Entry fee: None. Deadline: January 15. Prizes: Change each year. Check website.

For more information contact:
League of Canadian Poets
54 Wolseley St.
Toronto ON M5T 1A5
Phone: (416) 504-1657 - Fax: (416) 504-0096
E-mail: league@ican.net
Web: www.poets.ca or www.youngpoets.ca

**The Bronwen Wallace Award**

Guidelines: Open to Canadian citizens or landed immigrants, under the age of 35, as yet unpublished in book form and without a book contract, but whose work must have appeared in at least one independently edited magazine or anthology. Alternates each year in the genres of poetry and short fiction. (Odd years–fiction).
Entry fee: None. Deadline: January 15. Prize: $1,000.

For more information contact:
The Writers' Trust of Canada
40 Wellington St. E., Suite 300
Toronto ON M5E 1C7
Phone: (416) 504-8222 - Fax: (416) 504-9090
E-mail: info@writers.trust.com
Web: www.writerstrust.com

**Ottawa Book Award/Prix du Livre d'Ottawa**

Guidelines: Open to books by Ottawa area authors published in English or French in the preceding two years. The contest alternates between Fiction (including Poetry) and Nonfiction. The contest for 2003 is for Fiction and Poetry.
Entry fee: None. Deadline: January 20. Prizes: $2,500 prize awarded to both an English and French author.

For more information contact:
Faith Seltzer
Office of Cultural Affairs
110 Laurier Avenue West
Ottawa ON K1P 1J1
Phone: (613) 580-2424 (ext. 27412)
E-mail: Faith.Seltzer@city.ottawa.on.ca
Web: www.city.Ottawa.on.ca

### Edward Goff Penny Memorial Prizes for Young Canadian Journalists

Guidelines: Journalists aged 20 to 25 may submit examples of their work from the previous year in each of two circulation categories: under 25,000 and over 25,000. Four senior editors judge for style, interest, persuasiveness and originality.
Entry fee: None. Deadline: January 25. Prizes: $3,000 for each category.

For more information contact:
Penny Prizes
Canadian Newspaper Association
890 Yonge Street, Suite 200
Toronto ON M4W 3P4
Phone: (416) 923-3567 - Fax: (416) 923-7206.
E-mail: n/a
Web: www.cna-acj.ca/penny/

### National Capital Writing Contest

Guidelines: Open to writers in the National Capital Region writing in English for original, unpublished work of the author. Contest alternates annually prose/poetry. Prose categories (2003): Article; Adult Short Story; Juvenile Short Story. Maximum 2,500 words. Poetry categories (2004): Free Verse (to 42 lines); Traditional, structured poem; Haiku (three haiku = one entry). Unlimited entries. Blind judging. If multiple entries sent, only one envelope is necessary.
Entry fee: Poetry $3/entry (members 1 free, more $2); Prose $5/entry (members 1 free, more $3). Deadline: January 30. Prizes: $100 (cheque); $50; $25 (bookstore gift certificates).

For more information contact:
Ottawa Branch
Canadian Authors Association
Phone: (613) 829-8220 - Fax: (613) 829-4616
E-mail: gillfoss@attcanada.ca (information only)
Web: pending.

### New Muse Award

Guidelines: Open to Canadian writers without a first short story collection or novel published. The New Muse Manuscript award is looking for book-length fiction manuscripts.
Entry fee: $20. Cheque/money order payable to Broken Jaw Press. Deadline: January 30. Prize: $500 and trade publication.

For more information contact:
Broken Jaw Press
PO Box 596, Station A
Fredericton NB E3B 5A6
Phone/fax: (506) 454-5127
E-mail: jblades@nbnet.nb.ca
Web: www.brokenjaw.com/newmuse.htm

### Archibald Lampman Award

Guidelines: Open to a book of poems published in the previous calendar year by a poet living in the National Capital Region. Submit three copies of eligible books (at least 48 pages). No books are returned. Award presented at Ottawa Book Awards ceremony in April.
Entry fee: None. Deadline: January 31. Prize: $500.

For more information contact:
*Arc* Poetry Society
PO Box 7219
Ottawa ON K1L 8E4
E-mail: arc.poetry@cyberus.ca
Web: www.cyberus.ca/~arc.poetry

### Annual Acrostic Story Contest

Guidelines: Entries must begin with a given opening, different each year, assigned by The Brucedale Press, and follow in 26 sentences the English alphabet. TWO copies, one with entry form attached, the other unidentified, to be sent by postal mail only. Full guidelines by e-mail, on our website, or by request with SASE. Opening words will be announced in our Fall newsletters.
Entry fee: $5/story. Deadline: January 31. Prizes: First – 25% of entry fees; Second – 15%; Third – 10% and up to three Honourable Mentions. All winners published in *The Leaf* newsletter.

For more information contact:
The Brucedale Press
PO Box 2259
Port Elgin ON N0H 2C0
Phone: (519) 832-6025

E-mail: brucedale@bmts.com
Web: www.bmts.com/~brucedale

**Short Grain Writing Contest**

Guidelines: Categories — Dramatic Monologue: Self-contained speech by single character to 500 words. Postcard Story: A work of narrative fiction up to 500 words. Prose Poem: A lyric poem written as a prose paragraph up to 500 words. Long Grain of Truth: A nonfiction creative prose piece up to 5000 words. Entries must be original, unpublished, not submitted elsewhere for publication or broadcast, nor accepted elsewhere for publication or broadcast for which they are also eligible to win a prize.
Entry fee: $22 for two entries in a single category. For an additional $5 you may enter one piece in ANY category of your choice. Cheque/money order payable to Short Grain Contest. U.S. and international entrants must pay in U.S. funds; add $4 postage for a total of $26 for the basic entry fee. Entry fee includes a one-year subscription to *Grain* (4 issues). Deadline: January 31. Prizes: Twelve $500 prizes (three prizes in four categories) and publication in the fall issue of *Grain*.

For more information contact:
*Grain* magazine
PO Box 67
Saskatoon SK  S7K 3K1
Phone: (306) 244-2828 - Fax: (306) 244-0255
E-mail: grain.mag@sk.sympatico.ca
Web: www.skwriter.com/grain

**Last Poems Poetry Contest**

Guidelines: Maximum of 4 poems per entry. Submissions not limited in topic or subject.
Entry fee: $15 (includes 1-year, 3-issue subscription). Deadline: January 31. Prize: $250 cash and publication in the spring issue of *sub-Terrain* magazine.

For more information contact:
*sub-Terrain* Magazine
PO Box 3008, MPO
Vancouver BC  V6B 3X5
Phone: (604) 876-8710 - Fax: (604) 879-2667
E-mail: subter@portal.ca
Web: www.anvilpress.com/subterrain

### *PRISM international* Annual Short Fiction Contest

Guidelines: Open to original, unpublished material, not under consideration elsewhere. We will purchase first North American serial rights for all work accepted for publication. Entries no longer than 25 pages. No electronic submissions. Contest open to anyone except students or instructors in the Creative Writing Program at the University of British Columbia. Works of translation are eligible. Blind judging. Only the title should appear on each page of the manuscript. Manuscripts not returned.
Entry fee: $22 plus $5 per extra entry (includes 1-year subscription). Out-of-Canada please pay in U.S. funds. Make cheques payable to *PRISM international*. Deadline: January 31. Prize: $2,000 Grand prize; $200 for 5 runners-up and publication at $20/page (or U.S. equivalent).

For more information contact:
*PRISM international*
Creative Writing Program, UBC
Buch. E 462 – 1866 Main Mall
Vancouver BC V6T 1Z1
Phone: (604) 822-2514 - Fax: (604) 822-6616
Web: prism.arts.ubc.ca/

### Mary Buchanan and James McIntyre Award for Unintentional Humour in Canadian Poetry

Guidelines: Entries should be unintentionally humourous (bathetic) poems by Canadian poets.
Entry fee: None. Deadline: January 31. Prize: Publication of poem.

For more information contact:
D.M.R. Bentley, Editor
*Canadian Poetry*, Department of English
University of Western Ontario
London ON N6A 3K7
Phone: (519) 661-3404 - Fax: (519) 661-3776
Web: www.arts.uwo.ca/canpoetry

### Danuta Gleed Literary Award

Guidelines: Open to first collections of short fiction in the English language by a Canadian published in the previous calendar year. Winners announced on Canada Book Day. Send 4 copies of book along with a cover page outlining author, title, and publisher. Contact Penny Dickens, Executive Director, for further information.
Entry fee: None. Deadline: January 31. Prizes: $5000; 2nd and 3rd prizes $500.

For more information contact:
The Writers Union of Canada
40 Wellington Street, Third Floor
Toronto ON M5E 1C7
Phone: (416) 703-8982 (ext. 221)
E-mail: twuc@the-wire.com
Web: www.writersunion.ca

## February

### Aventis Pasteur Medal for Excellence in Health Research Journalism

Guidelines: Open to reporting of health research in print form. Articles must be published in Canadian newspapers or magazines during the previous calendar year. Entries may be submitted directly by journalists or recommended by others (e.g. editors, colleagues, scientific societies, or the public) and should include the article to be judged (one original exactly as it appeared in the publication and four copies with name, publication, and date removed to ensure anonymity); evidence of publication; applicant's name, title, mailing address, phone/fax numbers, and e-mail address.
Entry fee: None. Deadline: February 22. Prize: $2,500 bursary and medal.

For more information contact:
Canadians for Health Research
PO Box 126
Westmount PQ H3Z 2T1
Phone: (514) 398-7478 - Fax: (514) 398-8361
E-mail: info@chrcrm.org
Web: www.chrcrm.org

### The Capital Crime Writers Mystery Short Story

Guidelines: Open to CCW members and residents of the National Capital Region only. Story must be an original short crime fiction in English to a maximum of 3,500 words. Limit one story per person. Prizes will be awarded at the Ottawa Literary Awards ceremony in April.
Entry fee: $5 (includes 1-year subscription to *Storyteller* magazine). Make cheque payable to Capital Crime Writers. Deadline: February (but check each year for minor changes). Prizes: $60 and $50 gift certificate from Grand & Toy; $50; $40.

For more information contact:
Mystery

185 Hopewell Ave.
Ottawa ON K1S 2Z4
E-mail: pikeville@sympatico.ca

**The Hilda Neatby Prize in Women's History**

Guidelines: Open to academic articles published in Canadian journals or books during the previous year and deemed to make an original and scholarly contribution to the field of women's history. Send nominations and 3 copies of the nominated article. See website for details.
Entry fee: None. Deadline: February 1. Prizes: Two prizes of $100 are awarded, one for best article in each official language.

For more information contact:
Canadian Historical Association
c/o The Hilda Neatby Prize Committee
395 Wellington St.
Ottawa ON K1A 0N3
Phone: (613) 233-7885 - Fax: (613) 567-3110
Web: www.cha-shc.ca

**The Larry Turner Award for Nonfiction**

Guidelines: Open to unpublished literary or personal essays, articles, memoirs, travel pieces, etc., in English, to 2,500 words. No limit. Send 2 copies, one with no author identification and one with full identification, including e-mail if applicable. Winners published in *The Grist Mill*, and receive a free contributor's copy plus a 1-year subscription. Bios on request.
Entry fee: $10/entry (includes 1-year subscription to *The Valley Writers' News*). Cheques payable to Valley Writers' Guild. Deadline: First Friday in February. Prizes: Grand Prize — $500 and an engraved plaque; $200/$100 and up to 3 Honourable Mentions of $20 each.

For more information contact:
The Valley Writers' Guild
PO Box 534
Merrickville ON K0G 1N0
E-mail: vwg@storm.ca
Web: www.storm.ca/~vwg

**God Uses Ink Annual Writing Awards**

Guidelines: Categories — novel, nonfiction book, short fiction, personal article/essay, third-person article. Open to writing by Christians with Canadian citizenship only for material published during the previous calendar year from anywhere in the world, in secular or Christian media. See website for full details and entry form.

Entry fee: Set annually. Deadline: Early February. Prizes: Announced annually.

For more information contact:
The Word Guild
PO Box 487
Markham ON L3P 3R1
Phone: (905) 471-1447
E-mail: contest@thewordguild.com
Web: www.thewordguild.com

**Scarborough Arts Council Poetry Contest**

Guidelines: Open to Canadian citizens residing in Canada or landed immigrants able to vote in Canada. Submit up to three poems, typewritten, 30 lines maximum. Send two copies of each poem with the name, address and phone number of the poet in the upper right-hand corner of every page. Mss. not returned.
Entry fee: $15. Deadline: Mid-February (dates may vary slightly). Prize: $250 first prize; three honourable mentions.

For more information contact:
Scarborough Arts Council
1859 Kingston Road
Scarborough ON M1N 1T3
Phone: (416) 698-7322 - Fax: (416) 698-7972
E-mail: programs@scarborougharts.com
Web: www.scarborougharts.com

**Monica Ladell Poetry Prize**

Guidelines: Open only to residents of the Scarborough Region of Toronto. Other rules follow the general category above.
Entry fee: $15. Deadline: Mid-February (dates may vary slightly). Prize: $50.

For more information contact:
Scarborough Arts Council
1859 Kingston Road
Scarborough ON M1N 1T3
Phone: (416) 698-7322 - Fax: (416) 698-7972
E-mail: programs@scarborougharts.com
Web: www.scarborougharts.com

**Youth Prize for Poetry**

Guidelines: Open to youths 13–19 years of age only, residing the Toronto area. Entries must include school attended. Other rules follow the general category above.

Entry fee: $15. Deadline: Mid-February (dates may vary slightly). Prizes: $50; $30; $20

For more information contact:
Scarborough Arts Council
1859 Kingston Road
Scarborough ON M1N 1T3
Phone: (416) 698-7322 - Fax: (416) 698-7972
E-mail: programs@scarborougharts.com
Web: www.scarborougharts.com

**Postcard Story Competition**

Guidelines: Genre is open: poetry, prose, dialogue, etc. Max. 250 words. Entries must be original and unpublished, in English, typed and double-spaced. Include a separate cover letter with name, address, telephone, e-mail, and word count. Blind judging. Entries not returned.
Entry fee: $5, made payable to the Writers' Union of Canada. Deadline: February 14. Prize: $500.

For more information contact:
The Writers' Union of Canada
40 Wellington St. E., 3rd Floor
Toronto ON M5E 1C7
Phone: (416) 703-8982 (ext. 223) - Fax: (416) 506-7656
E-mail: projects@writersunion.ca
Web: www.writersunion.ca

**Writers' Federation of New Brunswick Literary Competition (prose and poetry)**

Guidelines: Open to writers outside the province. Entry must be original, typewritten single-sided and not previously published or submitted elsewhere. Prose (Fiction and Nonfiction): 15 pages double-spaced or 4,000 words. Poetry: A maximum of 100 lines or 5 poems. In the Children's Literature category, poetry submissions must have a minimum of 10 poems (starting in 2003). Name and address of the writer, title of the ms. and category must be attached to the entry on a separate page. Some restrictions apply. Check with WFNB for full details.
Entry fee: $10 (members/students); $15 non-members. Deadline: February 14. Prizes: $150; $75; $50.

For more information contact:
Writers' Federation of New Brunswick
PO Box 37, Station A
Fredericton NB E3B 4Y2
Phone: (506) 459-7228

E-mail: wfnb@nb.aibn.com
Web: www.sjfn.nb.ca/~wfnb/index.htm

### The Richards Prize

Guidelines: Open to collections of short stories, short novels, or a substantial portion of a longer novel (not to exceed 30,000 words). Work must be unpublished although some individual stories may have been previously published. Rules follow those of general WFNB competition above.
Entry fee: $15. Deadline: February 14. Prize: $400.

For more information contact:
Writers' Federation of New Brunswick
PO Box 37, Station A
Fredericton NB E3B 4Y2
Phone: (506) 459-7228
E-mail: wfnb@nb.aibn.com
Web: www.sjfn.nb.ca/~wfnb/index.htm

### The Alfred G. Bailey Prize

Guidelines: Open to poetry manuscript of least 48 pages not previously published, in whole or in part, in book/chapbook form (individual poems published or accepted for publication in periodicals may be included). Number of lines of poetry per page immaterial. Rules follow those of general WFNB competition above.
Entry fee: $15. Deadline: February 14. Prize: $400.

For more information contact:
Writers' Federation of New Brunswick
PO Box 37, Station A
Fredericton NB E3B 4Y2
Phone: (506) 459-7228
E-mail: wfnb@nb.aibn.com
Web: www.sjfn.nb.ca/~wfnb/index.htm

### The Sheree Fitch Prize

Guidelines: Open to youth, 14–18 years of age as of January 1 of the year of the contest. Entries in the 2003 contest will be prose and thereafter will alternate between poetry and fiction. Submit maximum 5 poems or 100 lines in total.
Entry fee: None. Deadline: February 14. Prizes: $150; $100; $50.

For more information contact:
Writers' Federation of New Brunswick
PO Box 37, Station A
Fredericton NB E3B 4Y2

Phone: (506) 459-7228
E-mail: wfnb@nb.aibn.com
Web: www.sjfn.nb.ca/~wfnb/index.htm

**PEI Council of the Arts Awards**

Guidelines: Full guidelines for all awards available from PEI Council of the Arts.

**Milton Acorn Poetry Award**

Guidelines: Open to unpublished work from residents of Prince Edward Island only.
Entry fee: $10. Deadline: February 15. Prizes: $500; $200; $100.

**Sentner Memorial Short Story Award**

Guidelines: Open to unpublished work from residents of PEI only.
Entry fee: $10. Deadline: February 15. Prizes: $500; $200; $100.

**Lucy Maud Montgomery PEI Literature for Children Award**

Guidelines: Open to unpublished work from residents of PEI only.
Entry fee: $10. Deadline: February 15. Prizes: $500; $200; $100.

**Feature Article Award**

Guidelines: Open to published articles by residents of PEI only.
Entry fee: $10. Deadline: February 15. Prizes: $500; $200; $100.

**Cavendish Area Tourist Association Creative Writing Awards for Young People**

Guidelines: Available by e-mail.
Entry fee: None. Deadline: February 15. Prizes: $75; $50; $25 in three categories: High School; Junior High; Elementary.

For more information for above awards contact:
PEI Council of the Arts Awards
115 Richmond St.
Charlottetown PE  C1A 1H7
Phone: (902) 368-4410 - Fax: (902) 368-4418
E-mail: artscouncil@pei.aibn.com

**Arthur Ellis Awards**

Guidelines: Open to first publication of crime fiction or nonfiction, regardless of language, in the preceding year by a writer, regardless of nationality, who is resident in Canada or by a Canadian writer resident abroad. Categories: best crime novel; best first crime novel; best true crime; best juvenile crime fiction; best crime short story; best crime book in the French language; best play; best reference/criticism/anthology.
Entry fee: None. Deadline: Currently February 15 (but may go back to

January 31). Prizes: Arthur Ellis statuette plus cash prizes for best crime novel and best first crime novel.

For more information contact:
Crime Writers of Canada
3007 Kingston Rd.
Toronto ON M1M 1P1
Phone: (416) 597-9938
E-mail: info@crimewriterscanada.com
Web: www.crimewriterscanada.com

**The W.O. Mitchell Literary Prize**

Guidelines: Open to writers who have produced an outstanding body of work, have acted during their careers as "caring mentor" for writers, and have published a work of fiction or had a new stage play produced during the three-year period specified for each competition. Prize is awarded every third year to a writer who works in French.
Entry fee: None. Deadline: February 15. Prize: $15,000.

For more information contact:
The Writers' Trust of Canada
40 Wellington St. E., Suite 300
Toronto ON M5E 1C7
Phone: (416) 504-8222 - Fax: (416) 504-9090
E-mail: info@writers.trust.com
Web: www.writerstrust.com

**Odes of March Poetry Contest**

Guidelines: Open to persons of Christian faith, but poems need not be religious. We encourage poets to write outside religious cliché. The focus here is on the poet — not necessarily the poetry — being Christian. All Entry fees (in excess of basic operating costs) are returned to the entrants as prizes, so prizes listed below are minimum amounts paid. For specific rules visit our site.
Entry fee: $10 per poem (maximum 5). Deadline: February 15. Prizes: $200; $100; three honorable mentions of $25.

For more information contact:
New Leaf Works
121 Morin Maze
Edmonton AB T6K 1V1
Phone: (780) 461-0221
E-mail: newleafworks@snowfaux.com
Web: www.snowfaux.com

### Western Magazine Awards Foundation

Guidelines: Open to magazine publishers, editors, art directors and freelance contributors working in British Columbia, Alberta, Saskatchewan, Manitoba, Yukon and the Northwest Territories in the following categories: Magazine writing, Photography, Illustration and Art direction. Send one cheque or money order for the total number of entries submitted (made payable to the Western Magazine Awards Foundation) with your entries.
Entry fee: $27 (+ GST) if the entry appeared in a magazine with a circulation of 20,000 or less; or $35 (+ GST) if the entry appeared in a magazine with a circulation of more than 20,000. Deadline: February 22. Prizes: All written and visual category winners receive $500. Magazine of the Year and Lifetime Achievement Award winners do not receive a cash prize. All winners receive certificates.

For more information contact:
Web: www.westernmagazineawards.com/

### Tom Fairley Award

Guidelines: Open to both freelance and in-house editors for outstanding contribution to a work published in Canada in English or French during the previous calendar year, with supporting documentation due a week or two later. Open to any type of written project — book, magazine, government or corporate report, software documentation or any other type of editorial work is eligible. Nominees are limited to one submission per year that can comprise a single item or several items from a related series of titles. Self-nominations are encouraged. For detailed submission information check website.
Entry fee: None. Deadline: Late February. Prize: $2,000.

For more information contact:
Editors' Association of Canada
502–27 Carlton St.
Toronto ON  M5B 1L2
Phone: 1-866-CAN-EDIT or (416) 975-1379 - Fax: (416) 975-1637
E-mail: fairley_award@editors.ca
Web: www.editors.ca

### The City of Calgary W.O. Mitchell Book Prize

Guidelines: Open to books published in English or French no later than December 31 of the preceding year by Calgary authors who must have lived in Calgary for a minimum of two years. Eligible work is: fiction; poetry; nonfiction; children's literature and drama. Send four copies of the submission. If there is more than one author chosen, the prize is

divided equally.
Entry fee: None. Deadline: February 28. Prize: $2,000.

For more information contact:
Writers Guild of Alberta Awards Program
Percy Page Centre
11759 Groat Road
Edmonton AB T5M 3K6
Phone: (780) 422-8174 or 1-800-665-5354
E-mail: heather@writersguild.ab.ca
Web: www.writersguild.ca

**The City of Edmonton Book Prize**

Guidelines: Open to books by authors 18 years of age and over on subjects that deal with some aspect of the City of Edmonton — history, geography, current affairs, its arts or its people — or are written by an Edmonton author. Entries may be fiction, nonfiction, poetry or drama written for adults or children and published during the twelve months ending on March 15 of the year preceding the award year. Send 5 copies.
Entry fee: None. Deadline: February 28. Prize: $2,000.

For more information contact:
Writers Guild of Alberta Awards Program
Percy Page Centre
11759 Groat Road
Edmonton AB T5M 3K6
Phone: (780) 422-8174 or 1-800-665-5354
E-mail: heather@writersguild.ab.ca
Web: www.writersguild.ca

**Jon Whyte Memorial Essay Prize**

Guidelines: Open to essays submitted by Alberta residents only. There is no theme. This competition is co-sponsored by the Banff Centre for the Arts and the Writers Guild of Alberta.
Entry fee: None. Deadline: February 28. Prizes: $1,000; two $500 prizes for runners-up.

For more information contact:
Writers Guild of Alberta Awards Program
Percy Page Centre
11759 Groat Road
Edmonton AB T5M 3K6
Phone: (780) 422-8174 or 1-800-665-5354
E-mail: heather@writersguild.ab.ca
Web: www.writersguild.ab.ca

## Best Article on the History of Sexuality in Canada Competition (alternate even years)

Guidelines: Open to scholarly work in the burgeoning field of the history of sexuality in Canada that makes an original contribution to the study of the sexual past from any period in the history of what is now called Canada. Entries may be in English or French. Nominations may be made by faculty, students, editors, publishers or self-nomination. Send three copies of the article. Write for complete requirements.
Entry fee: None. Deadline: February 28. Prize: Not specified.

For more information contact:
The Canadian Committee on the History of Sexuality
c/o Steven Maynard, Department of History
Queen's University
Kingston ON K7L 3N6

## City of Toronto Book Awards

Guidelines: Fiction and nonfiction books published in English for adults/and or children that are evocative of Toronto and are of artistic and literary merit are eligible. Reprints, textbooks and manuscripts are not eligible. There are no separate categories, and all books are judged together. Submit six copies of entry along with name, address, phone, fax, e-mail address.
Entry fee: None. Deadline: February 28. Prizes: $15,000 in prize money. Shortlisted authors (usually four to six) receive $1,000 each. Winner awarded remainder.

For more information contact:
Toronto Book Awards Committee
c/o Toronto Protocol, City Clerk's Office
City Hall, West Tower, 10th Floor
100 Queen Street West
Toronto ON M5H 2N2
Phone: (416) 392-8191 - Fax: (416) 392-1247
E-mail: bkurmey@city.toronto.on.ca
Web: www.city.toronto.on.ca/ourcity/tba_index.htm

## The Open Window Poetry Contest

Guidelines: Open to poems on any theme, any length, any style for an annual international anthology of poetry. Send 3 poems, previously unpublished. See website for full information.
Entry fee: $15 (inc. copy of full colour cover, perfect bound book). Deadline: February 28. Prizes: 10 cash prizes from $100; up to 12 honourable mentions; up to 300 runner-up poems published.

For more information contact:
Hidden Brook Press
412–701 King Street West
Toronto ON M5V 2W7
Phone: (416) 504-3966
E-mail: contestinfo@hiddenbrookpress.com
Web: www.hiddenbrookpress.com

## March

### Best New Writer Prize for Creative Nonfiction

Guidelines: Open to writers whose first publishing credit (outside of a school or university publication) must have been within the last five years and unpublished writers for original, unpublished work to maximum 4,000 words. Submit personal and journalistic pieces in essay form with a strong voice, attention to narrative, experimental styles and, of course, compelling subject matter in a style that combines literature and journalism. Entries present holistic pictures of their subject, using concrete examples and narration to support a thesis and are based on exhaustive research, present subject matter grounded in real-world facts and offer insight into important social, cultural and/or political issues. Multiple entries permitted. Blind judging.
Entry fee: None. Deadline: March 1. Prize: $250.

For more information contact:
*This Magazine* Best New Writer Prize
401 Richmond Street West, Suite 396
Toronto ON M5V 3A8
Phone: (416) 979-8400 - Fax: (416) 979-1143
E-mail: thismag@web.net
Web: www.THISmag.org

### The Malahat Long Poem Contest

Guidelines: Open to a long poem or cycle of poems up to a maximum of 20 pages. Submissions previously published or accepted for publication elsewhere will not be considered. Blind judging. For manuscript return enclose a SASE with sufficient Canadian postage.
Entry fee: $30 (includes 1-year's subscription). Deadline: March 1. (Note: held in alternate years with Malahat Novella Contest.) Prizes: Two prizes of $400 plus payment for publication at our regular rate of $30 per page.

For more information contact:
*The Malahat Review*

The University of Victoria
PO Box 1700 Stn. CSC
Victoria BC V8W 2Y2
Phone: (250) 721-8524
E-mail: malahat@uvic.ca (enquiries only)
Web: web.uvic.ca/malahat/

**The Malahat Novella Contest**

Guidelines: Entries limited to 30,000 words. Submissions previously published or accepted for publication elsewhere are not eligible. Blind judging. Please write your name and address on a separate page. For ms. return please send SASE with sufficient Canadian postage or IRCs.
Entry fee: $30 (includes 1-year subscription). Deadline: March 1. (Note: held in alternate years with Malahat Long Poem Contest.) Prize: $500, plus payment for publication at our regular rate of $30 per magazine page.

For more information contact:
*The Malahat Review*
The University of Victoria
PO Box 1700 Stn. CSC
Victoria BC V8W 2Y2
Phone: (250) 721-8524
E-mail: malahat@uvic.ca (enquiries only)
Web: web.uvic.ca/malahat/

**The Ottawa Public Library Short Story Contest**

Guidelines: Open to English and French writers in the Greater Ottawa area over 18 years of age. All manuscripts to 2,500 words must be the author's original, unpublished work and sent as hardcopy. Format: typed/printed, double-spaced, single-sided in readable font. Mss. not returned. Blind judging. Entries may be delivered to any of the 33 branches during normal business hours.
Entry fee: $5/story. Deadline: March 1. Prizes: $500; $250; $100.

For more information contact:
Nepean Centrepointe Branch
101 Centrepointe Drive
Ottawa ON K2G 5K7
Phone: (613) 727-6700 (ext. 308)
E-mail: patricia.chuba@library.ottawa.on.ca
Web: www.library.ottawa.on.ca

### Other Voices Creative Nonfiction Contest

Guidelines: Open to original submissions on any subject up to 5,000 words (standard contest format). No simultaneous submissions. Manuscripts will not be returned. Include an SASE or e-mail address for reply. Entry fee: $22. Deadline March 1.

For more information contact:
Other Voices Publishing Society
PO Box 52059
8210–109 St.
Edmonton AB  T6G 2T5
Web: www.othervoices.ab.ca

### Sunburst Award for Canadian Literature of the Fantastic

Guidelines: Open to a novel or short story collection classed as literature of the fantastic, which includes science fiction, fantasy, horror, magic realism, and surrealism, as well as mainstream books incorporating elements of these by a Canadian citizen (residing in or outside Canada) or landed immigrant. The work must be substantially text-based and have been published in book form (not electronic format) and released during the previous calendar year. Note: If the jury did not consider an eligible book in the year in which it was published, it can be considered the following year. However, once a book has been considered, it becomes ineligible. Send 6 copies of the book. Translations into English may be considered on an equal footing with works written originally in English, however, only the first translation of a work is eligible. Entry fee: None. Deadline: March 1. Prize: $1,000 plus an engraved bronze medallion.

For more information contact:
The Sunburst Award
106 Cocksfield Ave.
Toronto ON  M3H 3T2
Phone: (416) 636-4691 - Fax: (phone first)
E-mail: mici@sunburstaward.org
Web: www.sunburstaward.org

### The Joker is Wild Humour Contest

Guidelines: Open to writers living within commuting distance of Ottawa. Prose (fiction or nonfiction) to 1,000 words, double-spaced. Verse (rhyming or free verse) to 40 lines, single-spaced. Entries must be in English and unpublished. Send 2 copies, one with author identification and one without. No limit. Prize presentation at the annual literary awards at the National Library, in April. All 12 winners will be published

in *The Grist Mill*, and receive a free copy.
Entry fee: $4/entry, payable to Valley Writers' Guild. Deadline: First Friday in March. Prizes: $100; $25; $10 and 3 Honourable Mentions in both categories.

For more information contact:
The Valley Writers' Guild
PO Box 32
Spencerville ON  K0E 1X0
E-mail: vwg@storm.ca
Web: www.storm.ca/~vwg

### Kenneth R. Wilson Awards

Guidelines: Open to all business publications published in English and/or French. Editorial staff, contributors, freelancers, design staff and people engaged in cooperative efforts with the editor may enter. Only material published in the previous year is eligible. Entries must consist of a single article or a series of articles provided a common theme and a single purpose are maintained. In the case of a series, the majority of the installments must have been published within the calendar year, but the complete series should be submitted for judging.
Entry fee: None. Deadline: March 8. Prizes: $1,000 for Gold winner; $500 for Silver winner in each of 17 categories.

For more information, contact:
Alison Wood
Canadian Business Press
c/o Philip Boyd & Associates
649 Queensway West
Mississauga ON  L5B 1C2
Phone: (905) 896-0261, or Toronto office: (416) 963-5132

### The Claremont Review Poetry Contest

Guidelines: Open to young poets 13–19 years of age. Send 3 poems. No faxed or e-mail submissions accepted. Blind judging, Make cheque or money order to *The Claremont Review*. Send SASE for results only.
Entry fee: $15 (includes 1-year subscription to the magazine). Deadline: March 15. Prizes: $300; $200; $100.

For more information contact:
Editors
*The Claremont Review*
4980 Wesley Road
Victoria BC  V8Y 1Y9

### Duncan Campbell Scott Essay Contest

Guidelines: Open to those who live within 100 kilometres of Parliament Hill, Ottawa, for essays on some aspect of Canadian culture, broadly defined, in English, between 1,500 and 2,000 words. Each entry must be original, unpublished in any format, not submitted for publication in any format, for broadcast or in a contest that awards a prize. One entry per person. Blind judging. For return of entries send SASE.
Entry fee: None. Deadline: March 15. Prize: $250.

For more information contact:
DCS Essay Contest
130C Greenfield Ave.
Ottawa ON K1S 5L2
E-mail: artconn@istar.ca

### City of Ottawa 55-plus Short Story Contest

Guidelines: Open to residents of Ottawa 55 years or older, for original and unpublished works, 2000 words or less.
Entry fee: $5/per entry. Deadline: March 15. Prizes: $200; $100; $50.

For more information contact:
City of Ottawa Short Story Contest
Heron Seniors' Centre
1480 Heron Road
Ottawa ON K1V 6A5
Phone: (613) 247-4802 - Fax: (613) 247-4803
E-mail: Noreen.Carisse@city.ottawa.on.ca

### Okanagan University College Short Story Contest

Guidelines: Open to Okanagan writers for original, unpublished stories of between 1,000 and 5,000 words, typed on 8.5 x 11 inch plain white paper and double-spaced. No limit on number of entries per writer.
Entry fee: $10/entry. Deadline: March 29. Prizes: $500; $200; $100 and a chance to have stories read on CBC.

For more information contact:
Secretary
c/o English Dept.
Faculty of Arts
Okanagan University College
3333 College Way
Kelowna BC V1V 1V7
Phone: (250) 492-4305 (ext. 3221)

### The Norma Fleck Award for a Canadian Children's Nonfiction Book

Guidelines: Open to books based on an original subject or exploring a familiar subject in a new and interesting way written and illustrated by Canadian citizens or landed immigrants. The award goes to the author unless 40% or more of the text area is composed of original illustrations, in which case the award will be divided equally between author and illustrator. $5,000 in matching funding available to publisher for promotional purposes. There will be five shortlisted books resulting in one winner and four honour books. Contact Canadian Children's Book Centre for eligible categories of nonfiction books.
Entry fee: None. Deadline: March 30 but may vary. Prize: Value: $10,000.

For more information contact:
Program Coordinator
Canadian Children's Book Centre
101–40 Orchard View Blvd.
Toronto ON  M4R 1B9
Phone: (416) 975-0010 - Fax: (416) 975-8970
E-mail: info@bookcentre.ca
Web: www.bookcentre.ca (under Children's Book Awards)

### Cranberry Tree Press Annual Anthology Contest

Guidelines: Posted on website. Theme changes each year.
Entry fee: $10. Deadline: Usually March 31. Prizes: $100; $50; $35 plus publication of top 25 poems (amounts subject to change).

For more information contact:
Cranberry Tree Press
5060 Tecumseh Road E., Suite 173
Windsor ON  N8T 1C1
Phone: (519) 945-8106 - Fax: (519) 948-6861
E-mail: mail@cranberrytreepress.com
Web: www.cranberrytreepress.com

### Annual Norman Kucharsky Award

Guidelines: Open to members of the Periodical Writers' Association of Canada (PWAC) in good standing at deadline date and the date of the PWAC AGM, for a previously published, nonfiction, periodical article pertaining generally to the fields of the arts or culture. Eligible articles published in the previous year must be at least 500 words. Limit two per member. Send original tear sheets or photocopies, with the name of the publication and the date clearly shown and byline obscured. Blind judging. Send three copies of each article. The winning article will, with the winner's permission, be published in *Contact* and/or posted on website. Entry fee: None. Deadline: March 31. Prize: The winner will have his/her PWAC national dues paid for the following membership year.

For more information contact:
PWAC National Office
54 Wolseley St, Suite 203
Toronto ON  M5T 1A5
Phone: (416) 504-1645 - Fax: (416) 504-9079
E-mail: pwac@web.net
Web: www.pwac.ca

### *Canadian Writer's Journal* Semi-annual Short Fiction Contest

Guidelines: Open to original, unpublished stories, any genre, maximum length 1,200 words (accurate word count please). Blind judging. Name, address and a short biography of the author to be submitted on a separate sheet to accompany the entry. Manuscripts destroyed at the end of the competition. Send #10 (business size) SASE for contest results only. Winners announced in *CWJ* and on the website. Entry gives permission to include all the annual winners in a collection titled *Choice Works*, which is published separately.
Entry: $5/story. Deadline: March 31. Prizes: $100; $50; $25; honourable mentions receive 1-year subscription to the magazine.

For more information contact:
*Canadian Writer's Journal*
PO Box 5180
New Liskeard ON  P0J 1P0
Web: www.cwj.ca

## April

### The Bony Pete

Guidelines: Open to original, unpublished fiction and mystery stories (crime, suspense, private eye, amateur or professional), maximum 5,000 words, featuring Toronto at any time in history. Ms. must be typed, double spaced, on one side of regular white paper using 12-point Courier/Times Roman in a flush left mode and submitted in contest form: title and page number upper right (no author name), cover sheet with entrant's information, story title, approximate word count. Contest is open ONLY to registered attendees of Bloody Words. No copies will be returned.

Entry fee: $5 (but contestant must be attending Bloody Words to enter). Deadline: April 1. Prize: $100 and nine-inch skeleton of our mascot, Bony Pete.

For more information contact:
Caro Soles
Bloody Words Mystery Conference
12 Roundwood Court
Toronto ON M1W 1Z2
Phone: (416) 497-5293 - Fax: (416) 497-5293
E-mail: info@bloodywords.com
Web: www.bloodywords.com

**Winnipeg *Free Press*/Writers' Collective Short Story Contest**

Guidelines: Call or e-mail for form that contains complete details. Entry fee: $5 members; $10 non-members. Deadline: April 1. Prizes: $50–$200 including 1-year membership in Collective and 6 issues of the magazine.

For more information contact:
4th Floor Library
University of Winnipeg
515 Portage Ave.
Winnipeg MB R3B 2E9
Phone: (204) 786-9468
E-mail: writerscollective@uwinnipeg.ca
Web: scholar.uwinnipeg.ca/groups.writerscollective/

***Seeds* Poetry Contest**

Guidelines: See website for full information for this annual international anthology of poetry. Send 3 previously unpublished poems, any theme, any length, any style.
Entry fee: $12. Deadline: April 1. Prizes: 9 cash prizes $50–$10; 15–25 honourable mentions.

For more information contact:
Hidden Brook Press
412–701 King Street West
Toronto ON M5W 2W7
Phone: (416) 504-3966
E-mail: contest@hiddenbrookpress.com
Web: www.hiddenbrookpress.com

**No Love Lost Poetry Award**

Guidelines: All themes, types and styles of poetry welcome including B/W art - send jpg. For full entry details check website or e-mail.

Entry fee: $12 (inc. copy of B/W saddle stitched book). Deadline: April 1. Prizes: $50; $25; $15; and 6 at $10. 15 to 25 honourable mentions.

For more information contact:
Hidden Brook Press
412–701 King Street West
Toronto ON  M5V 2W7
Phone: (416) 504-3966
E-mail: contestinfo@hiddenbrookpress.com
Web: www.hiddenbrookpress.com

**ConVersion Short Story Contest**

Guidelines: Open to science fiction, fantasy and horror to a maximum of 5,000 words.
Entries must be submitted in competition format for blind reading/judging. Mail 3 copies of each entry. No e-mail entries, please. For complete guidelines see website. Journeyman level: Open to writers with fewer than 12 published short stories (paid) or 1 to 2 novels in the genre. Apprentice level: Open to writers with fewer than 3 published short stories (paid) or 1 novel in the genre.
Entry fee: $5, unless paid member of ConVersion Science Fiction/Fantasy Convention. Deadline: April 1. Prizes: Journeyman: $250; $200; $150; 2 honorable mentions: $50 gift certificate. Apprentice: $200; $150; $100; 2 honorable mentions: $25 gift certificate.

For more information contact:
Calgary Science Fiction and Fantasy Society
PO Box 61178
Kensington Postal Outlet
Calgary AB  T2N 4S6
E-mail: rmherrin@ucalgary.ca (for 2002–2004 only)
Web: www.con-version.org/story.html

**The Governor General's Literary Awards**

Guidelines: Open to first-edition trade books in English and French written, translated or illustrated by Canadian citizens or permanent residents of Canada submitted by the publisher. Categories: Children's Literature (text); Children's Literature (illustration); Drama; Fiction; Poetry; Literary Nonfiction; and Translation. In the case of translations, the original work, written in English or French, must also be a Canadian-authored title. For complete guidelines and exempted categories check website.
Entry fee: None. Deadlines: April 15 for books published September 1 to March 31; August 7 for books published March 1 to September 30 (dates

subject to change). Prizes: $15,000/category/each language plus leather-bound copy of book.

For more information contact:
Canada Council for the Arts
Writing and Publishing Section
350 Albert St.
PO Box 1047
Ottawa ON K1P 5V8
Phone: 1-800-253-5588 (ext. 5576) or (613) 566-4414 (ext. 5576)
Fax: (613) 566-4410
E-mail: joanne.larocque-poirier@canadacouncil.ca
Web: www.canadacouncil.ca
For other writing prizes offered by Canada Council:
www.canadacouncil.ca/prizes/prli01-e.asp

**The Vernon & District Mood Disorders Society Poetry Contest**

Guidelines: Open to work on any topic in good taste in two categories: Adult and Youth. Write "I give permission to publish," sign and date. Include: mailing address, name, age, and fee. Cheques made out to the society. Funds go towards our youth program.
Entry fee: $5/1st poem; $1/each additional poem. Deadline: April 15. Prizes: $50 and plaque inscribed with winning poem in both categories. Publication in newsletter.

For more information contact:
The Vernon & District Mood Disorders Society
2100–28th Crescent
Vernon BC V1T 1V2
Phone: (250) 558-6900 - Fax: same
E-mail: pharding@junction.net
Web: pending.

***EVENT* Creative Nonfiction Contest (annual contest)**

Guidelines: Open to manuscripts exploring the creative nonfiction form. (Check your library for back issues of *Event* with previous winning entries and judges' comments.) Previously published material, or material accepted elsewhere for publication not eligible. Maximum entry length is 5,000 words, typed, double-spaced. Multiple entries are allowed but each entry must be accompanied by a $25 Entry fee. Blind judging. Include an SASE (Canadian postage/IRCs only). Douglas College employees may not enter. Make cheque or money order payable to *Event*.

Entry fee: $25/entry (includes GST and a 1-year subscription to *Event*). Deadline: April 15. Prizes: Three winners will each receive $500 plus payment for publication in *Event*. Other manuscripts may be published.

For more information contact:
The Douglas College Review
PO Box 2503
New Westminster BC V3L 5B2
Phone: (604) 527-5293 - Fax: (604) 527-5095
E-mail: event@douglas.bc.ca
Web: event.douglas.bc.ca

**The Tree House Poetry Contest (Youth)**

Guidelines: Open to contestants between 6-18 years of age. Please send three poems. Poems will be read on The World Poetry Radio Show and published in *The World Poetry Electronic Newsletter* in The Tree House Section.
Entry fee: None. Deadline: April 15. Prizes: $10; $ 5:00; six pencils.

For more information contact:
Patricia Star Downey
702–31 Elliot St.
New Westminster BC V3L 5C9
Phone: (604) 526-4729 - Fax: same
E-mail: ariadne_sawyer@telus.net
or astarte_sita@yahoo.com

**Writing for Children Competition**

Guidelines: Open to Canadian citizens or landed immigrants who have not been published in book form and who do not have a contract with a publisher. Genre is open: poetry, prose, dialogue, etc. Max. 1,500 words. Entries must be original and unpublished, in English, typed and double-spaced. Blind judging. Entries will not be returned.
Entry fee: $15 payable to the Writers' Union of Canada. Deadline: Canada Book Day (April 23). Prize: $1,500. The winners and finalists will also have their work submitted to three (3) publishers of children's literature.

For more information contact:
The Writers' Union of Canada
40 Wellington St. E., 3rd Floor
Toronto ON M5E 1C7
Phone: (416) 703-8982 (ext. 223) - Fax: (416) 506-7656
E-mail: projects@writersunion.ca
Web: www.writersunion.ca

**Write Your Heart Out**

Guidelines: Open to all contemporary romance novel manuscripts. First 3 chapters and two-page synopsis, no explicit sexual content or paranormal. Manuscripts do not have to be complete but must be previously unpublished and not be simultaneously submitted elsewhere. Manuscripts will not be returned. Visit website for more details.
Entry fee: $10 U.S./$15 CDN. Deadline: April 30. Prizes: $500 CDN; $100 CDN and 10 consolation detailed critique prizes.

For more information contact:
Ponder Publishing Inc.
PO Box 23037
RPO McGillivray
Winnipeg MB R3T 5S3
Phone: (204) 269-2985 - Fax: (204) 888-7159
E-mail: service@ponderpublishing.com
Web: www.ponderpublishing.com

**Copyright Contest**

Guidelines: Open to Canadian residents in 2 categories: 13–18 and 19–25 years of age in the form of an essay, short story or poem in English to a maximum of 500 words, with a creative approach to copyright issues in your life. (Note: make sure to properly reference any materials you use.) Include the following information with your submission: name, address, e-mail address, age, phone number. To find out more about copyright in Canada and around the world, check out the following websites:
http://www.strategis.gc.ca/sc_mrksv/cipo/welcome and
http://www.wipo.org and http://www.cb-cda.gc.ca/.
[While the copyright of the work remains with the creator, The Writers' Trust of Canada and Access Copyright™ may use winning contest submissions for promotional material during a two-year period following the close of the contest. The creator(s) of the work will be acknowledged on any material produced.]
Entry fee: None. Deadline: April 30. Prizes: $500; $100; 10 book prizes in each category.

For more information contact:
Access Copyright
1 Yonge Street, Suite 1900
Toronto ON M5E 1E5
Fax: (416) 868-1621
E-mail: essaycontest@accesscopyright.ca
Web: www.accesscopyright.ca

### Annual BC High School Writing and Design Contest

Guidelines: Open to students attending high school in BC during the year previous and the contest school year only. Two age categories: Junior (grades 7–10); Senior (grades 11–12).
Entry fee: $10 (all entrants receive 1 copy of anthology); $5/additional submission. (Group rates and financial assistance also available.) Deadline: April 30. Prizes: 42 students share $7,000 and publication in annual anthology of poetry, short fiction, essay. Art: $500 to winners in each genre, $100 for honourable mentions.

For more information contact:
Ripple Effect Press
PO Box 2836
349 W. Georgia St.
Vancouver BC V6B 3X2
Phone: (604) 879-7327 - Fax: (604) 879-7321
E-mail: info@rippleeffect.ca
Web: www.rippleeffect.ca

### Shaunt Basmajian Chapbook Award

Guidelines: Open to manuscripts of poems up to 24 pages in length. Poems may be published (other than chapbook or book form) or unpublished, and may be in any style or tradition. All entrants will receive a copy of the winning chapbook. No limit on number of entries.
Entry fee: $15/chapbook ms. Deadline: April 30. Prize: Winner will receive 50 copies of the resulting chapbook and $100 CDN cash.

For more information contact:
The Canadian Poetry Association
PO Box 22571
St. George Postal Outlet
264 Bloor St. W.
Toronto ON M5S 1V8
E-mail: writers@sympatico.ca
Web: www.mirror.org/cpa/

### The Edna Staebler Award for Creative Nonfiction

Guidelines: Open to books of creative nonfiction published in the preceding year by developing writers who have had no more than two books published. The book must have a Canadian locale and/or significance and be distinguished by first-hand research, well-crafted, interpretive writing related to the writer's personal discovery or experience and exhibiting a creative use of language or approach to the subject matter. Send six copies of the book. These will not be returned. Entry form re-

quired.
Entry fee: None. Deadline: April 30. Prize: $3,000

For more information contact:
Kathryn Wardropper, Awards Administrator
The Edna Staebler Award for Nonfiction
Laurier Bookstore
Wilfred Laurier University
Waterloo ON N2L 3C5
Phone: (519) 884-1970 (ext. 3109) - Fax: (519) 884-8202
E-mail: kwardrop@wlu.ca

**Illustrated Postcard Story Competition**

Guidelines: Open to unpublished postcard stories, maximum 300 words (a postcard story is a short piece of fiction or nonfiction) judged on literary merit alone. Limit two entries per person, typed on a single sheet of 8.5 x 11 inch plain paper, single-spaced. Blind judging. There is no entry form. Entrants are encouraged to illustrate their stories.
Entry fee: $10 cheque payable to Victoria School of Writing Postcard Story Competition. Deadline: April 30. Prizes: Full scholarship to the July 15 to 20 Victoria School of Writing ($575); half scholarship to the Victoria School of Writing ($288); quarter scholarship ($144). Winning stories will be published in the Victoria *Times Colonist.*

For more information contact:
The Victoria School of Writing
PO Box 8152
Victoria BC V8W 3R8

## May

### *Pottersfield Portfolio* Annual Compact Fiction/Short Poem Competition

Guidelines: Open to Canadian writers and expatriates only. Three categories: Fiction: maximum 1500 words; Poetry: maximum 20 lines (one per page); Nonfiction: maximum 1500 words exploring the open-ended theme of "journeys." Maximum 3 poems or 2 stories or 2 nonfiction pieces, previously unpublished or accepted elsewhere. Entry fee entitles you to a 1-year subscription (2 issues). Blind judging. Please type your name, address, phone/fax number, story or poem titles, and (for the fiction and essay category) an accurate word count on a separate sheet. Entries cannot be returned. Send SASE for results only.
Entry fee: $20 for first entry in any category plus additional $5 for each

subsequent entry. Deadline: May 1. Prize: $200 each category and publication in autumn issue of magazine.

For more information contact:
Douglas A. Brown, Managing Editor
*Pottersfield Portfolio*
PO Box 40, Station A
Sydney NS B1P 6G9
Web: www.portfolio.com and www.magomania.com

**F.G. Bressani Prize (biennial)**

Guidelines: Poetry and Novel categories open only to Canadian writers of Italian origin of 16 years of age and over writing in Italian, English or French, for work published within the past five years. Submit 3 copies with address/phone number of author or publisher on the title page only. Short Fiction (novellas, short stories, creative nonfiction) open to all writers dealing with subjects pertaining to the Italian culture and/or immigration experiences lived by Italians. Entries must have been published during the past 5 years. Submit 3 copies as above. No essays.
Entry fee: None. Deadline: May 1. Prizes: $500 each category.

For more information contact:
Italian Cultural Centre
3075 Slocan St.
Vancouver BC V5M 3E4
Phone: (604) 430-3337 - Fax: (604) 430-3331
E-mail: cultural_mmngr@iccs.bc.ca

**The Marianna Demptster Award**

Guidelines: Open only to writers in the Atlantic Provinces. Awarded for the best children's book for the ten and under age group published either in the year of the award or the preceding one.
Entry fee: $10. Deadline: May 1. Prize: $100.

For more information contact:
Canadian Authors Association, Nova Scotia Branch
c/o Evelyn Brown
15 MacRea Ave.
Dartmouth NS B2Y 1Z4
Phone: (902) 466-2558
E-mail: raemacpub@ns.sympatico.ca

**The Lilla Stirling Award**

Guidelines: Open only to writers in the Atlantic Provinces. Awarded for the best children's book for the ten and over age group published ei-

ther in the year of the award or the preceding one.
Entry fee: $10. Deadline: May 1. Prize: $100.

For more information contact:
Canadian Authors Association, Nova Scotia Branch
c/o Evelyn Brown
15 MacRea Ave.
Dartmouth NS B2Y 1Z4
Phone: (902) 466-2558
E-mail: raemacpub@ns.sympatico.ca

**The John Spenser Hill Award for Fiction**

Guidelines: Open to short stories, unpublished, in English to 2,500 words. No limit. Blind judging. Winners receive a 1-year subscription to *The Valley Writers' News*. Bios will be solicited.
Entry fee: $10 per submission, payable to Valley Writers' Guild. Deadline: First Friday in May. Prizes: Grand Prize is $500 and an engraved plaque. Secondary prizes of $200; $100 and up to three honourable mentions at $20 each plus publication in *The Grist Mill*.

For more information contact:
The John Spenser Hill Award for Fiction
c/o The Valley Writers' Guild
PO Box 534
Merrickville ON K0G 1N0
E-mail: vwg@storm.ca
Web: www.storm.ca/~vwg

**The Annual Short Story Contest**

Guidelines: Unpublished fiction of 2,000 words on any topic/subject is eligible. Additional stories may be submitted with a supplementary fee of $15/story.
Entry fee: $15 (includes 1-year/3-issue subscription). Deadline: May 15. Prize: $500 and publication in the summer issue of *sub-Terrain* magazine

For more information contact:
*sub-Terrain* Magazine
PO Box 3008, MPO
Vancouver BC V6B 3X5
Phone: (604) 876-8710 - Fax: (604) 879-2667
E-mail: subter@portal.ca
Web: www.anvilpress.com/subterrain

**The Isabel Miller Young Writers Award (Poetry or Fiction)**

Guidelines: Open to original, unpublished work of Alberta residents 12 to 18 years of age not submitted elsewhere for publication or perfor-

mance, typed, double-spaced, on 8.5 x 11 inch paper in a legible font. No limit on number of entries/person. A covering page must be attached to your submission. On the covering page, please provide the following information: your name, complete mailing address, and telephone number; age and date of birth, and title of your piece. An absolutely accurate word count is required. Poems: up to 500 words (not including title). Stories: up to 1,000 words (not including title). Blind judging. Entries will not be returned.
Entry fee: $5/piece of writing. If a classroom teacher is submitting a class set of writing, the entry fee is $20 for the class. Deadline: May 15. Prizes: First Prize: $300 (cash prize or partial scholarship to attend YouthWrite, the WGA's summer writing camp for kids); Second Prize: $200 (cash prize or partial scholarship to attend YouthWrite); Third Prize: $100 (cash prize or partial scholarship to attend YouthWrite).

For more information contact:
Writers Guild of Alberta Awards Program
Percy Page Centre
11759 Groat Road
Edmonton AB T5M 3K6
Phone: (780) 422-8174 or 1-800-665-5354 - Fax: n/a
E-mail: heather@writersguild.ab.ca
Web: www.writersguild.ab.ca

**Milton Acorn Prize for Poetry**

Guidelines: Open to poems up to 30 lines, typed or neatly printed. Photocopied submissions accepted. Cheques payable to: *Poetry Forever.* Blind judging. Entries will not be returned. Please include SASE for list of winners. Purpose of contest: to fund the publication of full-size collections by the People's Poet, Milton Acorn (1923–1986).
Entry fee: $3/poem. Deadline: May 15. Prizes: First; second; third place prizes. The amount varies but no less than $100. The top three poems will receive broadsheet publication.

For more information contact:
*Poetry Forever*
PO Box 68018
Hamilton ON L8M 3M7
Phone: (905) 312-1779
E-mail: james@meklerdeahl.com

**VanCity Book Prize**

Guidelines: Open to authors who have resided in BC for three of the past five years for books pertaining to women's issues, published any-

where in the world. Submission by publisher only.
Deadline: May 15. Prize: $4,000 ($3,000 to author; $1,000 to BC women's charity of choice).

For more information contact:
c/o BC Book World
3516 West 13th Avenue (rear)
Vancouver BC V6R 2S3
Phone: (604) 877-7641 - Fax: (604) 877-7639

**Starship Story Contest (2 categories: 9 and under; 10–15)**

Guidelines: Open to original and unpublished stories, written on a computer or typewriter, double-spaced and to a maximum of 600 words. One entry per person. No fax or e-mail submissions. Blind judging. Send separate sheet with name, address, phone number and 25–30 word biographical sketch. For complete set of rules call the phone number above.
Entry fee: None. Deadline: May 30. Prizes: 7 winners will be published in "Starship," receive a backpack and $100 each.

For more information contact:
*The Sunday Star*
One Yonge St.
Toronto ON M5E 1E6
Phone: (416) 350-3000 (press category 3443)

**Quebec Writers' Federation Awards**

A. M. Klein Prize for Poetry
Hugh MacLennan Prize for Fiction
Mavis Gallant Prize for Nonfiction

Guidelines: The Translation Prize alternates on an annual basis for a translation from French to English/English to French with a 2-year eligibility span for each. Criteria differ. Consult website. Books for remaining prizes must have been written in English by an author who has been a resident of Quebec for at least 3 of the past 5 years prior to publication date. If coauthored, 50% of authors must meet this specification. Submit 4 copies. Entry form(s) required.
Entry fee: $10/title. Deadlines: May 30 for books published October 1–May 15. August 15 for books (or bound proofs) published May 16–September 30. Translation Award Prizes: $2,000 for each award. First Book Award Prize: $1,000.

For more information contact:
1200 Atwater Ave., Suite 3
Montreal, PQ H3Z 1X4
Phone: (514) 933-0878 - Fax: (514) 934-2485

E-mail: qspell@total.net
Web: www.qwf.org

**Burnaby Writers' Society Contest**

Guidelines: Open to BC residents only. Contest category, and guidelines vary each year. Check website for current information, or send SASE to above address.
Entry fee: $5/entry (changes annually). Deadline: May 31. Prizes: $200; $100; $50 and honourable mentions.

For more information contact:
Burnaby Writers' Society
c/o 6584 Deer Lake Ave.
Burnaby BC V5G 3T7
E-mail: lonewolf@portal.ca
Web: www.bws.bc.ca

**Northern Ontario Poetry Competition**

Guidelines: Open only to residents of Northern Ontario with a postal code beginning with the letter "P." Poems must be titled, previously unpublished, and typed in black ink, one per page, on 8.5 x 11 inch white bond paper. Photocopies and letter quality computer printouts accepted. Poems not to exceed 50 lines, including the title. Line length exceeding 44 characters including punctuation and spaces may be broken at the discretion of the anthology committee. Once a line has to be broken due to its length, it will count as two lines. Only the title and the poem itself should appear on the page. Blind judging. All those chosen by the judge to be included in the anthology will receive a certificate and a complimentary copy of the anthology.
Entry fee: $3/poem by cheque or money order to White Mountain Publications. Deadline: May 31. Prizes: First, second and third plus honourable mentions published in Anthology.

For more information contact:
*Canadian Writer's Journal*
PO Box 5180
New Liskeard ON P0J 1P0
Phone: (705) 647-5424 - Fax: (705) 647-8366
Toll-free: 1-800-258-5451
Web: www.cwj.ca

## June

### City of Vancouver Book Award

Guidelines: Open to books in any genre that demonstrate excellence and contribute to the appreciation and understanding of Vancouver's history, unique character or the achievements of its residents. Consult website for eligibility and evaluation criteria.
Entry fee: $25. Deadline: June. Prize: $2,000.

For more information contact:
Office of Cultural Affairs
453 W. 12th Ave.
Vancouver BC V5Y 1V4
Phone: (604) 871-7487 - Fax: (604) 871-6048
E-mail: oca@city.vancouver.bc.ca
Web: www.city.vancouver.bc.ca/oca

### Great Blue Heron Poetry Contest

Guidelines: Open only to original, previously unpublished material not accepted for publication elsewhere. Total entry not to exceed 4 pages or a maximum of 150 lines. It can be one longer poem, or several shorter poems (typed and double-spaced). No electronic submissions. Blind judging. Entries not returned. Only winners notified. Make cheques or money orders payable to *The Antigonish Review*. Full details, guidelines, queries, see website.
Entry fee: $25 (includes a one-year subscription to *The Antigonish Review*). Deadline: June 1. Prizes: $800; $500; $300, all three with publication.

For more information contact:
*The Antigonish Review* Contest
PO Box 5000
St. Francis Xavier University
Antigonish NS B2G 2W5
Phone: (902) 867-3962
E-mail: TAR@stfx.ca
Web: www.antigonishreview.com

### Alberta Playwriting Contest

Guidelines: Open to all Albertans whose primary residence has been Alberta for at least one year immediately prior to submission, including non-administrative members of APN. Each submission must be accompanied by a completed Declaration and Entry form. Full-length category must have running time of minimum 75 minutes (not including intermissions). Discovery category does not have a minimum running time. Note:

High school exception for Discovery category. For eligibility restrictions consult website.
Entry fee: $40 Non-refundable cheque/money order to Alberta Playwrights' Network. Deadline: June 1. Prizes: Full Length $3,500; Discovery $1,500.

For more information contact:
Alberta Playwrights' Network
2nd Floor, 1134 8th Avenue SW
Calgary AB T2P 1J5
Phone: (403) 269-8564 - Fax: (403) 265-6773
Toll-free: 1-800-268-8564
E-mail: apn@nucleus.com
Web: www.nucleus.com/~apn

**The Lawrence House Short Story Contest**

Guidelines: Open to fiction of 2,500 words maximum, in English. Blind judging. Send cover letter with contact information. SASE for results only.
Entry fee: $20 payable to Lawrence House Centre for the Arts. Deadline: June 15. Prizes: $500; $250; $100.

For more information contact:
Lawrence House Centre for the Arts
127 S. Christina St.
Sarnia ON N7T 2M8
Web: www.lawrencehouse.ca

**The "The Motion of Metaphor" Contest**

Guidelines: Both free verse and rhymed poems to a maximum of 50 lines each. Spaces between the stanzas count as lines. Blind judging. Enclose SASE for winners list.
Entry fee: $2/poem or $5/3 poems. Deadline June 15. Prizes: $50 for best Rhyming Poem; $50 for best free verse poem; $50 for best haiku poem — includes publication in the *We Are T.O.P.S.* newsletter.

For more information contact:
The Ontario Poetry Society
c/o I.B. Iskov, Contest Coordinator
31 Marisa Court
Thornhill ON L4J 6H9
Phone: (905) 738-0309 - Fax: (905) 738-8256
E-mail: iskov_tops@hotmail.com
Web: www.mirror.org/tops

### Orion Prize for Poetry

Guidelines: Open to poems up to 30 lines, typed or neatly printed. Photocopied submissions accepted. Blind judging. Cheques payable to: *Poetry Forever*. Entries will not be returned. Include SASE for a list of winners. Purpose of Contest: to fund the publication of a full-size collection by Ottawa poet Marty Flomen (1942–1997).
Entry fee: $3/poem. Deadline: June 15. Prizes: First, second, and third place prizes but no less than $100. The top three poems will receive broadsheet publication.

For more information contact:
*Poetry Forever*
PO Box 68018
Hamilton ON  L8M 3M7
Phone: (905) 312-1779
E-mail: james@meklerdeahl.com

### George Cadogan Memorial Award

Guidelines: Genre changes annually. Open to all Canadian residents for previously unpublished work. No simultaneous submissions please. Submission must be typed or computer-generated, printed on one side of the page. Include title and page number on each page of your entry. Blind judging. Manuscript will not be returned unless accompanied by an SASE with sufficient postage. Only winners will be notified by telephone or e-mail.
Entry fee: $5 payable to Canadian Authors Association. For written evaluation add $5. Deadline: June 30. Prizes: Plaque for winner with first, second and third cash prizes and publication in *Voices & Visions*.

For more information contact:
CAA Poetry Contest
c/o Community Services Dept., 7th Flr.
City of Kitchener
200 King St. W.
PO Box 1118
Kitchener ON  N2G 4G7
Phone: (519) 571-1315
E-mail: gkreller@golden.net

### John Glassco Translation Prize

Guidelines: Open to the first published, book-length work of literary translation in English or French by a Canadian citizen or landed immigrant.
Entry fee: None. Deadline: June 30. Prize: $1,000.

For more information contact:
Association des traducteurs et traductrices littéraires du Canada/
Literary Translators' Association of Canada
ATTN: Patricia Godbout
SB 335 – Concordia University
1455, boul. de Maisonneuve ouest
Montreal PQ H3G 1M8
Phone: (514) 848-8702 - Fax: (514) 848-4514
E-mail: Ltac@alcor.concordia.ca
Web: www.geocities.com/ltac_attlc

**Eden Mills Literary Contest (Short Story/Poetry)**

Guidelines: Open to new or modestly published writers age 16 and over. Short story (max. 2,500 words); poetry (max. 5 poems).
Entry fee: $10 payable to Eden Mills Writers' Festival. Deadline: June 30. Prizes: $500; $200; $100.

For more information contact:
Eden Mills Writers' Festival
c/o Randa Wright
212 Barden St.
Eden Mills ON N0B 1P0
Phone: (519) 856-9450
E-mail: deluxe@golden.net
Web: edenmillswritersfestival.ca

**Poetry Anthology Contest**

Guidelines: Open only to residents of the Regional Municipality of Niagara. Poems (one per page) must be titled, previously unpublished, not being considered elsewhere, typed or printed in black ink on 8.5 x 11 inch white bond paper (True Roman 10 point font). Line length exceeding 44 characters (inc. punctuation and spaces) may be broken at the discretion of the committee. No epic poems please. No staples. Blind judging. Send a stamped, self-addressed #10 business envelope to be used for your invitation to awards evening and launch of the subsequent anthology. Poets retain all but first publication rights. Poems receiving honourable mention and Judge's Selections will also appear in the anthology.
Entry fee: $5/poem, $12/3 poems, payable to CAA Niagara Branch. Deadline: June 30. Prizes: $100; $50; $25.

For more information contact:
The Niagara Branch of the Canadian Authors Association
Poetry Anthology Contest

PO Box 9
Grimsby ON L3M 4G1
Phone: (905) 871-4276 or (905) 468-5517
Web: www.sympatico.ca/gplewis/

**CPA Annual Poetry Contest**

Guidelines: Poems published in *Poemata* or on website. See website or check e-mail for entry details.
Entry fee: $5/poem. Deadline: June 30. Prizes: $50; $40; $30; $20; $10; $5 and up to 10 honourable mentions.

For more information contact:
The Canadian Poetry Association, BC Chapter
PO Box 3
Clinton BC V0K 1K0
E-mail: writers@sympatico.ca
Web: www.mirror.org/cpa/

**Poem of the Year Contest**

Guidelines: Entrants may submit up to four unpublished poems, each no more than 100 lines in length. Blind judging. No poems will be returned. Winning poems, along with two honourable mentions and up to seven Editor's Choices, published in the winter issue of *Arc* Magazine.
Entry fee: $18 Canadian (includes a 1-year subscription). Deadline: June 30. Prize: $1,000; $750; $500 (all plus publication).

For more information contact:
*Arc Poetry* Society
Box 7219
Ottawa ON K1L 8E4
E-mail: arc.poetry@cyberus.ca
Web: www.cyberus.ca/~arc.poetry

## July

**The Great Canadian Literary Hunt**

Guidelines: Open to poetry of up to 100 lines and short stories of up to 5,000 words maximum. Entries must be original and unpublished. Multiple entries permitted. Blind judging. Send SASE for winners only. Contest updates in free online newsletter. To subscribe send blank e-mail to: greatcanadianliteraryhunt-subscribe@yahoogroups.com.
Entry fee: $10/fiction entry. $10/two poems. Payable to *This Magazine*. Deadline: July 1. Prizes(s): Fiction: $750; $500; $250. Poetry: $750; $500; $250 and publication in *This Magazine*.

For more information contact:
*This Magazine*
401 Richmond St. W., Suite 396
Toronto ON M5V 3A8
Phone: (416) 979-8400 - Fax: (416) 979-1143
E-mail: thismag@web.net
Web: www.THISmag.org

**Banff Mountain Book Festival**

Guidelines: Open to awards in four categories: Mountain Literature; Mountain Exposition; Mountain Image and Adventure Travel, with one Grand Prize winner, regardless of category. Submissions must be in English, except for the Mountain Image, where all languages are acceptable. Send 7 copies of each submission to the Festival Office in Banff.
Entry fee: None. Deadline: July 15. Prizes: Over $5,000 to be awarded.

For more information contact:
Banff Centre for Mountain Culture
PO Box 1020
107 Tunnel Mountain Drive
Banff AB T1L 1H5
Phone: (403) 762-6347 - Fax: (403) 762-6177
E-mail: mountainculture@banffcentre.ca
Web: www.banffcentre.ca/mountianculture

**Tidepool Prize for Poetry**

Guidelines: Open to poems of up to 30 lines, typed or neatly printed. Photocopied submissions accepted. Cheques payable to: *Poetry Forever.* Entries will not be returned. Include SASE if you wish to receive a list of winners. Blind judging. Purpose of Contest: to fund the publication a full-size collection by Hamilton poet Herb Barrett (1912–1995).
Entry fee: $3/poem. Deadline: July 15. Prizes: First, second, and third place prizes, no less than $100. Other Prizes: The top three poems will receive broadsheet publication.

For more information contact:
*Poetry Forever*
PO Box 68018
Hamilton ON L8M 3M7
Phone: (905) 312-1779 - Fax: n/a
E-mail: james@meklerdeahl.com

### Canadian Poetry Association BC Chapter Annual Poetry Contest

Guidelines: See website or e-mail. Winning poems and honourable mentions will appear in the *Dogwood Express II* contest anthology published by Little Red Hen Publishing.
Entry fee: $10/three poems. Deadline: July 15. Prizes: $50; $40; $30; $20; $10; $5 and up to 10 honourable mentions.

For more information contact:
Canadian Poetry Association
E-mail: writers@sympatico.ca
Web: www.mirror.org/cpa/

### Saskatchewan Book Awards

Categories: 12 Awards are given each year. Book of the Year; Fiction; Nonfiction; First Book (*Brenda Macdonald Riches Award*); Regina Book Award; Saskatoon Book Award; Poetry (*Anne Szumigalski Award*); Children's Literature; Scholarly Writing; Awards for Saskatchewan Publishers; Award for Publishing; First Peoples Publishing; Publishing in Education.

Guidelines: Books may be entered for more than one award. Submit four copies/title for the first submission, thereafter send three copies/category. Submissions from publishers or writers.
Entry fee: $15/title/category. Deadline: For books published September 15–July 31 the deadline is July 31. (For books published in August & September, see September 15). Prize: $1,500.

For more information contact:
Saskatchewan Book Awards
PO Box 1921
Regina SK S4P 3E1
Phone: (306) 569-1585 - Fax: (306) 569-4187
E-mail: director@bookawards.sk.ca
Web: www.bookawards.sk.ca

### Canadian National Playwriting Competition

Guidelines: Open to all professional and nonprofessional playwrights resident in Canada. Plays must be original, not produced (at time of postmark), Canadian stage plays submitted in English. (Musicals not eligible.) Script must be typewritten or word processed on one side of the paper only, double-spaced between speaking parts. Entrants declare themselves available to participate in the New Play Festival in Kamloops, BC, the following April. Submissions must be made under a pseudonym. For complete details check website.

Entry fee: $35/play regardless of category. Critique fee an additional $25. Deadline: Fourth Monday in July. Prizes: Full length—$1,500; One Act—$1,000; Special Merit—$750.

For more information contact:
Theatre BC
PO Box 2031
Nanaimo BC V9R 6X6
Phone: (250) 714-0203 - Fax: (250) 714-0213
Web: www.theatrebc.org/playcomp

**The Pearson Writers' Trust Nonfiction Prize**

Guidelines: Open to first edition trade books by Canadian citizens or permanent residents, published between January 1 and December 31. Announcement Date: March.
Entry fee: None. Deadlines: July 31 and November 15. Prizes: $10,000; $1,000 for up to four shortlisted authors.

For more information contact:
The Writers' Trust of Canada
40 Wellington St. E., Suite 300
Toronto ON M5E 1C7
Phone: (416) 504-8222 - Fax: (416) 504-9090
E-mail: info@writers.trust.com
Web: www.writerstrust.com

**The Shaughnessy Cohen Prize for Political Writing**

Guidelines: Open to first edition nonfiction trade books by Canadian citizens or permanent residents, published between January 1 and December 31 for work that enlarges the understanding of contemporary Canadian political and social issues.
Entry fee: None. Deadlines: July 31 and November 15. Prize: $10,000; $1,000 for up to four shortlisted authors.

For more information contact:
The Writers' Trust of Canada
40 Wellington St. E., Suite 300
Toronto ON M5E 1C7
Phone: (416) 504-8222 - Fax: (416) 504-9090
E-mail: info@writers.trust.com
Web: www.writerstrust.com

**Rogers Writers' Trust Fiction Prize**

Guidelines: Open to first edition fiction trade books by Canadian citizens or permanent residents, published between January 1 and December 31. Announcement date and location: March.

Entry fee: None. Deadlines: July 31 and November 15. Prizes: $10,000; $1,000 for to up to four shortlisted authors.

For more information contact:
The Writers' Trust of Canada
40 Wellington St. E., Suite 300
Toronto ON M5E 1C7
Phone: (416) 504-8222 - Fax: (416) 504-9090
E-mail: info@writers.trust.com
Web: www.writerstrust.com

**The Drainie-Taylor Biography Prize**

Guidelines: Open to first edition trade books of literary biography, autobiography or personal memoir by Canadian citizens or permanent residents published between January 1 and December 31. Translations into English are eligible and will be considered in the year in which the English translation is published. (Should a translation win, the prize will be divided as follows: $7,500 to the author, $2,500 to the translator.) Announcement date and location: March.
Entry fee: None. Deadlines: July 31 and November 15. Prize: $10,000.

For more information contact:
The Writers' Trust of Canada
40 Wellington St. E., Suite 300
Toronto ON M5E 1C7
Phone: (416) 504-8222 - Fax: (416) 504-9090
E-mail: info@writers.trust.com
Web: www.writerstrust.com

**Tara Singh Hayer Memorial Award**

Guidelines: Open to work that highlights cases of media repression in another country, attempts at or actual censorship, work involving difficult-to-obtain access to information requests or instances in which the journalist faced significant risks or threats, physical or otherwise, to practise his or her profession. Applications are invited from Canadian journalists working for news media organizations full-, part-time or freelance. Submissions in French or English may be in the form of video tapes, audio tapes, articles or columns aired or published between July 1 and June 30 of the preceding year. Candidates must be nominated by someone else. For complete submission details see website.
Entry fee: None. Deadline: July 31. Prize: $2,000 and framed plaque.

For more information contact:
Canadian Journalists for Free Expression
489 College Street, Suite 403

Toronto ON M6G 1A5
Phone: (416) 515-9622 - Fax: (416) 515-7879
E-mail: cjfe@cjfe.org
Web: www.cjfe.org

## August

### The Creative Nonfiction Contest

Guidelines: Open to submissions of 2,000 to 4,000 words maximum, not limited to any particular topic or subject. Creative nonfiction doesn't report as much as it tells. It's a story conveying not just the facts, but an experience, a tale complete with true events, utilizing the tools of fiction — if necessary — to present itself. Additional stories may be submitted with a supplementary fee of $5/story.
Entry fee: $15, includes 1-year/3-issue subscription. Deadline: August 1.
Prize: Grand prize: $250 and publication in the winter issue of *sub-Terrain* magazine.

For more information contact:
*sub-Terrain* magazine
PO Box 3008, MPO
Vancouver BC V6B 3X5
Phone: (604) 876-8710 - Fax: (604) 879-2667
E-mail: subter@portal.ca
Web: www.anvilpress.com/subterrain

### Atlantic Writing Competition for Unpublished Manuscripts

Guidelines: Open to anyone resident in the Atlantic Provinces for at least six months prior to August of competition year. Only one entry/category is allowed. Writers whose work has been professionally published in book form or frequently in periodical or media production may not enter in the genre in which they have been published or produced. Entries must be the original, unpublished work of the writer, and must not have been accepted for publication or submitted elsewhere. Previously entered work may not be resubmitted. Judges return written comments when the competition is concluded. Entry forms available from the WFNS office by March.
Entry fee: $15 ($10 for WFNS members); $25 for novel ($20 for WFNS members). Deadline: First Friday in August. Prizes: Novel — $200, $150, $100; Writing for Children — $150, $75, $50; Poetry — $100, $75, $50; Short Story — $100, $75, $50; Essay/Magazine Article — $150, $75, $50.

For more information contact:
Writers' Federation of Nova Scotia
1113 Marginal Road
Halifax NS B3H 4P7
Phone: (902) 423-8116 - Fax: (902) 422-0881
E-mail: talk@writers.ns.ca
Web: www.writers.ns.ca/competitions or www.writers.ns.ca

### The Giller Award

Guidelines: Open to full-length novels or collections of short stories in English by a Canadian citizen or permanent resident published by a professional publisher in Canada. Submission packages are sent to publishers, who send their selection of eligible books to the Foundation. Shortlisted publishers are asked to contribute a nominal sum to marketing/promotion efforts.
Entry fee: None. Deadline: Mid-August. Prize: $25,000.

For more information contact:
The Doris Giller Foundation
4 Kintyre Avenue
Toronto ON M4M 1M1
Phone: (416) 466-33647 - Fax: (416) 466-1290
E-mail: elanar@sympatico.ca
Web: www.thegillerprize.ca

## September

### The Albert B. Corey Prize (biennial)

Guidelines: Open to works dealing with some aspect of Canadian-American relations or the history of both countries. Send one copy of the book to each of the judges. For current information contact the Association.
Entry fee: None. Deadline: Fall. Prize: $1,000.

For more information contact:
Canadian Historical Association
395 Wellington Street
Ottawa ON K1A 0N3
Phone: (613) 233-7885 - Fax: (613) 567-3110
Web: www.cha-sch.ca

### The International 3-Day Novel-Writing Contest

Guidelines: Every Labour Day weekend entrants participate from around the world. Research and outlines prior to the contest permissible, but actual writing must take place over the long weekend. For a complete

copy of the rules send an SASE (enclose International Reply Coupon if residing outside Canada) to the above address or visit our website.
Entry fee: $35. Deadline: Registration must be postmarked by Friday of the Labour Day weekend. Prize: Publication.

For more information contact:
Anvil Press Publishers
204A–175 East Broadway
Vancouver BC V5T 1W2
Phone: (604) 876-8710 - Fax: (604) 879- 2667
E-mail: subter@portal.ca
Web: www.anvilpress.com

**The Literati Short Story Contest**

Guidelines: See website or send SASE for details.
Entry fee: $10. Deadline: September 15. Prize: Varies — up to $5,000.

For more information contact:
Scribendi
4 Sherman Street
Thamesville ON N0P 2K0
E-mail: contactus@scribendi.com
Web: www.scribendi.com/contest.htm

**Saskatchewan Book Awards**

Deadline: September 15 for books published in August and September. For list of categories see entry under July 15.

**The MacLean Hunter Endowment for Literary Nonfiction**

Guidelines: Open to anyone except students or instructors in the Creative Writing Program at the University of British Columbia. Entries must be original, unpublished material, not under consideration elsewhere. We will purchase first North American serial rights for all work accepted for publication. Entries must be no longer than 25 pages. No e-mail entries. Works of translation are eligible. Blind judging. Title only on each page of the manuscript.
Entry fee: $25/one piece of nonfiction, plus $5 for each additional piece. Payment from non-Canadian entrants in U.S. funds. Please make cheques payable to *PRISM international*. Deadline: September 30. Prize: $1,500 and $20/page for publication as well as a 1-year subscription.

For more information contact:
Creative Writing Program, UBC
Buch. E 462 – 1866 Main Mall
Vancouver BC V6T 1Z1
Web: www.arts.ubc.ca/prism

### National Campus Symposium Retail Award

Guidelines: Entrants must have participated in CPC directed campaigns.
Entry fee: None. Deadline: September 30. Prize: Certificate.

For more information contact:
Canadian Publishers' Council
250 Merton Street, Suite 203
Toronto ON M4S 1B1
Phone: (416) 322-7011 (ext. 226) - Fax: (416) 322-6999
E-mail: coneill@pubcouncil.ca
Web: www.pubcouncil.ca

### The Acorn-Rukeyser Chapbook Contest

Guidelines: Open to poetry manuscripts of up to 30 pages. Poems may be published or unpublished. Manuscripts must be typed or word processed. Simultaneous submissions are acceptable. Blind judging. Copyright remains with the author. All entries returned after the winner is published. Winner notified in spring. All entrants receive a copy by Labour Day.
Entry fees: $12 (CDN); $10 (U.S.); £5 (UK). Make cheques payable to Mekler & Deahl, Publishers. Deadline: September 30. Prizes: Winner $100 (U.S.), publication and 50 copies of the book; Runner-up: $100 (U.S.).

For more information contact:
Mekler & Deahl, Publishers
237 Prospect Street South
Hamilton ON L8M 2Z6
Phone: (905) 312-1779
E-mail: james@meklerdeahl.com

### Canadian Writer's Journal Semi-annual Short Fiction Contest

Guidelines: Open to original, unpublished stories, any genre, maximum length 1,200 words (accurate word count please). Blind judging. Manuscripts destroyed at end of the competition. Send #10 (business size) SASE for contest results only. Winners announced in CWJ and on the website. Entry gives permission to include all the annual winners in a collection entitled *Choice Works*, which is published separately.
Entry fee: $5/story. Deadline: September 30. Prizes: $100; $50; $25; honourable mentions receive 1-year subscription to the magazine.

For more information contact:
The Canadian Writers' Journal

PO Box 5180
New Liskeard ON P0J 1P0
Web: www.cwj.ca

## October

### Write Your Heart Out Romance Novel Contest.

Guidelines: Open to original, unpublished contemporary romance novel manuscripts with no explicit sexual content or paranormal storylines. Send the first 3 chapters and two-page synopsis with estimated word count of the completed manuscript. Title page must include your name, address, phone number, e-mail address if applicable, and whether the entire manuscript is finished. Multiple entries allowed but no simultaneous submissions. Previous winners not eligible. Manuscripts will not be returned. For complete guidelines visit website.
Entry fee: $15(CDN) or $10(U.S.). Deadline: Check website. Prizes: $500 (CDN) and possible book contract; $100 (CDN); plus 10 consolation prizes of a detailed critique of your first three chapters and synopsis by our editorial team.

For more information contact:
Ponder Publishing Inc.
PO Box 23037 RPO McGillivray
Winnipeg MB R3T 5S3
Web: www.ponderpublishing.com/

### Canadian Nurses Association Awards of Excellence

Guidelines: Open to print and broadcast media reports that foster greater public understanding of the Canadian health care system by informing and educating Canadian audiences about health care, the role of health organizations and health care professionals.
Entry fee: None. Deadline: October. Please consult the CNA website for exact date. Prizes: Award of Excellence and Award of Merit in each of two categories.

For more information contact:
Canadian Nurses Association
50 Driveway
Ottawa ON K2P 1E2
Phone: (613) 237-2159 (ext. 310) - Fax: (613) 237-3520
E-mail: csaindon@cna-nurses.ca
Web: www.cna-nurses.ca

### *FreeFall* Magazine Fiction & Poetry Contest

Guidelines: Open to fiction: max 3,000 words; poetry: 5 poems/entry. An entry form and a separate cover sheet listing category, title, and word count must accompany each entry. Blind judging. Do not fold or staple. No electronic or fax submissions accepted. Entry form and details on website.
Entry fee: $10/entry. Deadline: October 1. Prizes: Fiction: $200, $100; Poetry: $200, $100.

For more information contact:
*FreeFall* magazine
Fiction and Poetry Contest
c/o Alexandra Writers' Centre Society
922 – 9 Avenue SE
Calgary AB T2G 0S4
Phone: (403) 264-4730 - Fax: (403) 264-4730
E-mail: awcs@telusplanet.net
Web: www.alexandrawriters.org

### Francois-Xavier Garneau Medal (awarded every 5 years)

Guidelines: Open to a Canadian citizen or landed immigrant for an outstanding scholarly book in either official language, published in the field of history. Entries to be mailed to judges selected for the year of competition.
Entry fee: None. Deadline: October 1. Prize: $2,000 and a specially minted medal engraved with recipient's name.

For more information contact:
Canadian Historical Association
395 Wellington Street
Ottawa ON K1A 0N3
Phone: (613) 233-7885 - Fax: (613) 567-3110
Web: www.cha-sch.ca

### Awesome Authors Youth Writing Contest
### Super auteurs concours d'critures pour les jeunes

Guidelines: Open to children resident in the City of Ottawa in three age groups: 9–11; 12–14; 15–17 for original, unpublished poetry and short stories. Entries may be dropped of at any library branch in the amalgamated City of Ottawa.
Entry fee: None. Deadline: October 11. Prizes: $50; $30; $20 for both English and French winners in each category.

For more information contact:
Jane Venus

Manager Children's and Youth Services
Ottawa Public Library
101 Centrepointe Drive
Ottawa ON  K2G 5K7
Phone: (613) 727-6700
Web: www.library.Ottawa.on.ca

**No Love Lost Poetry contest**

Guidelines: Open to previously unpublished poems on the following topics: love, hate, lust, desire, passion, jealousy and ambivalence (including brotherly, sisterly, parental love, love of country, city etc.) for an annual international anthology of poetry. Send three poems. See website for full information.
Entry fee: $15 (includes copy of full-colour cover perfect bound book). Deadline: October 30. Prizes: 10 Cash Prizes from $10 to $100 plus up to 12 honourable mentions and up to 300 runner-up poems published.

For more information contact:
Hidden Brook Press
412 – 701 King Street West
Toronto ON  M5V 2W7
Phone: (416) 504-3966
E-mail: contestinfo@hiddenbrookpress.com
Web: www.hiddenbrookpress.com

**Winnipeg *Free Press*/Writers' Collective Nonfiction and Poetry Contests**

Guidelines: Call or e-mail for entry form that includes full details. Entry fee: $5/members; $10/non-members. Deadline: October 31. Prizes: $50–$200 plus one-year membership in Writers' Collective including six issues of the magazine.

For more information contact:
4th Floor Library
University of Winnipeg
515 Portage Avenue
Winnipeg MB  R3B 2E9
Phone: (204) 786-9468
E-mail: writerscollective@uwinnipeg.ca
Web: scholar.uwinnipeg.ca/groups/writerscollective/

**The Cecilia Lamont Literary Contest (poetry and prose)**

Guidelines: Open to poetry (to 36 lines) and prose (short stories, articles, fiction or nonfiction to 1,000 words) not previously published for a fee. Blind judging. Mss. to show title only. By entering this contest, par-

ticipants grant the White Rock and Surrey Writers' Club the right to feature their entries in future club publications (if any), but subsequent publishing rights remain with the author. Entries not complying with the length limits will be disqualified.
Entry fee: $6/piece submitted, reduced to $5/piece for 4 or more, which can be a mix of categories, payable to: White Rock and Surrey Writers' Club. Deadline: October 31. Prizes: $75/engraved plaque; $50/certificate; $25/certificate; Three honourable mentions: book and certificate in each category.

For more information contact:
The Cecilia Lamont Literary Contest
c/o Community Arts Council of White Rock & District
15242 Russell Avenue
White Rock BC  V4B 2P6
Phone: (604) 536-8333 - Fax: (604) 536-8335
E-mail: robin.rankine@whiterockartscouncil.com

### The Sandburg-Livesay Anthology Contest

Guidelines: Open to poems published or unpublished, any length up to 70 lines. Up to 10 poems may be submitted per entry fee. Blind judging. Poems will be judged individually; more than one poem by a single author may be accepted for publication. Copyright remains with the author. Winners will be notified in late spring. All entrants will be notified and receive a copy of the anthology, a $20 value, by Labour Day. Entrants with poetry in the anthology will receive one additional copy.
Entry fee: $15(CDN); $12(U.S.); £6(UK) payable by cheque to Mekler & Deahl, Publishers. Deadline: October 31. Prizes: $250 (U.S.); $150 (U.S.); $100 (U.S.) all with anthology publication. Other prizes: anthology publication.

For more information contact:
Mekler & Deahl, Publishers
237 Prospect Street South
Hamilton ON  L8M 2Z6
Phone: (905) 312-1779
E-mail: james@meklerdeahl.com

### Annual BC Alternative Writing and Design Contest

Guidelines: Open to BC residents (past and present) only. Looking for innovative, edgy, humorous and experimental work in all genres.
Entry fee: $12 (all entrants receive 1 copy of anthology); $6/additional submission. Deadline: October 31. Prizes: 24 authors share $2,500 and publication in annual anthology of Poetry; Short Fiction; Creative Rant;

Cover Art. $400 to winners in each genre, honorarium for honourable mentions.

For more information contact:
Ripple Effect Press
PO Box 2836
349 W. Georgia Street
Vancouver BC V6B 3X2
Phone: (604) 879-7327 - Fax: (604) 879-7321
E-mail: info@rippleeffectpress.com
Web: www.rippleeffectpress.com

## November

### Pat Lowther Memorial Award

Guidelines: Found on website.
Entry fee: $15/title. Deadline: November. Prize: $1,000.

For more information contact:
League of Canadian Poets
54 Wolseley Street, Suite 204
Toronto ON M5T 1A5
Phone: (416) 504-1657 - Fax: (416) 504-0096
E-mail: league@poets.ca
Web: www.poets.ca

### Gerald Lampert Memorial Award

Guidelines: Found on website.
Entry fee: $15/title. Deadline: November. Prize: $1,000.

For more information contact:
League of Canadian Poets
54 Wolseley Street, Suite 204
Toronto ON M5T 1A5
Phone: (416) 504-1657 - Fax: (416) 504-0096
E-mail: league@poets.ca
Web: www.poets.ca

### The Ray Burrell Award for Poetry

Guidelines: Open to poetry, any style, unpublished, in English, single-spaced, to 60 lines. No limit. Send two copies. Blind judging. All winning entries will be published in *The Grist Mill*, with free contributors' copy and 1- year subscription to *The Valley Writers' News*. Bios will be solicited. Results TBA no later than the end of January.
Entry fee: $5/poem, payable to Valley Writers' Guild. Deadline: First Fri-

day in November. Prizes: $500 and an engraved plaque; $200/$100 and up to three honourable mentions of $20 each.

For more information contact:
The Ray Burrell Award for Poetry
c/o Valley Writers' Guild
PO Box 534
Merrickville ON K0G 1N0
E-mail: vwg@storm.ca
Web: www.storm.ca/~vwg

**Short Prose Competition for Developing Writers**

Guidelines: Open to Canadian citizens or landed immigrants who have not been published in book form and who do not have a contract with a publisher. Entries must be original, unpublished and either fiction or nonfiction of maximum 2,500 words in English. Blind judging. Entries will not be returned.
Entry fee: $25 payable to the Writers' Union of Canada. Deadline: November 3. Prize: $2,500 plus publication in a Canadian literary journal.

For more information contact:
The Writers' Union of Canada
40 Wellington Street E., 3rd Floor
Toronto ON M5E 1C7
Phone: (416) 703-8982 (ext. 223) - Fax: (416) 506-7656
E-mail: projects@writersunion.ca
Web: www.writersunion.ca

**Nelson Reese Poetry Prize (Catullus Theme)**

Guidelines: Take any Catullus poem and re-wire it.
Entry fee: None. Deadline: November 10. Prize: Cash prize and publication.

For more information contact:
NOTHO.NET
4127 avenue Colonial
Montreal PQ H2W 2C2
E-mail: nath@notho.net
Web: notho.net

**The Ann Connor Brimer Award**

Guidelines: Open to both fiction and nonfiction books, by authors alive and living in Atlantic Canada, intended for youth up to age 15, published in the preceding calendar year. No textbooks. Illustration not a consideration. The book must be in print and readily available. Send 3 copies to accompany the nomination form. Prize awarded in May at the

Atlantic Writing Awards.
Entry fee: None. Deadline: November 15. Prize: $1,000 plus a framed certificate.

For more information contact:
Nova Scotia Library Association
PO Box 36036
Halifax NS B3J 3S9
Phone: (902) 490-5875 - Fax: (902) 490-5893
E-mail: mahm1@nsh.library.ns.ca
Web: nsla.ns.ca/awards.html#ConnorBrimer

**The Writers' Trust of Canada:**
**Drainie-Taylor Biography Prize;**
**Rogers Writer's Trust Fiction Prize;**
**Shaughnessy Cohen Prize for Political Writing;**
**Pearson Writer's Trust Nonfiction Award.**

Guidelines: See Writer's Trust Awards listed for July 31. Deadline: November 15.

For more information contact:
The Writers' Trust of Canada
40 Wellington Street East, Suite 300
Toronto ON M5E 1C7
Phone: (416) 504-8222 - Fax: (416) 504-9090
E-mail: info@writers.trust.com
Web: www.writerstrust.com

**The Betty Drevniok Award**

Guidelines: Send up to 10 original, unpublished haiku not currently under consideration elsewhere. Haiku must be typed or neatly printed in triplicate on 3" x 5" cards. One card/set must only include author's name and address in upper corner. No entries returned.
Entry fee: $4/haiku. Deadline: November 30. Prizes: $100; $50; $25.

For more information contact:
Haiku Canada
c/o Ann Goldring
4162 Vandorf Road
Stouffville ON L4A 7X5

**The Herb Barrett Award**

Guidelines: Open to haiku or short poems, published or unpublished; must be no more than 4 lines long. Haiku may or may not follow the traditional 17-syllable form, but should be in the haiku tradition. Up to 10 haiku or short poems in the haiku tradition per entry fee. Blind judging.

One poem/page. Copyright remains with the author. Winners will be notified in summer. All entrants will receive one copy of the anthology by Labour Day. Entrants with poetry in the anthology will receive one additional copy.
Entry fees: $12(CDN); $10(U.S.); £5(UK) payable by cheque to Mekler & Deahl, Publishers. Deadline: November 30. Prizes: $200 (U.S.); $150 (U.S.); $100 (U.S.). Other prizes: anthology publication.

For more information contact:
Mekler & Deahl, Publishers
237 Prospect Street South
Hamilton ON L8M 2Z6
Phone: (905) 312-1779
E-mail: james@meklerdeahl.com
Web: www.meklerdeahl.com

**Bliss Carman Poetry Award**

Guidelines: Send up to 3 original, unpublished poems/entry, not submitted elsewhere for publication or broadcast, or to another competition. Maximum 150 lines. Blind judging. No faxed or e-mailed submissions accepted. Entries will not be returned.
Entry fee: $27. Deadline: November 30. Prizes: $500; $300; $200.

For more information contact:
Prairie Fire Press, Inc.
423 – 100 Arthur Street
Winnipeg MB R3B 1H3
Phone: (204) 943-9066 - Fax: (204) 942-1555
E-mail: prfire@escape.ca
Web: www.prairiefire.mb.ca

**Short Fiction Award**

Guidelines: One story/entry, maximum 15,000 words with no identification. Story must be original, unpublished, not submitted elsewhere for publication or broadcast, or to another competition. No faxed or e-mailed submissions accepted. Entries will not be returned.
Entry fee: $27. Deadline: November 30. Prizes: $500; $300; $200.

For more information contact:
Prairie Fire Press, Inc.
423 – 100 Arthur Street
Winnipeg MB R3B 1H3
Phone: (204) 943-9066 - Fax: (204) 942-1555
E-mail: prfire@escape.ca
Web: www.prairiefire.mb.ca

### Creative Nonfiction Award

Guidelines: Open to original, unpublished essays not submitted elsewhere for publication or broadcast, or to another competition. Maximum length 5,000 words. One essay/entry. Blind judging. No faxed or e-mailed submissions accepted. Entries will not be returned.
Entry fee: $27. Deadline: November 30. Prizes: $500; $300; $200.

For more information contact:
Prairie Fire Press, Inc.
423 – 100 Arthur Street
Winnipeg MB R3B 1H3
Phone: (204) 943-9066 - Fax: (204) 942-1555
E-mail: prfire@escape.ca
Web: www.prairiefire.mb.ca

### Winners' Circle Short Story Contest

Guidelines: Open to unpublished stories to maximum of 4,000 words, double-spaced, wide margins. Blind judging. Story title only on each page of manuscript. Include SASE for manuscript evaluation. Limit: 5 entries per writer. Winning stories published in an anthology.
Entry fee: $20. Deadline: November 30. Prize: Grand prize: $500. Others: $150; $100; $50.

For more information contact:
Toronto and Central Ontario Branch
Canadian Authors Association
PO Box 11041
97 Guildwood Parkway
Toronto ON M1E 5G5
Web: www.tacob.org

### John Bullen Prize

Guidelines: Open to historical dissertations written by Canadian citizens or landed immigrants living in Canada who have been accepted for the doctoral degree at a Canadian university during the previous academic year. Each complete submission must include the following: a copy of the dissertation; a copy of a letter from the university's Faculty of Graduate Studies attesting that the dissertation was accepted for the doctoral degree in the period specified; and a copy of a letter of presentation from the department Head, Chair, or Graduate Chair. For complete guidelines consult the website.
Entry fee: None. Deadline: November 30. Prize: $500.

For more information contact:
Canadian Historical Association

395 Wellington Street
Ottawa ON K1A 0N3
Phone: (613) 233-7885 - Fax: (613) 567-3110
Web: www.cha-shc.ca

### The Donner Prize

Guidelines: Open to provocative, readable, and inspiring books on Canadian public policy that cover a broad spectrum of issues, including healthcare, social issues, educational reform, public finance, environment, regulatory/legal reform, urban affairs, youth issues, and social policy. The author must be Canadian, and the publisher of the book must be either Canadian or American.
Entry fee: None. Deadline: November 30. Prizes: $25,000 and $10,000 each to two runners-up.

For more information contact:
Donner Canadian Foundation Prize Manager
Meisner Publicity
112 Braemore Gardens
Toronto ON M6G 2C8
Phone: (416) 656-3722 - Fax: (416) 658-5205
E-mail: meisner@interlog.com
Web: www.donnerbookprize.com

### Municipal Chapter of Toronto IODE Book Award

Guidelines: Open to residents of Toronto (GTA) only. Award given annually to author and/or illustrator of children's book published by Canadian publisher, for ages 6 through 12.
Entry fee: None. Deadline: End of November. Prize: $1,000.

For more information contact:
Municipal Chapter of Toronto IODE Book Award
40 St. Clair Ave. East
Toronto ON M4T 1M9
Phone: (416) 925-5078 - Fax: (416) 925-5127
E-mail: iodetoronto@lefca.com

## December

### The McNally Robinson Book of the Year Award

Guidelines: Open to non-academic books of fiction, poetry, creative nonfiction, nonfiction and drama. Entries must be written in English by a living author who will have been a resident in Manitoba for three of the last five years as well as one of the past two years. Please note that books written by more than one author are eligible as long as all authors meet

the residency criteria.
Entry fee: $25/title. Deadline: December. Prize: $3,000.

For more information contact:
The Manitoba Writers' Guild
206 – 100 Arthur Street
Winnipeg MB R3B 1H3
Phone: (204) 942-6134 - Fax: (204) 942-5754
E-mail: mbwriter@escape.ca

**The McNally Robinson Books for Young People Award (Young Adult/Children)**

Guidelines: Open to non-academic books of fiction, poetry, creative nonfiction, nonfiction and drama written in English by a living author. Eligible authors will have been a resident in Manitoba for three of the last five years as well as one of the past two years. Please note that books written by more than one author are eligible as long as all authors meet the residency criteria.
Entry fee: $25/title. Deadline: December. Prize: $1,500 for each of two authors.

For more information contact:
The Manitoba Writers' Guild
206 – 100 Arthur Street
Winnipeg MB R3B 1H3
Phone: (204) 942-6134 - Fax: (204) 942-5754
E-mail: mbwriter@escape.ca

**The Eileen McTavish Sykes Award for Best First Book**

Guidelines: Open to authors of a first professionally published, non-academic book, written in English by a living author. Books of fiction, poetry, creative nonfiction, nonfiction and drama published between January 1 and December 31 of the competition year will be considered. Eligible authors will have been a resident in Manitoba for three of the last five years and one of the past two years. If the book has more than one author all must meet the residency criteria.
Entry fee: $25/title. Deadline: December. Prize: $1,500.

For more information contact:
The Manitoba Writers' Guild
206 – 100 Arthur Street
Winnipeg MB R3B 1H3
Phone: (204) 942-6134 - Fax: (204) 942-5754
E-mail: mbwriter@escape.ca

### Le Prix littraire (biennial, even years)

Guidelines: Open to Manitoba authors writing in French who have published books or produced plays. Entries must be a non-academic, single title, written in French by a living author who has been resident in Manitoba for three of the last five years as well as one of the last two years. Books of fiction, poetry, creative nonfiction and playwriting will be considered.
Entry fee: None. Deadline: December. Prize: $3,500.

For more information contact:
The Manitoba Writers' Guild
206 – 100 Arthur Street
Winnipeg MB R3B 1H3
Phone: (204) 942-6134 - Fax: (204) 942-5754
E-mail: mbwriter@escape.ca

### The William Kennedy Isbister Award for Nonfiction

Guidelines: Open to non-academic, single title, adult books of nonfiction, written in English by a living author and published between January 1 and December 31 of year of submission. Eligible authors will have been resident in Manitoba for three of the last five years as well as one of the last two years.
Entry fee: $25. Deadline: December. Prize: $3,500.

For more information contact:
The Association of Manitoba Book Publishers
404 – 100 Arthur Street
Winnipeg MB R3B 1H3
Phone: (204) 947-3335
E-mail: assocpub@mb.sympatico.ca

### The Margaret Laurence Award for Fiction

Guidelines: Open to non-academic, single title adult fiction books written in English by a living author published between January 1and December 31 of the year of submission. Eligible authors will have been resident in Manitoba for three of the last five years as well as one of the last two years.
Entry fee: $25. Deadline: December. Prize: $3,500.

For more information contact:
The Association of Manitoba Book Publishers
404 – 100 Arthur Street
Winnipeg MB R3B 1H3
Phone: (204) 947-3335
E-mail: assocpub@mb.sympatico.ca

**Newfoundland and Labrador Book Awards**

Guidelines: Open to poetry and nonfiction; fiction and children's literature given on alternate years (poetry/nonfiction on even years; fiction/children on odd years). Author prize only, no award for illustrator. Eligible are single-authored books that may have been published anywhere in Canada BUT the author must have lived in the province of Newfoundland and Labrador for any combination of 36 of the last 60 months, including the five years to the December 31 date of entry. Send four copies of each entry accompanied by a letter stating the category being entered and the eligibility requirements being met. Author or publisher may enter.
Entry fee: None. Deadline: December. Prizes: $1,000 per category.

For more information contact:
Writers' Alliance of Newfoundland and Labrador
PO Box 2681
St John's NF  A1C 5M5
Phone: (709) 739-5251 - Fax: (709) 739-5931
E-mail: wanl@nfld.com
Web: writersalliance.nf.ca

**Wallace K. Ferguson Prize**

Guidelines: Open to Canadian citizens or landed immigrants who have published an outstanding scholarly book in a field of history other than Canadian history, during the past year. Authors of eligible books are encouraged to check with their publishers to ensure their work has been submitted. Some restrictions apply. For judges and complete requirements consult the website.
Entry fee: None. Deadline: December 1. Prize: $1,000.

For more information contact:
Canadian Historical Association
395 Wellington Street
Ottawa ON  K1A 0N3
Phone: (613) 233-7885 - Fax: (613) 567-3110
Web: www.cha-shc.ca

**Sir John A. Macdonald Prize**

Guidelines: Open to nonfiction work of Canadian history "judged to have made the most significant contribution to an understanding of the Canadian past." Authors of eligible books are encouraged to check with their publishers to ensure their work has been submitted. Some restrictions apply. For judges and complete requirements consult the website.
Entry fee: None. Deadline: December 1. Prize: $1,000.

For more information contact:
Canadian Historical Association
395 Wellington Street
Ottawa ON K1A 0N3
Phone: (613) 233-7885 - Fax: (613) 567-3110
Web: www.cha-shc.ca

**Atlantic Poetry Prize**

Guidelines: Open to full-length books of adult poetry written by Atlantic Canadians, and published as a whole for the first time in the previous calendar year. Entrants must be native or resident of Newfoundland, Prince Edward Island, Nova Scotia, or New Brunswick and have spent a substantial portion of their lives there, or have lived in one or a combination of these provinces for at least 24 consecutive months prior to entry deadline date. Publishers: send four copies and a letter attesting to the author's status as an Atlantic Canadian and the author's current mailing address and telephone number.
Entry fee: None. Deadline: First Friday in December. Prize: $1,000.

For more information contact:
Writers' Federation of Nova Scotia
1113 Marginal Road
Halifax NS B3H 4P7
Phone: (902) 423-8116 - Fax: (902) 422-0881
E-mail: talk@writers.ns.ca
Web: www.writers.ns.ca

**Evelyn Richardson Memorial Nonfiction Award**

Guidelines: Open to full-length books of nonfiction written by Nova Scotians, and published as a whole for the first time in the previous calendar year. Publishers: send four copies and a letter attesting to the author's status as a Nova Scotian and the author's current mailing address and phone number. Nova Scotia's highest award for a book of nonfiction written by a Nova Scotian.
Entry fee: None. Deadline: First Friday in December. Prize: $1,000.

For more information contact:
Writers' Federation of Nova Scotia
1113 Marginal Road
Halifax NS B3H 4P7
Phone: (902) 423-8116 - Fax: (902) 422-0881
E-mail: talk@writers.ns.ca
Web: www.writers.ns.ca

## Thomas Head Raddall Atlantic Fiction Award

Guidelines: Open to full-length books of fiction written by Atlantic Canadians, and published as a whole for the first time in the previous calendar year, are eligible. Entrants must be native or resident of Newfoundland, Prince Edward Island, Nova Scotia, or New Brunswick and have spent a substantial portion of their lives there, or have lived in one or a combination of these provinces for at least 24 consecutive months prior to entry deadline. Publishers: send four copies and a letter attesting to the author's status as an Atlantic Canadian and the author's current mailing address and telephone number.
Entry fee: None. Deadline: First Friday in December. Prize: $10,000.

For more information contact:
Writers' Federation of Nova Scotia
1113 Marginal Road
Halifax NS B3H 4P7
Phone: (902) 423-8116 - Fax: (902) 422-0881
E-mail: talk@writers.ns.ca
Web: www.writers.ns.ca

## Cunard First Book Award

Guidelines: Open to full-length books of fiction, nonfiction or poetry written by Atlantic Canadians, and published as a whole for the first time in the previous calendar year. Entrants must have spent a substantial portion of their lives in Atlantic Canada, or lived in one or a combination of these provinces for at least 24 consecutive months prior to entry deadline. Entries submitted to the Atlantic Poetry Prize, Evelyn Richardson Nonfiction Award, Thomas Head Raddall Atlantic Fiction Award, Dartmouth Book Award, and/or Ann Connor Brimer Award are automatically entered in the competition. Publishers: send four copies and a letter attesting to the author's regional status, current mailing address and phone number.
Entry fee: None. Deadline: First Friday in December. Prize: $500.

For more information contact:
Writers' Federation of Nova Scotia
1113 Marginal Road
Halifax NS B3H 4P7
Phone: (902) 423-8116 - Fax: (902) 422-0881
E-mail: talk@writers.ns.ca
Web: www.writers.ns.ca

### Dartmouth Book Awards

Guidelines: Open to new books published in award year about Nova Scotia and/or its people. See website for criteria details.
Entry fee: $10/title. Deadline: Early December. Prizes: $1,200 for fiction; $1,200 for nonfiction.

For more information contact;
Jennifer Evans
Dartmouth Book Awards Committee
60 Alderney Drive
Dartmouth NS B2Y 4P8
Phone: (902) 490-5991 - Fax: (902) 490-5889
E-mail: msje1@nsh.library.ns.ca
Web: www.region.halifax.ns.ca/bookawards/index.html

### The Trillium Book Award/Prix Trillium

Guidelines: Open to books in any genre: fiction, nonfiction, drama, children's books, and poetry by Ontario writers who have lived in Ontario for at least three out of the past five years and who have been published anywhere in the world, submitted by their publishers. Titles must have been published for the first time in the previous calendar year, remain in print in that year and be available for sale in the following spring. Submit 4 copies for jury and promotional use: these will not be returned. Anthologies, new editions, reissues and translations are not eligible.
Entry fee: None. Deadline: December 11. Prizes: $12,000 (author); $2,500 (publisher) in each official language.

For more information contact:
Ministry of Tourism, Culture and Recreation
Arts and Cultural Industries Branch
400 University Avenue, 5th Floor
Toronto ON M7A 2R9
Phone: (416) 314-7786 - Fax: (416) 314-7460
E-mail: edward.yanofsky@mczcr.gov.on.ca
Web: www.tourism.gov.on.ca

### *Fiddlehead* Award for Best Story

Guidelines: Open to short stories up to 20 typed pages. No simultaneous submissions, or manuscripts previously accepted for publication. Blind judging. Ms. will not be returned.
Entry fee: $24. Deadline: December 15. Prize: $1,000.

For more information contact;
*The Fiddlehead*

Campus House
11 Garland Court
PO Box 4400
Fredericton NB E3B 5A3
Phone: (506) 453-3501
E-mail: fid@nbnet.nb.ca
Web: www.lib.unb.ca/Texts/Fiddlehead

**Canadian Authors Association National Literary Awards**

Guidelines: Open to full-length books published in competition year by Canadian citizens or landed immigrants in the following categories: MOSAID Technologies Award for Fiction; John Chalmers Award for Poetry; Lela Common Award for Canadian History; The Birks Family Foundation Award for Canadian Auto/Biography; The Jubilee Award (for a collection of short stories by one author). No limit on number of titles entered.
Entry fee: $25/title. Deadline: December 15. Prizes: $2,500 and engraved silver medal.

For more information contact:
Canadian Authors Association
320 South Shores Road
PO Box 419
Campbellford ON K0L 1L0
Phone: (705) 653 0323 - Fax: (705) 653-0593
Toll-free: 1-866-216-6222
E-mail: canauth@redden.on.ca
Web: www.CanAuthors.org

**The Carol Bolt Award for Drama**

Guidelines: Open to plays published or performed in the previous year. No limit on number of plays entered.
Entry fee: $20/title. Deadline: December 15. Prize: $1,000 and engraved silver medal.

For more information contact:
Canadian Authors Association
320 South Shores Road
PO Box 419
Campbellford ON K0L 1L0
Phone: (705) 653 0323 - Fax: (705) 653-0593
Toll-free: 1-866-216-6222
E-mail: canauth@redden.on.ca
Web: www.CanAuthors.org

### CAA Award for Juvenile Short Story

Guidelines: Open to stories published in Canadian magazines or anthologies during the competition year.
Entry fee: None. Deadline: December 15. Prize: $2,500 and certificate.

For more information contact:
Canadian Authors Association
320 South Shores Road
PO Box 419
Campbellford ON  K0L 1L0
Phone: (705) 653 0323 - Fax: (705) 653-0593
Toll-free: 1-866-216-6222
E-mail: canauth@redden.on.ca
Web: www.CanAuthors.org

### Ralph Gustafson Prize for Best Story and Best Poem

Guidelines: Open to fiction: up to 25 pages/entry; poetry: up to 5 poems/entry; Blind judging. No simultaneous submissions. No work previously published or accepted for publication. Entries will not be returned. Winners published in the spring issue of *The Fiddlehead.*
*Entry fee: $24. Deadline: December 15. Prizes: $1,000 each for poetry and fiction, plus two $100 honourable mentions.*

For more information contact:
*The Fiddlehead*
Campus House
11 Garland Court
PO Box 4400
Fredericton NB  E3B 5A3
Phone: (506) 453- 3501
E-mail: fid@nbnet.nb.ca
Web: www.lib.unb.ca/Texts/Fiddlehead

### Science in Society Book Awards

Guidelines: Open to Canadian citizens or residents of Canada for books published in Canada during the previous year in either English or French. Entries must deal with aspects of basic or applied science or technology, historical or current, in any area including health, social or environmental issues, regulatory trends etc. Judging criteria: literary excellence, scientific content and accuracy, initiative, originality, clarity of interpretation and value in promoting greater understanding of science to general readership. Submit 6 copies of book and a brief curriculum vitae of the author(s). Include fully completed entry form with each submission.

Entry fee: None. Deadline: December 15. Prizes: $1,000 one for general readership; one suitable for children

For more information contact:
CSWA Awards
PO Box 1543
Kingston ON K7L 5C7
Phone: 1-800-796-8595 - Fax: (613) 548-8577

**The BC Book Prizes:**
**The Hubert Evans Nonfiction Prize;**
**The Roderick Haig-Brown Regional Prize;**
**The Sheila A. Egoff Children's Literature Prize;**
**The Dorothy Livesay Poetry Prize;**
**The Ethel Wilson Fiction Prize;**
**The Bill Duthie BC Booksellers' Choice Award.**

Guidelines: The full details for each prize are on the website. Entry fee: $25. Deadline: December 24. Prizes: Approx $2,000.

For more information contact:
The BC Book Prizes
207 West Hastings Street, Suite 902
Vancouver BC V6B 1H7
Phone: (604) 687-2405 - Fax: (604) 669-3701
E-mail: info@rebuscreative.net
Web: www.harbour.sfu.ca/bcbook/

**The Griffin Prize for Excellence in Poetry**

Guidelines: Publishers only may enter books. Translations are eligible. The entry form is available online. See website for full requirements. Entry fee: Certain conditions agreed to by publishers. Deadline: December 31. Prize: $80,000 divided into two categories — Canadian and International.

For more information contact:
The Griffin Prize
6610 Edwards Boulevard
Mississauga ON L5T 2V6
Phone: (905) 565-5993 - Fax: (905) 564-3645
E-mail: info@griffinpoetryprize.com
Web: www.griffinpoetryprize.com/welcome.html

**Writers Guild of Alberta Awards program:**
**Henry Kreisel Award for Best First Book**

Guidelines: Open to Alberta authors with books published anywhere in the world between January 1 and December 31 of the preceding year.

To be eligible, authors must have been resident in the province for at least 12 of the 18 months prior to the entry date. Eligible plays must be submitted with copies of contracts of performances. Registered plays having a minimum of three consecutive public performances during premiere engagements may be entered. Except in the drama category unpublished manuscripts and anthologies are not eligible. Full-length radio plays that have been published in anthologies are eligible. Mail 5 copies of each book or registered play. Works may be submitted by authors, publishers or any interested parties.
Entry fee: None. Deadline: December 31. Prize: $1,000 and leather-bound copy of winning book.

**Gwen Pharis Ringwoood Award for Drama**

Guidelines: As above. An additional 3 copies of each book must be submitted for plays that are also entering the Best First Book category.
Entry fee: None. Deadline: December 31. Prize: $1,000 and leather-bound copy of winning book.

**Stephan G. Stephansson Award for Poetry**

Guidelines: As above. Eligible verse plays must be submitted with copies of contracts of performances. An additional 3 copies of each book must be submitted for if they are also entering the Best First Book category.
Entry fee: None. Deadline: December 31. Prize: $1,000 and leather-bound copy of winning book.

**R. Ross Annett Award for Children's Literature**

Guidelines: As above. Unpublished manuscripts and anthologies are not eligible. An additional 3 copies of each book must be submitted for books that are also entering the Best First Book category.
Entry fee: None. Deadline: December 31. Prize: $1,000 and leather-bound copy of winning book.

**Georges Hugnet Award for Novel**

Guidelines: As above. Unpublished manuscripts and anthologies are not eligible. Mail 5 copies of each book and an additional 3 copies if it is also entered for the Best First Book Award.
Entry fee: None. Deadline: December 31. Prize: $1,000 and leather-bound copy of winning book.

**Wilfred Eggleston Award for Nonfiction**

Guidelines: As above. Unpublished manuscripts and anthologies are not eligible. Mail 5 copies of each book and an additional 3 copies if it is also entered for the Best First Book Award.

Entry fee: None. Deadline: December 31. Prize: $1,000 and leather-bound copy of winning book.

**Howard O'Hagan Award for Short Fiction**

Guidelines: As above. Unpublished manuscripts and anthologies are not eligible. Mail 5 copies of each story.
Entry fee: None. Deadline: December 31. Prize: $1,000 and leather-bound copy of winning book.

For more information contact:
Writers Guild of Alberta Awards Program
Percy Page Centre
11759 Groat Road
Edmonton AB T5M 3K6
Phone: (780) 422-8174 or 1- 800-665-5354
E-mail: heather@writersguild.ab.ca
Web: www.writersguild.ab.ca

**Poet's Corner Award**

Guidelines: Award is given to the author of the best Canadian-authored, book-length poetry manuscript received.
Entry fee: None. Deadline: December 31. Prize: $500 plus trade publication.

For more information contact:
Broken Jaw Press
PO Box 596, Station A
Fredericton NB  E3B 5A6
Phone: (506) 454-5127
E-mail: jblades@nbnet.ca
Web: www.brokenjaw.com/poetscorner.htm

**Geoffrey Bilson Award for Historical Fiction for Young People**

Guidelines: Open to work of historical fiction for young people. The award winner is decided by a jury selected by the Canadian Children's Book Centre. Contact CCBC for current criteria.
Entry fee: None. Deadline: December 31. Prize: $1,000.

For more information contact:
Brenda Halliday, Librarian
101 – 40 Orchard View Blvd.
Toronto ON  M4R 1B9
Phone: (416) 975-0010 - Fax: (416) 975-8970
E-mail: brenda@bookcentre.ca
Web: www.bookcentre.ca (under Children's Book Awards)

### The National Chapter of Canada IODE Violet Downey Book Award

Guidelines: Open to English language books containing at least 500 words of text (preferably with Canadian content) in any category, suitable for children aged 13 and under. The book must be written by a Canadian citizen, and must have been published in Canada during the calendar year immediately preceding the National Chapter annual meeting held in May. Fairy tales, anthologies and books adapted from another source are not eligible.
Entry fee: None. Deadline: December 31. Prize: $3,000.

For more information contact:
The National Chapter of Canada IODE
40 Orchard View Blvd., Suite 254
Toronto ON M4R 1B9
Phone: (416) 487-4416 - Fax: (416) 487-4417
E-mail: iodecanada@sympatico.ca
Web: www.iodecanada.ca

### *The Sunday Star* Short Story Contest

Guidelines: Open to Canadian citizens or residents 16 years and older with no affiliation to the newspaper or those immediately connected with it. Entries limited to one original, unpublished entry per person to a maximum of 2,500 words. Blind judging. A 25–50 word biographical sketch on a separate sheet of paper must be included. No school assignments. Pseudonyms not permitted.
Entry fee: $5 by cheque or money order payable to *The Sunday Star* Short Story Contest. Deadline: December 31. Prizes: $10,000; $3,000; $1,000 and seven honourable mentions receive $200, all with publication.

For more information contact:
Short Story Contest
*The Sunday Star*
One Yonge Street
Toronto ON M5E 1E6
Phone: (416) 350-3000 (press 2747)
Web: www.thestar.com (click on contests)

### The British Columbia Historical Federation Awards

Guidelines: Open to books presenting any facet of BC history, published in the contest year, which include names, dates, and places with relevant maps and pictures. Not limited to BC writers. Reprints and revisions are ineligible. Send two copies of the book, which will become the property of the Federation. Include name and address of person submit-

ting the book, the selling price of all editions and the address from which it may be purchased. Include shipping and handling costs if bought by mail order.
Entry fee: None. Deadline: December 31. Prizes: $300; $200; $100 and honourable mentions plus certificate of merit.

### The Lieutenant Governor's Medal for Historical Writing

Guidelines: For a book that contributes significantly to the recorded history of BC.
Entry fee: None. Deadline: December 31. Prize: Medal.

For more information contact:
Lloyd Atchison
#10 – 6488 168th Street
Surrey BC V3S 8Z1
Phone: (604) 576-4959
E-mail: atchis@axionet.com

### Best Article Award

Guidelines: Open to articles to a maximum of 3,000 words, submitted for publication in the *BC Historical News* by amateur historians or students. Entries to be typed, double-spaced and accompanied by photographs if available, and substantiated with footnotes where applicable. Photos should be accompanied with the following information: source, permission to publish, archival number if applicable and a brief caption. Photos will be returned to the writer.
Entry fee: None. Deadline: Ongoing. Prize: Not specified.

For more information contact:
Fred Braches
Editor, *BC Historical News*
PO Box 130
Whonnock BC V2W 1V9

### The Stephen Leacock Memorial Medal for Humour

Guidelines: Open to be Canadian citizens or landed immigrants, living at the time of publication and writing in English. The major emphasis of each entry must be on humour, but literary merit is equally important. All entries must have been published in the competition year and carry an ISBN. In the case of a translation from another language, the translation must have been published in the current year. Submit ten copies of the book, a biographical sketch and photo (at least 5" x 7" and b/w if possible) of the author. After judging, the books are added to the Associates' collections of Canadian humour, and are nonreturnable. The winning author will attend the Awards dinner in Orillia and give an address.

(Please make sure that your author is aware of this obligation.) Check website for full details.
Entry fee: $40. Cheque payable to the Stephen Leacock Associates. Deadline: December 31 of the current year, but earlier submissions are appreciated. Prize: $10,000 and Laurentian Bank medal.

For more information contact:
Ms. Judith D. Rapson
Chair, Award Committee
4223 Line 12 North RR #2
Coldwater ON L0K 1E0
Phone: (705) 835-3218 - Fax: (705) 835-5171
E-mail: drapson@bconnex.net
Web: www.leacock.ca

**The Petra Kenney International Poetry Competition**

Guidelines: Open to poems up to 80 lines. Send 2 copies. No staples, please. Blind judging. Awards ceremony held every May at Canada House, Trafalgar Square, London, England.
Entry fee: $7/poem. Deadline: December 31. Prizes: $2,000; $1,000; $500 and 3 commendations at $250.

For more information contact:
The Executive Director
38 Langmuir Crescent
Toronto ON M6S 2A7
Phone: (416) 769-2964 - Fax: (416) 769-5752
E-mail: molly.y@sympatico.ca
Web: www.petrapoetrycompetition.co.uk

—

Gill Foss is a journalist, editor and award-winning poet whose work has appeared in several anthologies as well as being read on radio. She has organized and judged prose and poetry contests at both the local and national levels. Gill is currently the President of the Canadian Authors Association.

# Federal and Provincial Grants for Writers

*by Karleen Bradford & Gill Foss*

The number of writers applying for grants in Canada today is growing steadily. The number of grants is decreasing. That's the bad news. But there is still a lot of good news. There are grants out there, and writers are receiving them. But applying for them takes skill and know-how. It's a skill all on its own, and one writers would be wise to learn before throwing themselves into the maelstrom.

The most important thing to do, before anything else, is to learn as much as possible about the preparation of an effective grant application and, please, don't waste your time and others' by applying for grants for which you are not qualified. Study the application forms carefully. Then follow the requirements stringently. Make the effort to prepare everything requested as carefully as you can, and be sure it is presented in as professional a manner as possible.

Many grant applications will ask you for a sample of your writing. Choose carefully. This will be the most important aspect of your application. Juries will base their decisions mostly on it. Keep to the word or page count requested. Prepare the piece with as much nitpicking care as you would when you send it off to a publisher. Even if your manuscript is in the first-draft stage, polish the sample until it is as perfect as possible. The sample does not necessarily have to come from your first chapter. Choose a selection that will give a good idea of who your characters are, and what the problems are that beset them.

Let the jurors know that your theme is a meaningful one, and that you are capable of exploring it.

If your work is nonfiction, the topic will be of equal importance with the quality of the writing. Juries must be convinced that your project is of vital importance.

In either fiction or nonfiction, you are usually quite at liberty to send a selection taken from various pieces of work, unless requested otherwise but, if you are applying for a work-in-progress grant, it goes without saying that you send a sample from that work. Again, even though the work may still be in progress, make certain that the sample is a finished, polished piece of writing.

If a description of your project is required, prepare this with as much care and thought as you would prepare the sample of writing. The same points will be important. You must convince the jurors of the importance of your work and of your ability to do it. The quality of the writing in this sample must accurately reflect the quality of the writing in your work.

Send references only when requested. The same thing goes for blurbs or reviews of previous work.

In short — find out what the rules are, follow them, and be professional. Good luck! (If you don't succeed at first — you know what to do.)

—

Karleen Bradford is the award-winning author of 17 works of fiction and nonfiction for children and young adults. Her latest novels include *Whisperings of Magic,* (Harper Collins Publishers Ltd., 2001) and *With Nothing But Our Courage, The Loyalist Diary of Mary MacDonald*, (Scholastic Canada Ltd., Dear Canada Series 2002).

—

## Federal Grants for Writers

### Compiled by Gill Foss

The following is a list of the major grants available to writers across Canada at the time of publication, but they are not necessarily the only ones. Your municipality may offer assistance through its Department of Arts and Culture and local foundations may be available to fund certain projects. Good luck with your applications!

### The Canada Council for the Arts Grants for Professional Writers

Applicants may apply to one of three categories: **Emerging Writer**; **Mid-Career Writer**; **Established Writer**.

- The entry level is one book published by a professional publisher or four major publications in literary journals or recognized magazines.
- Grants are available in amounts up to $10,000 in the **Emerging Writer** category, and up to $20,000 in the others.
- Grants over $10,000 are available only to writers who have a minimum of two books published by professional publishers.
- One deadline per year: October 1.

For further information contact:
Bianca Côté , Program Officer, Writing and Publishing Section
Phone: (613) 566-4414 (ext. 5537) - Fax: (613) 566-4410

Toll-free: 1-800-263-5588 (ext. 5537)
E-mail: bianca.cote@canadacouncil.ca
Web: www.canadacouncil.ca/grants/publishing/

**Grants to Aboriginal Writers, Storytellers and Publishers**

This program provides assistance for the creation, production and dissemination of First Peoples literary and oral arts. There are two components to this program. **Creative writing grants** support new projects of fiction, poetry, orature, children's literature, legends/mythology or literary nonfiction in English, French or Aboriginal languages. **Publishing grants** support Aboriginal publishers and collectives for projects in English, French and Aboriginal languages. Not available for self-publishing projects.

Creative writing grants offer two levels of support:

- Professional writers/storytellers may apply for a maximum of $10,000.
- Developing writers/storytellers for a maximum of $3,000.
- Publishing grants provide a maximum of $20,000.
- One deadline per year: May 15.

For further information and application form contact:
Paul Seesequasis, Writing and Publishing Section Officer
Phone: (613) 566-4414 (ext. 5482) - Fax: (613) 566-4410
Toll-free: 1-800-263-5588 (ext. 5482)
Hearing impaired callers with TTY machine call: (613) 565-5194
E-mail: paul.seesequasis@canadacouncil.ca
Web: www.canadacouncil.ca

## Provincial Grants for Writers

### Alberta

Writers who have been published, produced or aired may apply for: **Art Production** — money to stay at home and write; **Training** — course, retreats, master classes etc.; **Travel/marketing** — attending a launch or premiere of one's work, promo tours, etc.; **Research.**

Writers who have not been published are eligible for the training portion of the grant only.

For further information and guidelines, please contact:
Writing and Publishing Consultant
The Alberta Foundation for the Arts

9th Floor, Standard Life Centre
10405 Jasper Avenue
Edmonton AB  T5J 4R7
Web: www.affta.ab.ca

## British Columbia

Assistance is available to professional British Columbia creative writers through the British Columbia Arts Council for specific creative projects. Two levels of funding are available. **Emerging Writers** may request up to a maximum of $5,000 during one fiscal year; **Senior Writers** may request up to a maximum of $10,000 during one fiscal year. Awards are intended to assist creative writers by providing time to work on the proposed project.

Eligible genres include drama, fiction, juvenile, nonfiction and poetry. Program guidelines, closing dates, application forms and additional information regarding the programs of the British Columbia Arts Council are available through the Council's web page.

For further information contact:
Walter K. Quan, Coordinator, Arts Awards Programs
PO Box 9819, Stn Prov. Govt.
Victoria BC  V8W 9W3
Phone: (250) 356-1728 - Fax: (250) 387-4099
E-mail: jeremy.long@gems5.gov.ba.ca
Web: www.bcartscouncil.gov.bc.ca

## Manitoba

### Writers A Grant

Deadlines: May 15; September 15.
This grant assists professional Manitoba writers who show a high standard of work and exceptional promise with concentrated work on a major writing project. Applicants must have had two major works published professionally in book form or 250 pages published in literary periodicals. The maximum grant is $10,000.

### Writers B Grant

Deadlines: May 15; September 15.
This grant assists professional Manitoba writers in the early stages of their careers with concentrated work on a major writing project. Applicants must have had one major work published professionally in book form or 120 pages published in literary periodicals. The maximum grant is $5,000.

**Writers C Grant**
Deadlines: May 15; September 15.
This grant assists emerging writers with manuscript development. Applicants must show a high standard of written work and exceptional promise, and must have a modest publication background. The maximum grant is $2,000.

**Short-Term Project Grants**
Deadline: Four weeks prior to project.
This grant assists published professional Manitoba writers and editors with projects of short duration related to current artistic work or significant career opportunities. Only one award may be received in a fiscal year. The maximum award is $1,000.

**Art Ventures**
Deadline: February 7.
This program assists projects which explore new directions in the arts or which represent a departure from past practice of the individual.

**ACCESS**
Deadline: February 7.
ACCESS supports projects that assist artists in overcoming barriers to equal opportunities while making the transition to professional status.

For further information contact:
Mark Morton, Writing and Publishing Officer
Phone: (204) 945-0422 - Fax: (204) 945-5925
E-mail: mmorton@artscouncil.mb.ca
Web: www.artscouncil.mb.ca

## New Brunswick

**Creation Grant** available for professional artists for the research, development and execution of original projects in the arts. Maximum grant is $7,000 per two-year period. Applicants must be residents of New Brunswick.

**Documentation Grant** available for professional artists to provide support for original documentation of arts activities, arts products or art history. Preference given to proposals concerning New Brunswick art or artists. Maximum grant is $6,000 per two-year period.

For more information contact:
Program Officer/Agent de programme
New Brunswick Arts Board
Conseil des arts du Nouveau-Brunswick
634 rue Queen Street, Suite 300

Fredericton NB E3B 1C2
Phone: (506) 460-5888
Toll-free: 1-866-460-ARTS
E-mail: rbarriault@artsnb.ca
Web: www.artsnb.ca

## Newfoundland and Labrador

**Project Grants** support production costs, operating costs, travel costs, study costs, and living expenses relating to a specific project to be undertaken by an artist, arts group or organization.

For more information contact:
Newfoundland & Labrador Arts Council
PO Box 98, Station C
St John's NF A1C 5H5
Phone: (709) 726-2212 - Fax: (709) 726-0619
E-mail: kmurphy@newcomm.net
Web: www.nlac.nf.ca

## Nova Scotia

### Nova Scotia Arts Council

Offers a range of programs to encourage creation, presentation, professional development, research, commissioning, touring and travel activities in all the arts disciplines. These programs are available to professional individual artists.

**Professional Development**: Assistance up to $3,000 for formal study programs, mentoring, apprenticeships, conferences, etc. Deadlines: June 30; January 15.

**Creation Grants**: Assistance up to $12,000 to help with the creation of new work by contributing to the artists project and living costs. Deadline: June 30; January 15.

**Presentation Grants**: Assistance up to $5,000 to assist with the direct costs of public presentation of the artist's work. Deadline: June 30; January 15.

For more information contact:
Nova Scotia Arts Council
PO Box 1559
Halifax NS B3J 2Y3
Phone: (902) 422-1123 - Fax: (902) 422-1445
E-mail: nsartscouncil@ns.sympatico.ca
Web: www.novascotiaartscouncil.ns.ca/home.html

### Nova Scotia Talent Trust

The Nova Scotia Talent Trust provides scholarships to Nova Scotians who demonstrate exceptional potential and commitment to become established artists in their chosen fields. Applicants of any age may apply but priority is given to support those who are not yet established and who are undertaking programs of study which will advance their artistic development and who are pursing career paths that can lead to them becoming established artists.

For more information contact:
Nova Scotia Talent Trust
PO Box 456
Halifax NS B3J 2R5
Phone: (902) 424-0710 - Fax: (902) 424-0710
E-mail: nstt@nstalenttrust.ns.ca
Web: www.nstalenttrust.ns.ca

## Ontario

### The Ontario Arts Council

The Ontario Arts Council offers two programs, Writers' Reserve and Works-in-Progress, to emerging and established professional writers who are permanent Ontario residents and Canadian citizens or landed immigrants.

**Writers' Reserve** grants are made upon the recommendation of Ontario book publishing companies or periodicals that have been designated third-party recommenders by the Ontario Arts Council. Writers can apply to create new work in one of the following areas: fiction, poetry, literary criticism, commentary on the visual or performing arts, history, biography, autobiography, political or social issues, science, travel or belles lettres. These categories also apply to writing for children, multimedia CD-ROM or edited electronic media (other than radio or film scripts). The maximum assistance to a writer through this program in one fiscal year is $10,000; the minimum grant is $1,500. (However, any one publisher's total recommendation for any single writer may not exceed $5,000 in one fiscal year.)

**Works-in-Progress** grants are to assist writers with the completion of book-length works of literary merit in poetry and prose. The value of each Works-in-Progress grant is $12,000.

For further information contact:
Ontario Arts Council
151 Bloor Street West

Toronto ON  M5S 1T6
Phone: (416) 961-1660
Toll-free in Ontario: 1-800-387-0058
E-mail: info@arts.on.ca
Web: www.arts.on.ca

**The Toronto Arts Council**

Applicants must have resided in the City of Toronto for at least one year prior to the date of application. Grants are for the creation of new work or for work-in-progress in the area of literary arts:
$1,500 for writers whose work has never been published or produced.
$4,500 for previously published or produced writers.

For further information contact:
Grants Officer
Toronto Arts Council
141 Bathurst Street
Toronto ON  M5V 2R2
Phone: (416) 392-6802 (ext. 205)
E-mail: sara@torontoartscouncil.org
Web: www.torontoartscouncil.org/grant-main.htm

## Prince Edward Island

Maximum grant available to an individual artist is $4,000. **Travel and study grants** of up to $1,000 are also available.
**Professional Development/Study**:
Maximum grant $1000. Residency requirements are six of last 12 months. Maximum grant available for an organization or small group is $7,000. Travel maximum grant is $1,000. Residencey requirements are six of last 12 months.

For further information contact:
Prince Edward Island Council of the Arts
115 Richmond Street
Charlottetown PE  C1A 1H7
Phone: (902) 368-4410
E-mail: artscouncil@pei.aibn.com

## Québec

**Type "A"** grants available for research and creative writing. **Type "B"** grants are for literary events and **Type "C"** grants for professional development.

For further information contact:
Québec Office:

Conseil des arts et des lettres du Québec
79, boul. Rene-Levesque Est, 3e etage
Québec QC H1R 5N5
Phone: (418) 643-1707 - Fax: (418) 643-4558
Toll-free: 1-800-897-1707

Montreal Office:
Conseil des arts et des lettres du Québec
500, place d'Armes, 15e etage
Montreal QC H2Y 2W2
Phone: (514) 864-3350 - Fax: (514) 864-4160
Toll-free: 1-800-608-3350
Web: www.calq.gouv.qc.ca

## Saskatchewan

**Creative Grants** available to assist Saskatchewan's artists and emerging artists. "A" Grants of up to $20,000, "B" Grants of up to $12,000, and "C" Grants of up to $4,000.

**Professional Development Grants** available to assist individuals from Saskatchewan to pursue excellence in the arts through study in a formal setting or in an informal setting such as apprenticeships or mentorships. "A" Grants of up to $10,000, "B" Grants of up to $7,500, and "C" Grants of up to $4,000.

**Research Grants** available to assist individuals from Saskatchewan to pursue research in the arts such as general research, independent curatorial research and research on new techniques or new technologies. "A" Grants of up to $5,000, "B" Grants of up to $3,500, and "C" Grants of up to $1,500.

**Travel Grants** available to assist individuals from Saskatchewan to pursue travel related to their arts practice covering up to 50% of eligible travel costs plus assistance of up to $100 dollars a day for a maximum of five days.

The deadlines for all the above are October 1 and March 15 annually.

For further information contact:
Grants Coordinator
Saskatchewan Arts Board
2135 Broad Street
Regina SK S4P 3V7
Phone: (306) 787-4131 - Fax: (306) 787-4199
Toll-free: 1-800-667-7526

E-mail: grants@artsboard.sk.ca
Web: www.artsboard.sk.ca

## Yukon

**Advanced Artist Award**: Grants to individual artists toward projects contributing to their personal artistic development. Up to $5,000 for "A" level artists, up to $2,500 for "B" level artists. "A" level artists should have some national prominence and "B" level artists should have had a least some local recognition. One year continuous residency in the Yukon prior to application is a requirement.

Deadlines: April 1 and October 1.

For further information contact:
Laurel Parry, Arts Consultant,
Arts and Cultural Industries Branch
Dept. of Tourism, Business and Culture
Government of Yukon
Box 2703 (L-3)
Whitehorse YT Y1A 2C6
Phone (867) 667-5264 - Fax: (867) 393-6456
Toll-free: 1-800-661-0408 (ext. 5264)
E-mail: laurel.parry@gov.yk.ca

**Arts Fund**: Grants to assist community groups and collectives to undertake arts-related projects including the visual, performing or literary arts. Aim is to foster the creative development of the arts in the Yukon.

Deadlines: March, June, September, and December 15.

For further information:
Janice Brodie, Arts Fund Coordinator
Arts and Cultural Industries Branch
Dept. of Tourism, Business and Culture
Government of Yukon
Box 2703 (L-3)
Whitehorse YT Y1A 2C6
Phone: (867) 667- 3535 - Fax: (867) 393-6456
Toll-free: 1-800-661-0408 (ext. 3535)
E-mail: artsfund@gov.yk.ca

—

Gill Foss is a freelance journalist and an award-winning poet whose work has appeared in several anthologies. She is National President of the Canadian Authors Association, a professional member of the Periodical Writers Association of Canada and an Associate member of the Editors Association. She has not yet applied for a grant but, now having this information, will likely do so!

# Writing Schools, Workshops and Retreats

*by Sandra Phinney*

Writers are an inquisitive lot. They seek to learn as much as they can. The good news is that Canada has an abundance of learning opportunities for writers. Whether you are a beginner looking for tools and inspiration, or a seasoned pro who needs a challenge, there is a veritable smorgasbord of "writerly" activities to select from.

Degree and diploma programs offer one- to five-year courses of study in journalism or creative writing. And short-term workshops, retreats, writing festivals and special events abound. These can be a couple of hours, a day, or up to several months in duration. Genres vary and run the gamut from writing verse for greeting cards to writing literary poems, short stories and novels. The medium can be radio, newspapers, magazines, stage or film.

Perhaps you've begun a family memoir ... or thought about starting a freelance business ... or you want to write a play. Somewhere, there is a workshop or course that will suit you to a "T." If you earn you living as a writer, and yearn for professional development, there are ample opportunities for you to do so. And if you are looking for a career as a journalist or aspire to be a literary icon, some of the best schools in the world are right on your doorstep.

The following information is designed to inform you of the choices that exist across the country — and to whet your appetite. Spread your wings! Hone your skills or try something you've never attempted before.

## Degree and Diploma granting programs related to Journalism and Creative Writing

### University of British Columbia

The School of Journalism offers a two-year Master of Journalism (MJ) degree. The School teaches the fundamental skills of researching, reporting and writing for all media. Courses in journalistic issues and ethics also cover all forms of media. The research emphasis is focused on current journalistic issues, especially the impact of new media on conventional means of communication.

School of Journalism
University of British Columbia
6388 Crescent Road
Victoria BC V6T 1Z2
Phone: (604) 822-6688
E-mail: journal@interchange.ubc.ca
Web: www.journalism.ubc.ca/

**University of British Columbia**

The Creative Writing Program at UBC offers a two-year studio course of resident study. Applicants choose from one of two joint degrees: MFA in Stage Playwriting (Creative Writing and Theatre) or MFA in Screenwriting (Creative Writing and Film Studies). UBC also offers a diploma program in Applied Creative Nonfiction. Prerequisite is a Bachelor's degree or equivalent in any discipline and some writing experience in creative nonfiction, fiction or translation.

UBC Creative Writing Program
Buchanan Room E462
866 Main Mall
Vancouver BC V6T 1Z1
Phone: (604) 822-0699
E-mail: patrose@interchange.ubc.ca
Web: www.creativewriting.ubc.ca/

**University of Victoria**

The Writing Department at the university offers the a variety of program options including a Major (in drama, fiction, poetry, nonfiction; also a Writing/Theatre option); a Professional Writing Minor (interdisciplinary, with the English Department) and the Harvey Southam Diploma in Writing and Editing (a postgraduate co-op program in journalism and publishing).

The Department of Writing
University of Victoria
PO Box 1700, STN CSC
Victoria BC V8W 2Y2
Phone: (250) 721-7306
E-mail: writing@finearts.uvic.ca
Web: www.finearts.uvic.ca/writing/

**Simon Fraser University Writing and Publishing Program**

The Writing and Publishing Program offers professional certificates in six areas: Business Writing; Public Relations and Marketing Communications; Editing; Publishing; Technical Communication; and Creative and Professional Writing. Courses can also be taken as freestanding credits.

The Writing and Publishing Program
Continuing Studies
Simon Fraser University at Harbour Centre
515 West Hastings Street
Vancouver BC V6B 5K3
Phone: (604) 291-5093
E-mail: wpp@stu.ca
Web: www.sfu.ca/cstudies/wp/

**Malaspina University-College**

The Department of Creative Writing and Journalism at Malaspina University-College offers comprehensive degree programs (Bachelor of Arts, Major and Minor) in Creative Writing. Professional-level skills are developed in various literary genres including poetry, short fiction, plays, screenplays, news articles and feature stories.

Malaspina University-College
900 Fifth Street
Nanaimo BC V9R 5S5
Phone: (250) 753-3245
E-mail: Advising@mala.bc.ca
Web: www.mala.bc.ca/www/discover/main.htm

**University of Calgary**

The University of Calgary offers an MA or Ph.D in English with a Creative Writing option. Students considering a Creative Writing Option at the MA or Ph.D. level are admitted to the program on the basis of their academic preparation and fulfill the same requirements, including course work, as other MA and Ph.D. candidates.

University of Calgary
2500 University Drive NW
Calgary AB T2N 1N4
Phone: (403) 220-5470
E-mail: enggrad@ucalgary.ca
Web: www.english.ucalgary.ca/graduate/index.html

**York University**

The Creative Writing Program at York University is an Honours BA Program offered by the Faculty of Arts. In the early years, the program acquaints students with various ways of writing; in the later years, the programs exposes students to the history of formal experimentation and growth in particular genres, encouraging specialization in two genres.

Creative Writing Office
210 Vanier College
York University
4700 Keele Street
Toronto ON M3J 1P3
Phone: (416) 736-5910
E-mail: suepar@yorku.ca
Web:
www.yorku.ca/human/undergrad/Programs/CreativeWriting.html

**University of Windsor**

The Department of English offers programs leading to an MA in English and Creative Writing. The English and Creative Writing program allows students to combine graduate-level study of literature with advanced work in creative writing in a two-term workshop and by developing a significant independent writing project.

Department of English
2100 Chrysler Hall North
University of Windsor
Windsor ON N9B 3P4
Phone: (519) 253-3000 (ext. 2288)
E-mail: hallen@uwindsor.ca
Web: www.cs.uwindsor.ca/units/english/html/graduate.html

**University of Western Ontario**

This institution offers a post-graduate degree — Master of Arts in Journalism — that can be completed within one year.

University of Western Ontario
Faculty of Information and Media Studies
Middlesex, College
London ON N6A 5B7
Phone: (519) 661-4017
E-mail: journalism@julian.uwo.ca
Web: www.fims.uwo.ca/journalism

### Carleton University

This institution offers a four-year Bachelor of Journalism degree and a one-year Masters of Journalism program.

Carleton University
1125 Colonel By Drive
Ottawa ON K1S 5B6
Phone: (613) 520-3663, Undergraduate Office
E-mail: liaison@carleton.ca
Phone: (613) 520-2525, Graduate Studies
E-mail: Graduate_Studies@carleton.ca
Web: www.carleton.ca/

### Ryerson Polytechnic University

A four-year journalism degree, and a two-year journalism program for those with a bachelor's degree from an accredited university, is available from this university.

Ryerson Polytechic University
50 Victoria Street
Toronto ON M5B 2K3
Phone: (416) 979-5136
E-mail: g1allen@ryerson.ca or jyip@ryerson.ca
Web: www.ryerson.ca/

### Concordia University

Concordia University offers an MA in Creative Writing and an undergraduate Bachelor of Arts in journalism degree as well as an 11-month graduate journalism diploma.

Concordia University
1455 de Maisonneuve Blvd. W.
Montreal PQ H3G 1M8
Phone: (514) 848-2424
E-mail: communications@concordia.ca
Web: www.concordia.ca/

### University of New Brunswick

UNB offers an MA (Creative Writing). Candidates must have a BA with first or second class Honours in English or equivalent. Length of time is normally 20 months in residence.

Sir Howard Douglas Hall
3 Bailey Drive
PO Box 4400
Fredericton NB E3B 5A3

Phone: (506) 453-4864
E-mail: english1@unb.ca
Web: www.unbf.ca/arts/english/

**University of Kings College**

This university offers a four-year Bachelor of Journalism (Honours) degree, and a one-year postgraduate Bachelor of Journalism (BJ) degree for those who already possess a BA.

University of King's College
6350 Coburg Road
Halifax NS B3H 2A1
Phone: (902) 422-1271
E-mail: elizabeth.yeo@ukings.ns.ca
Web: www.ukings.ns.ca/

## Writing Schools, Workshops, Retreats

**Booming Ground**

Booming Ground consists of a week of intensive writing workshops, seminars and readings, through the Creative Writing Program at the University of British Columbia. Booming Ground is a work-oriented creative community, with classes aimed at mid-career, published writers, as well as those at earlier stages in their artistic development. Workshops are led by accomplished writers. Working closely with a small group of fellow writers, you will explore your own work, that of your peers and the creative process.

Booming Ground Writer's Community
Creative Writing Program, UBC
Buch. E 462, 1866 Main Mall
Vancouver BC V6T 1Z1
Phone: (604)822-2469
E-mail: bg@arts.ubs.ca
Web: www.arts.ubc.ca/bg

**Victoria School of Writing**

This annual event takes place at the St. Margaret's Girls School. Writers can enjoy five full days of workshops in humour, poetry, fiction, nonfiction, suspense fiction and memoirs. Each workshop is led by an experienced, award-winning writer, and includes a one-on-one consultation with the instructor. The Victoria School of Writing also offers workshops on creative writing, poetry, fiction and nonfiction throughout the year at the same location.

Victoria School of Writing Society
Box 8152
Victoria BC V8W 3R8
Phone: (250) 595-3000
E-mail: vicwrite@islandnet.com
Web: www.islandnet.com/vicwrite/

**Kootenay School of Writing**

KSW is a collectively operated, writer-run centre, that focuses on contemporary writing practice and poetics. KSW schedules regular readings and talks, seminars, writer-in-residence programs, and panel discussions. Most of the courses have a strong base in the avant-garde literature that is coming out of modernism or is a departure from mainstream programs.

Kootenay School Of Writing
201 – 505 Hamilton St.
Vancouver BC V6B 2R1
Phone: (604) 688-6001

**Surrey International Writers' Conference**

Over 60 workshops are staged during an October weekend in Surrey, BC. Workshops include something for everyone: novelists, journalists, poets, article writers, nonfiction writers, romance writers, writers for children, screenwriters, fantasy and science fiction writers. Beginner writers are welcome. There are opportunities for experienced writers to take master classes.

Rusty Nixon, Conference Coordinator
E-mail: rixon@telus.net
Phone: (604) 589-2221
Web: www.surreywritersconference.bc.ca/

**Summer Publishing Workshops, Simon Fraser University**

SFU offers an impressive series of Editing, Bookpublishing, Web, and Design workshops every summer. Courses range from one day to one week of intensive professional development.

151 – 515 West Hastings Street
Vancouver BC V6B 5K3
Phone: (604) 291-241
E-mail: pubworks@sfu.ca
Web: www.sfu.ca/pubworks

## Sunshine Coast School of Writing

This school offers a growing number of seminars, intensive weekend workshops, and writers' retreats. In time, it will offer longer-term workshops.

Contact person:
Carol Hodgson
RR4 451 Pratt Road
Gibsons BC V0N 1V4
Phone: (604) 886-8951
E-mail: c_hodgson@sunshine.net
Web: www.suncoastarts.com

## Praxis Centre

Praxis Centre for Screenwriters is a nonprofit organization devoted to the professional development of Canadian screenwriters and filmmakers. Located in Vancouver, the centre supports and stimulates the production of innovative Canadian feature films though screenplay and screenwriter development. The Script Analysis program provides detailed written feedback to screenwriters before they submit their scripts to producers or funding agencies. The centre also creates or sponsors a number of seminars, workshops, and presentations for screenwriters and filmmakers throughout the year.

Praxis Centre, School for the Contemporary Arts
The Mews
#300, 12 Water St.
Vancouver BC V6B 1A5
Phone: (604) 682-3100
E-mail praxis@sfu.ca
Web: www.praxisfilm.com/Home.html

## The Alberta League Encouraging Storytelling (T.A.L.E.S.)

The league sponsors two workshops on storytelling in conjunction with the T.A.L.E.S. Fort Edmonton Storytelling Festival on the Sunday and Monday mornings of the Labour Day Weekend, every year.

Gail de Vos
9850 91 Ave. NW
Edmonton AB T6E 2T6
Phone: (780) 439-7814
E-mail: gdevos@iris.slis.ualberta.ca

T.A.L.E.S. Strathcona offers a storytelling retreat at the Strathcona Wilderness Centre one weekend every April. The event includes workshops, panel discussions and story circles.

Helen Lavender
1374 Lakeview Road
Sherwood Park AB T8H 1L5
Phone: (780) 467-2924
E-mail: hlavender@telusplanet.net

### Edmonton's Stroll of Poets

This organization promotes poetry, and initiates a number of performance venues for poets. Along with a reading series, it also sponsors festivals and workshops.

Stroll of Poets Society
Mark Kozub
Box 35082, Oliver PO
Edmonton AB T5K 2R8
Phone:(780) 490-1414
E-mail: abeatnik@telusplanet.net
Web: www.incentre.net/stroll

### The University of Alberta Faculty of Extension Women's Program

This program provides practical writing experience combined with the know-how of publishing in Canada that can help lead your first drafts to published works. Guided by professional writers, the Faculty of Extension offers courses in Writing Basics, Fiction Writing, Nonfiction Writing and Publishing, Editing, New Media Writing, and Women's Writing.

Writing Program
Applied Arts, Faculty of Extension, U of A
University Extension Centre
93 University Campus NW
Edmonton AB T6G 2T4
Phone: (780) 492-3109
E-mail: susan.boychuk@ualberta.ca
Web: www.extension.ualberta.ca/writing/

### Banff Centre

The Writing and Publishing Department at Banff Centre offer a number of workshops and retreats throughout the year. *The Creative Nonfiction and Cultural Journalism Program* provides an opportunity for eight established nonfiction writers to develop a major essay, memoir, or feature piece. Banff Centre also has six- to eight-week self-directed writing residencies that provide time, space, and facilities for research, editing, and manuscript development. *The Wired Writing Studio* is a six-month program for poets and fiction writers. The Studio begins with two weeks on campus at The Banff Centre, interacting with an established writer/editor and other writing participants, and continues online: a twenty-week electronic extension of the experience. *The Writing Studio* is a five-week program intended specifically for those producing work of literary merit who are at an early stage in their careers. It offers an extended period of uninterrupted writing time, one-on-one editorial assistance from a number of notable writers/editors, and an opportunity for involvement with a community of working writers. One-week writing workshops provide an opportunity to write, consult with a professional editor, and get to know other writers.

Writing & Publishing
The Banff Centre
Box 1020
107 Tunnel Mountain Drive
Banff AB T1L 1H5
Phone: (403) 762-6278
E-mail: writing_publishing@banffcentre.ca
Web: www.banffcentre.ab.ca/writing/

**Banff Writing Retreat**

Sponsored by the Writers' Guild of Alberta and The Banff Centre for the Arts. A nine-day winter retreat with a Writer-in-Residence on site.

Writers Guild of Alberta
Percy Page Centre
11759 Groat Road
Edmonton AB T5M 3K6
Phone: (780) 422-8174
E-mail: mail@writersguild.ab.ca
Web: www.writersguild.ab.ca/

**Sage Hill**

Sage Hill Writing Experience offers a special working and learning opportunity to writers at different stages of development. Top quality instruction, a low instructor–writer ratio, and the rural and urban Saskatchewan settings offer conditions ideal for the pursuit of excellence in the arts of fiction, nonfiction, poetry and playwriting. Different workshops are provided at various times of the year. They include: The Summer Experience, Fall Poetry Colloquium and Teen Writing Experiences in Regina, Saskatoon, and Moose Jaw.

Sage Hill Writing Experience
Box 1731
Saskatoon SK S7K 3S1

Phone: (306) 652-7395
E-mail: sage.hill@sasktel.net
Web: www.lights.com/sagehill

**Writer's Collective**

This organization, located at the University of Winnipeg, offers a series of writing workshops at various times throughout the year. Topics include: Writing and Editing Basics; Beginnings, Middles and Ends; Romance Writing; Writing for Children; Poetry; and many more. The Writer's Collective also runs monthly writer's circle meetings which give participants the opportunity to receive feedback on their writing.

Writer's Collective
4th Floor Library
University of Winnipeg
515 Portage Avenue
Winnipeg MB  R3B 2E9
Phone: (204) 786-9468
E-mail: writerscollective@uwinnipeg.ca

**The Canadian Society of Children's Authors, Illustrators, and Performers**

This society represents a group of professionals in the field of children's culture with members from all parts of Canada. CANSCAIP supports and promotes children's literature through newsletters, workshops, meetings and other information programs.

CANSCAIP
c/o Northern District Library, Lower Level
40 Orchard View Blvd.
Toronto ON  M4R 1B9
Phone: (416) 515-1559
E-mail: office@canscaip.org
Web: www.canscaip.org/

**Centauri Arts**

Centauri Arts offers adults the opportunity of relaxing for one or two weeks in a residential retreat, while taking courses from well-known writers and artists. Concentrate on your own creative endeavors — the poetry, short story or novel you always wanted to write or the painting you'd like to complete — regardless of your level of experience. Courses take place in a beautiful village-like centre, one hour north of Toronto.

Centauri Arts
19 Harshaw Ave.
Toronto ON  M6S 1X9

Phone: (416) 766 7124
E-mail: directors@centauri.on.ca
Web: www.centauri.on.ca/arts/

**Humber School for Writers**

The 30-week program in *Creative Writing by Correspondence* was created specifically to help students explore and develop their creative writing skills via regular and electronic correspondence. The program offers aspiring authors an opportunity to have a novel, book of short stories, volume of poetry, or a work of creative nonfiction critiqued by one of the distinguished faculty.

Humber College
205 Humber College Blvd.
Toronto ON M9W 5L7
Phone: (416) 675-5084
E-mail: writers@humberc.on.ca.
Web: www.humberc.on.ca/~writers/correspondence/

**Society of Children's Book Writers and Illustrators**

This organization sponsors workshops and retreats geared for writers and illustrators of children's works.

Society of Children's Book Writers and Illustrators
c/o Noreen Kruzich Violetta
130 Wren St. RR1
Dunrobin ON K0A 1T0
Phone: (613) 832-1288
E-mail: portage@compmore.net
Web: www.scbwicanada.org/

**The Writers' Circle of Durham Region**

This umbrella organization group encourages and promotes the art and skill of writing, fosters literacy, and provides moral support to writers through education and networking, both independently and in cooperation with existing organizations. It offers a number of workshops throughout the year.

The Writers' Circle of Durham Region
PO Box 323
Ajax ON L1S 3C5
Phone: (905) 259-6520
E-mail: info@wcdr.org
Web: www.wcdr.org/

**Storytellers of Canada**

This organization has an annual four-day conference that includes workshops by storytelling elders and storytelling circles. Location varies from year to year. Ongoing festivals, events and workshops are sponsored throughout the year.

Storytellers of Canada
c/o Glenna Janzen
411 Kilman Road – RR 1
Ridgeville ON L0S 1M0
Phone: (905) 892-9186
E-mail: gjanzen@mergetel.com
Web: www.niagara.com/~sccc/

**The Storytellers School of Toronto**

This organization supports creative work in the art of storytelling. The school publishes *Appleseed Quarterly — The Canadian Journal of Storytelling*. It offers courses, promotes and subsidizes the work of storytellers in education; and produces the Toronto Festival of Storytelling.

The Storytellers School of Toronto
791 St. Clair Avenue W.
Toronto ON M6C 1B7
Phone: (416) 656-2445
E-mail: admin@storytellingtoronto.org
Web: www.storytellingtoronto.org/

**Writers Guild of Canada**

This organization frequently sponsors workshops programs devoted to the craft of writing screenplays for movies and television.

The Writers Guild
123 Edward Street, Suite 1225
Toronto ON M5G 1E2
Phone: (416) 979-7907
E-mail: info@wgc.ca
Web: www.writersguildofcanada.com/

**Maritime Writers' Workshop**

The University of New Brunswick is the site of the annual Maritime Writers' Workshop, held every July. It offers instruction in fiction, poetry and writing for children.

Screenwriting and creative nonfiction are offered alternatively. Participants choose from one of the four workshop categories. The program encourages serious work throughout the week, with attention to professional standards that govern manuscript preparation and editorial demands. In addition to daily workshop group meetings, the schedule includes lecture/discussions and public readings by each of the workshop leaders, time for writing, and a private, one-on-one meeting with the group instructor.

Maritime Writers' Workshop
College of Extended Learning
The University of New Brunswick
Continuing Education Centre
6 Duffie Drive, PO Box 4400
Fredericton NB E3B 5A3
Phone: (506) 453-4646
E-mail: oned@unb.ca
Web: www.unb.ca/extend/writers/writers.htm

### A Working Writers' Retreat

This retreat offers an opportunity to get away from the interruptions that hinder your progress in a creative project. There are no scheduled workshops, no meals to cook, no obligations to fulfill. Transform you inspiration from dreams to reality, and make new friendships along the way. Held spring and fall at Villa Madonna, in Rothsay, NB.

Kathy Diane Leveille
3 Sunnybank St.
Quispamsis NB E2E 1L1
Phone: (506) 849-3036
E-mail: leveill@nbnet.nb.ca

### South Shore Literary Club

This organization sponsors a gala writer's festival every two years in October at White Point Beach Lodge in Nova Scotia. Accomplished Canadian writers from various genres give workshops and readings throughout the event. Topics vary year to year and can cover everything from ghostwriting to character development in a novel; nature writing, starting a freelance business and calling on the muse for your poetry.

Arleyne Barrett Corkum
PO Box 486
Liverpool NS B0T 1K0
Phone: (902) 354-3855

### Community of Writers

The Community of Writers is a week's workshop in Tatamagouche, NS, for writers at all levels, from absolute beginner to the more accomplished. Mornings are for workshops and afternoons for writing (canoeing, swimming, hiking, napping, gazing into space, walking the labyrinth and attending personal conferences with facilitators). Evenings are shared experiences by writers and retreat participants. The Retreat Program is for more experienced writers, is smaller, and runs concurrently.

Community of Writers
Tatamagouche Centre
RR #3
Tatamagouche NS  B0K 1V0
Phone: (902) 422-2427
E-mail: comwrite@supercity.ns.ca
Web: www.tatacentre.ca

**Playwrights Atlantic Resource Centre**

This organization has a program called *Home Delivery* whereby playwrights can receive "dramaturgical" assistance on an on-going basis through the mail, by e-mail, by phone and/or by fax. The program enables playwrights to establish an ongoing relationship with a dramaturge, developing a new script in up to four consultations over a 12-month period. PARC also sponsors workshops and promotes an exchange of playwrights across Canada.

Playwrights Atlantic Resource Centre
c/o Jenny Munday
PO Box 269
68 Main Street, 3rd Floor
Guysborough NS  B0H 1N0
Phone: (902) 533-2077
E-mail: parcoffice@ns.sympatico.ca

**National and provincial writers' organizations can provide additional information for workshops, retreats and mentoring programs.**

Contact a national writing association such as the Canadian Authors Association, Periodical Writers Association of Canada, the Canadian Association of Journalists and the Editors Association of Canada for the chapter closest to you. Local or provincial chapters offer workshops on various topics throughout the year. See the "Organizations of Interest to Writers" listing starting on page 410 for details.

—

Sandra Phinney is a freelance writer in Yarmouth, Nova Scotia. She writes features for regional, national and international magazines, and mini-documentaries for CBC radio. Sandra gives workshops on various aspects of freelance writing and creative writing. In her spare time Sandra Phinney writes poetry and fiction. Visit her website at www3.ns.sympatico.ca/s.phinney/.

# Canadian Literary Agents

*by Murphy O. Shewchuk*

In Canada, the listing of literary agents is small, and the numbers appear to be shrinking. As we progress into the multimedia, multifaceted publishing world of the 21st century, the specialized knowledge and insight of an agent will be needed more than ever to effectively promote a writer's work and to meet the publisher's needs.

Although there are always exceptions to every generality, a review of the market listings and discussions with individual agents have created the following impressions of how best to approach a literary agent. It is worth noting that these same guidelines apply when dealing directly with a publisher.

**Return postage is necessary...**

Very few literary agencies will return inquiries or manuscripts that have not been submitted with a self-addressed return envelope accompanied by sufficient postage (SASE) to cover the full weight of the shipment. In the case of material originating from a U.S. or foreign source, the postage can be in the form of International Reply Coupons, but because of the high cost of Canadian postage, these should be double the normal mailing fees. A short note can be added to your covering letter if the return of your manuscript is not required.

**Query letters serve as an important first step...**

Although there are a few exceptions, most agents will not read unsolicited manuscripts. In most instances the preference is to first receive a detailed query letter (with SASE). If interested in the subject matter, the agency will ask for more information which may be in the form of sample chapters or the complete manuscript.

**Never submit first drafts...**

Prepare your query letters and manuscripts as cleanly and as perfectly as possible. As in any other business, first impressions are extremely important. Remember that you are also selling a product. To quote one agency, "We are not impressed by the credentials of a writer — amateur or professional — or by his or her pitching techniques, but by his or her story ideas and ability to build a well-crafted script."

**Representation is a personal service business...**

It is worth noting that most agents do not use freelance readers to help evaluate manuscripts. Evaluation is usually a very personal matter and is the basis from which the agent decides to expend the considerable energy needed to promote a work. They may call on specialists in certain fields, such as technical nonfiction, to assist with the assessment of a manuscript.

**Fees may be charged...**

An agent's time is his or her stock in trade. Most agencies earn a large part of their income from the fees they receive as a percentage of the royalties or other earnings from published or, in the case of film or drama, produced work. In general, these fees are 15 percent of the author's income for domestic sales and 20 to 30 percent for foreign sales and lecturing.

Once an agent decides to represent your work, most prefer written contracts which can be binding for a fixed period, often two years. Some agencies charge writers an additional amount for photocopying, courier, postage and telephone/fax, "if these are excessive."

Finding publishable material can be very time consuming and this is often considered part of the agency's cost of doing business. However, providing the author with written evaluations and suggestions for improvement is often beyond the scope of normal agent duties and fees may be charged for this work. Individual agency fees vary widely. One agency mentioned a fee of $200 for a 200-page double-spaced manuscript. Another charges a fee of $395 to read the manuscript and produce a three- or four-page constructive critique. Still another agent was in the process of evaluating her fee structure.

Because of changes in the literary marketplace and space limitations, we have chosen not to list specific fee structures. In all instances, you should ask for clarification of the agency's fee structure with your first letter of inquiry (accompanied by an SASE, of course).

The following list of agents is offered to begin your search. New agencies' businesses are often short-lived; long-time agencies often form new partnerships; policies and needs change.

Additional information on Canadian literary agents may also be found on the Internet at www.writersunion.ca/links.htm and www.writersguildofcanada.com/resources/agents.html.

**Aurora Artists Inc.**
19 Wroxeter Avenue
Toronto ON M4K 1J5
Phone: (416) 463-4634 - Fax: (416) 463-4889

Notes: "Film and television-based agency representing screenwriters. Accepting queries one to two pages in length and accompanied by an SASE."

**Johanna M. Bates Literary Consultants, Inc.**
101, 2212 34th Avenue SW
Calgary AB T2T 2C6
Phone: (403) 282-7370 - Fax: (403) 299-5467
E-mail: query@telusplanet.net
Web: www.batesliterary.com/

Notes: "As consultants and agents, we are able to lead you through the necessary steps to make publishing and self-publishing a success. Because we know our business, we can warn you of industry pitfalls and help you to steer clear of organizations that may not have your best interests in mind. Check our website for more detailed information about our professional services."

**The Bukowski Agency**
14 Prince Arthur Avenue, Suite 202
Toronto ON M5R 1A9
Phone: (416) 928-6728 - Fax: (416) 963-9978
E-mail: assistant@thebukowskiagency.com
Web: www.thebukowskiagency.com/

Notes: "We are primarily interested in literary fiction, with international potential. Some mass market fiction, no genre fiction other than suspense/mystery. We also accept some literary nonfiction, and some commercial nonfiction such as mind, body, spirit. No film/video. No children's literature, no scriptwriting, no poetry. Queries via post only to the attention of Denise Bukowski. Queries by phone, fax or e-mail will not receive a response."

**Anne McDermid & Associates**
92 Willcocks Street
Toronto ON M5S 1C8
Phone: (416) 324-8845 - Fax: (416) 324-8870

E-mail: info@mcdermidagency.com
Web: www.mcdermidagency.com/

Notes: "The agency represents literary novelists and commercial novelists of high quality, and also writers of narrative nonfiction in the areas of memoir, biography, literary travel, and investigative journalism. We are expanding the list in the areas of narrative science writing and history. We find that our newer clients are interested in pursuing markets via the Internet as well as through the traditional publishing methods. We do not represent children's writing, self-help, business or computer books, gardening and cookery, or fantasy, science fiction or romance.

"We do not accept telephone queries. Send initial query by post or by e-mail. Initial query should contain a description of the book, a sample chapter, some information about yourself (a full CV is preferred), a full submission history of the project, and representative reviews if you are previously published. A stamped self-addressed envelope (SASE) is required if you need the material returned, otherwise all material is recycled. In view of the proliferation of viruses, we no longer open unsolicited attachments to e-mails. No reading fees are charged. We normally reply within six to eight weeks."

**The Pamela Paul Agency Inc.**

12 Westrose Avenue
Toronto ON M8X 2A1
Phone: (416) 410-5395 - Fax: (416) 410-4949
E-mail: agency@interlog.com

Notes: This agency has a small list representing screenwriters and book authors — primarily literary fiction. No unsolicited manuscripts. Address written inquiries to the attention of Sue Munro. Include SASE. List includes Cable Ace and Governor General award winners.

**Beverley Slopen Literary Agency**

131 Bloor St. W., Suite 711
Toronto ON M5S 1S3
Phone: (416) 964-9598 - Fax: (416) 921-7726
E-mail: beverley@slopenagency.on.ca
Web: www.slopenagency.on.ca/

Notes: "We don't take on many new authors. Our clients usually come to us by referral or we approach them. Occasionally, we do respond to very short e-mail queries, but we don't open attachments or long electronic files. Our preference is a query letter and a few sample pages sent by old-fashioned mail with a self-addressed envelope and Canadian postage. Usually, if we would like to see more, we will contact the writer by phone or e-mail. We don't handle any poetry, very few children's titles, and almost no works in the categories of fantasy, horror or romance."

**Carolyn N. Swayze Agency**
WRPO PO Box 39588
White Rock BC V4B 5L6
Phone: (604) 538-3478 - Fax:(604) 531-3022
E-mail: cswayze@direct.ca

Notes: Literary fiction, some genre fiction (mysteries and suspense), and literary and commercial nonfiction. Handles a limited children's list. Does not accept poetry, scripts, screenplays or essays. Please inquire in writing, enclosing a brief bio, short synopsis of the available work and, if fiction, the first 50 to 100 pages. For nonfiction, please include an outline, sample chapter and market research. Always enclose SASE.

**Transatlantic Literary Agency**
72 Glengowan Road
Toronto ON M4N 1G4
Phone: (416) 488-9214 - Fax: (416) 488-4531
E-mail: tla@netcom.ca
Web: www.tla1.com/

Notes: "TLA provides a personalized service to all our authors and illustrators. We are selective about what we send out and work closely with our clients to get a manuscript in the best possible shape before submitting it to a publisher. Once a sale has been made we spend time facilitating the relationship between the creator and the publishing house." Consult the website for additional information.

—

Murphy O. Shewchuk is a freelance writer, photographer and book author with ten published books and hundreds of illustrated articles to his credit. He also does a wide variety of computer graphics projects including interpretive displays, maps and book publishing projects. Check his website at www.sonotek.com for more information.

# Contributors' Notes

**Linda Aksomitis** is in her Masters of Vocational/Technical Education program, writing and teaching various online courses. She has taught over 20,000 students in her *Writing for Children* course. *Becoming a Library Technician*, her latest book, will be released in 2003. Linda's resource page for emerging children's writers can be found at www3.sk.sympatico.ca/aksoml/.

**Kimberley Alcock** is a writer, teacher, editor and former publicist for several publishing houses. Her publicity work has included book launches, press conferences, and publicity campaigns for several prominent international and BC authors, including Nick Bantock, Farley Mowat, Andrew Morton, Lesley Forbes, Patrick Lane, and Linda Svendsen.

**Jonathan Ball** is a journalist and a writer of fiction, nonfiction, screenplay, and poetry. *Son of the Storm*, an independent feature film based on a script he co-wrote with David Navratil, is being directed by Joseph Novak for release in 2003.

**Ken Basarke** has sold poetry and stories to *Pulp Eternity, Parsec, Blue Food, Jackhammer, Electric Wine, Storisende Verlag, Hugo's New Brew, Writer Online, Planet Relish, Visionair and Fantasy, Folklore & Fairytales* as well as *Dragons, Knights & Angels* magazine. His novels, *The Ursine Fix* and *The K'nith* are at the publishers.

**Rosemary Bauchman** is the author of six nonfiction books, numerous articles, short stories, poems and book reviews. She has conducted creative writing classes and edited material for other writers, has been a judge for fiction and nonfiction awards.

**Karleen Bradford** is the award-winning author of 17 works of fiction and nonfiction for children and young adults. Her latest novels include *Whisperings of Magic,* (Harper Collins Publishers Ltd., 2001) and *With Nothing But Our Courage: The Loyalist Diary of Mary MacDonald*, (Scholastic Canada Ltd., Dear Canada Series 2002).

**Arthur Bray** lives in Ottawa and is the author of four nonfiction books, two on Unidentified Flying Objects and two on financial planning. He is currently working on another nonfiction book on an unrelated topic.

**Joan Eyolfson Cadham**, who took her own advice, freelances full-time from Foam Lake, Saskatchewan, selling (and winning awards for) feature articles, editorials and columns for weekly newspapers, national magazines and CBC radio. She also has two nonfiction books published by Shoreline Press in Ste Anne de Bellevue.

**Melanie Cameron** is Poetry Co-Editor of *Prairie Fire Magazine*. Her book, *Holding the Dark* (poetry, The Muses' Company, 1999), was shortlisted for the Eileen MacTavish Sykes Award for Best First Book by a Manitoban Writer, and she was shortlisted for the John Hirsch Award for Most Promising Manitoban Writer.

**Deborah Cannon** is an archaeologist and museologist. She is published by Simon Fraser University's Archaeology Press and the Canadian Journal of Archaeology. She has written several short stories, completed two novels, and is working on a third.

**Terry Ann Carter** is a teacher and poet working in Ottawa. After seven chapbooks, her first book of poetry, *Waiting for Julia*, was published by Third Eye Press, London, Ontario. She serves on the Education Committee for the League of Canadian Poets. Her paper on Chiyo-ni (18th century woman haiku master) was presented to the Annual Haiku Canada Weekend in Kingston and again at the International Haiku Festival in Montreal where her haiku "*yesterday's rain*" took first place.

**Claudia Carver** is a former social worker who writes on a wide variety of topics from gardening to sexual abuse to vegetarian cooking. She has won prizes for fiction in Waterloo County writing contests and frequently writes short humour pieces on the frustrations and absurdities of everyday life.

**Sharon Caseburg** is an editor, poet, and freelance writer. She has a Master's degree from the University of Manitoba and currently works for a Western Canadian literary house.

**R.G. Condie**, author, columnist, journalist, and editor, is a published writer whose nonfiction, fiction, and poetry has appeared in a wide variety of books, magazines, and newspapers. His *Psychology for Writers* was sold to America House Publishers. He was CAA's first Writer-in-Residence.

**Paul G. Cormack** is a former radio news editor from Toronto. He now lives in the north of Scotland with his wife and three children, writes short fiction and works as a freelance editor. He is also an experienced technical author for the oil industry in the North Sea. Paul has developed various Internet and Intranet sites on commission from multinational corporations, small businesses and local interest groups in the past five years.

**Jennifer Crump** is a freelance journalist whose work has recently appeared in *Reader's Digest, Canadian Geographic, Today's Parent, Writer's Digest* and *Worth*. She is also the author of the recently released Frommer's *Toronto with Kids* (Wiley, 2001). Jennifer lives in north-eastern Ontario.

**Donna D'Amour** was a freelance reporter for the *Chronicle-Herald* newspaper for several years. Her articles have appeared in *The Globe and Mail, Trade and Commerce, Saltscapes, 50-Plus*, and *Reading Today*. Her book, *Colouring the Road*, was published in 1995 by Lancelot Press. In 2001 she directed a weekly writer's workshop.

**Sher DiCiccio**, Executive Director of the Waterloo Community Arts Centre, has worked in Waterloo since 1977. She is a member of the Association of Cultural Executives, the Canadian Authors Association (past-president of the Waterloo-Wellington branch), and chairs the Arts and Culture Cash Grants Committee, City of Waterloo. She lives in Kitchener with husband Vic, and three teenage children.

**Betty Dobson** is a freelance writer while she pursues her bachelor's degree in English and Creative Writing. An award-winning poet and essayist, she has also received academic recognition for the quality of her short fiction. Her website is: www.writers.net/writers/inkspotter.

**Marjorie Doyle** worked as a broadcaster from 1988–1999. Her commentaries and reviews were aired regionally and nationally on CBC Radio. She also hosted a national CBC radio show for six years. She has published two books of nonfiction and is working on her third.

**Betty Dyck** is the Winnipeg-based author of three nonfiction books, editor of two church histories, a published poet and freelance writer who conducts workshops on writing creative nonfiction and family histories.

**Heather Ebbs** writes proceedings for government departments, non-governmental organizations, national associations and industry on subjects ranging from West Nile virus to new drug products. In addition to her writing, Heather is also an indexer and an award-winning editor. She is a past-president of the (Freelance) Editors' Association of Canada.

**Margaret Bunel Edwards** is an Ottawa writer with more than 600 stories and articles published in Canada and the United States. Her stories have appeared in anthologies by Holt, Rinehart & Winston; Ginn; Nelson; and Gage. She is the author of two picture books. Her young adult historical novel, *The Ocean Between*, was shortlisted for the Geoffrey Bilson Award.

**Joanna Emery**'s first picture book, *Melville Smellville*, was published by a small Nova Scotia Press, Small World Publishing, in December 2001. Her poems and articles have appeared in various children's magazines such as *Jack & Jill* and *Ladybug*. She lives in Dundas, Ontario with her husband and three children.

**Anne Fairley** has written many nonfiction pieces. However, she loves poetry both as a reader and a writer. Through the years she has used her love of the genre to share the pleasure with children and adults.

**Julie H. Ferguson**, a Vancouver-based freelance writer and author of two nonfiction books, leads workshops that provide writers with the knowledge, skills, and confidence to approach publishers with their work. Her website is at www.beaconlit.com.

**Eric Fletcher** telecommutes from his electronic cottage bordering Gatineau Park. He coauthored *Québec Off the Beaten Path* (2002) with his wife Katharine with whom he also writes travel columns, and is designing maps for three regional guidebooks. An expert on computer systems and publishing, he teaches and consults about electronic publishing. Contact Eric at: chesley@netcom.ca.

**Katharine Fletcher** is a freelance writer who seeks the unusual, whether it be hiking Greece's remote Peloponnese or discovering a funky Glasgow museum. She telecommutes from her electronic cottage bordering Gatineau Park's wilderness sector, a landscape providing rich inspiration for her travel, environment and lifestyle columns, articles and books. Contact Katharine at: chesley@netcom.ca.

**Peggy Fletcher** was born in St John's, Newfoundland and now lives in Sarnia, Ontario. She taught Creative Writing and English at Lambton College, and is Family Editor at the *Sarnia Observer*. Peggy has published four books of poetry, one of short stories, and this has been supplemented by work in anthologies and magazines in Canada, England, Australia and the United States.

**Gill Foss** is a freelance journalist and an award-winning poet whose work has appeared in several anthologies. She is National President of the Canadian Authors Association, a professional member of the Periodical Writers Association of Canada and an Associate member of the Editors Association. She writes a regular profile column for a seniors' publication and articles and advertorials for two Ottawa newspapers.

**Albert G. Fowler**, OMM, CD, a retired chaplain, military historian, and freelance writer, is author of the book *Peacetime Padres* and of a wide variety of freelance articles.

**Marilyn Fraser** has published *Cab & Crystal*, a Canadian magazine on earth sciences. She has been Toronto correspondent for an international corporate magazine. Other publishing credits include *Canadian Gemologist*, *CARP News*, *Mississauga News*, and *The Medium* (a university newspaper). Marilyn has published five chapbooks. She presently writes for canadianrockhound.com.

**Donna Gamache**, from MacGregor, Manitoba, has published numerous short stories for both children and adults, as well as *Spruce Woods Adventure*, a novel for middle-grade children. She has also given classes in writing fiction to both children and adults.

**Barbara Florio Graham** is a long-time member of the Periodical Writers Association, and chairs both PWAC's Mentoring Committee and Strategic Planning Committee. An author and online teacher, her books and courses are described at www.SimonTeakettle.com.

Netherlands born **Lini Richarda Grol**'s novels, plays, poetry and "scissor-cut illustrations" have been published worldwide. She is a Life Member of the Canadian Authors Association, the Professional Women Writers of America and various poet's associations. One of her original stories, *Lelawala: The Maid of the Mist*, became a musical. It premiered in Toronto in June, 2001.

**Russ Harvey** is a West Coast computer consultant and writes on computer and Internet issues. One of the tasks he routinely performs is recovery from the effects of virus infections on client computers. Check out his website at: www.russharvey.bc.ca/rhc/rhc.html.

**Marian Dingman Hebb** spent ten years as a book and magazine editor before becoming a lawyer and specializing in arts and entertainment law. She has advised authors on book contracts for close to two decades and has written self-help guides on book contracts entitled *Help Yourself to a Better Contract*, *Ghost Writing*, and *Writers' Guide to Electronic Publishing Rights*, all published by the Writers' Union of Canada.

**Yvonne Jeffery Hope** is a Canadian freelance writer/editor whose specialties include editing romantic fiction. Her current home is Cyprus, legendary island of Aphrodite, goddess of love.

**Matt Hughes** writes speeches for politicians and corporate executives. He has published three novels: *Fools Errant* and *Fool Me Twice*, Warner Aspect 2001, *Downshift*, Doubleday Canada 1997, and *Breaking Trail: The memoirs of Senator Len Marchand*, Caitlin Press 2000. His suspense fiction has appeared in *Blue Murder, Alfred Hitchcock* and *Storyteller.*

**Susan Ioannou**'s poetry, fiction, and essays have appeared in numerous anthologies and magazines across Canada. Her most recent of several books is the critically acclaimed literary study *A Magical Clockwork: The Art of Writing the Poem* (Wordwrights Canada, 2000). By day she works as an editor for ClearTEXT in Toronto.

**Linda Jeays** considers the tribute column she wrote for a franchised seniors' newspaper in Ottawa one of her most rewarding long-term assignments. She still enjoys the challenge of softening the heart of a new editor and opening up a fresh market for her work.

**Mark Jeays** is a computer programmer specializing in World Wide Web applications. He currently works at Transport Canada and has his own one-man business, Capital Computer Solutions. He inherits his word-skills from Linda Jeays, an experienced freelance writer.

**Robert H. (Bob) Jones** has won numerous awards for his books and magazine articles. Editor of the Blue Ribbon Books series for Johnson Gorman Publishers in Calgary, Alberta, he resides in Courtenay, BC, with Vera, who is also a writer/editor.

**Vera Jones** wrote a popular cooking column in the *Comox Valley Record* newspaper for seven years. Presently working as a freelance writer and editor at her home in Courtenay, British Columbia, her articles have recently appeared in *BC Outdoors* and *BC Sport Fishing*.

**Dr. Kenneth Kalman** is a poet and the author of several short stories on time travel. His poetry and fiction encompass the essence of both today and of historical times. He is an observer and student of history and archaeology, whose life's passion is the study of First Century Palestine, particularly the historical evidence for Jesus. His novel *Sara Church and the Jesus Diaries* is expected to be published in 2003.

**Hélèna Katz** is a Montreal journalist whose work has appeared in magazines and newspapers in both Canada and the United States. She has given workshops on marketing for freelancers, writing queries and recycling stories in Montreal, Ottawa, and eastern Canada. She can be reached at: hkatz@web.ca.

**Carol Kavanagh** is a registered psychologist who has published poetry and is currently working on short stories and a novel. A book by Julia Cameron, *The Artist's Way*, inspired her and she then took a course by that name, and began writing morning pages.

**Linda Kay**, graduate program director at Concordia University's School of Journalism, was a columnist for *The Chicago Tribune* before launching a freelance writing career in Canada in 1990. Her work has appeared in *Reader's Digest, Chatelaine, Newsweek, Inside Sports, The (Montreal) Gazette* and *The London Free Press*.

**Mark Kearney** is an award-winning journalist who has had his work published in more than 60 magazines and newspapers in North America. During his 25-year career, he has also coauthored six books, three of them best sellers. Mark has taught writing at the University of Western Ontario for 12 years.

**Eileen Kernaghan** has published poetry in magazines ranging from *PRISM international* to The *Magazine of Gothic Vampire Poetry*. She is one-fifth of the BC women's poetry group Quintet, who recently published their first collection, *Quintet: Themes & Variations* (Ekstasis Editions). She is also the author of five novels and coauthor of two nonfiction books.

**Bryan M. Knight**, MSW, PhD, is the author of several e-books, including: *Hypnosis: Software for Your Mind; SELF-HYPNOSIS: Safe, Simple, Superb; How To Avoid A Bad Relationship; Easily Hypnotize Anyone; How To Get Started as a Hypnotherapist;* and *Marketing Action Plan for Success in Private Practice*. His website, Hypnosis Headquarters, can be found at www.hypnosis.org.

**Shirley Byers Lalonde** lives near Kelvington, Saskatchewan. She is a contributing editor for *WITH*, a U.S. based teen magazine and has also practised naming fiction's children in such periodicals as *The United Church Observer, My Friend, Brio, On the Line and Listen*.

**Lisa Lange** is mother of two boys, Mitchell and Matthew, and wife of Richard. She is a full-time office worker, seamstress and writer, living in Victoria, BC. She is also a member of the Canadian Authors Association.

**Ruth Latta**'s poetry has appeared in a range of publications, from *Bywords* to *Whetstone*. She is the coauthor of two chapbooks of poetry, *Three's Company*, 1996 and *Polarities*, 2000. Her most recently published poem appears in the current issue of *The Grist Mill*, the Valley Writer's Guild's annual. Ruth's latest work is a biography of Grace MacInnis, coauthored by Joy Trott, and published by Xlibris, 2001. Visit her website at www.cyberus.ca/~rklatta/RuthLatta.html.

**Bernice Lever**, current President of CAA, Vancouver Branch, has retired from teaching English at Seneca College (Toronto) to live on Bowen Island, BC. She continues to publish, to lead writing workshops and to give readings. A literary editor, her seventh book of poems is *BLESSINGS*, Black Moss, 2000. She is Literary Chair of the Bowen Island Festival of the Arts which is held each summer. Known as "Granny Grammar," her composition text and much more are listed on her website: www.colourofwords.com.

**Alison Lohans** published her first book in 1983. Since then, twelve more of her books have been published for people aged four through adult. Alison will be Writer-in-Residence at Regina Public Library in 2002–2003. Her newest title is *Waiting for the Sun* (Red Deer Press, fall 2001).

**Rowland Lorimer** is the Director of the Master of Publishing program at the Canadian Centre for Studies in Publishing at Simon Fraser University. He is Professor of Communication and the past editor of the *Canadian Journal of Communication* of which he is now the publisher. He is honorary President of the Association for Canadian Studies.

**Deb Loughead** is the author of numerous children's books, including *All I Need and other poems for kids* (Moonstruck Press, 1998) and *The Twisting Road Tea Room* (Ragweed Press, 2001). Her stories, poems and articles for children and adults have appeared in publications across the country.

**Cheryl MacDonald** has written several biographical articles and two full-length biographies, *Emma Albani: Victorian Diva* and *Adelaide Hoodless: Domestic Crusader.* She is now working on a biography of poet Wilson MacDonald. In addition to writing, Cheryl has handled design and typesetting on several projects, including two books for the Port Dover Board of Trade, *Port Dover: A Place in the Sun* and *Port Dover: A Summer Garden.*

**Janice MacDonald**'s detective series set in Edmonton, Alberta, features Randy Craig, whom some folks claim is very much like the author herself. Janice insists that she is slimmer, and, of course, Janice is happily married with two lovely children.

**Bruce Madole** is a member of the Canadian Country Music Association (CCMA), the Songwriters Association of Canada (SAC), and the Nashville Songwriter's Association International (NSAI), and is a co-coordinator of the NSAI's Toronto Regional Workshop. He has had nine songs cut by Canadian recording artists.

**Carol Matthews** is a writer and editor living in Yarmouth, Nova Scotia. She edited *Commerce — Business Journal of Southwestern Nova Scotia*, for three years, as well as editing several newsletters. As a writer she specializes in gardening, nature and travel. She has written for several online web sites and e-zines.

**Walt McConville** has served the CAA Victoria and Islands Branch as newsletter editor, archivist, and vice president. He's written six books, three musicals, two plays, and over 500 poems, technical articles and short stories published in Canada, Peru, the United Kingdom and the United States. He currently tutors a CAA poetry group and composes *Canauthword* crossword puzzles for the CAA National Newsline.

**Ishbel Moore**, a prolific writer and mentor, thought she understood the writing process, until she began work on *Blood Tapestry*, a fantasy romance novel. To move her story beyond chapter one, she required a map. While drawing "Charmangea," Ishbel discovered how much magic a writer could experience if willing to learn a different kind of "outline."

**Colin Moorhouse** provides speech-writing services to clients across Canada. Senior members of government and industry have delivered "his" speeches, numbering over 1000, all over the world. He teaches a two-day speechwriting seminar at Simon Fraser University in Vancouver, and is in demand to give his two-hour workshops. He can be reached at Colin_Moorhouse@telus.net.

**Mark Morton** is the Writing and Publishing Officer at the Manitoba Arts Council. He also teaches English at the University of Winnipeg, and is the author of two nonfiction books.

**Devon L. Muhlert** uses the MBTI™ in workshops. A photojournalist since 1991, she has two trade book manuscripts-in-progress, in classic P fashion, and fiction forthcoming in *Queen's Quarterly*. She is a songwriter, musician, and music director — and taught creativity and photography for Continuing Education at Okanagan University College.

**Sheldon Oberman** is a storyteller, teacher and author of 12 books including *The Always Prayer Shawl*, *The White Stone in the Castle Wall* and *The Shaman's Nephew: A Life in the Far North*. He travels widely, storytelling as well as giving talks and creative workshops on personal, fictional and traditional stories. His website is: www.sheldonoberman.com.

**Denyse O'Leary** is a Toronto-based freelance writer and the author of *Faith@Science* (Winnipeg: J. Gordon Shillingford, 2001). O'Leary writes regularly on science and faith issues. She also teaches workshops on business practice for writers and editors. She has two adult daughters, two cats, three gardens, and a website, www.denyseoleary.com.

**Laura Byrne Paquet** is an Ottawa writer/editor who writes Regency romances for Kensington Publishing in New York, as well as freelance magazine and newspaper articles.

**Sheila T. Paynter** from Westbank, British Columbia wrote for *BC Farm and Garden in the* mid-1950s and a further guest column for *Valley Vistas* in the 1980s. She self-published three outdoors books in the

1990s. She is currently writing a monthly freelance column for *Westside Weekly*, an insert in the *Kelowna Daily Courier*.

**Lois J. Peterson**'s personal essays have been published in a range of print and online markets. She teaches others how to have their say in workshops in Creative Writing Diploma Program in Surrey, British Columbia. The editor of *WORDS literary journal*, she publishes fiction, poetry, essays, and memoir.

**Phil Philcox** and **Beverly Boe** are a husband–wife magazine and book writing team living in Panama City Beach, Florida. They have been freelance writers for over thirty years and have travelled around the world writing for book and magazine publishers in the U.S., Canada, Australia, England and Europe.

**Sandra Phinney** is a freelance writer in Yarmouth, Nova Scotia. She writes features for regional, national and international magazines, and mini-documentaries for CBC radio. Sandra gives workshops on various aspects of freelance writing and creative writing. In her spare time she writes poetry and fiction. Visit www3.ns.sympatico.ca/s.phinney/.

**Holly Quan** has been freelancing since 1988. She writes on travel, tourism, marketing, food and other topics for an assortment of trade and consumer publications throughout North America. She's also author of several guidebooks including *Adventures in Nature: British Columbia*. She lives in the foothills southwest of Calgary.

**Angie Riley** is a creative freelance writer based in Ottawa. She has written for websites, newspapers, small businesses and nonprofit organizations. She is currently seeking a publisher for her novels that are just as stylish as her freelance writing work.

**Elizabeth Ruth**'s 2000 CBC radio documentary, "Quantum Father," was selected as one of the year's best. Her debut novel, *Ten Good Seconds of Silence* was published to critical acclaim in 2001. Elizabeth is a graduate of the Humber School for Writers, teaches writing at George Brown College, and edits *Fireweed*. Visit www.elizabethruth.com.

**Ingrid Ruthig** is a poet, writer, architect, and poetry/visual arts editor for *lichen literary journal*. Her nonfiction has appeared in print and online both in Canada and the U.S., while her fiction and award-winning poetry have been published in various literary journals. She lives outside Toronto, Ontario.

**Robert J. Sawyer**'s 13 SF novels include the Nebula Award-winner *The Terminal Experiment*, the national best seller *Calculating God*, and the just-released *Hominids*. He lives in Mississauga, Ontario. Visit his website at sfwriter.com.

**Shirley A. Serviss** owned and operated a literary press for seven years and has served on the editorial boards of *Other Voices*, *Quest* and several anthologies. She currently edits *WestWord* for the Writers Guild of Alberta. She has two published poetry collections: *Model Families* and *Reading Between the Lines* (Rowan Books, 2000).

**Murphy O. Shewchuk** is a freelance writer, photographer and book author with ten published books and hundreds of illustrated articles to his credit. He also does a wide variety of computer graphics projects including interpretive displays, maps and book publishing projects. Check his website at www.sonotek.com for more information.

**Keith Slater** has been involved in theatre as a playwright, actor, director, or member of the technical crew for over 27 years. He has written about 15 full-length plays and a number of one-act or shorter pieces. He has received several nominations or awards for his theatre work, and has conducted many acting, directing and playwriting workshops. Keith has also published some 300 scientific articles, 20 books and 30 short stories.

**Madelon A. Smid** is the coauthor of national best seller *Smart Women* (Macmillan Canada). Her articles are published internationally. She teaches creative writing classes in Saskatchewan, and continues to write both fiction and nonfiction.

**Richard Smith** is an Associate Professor of Communication at Simon Fraser University (SFU). He is also Director of the Centre for Policy Research on Science and Technology at SFU's Harbour Centre campus in downtown Vancouver.

**Margaret Springer** has written and published dozens of children's stories, a picture book and two junior novels. She is also an instructor with the Institute of Children's Literature and a consulting editor for Boyds Mills Press.

**Jennifer Stewart** is a freelance writer based in Queensland, Australia. She has had her own Web-based writing business at www.write101.com since 1998 and has clients from every continent except Antarctica.

**Sandra Stewart** won a prize for one of her many articles for local festival publications. She has presented academic papers on children's literature and is currently working on a fantasy novel for young adults. She is a newcomer to e-circles.

**Nikki Tate** is an award-winning author of three series for young readers: *The Estorian Chronicles*, *The Tarragon Island Series*, and the *StableMates* novels. A dynamic speaker, Tate visits thousands of school children each year to talk about the writing process and is much in demand as a writing workshop leader.

**Christina Truman**'s work has been featured in numerous national venues including *The Globe and Mail, CBC Radio, Canadian Health and Fitness, Schizophrenia Digest*, and *PETS Magazine*. Her articles have also appeared in the *Windsor Star*, as well as numerous local publications. She resides in Amherstburg, Ontario with her husband.

**Barbara Turner-Vesselago** is the author of *Skelton at Sixty* (Porcupine's Quill), *Freefall: Writing Without a Parachute* (The Writing Space) and *No News But Kindness*, a finalist for the (cancelled) 2001 Chapters/Robertson Davies Book Prize. She teaches Freefall Writing Workshops in Canada, the United States, England and Australia. www.freefallwriting.com.

**Ian Walker** published an inspirational article in *Lifeglow*. His short fiction has appeared in magazines, newspapers, and anthologies. His first novel was published in 1995. He acknowledges the help and encouragement of writer's groups in cyberspace, and those close to home.

**David G. Weagle** is a freelance writer and editor in Kentville, Nova Scotia. A recent graduate of Acadia University, his credits include short stories in *Winners Circle 5* and *Wordscape 4*, a monthly column in *The Authors*, short story evaluations, and in-house writing and editing for RBC Royal Bank.

**Deborah Wright** was born and educated in England. After founding a post-secondary institution in Victoria, BC, where she taught English, Deborah went on to become a professional proofreader. Her clients suggested she write informative booklets on English language usage. They are being used at Canadian universities and are available at www.punctuationtips.com.